A UNIVERSAL AESTHETIC
Collectible Beads

A UNIVERSAL AESTHETIC
Collectible
Beads

Robert K. Liu

, Sweet, Sweet, Life is more and more sweet.

iful, Beautiful, The days are more and more beautiful.

TRADITIONAL CHINESE NEW YEAR COUPLET

Thank you to
my mother Mary Liu
my wife Carolyn L.E. Benesh
my sons David M. Liu and Jonathan A. Liu
and Patrick R. Benesh-Liu
for sharing the sweet days of my life.

Photographer: Robert K. Liu
Graphic Designer: Martie Tinsley Meyer
Editors: Robert K. Liu, Margaret K. Liu
Assistant Editors: Carolyn L. E. Benesh, Anne L. Ross
Glossary: Jamey D. Allen

ISBN 0-9641023-0-7
Library of Congress Catalog Number: 94-68696

Published in 1995 by Ornament, Inc., United States of America.
1230 Keystone Way, Vista, California, 92083
Mailing Address: Post Office Box 2349, San Marcos, California 92079

Printed and bound in Italy by Arnoldo Mondadori Editore, Verona.

HALF-TITLE PAGE An ancient glass eye bead from Syria showing effects of age, wear and burial; note pitting, cracks and partially intact eyes; 3.0 cm high; possibly Islamic, 700-1100 A.D. If this bead were intact and in its original state, would it now be considered garish? *Courtesy of Rita Okrent.*

TITLE PAGE Ancient, ethnographic and contemporary beads from each chapter have been deliberately intermingled, making them difficult to differentiate—old as well as new beads enjoy similar aesthetic and intrinsic value. Ancient carnelian bicone from Afghanistan is 6.7 cm long. Contemporary beadmakers include the late Kyoyu Asao, Dan Adams, Jamey Allen, Michael Barley, Tom Boylan, City Zen Cane, Fineline Studios, Patricia Frantz, Dudley Giberson, Heron Glass, Molly Vaughan Haskins, Tory Hughes, Howard Newcomb, Kris Peterson, Galina Rein, and Patricia Sage.

QUOTATION PAGE Neolithic tabular and rhomboid agate and carnelian beads from Afghanistan similar to contemporaneous beads from Mesopotamia. Largest bead is 3.3 cm long.

QUOTE extracted from *Letters from Mesopotamia: Official, Business, and Private Letters on Clay Tablets from Two Millennia.* Translated and with an introduction by A. Leo Oppenheim, © 1967 by The University of Chicago.

I have never before written to you for something
precious I wanted, but if you are truly my father,
get me a fine string full of beads. . . if you have
none at hand, dig it out of the ground wherever
such things are found and send it to me. . . it
should be full of beads and should be beautiful.

LETTER TO UZALUM FROM SON ADAD-ABUM, 1800 B.C.

ACKNOWLEDGMENTS

Writing a comprehensive book draws upon the cumulative experiences of one's life. It is essentially a self-driven exercise whereby personal resources are taxed often to the maximum. During the year and a half that I worked on this book, including the year it took for the actual writing of *Collectible Beads*, I had much time to consider what influences enabled me to complete this task.

The strength, resilience and integrity of my mother Mary's character has shaped my life in ways I cannot begin to articulate. It was her decision to uproot her life and bring her five children to the United States so that they might have superior educations. The difficulty of coping in a foreign land and the uncertainty of changing fortune reveals only a small part of her profound life experiences. Independent and highly intelligent, with a special sensitivity for the arts, she permitted her children complete choice in careers and life partners. I love and respect my mother very much and am deeply grateful for the gift of life she provided me.

Without the supportive and nurturing environment provided by Carolyn Benesh for more than twenty years it would not have been possible to carry out this project. It is the intertwining of our professional and personal lives that enriches and stimulates my thinking and perceptions. Indeed, without the moral and financial support of her parents Kathryn and Peter Benesh during troubled years of publishing our magazines, *The Bead Journal,* and then its successor, *Ornament,* we would not have survived. I will not forget their generosity.

My youngest son Paddy's interest and enthusiasm for the rich variety of life, including beads, have similarly kept my views and thoughts fresh and vital, and each day I am inspired by his presence. I will forever cherish that my late brother John, a superb engineer, showed me that art and science are naturally compatible. If my former mentor in graduate school had not loaned me that first crucial sum of money that lead me to leave a career in science to one of bead research and publishing on personal adornment, this book may never have been written: Thank you Boyd and MaryEv Walker. I also thank Phil Shima, our first designer, for teaching me so well the basics of good artifact photography.

Ornament's staff has participated in this difficult but meaningful first book project, and I appreciated their compassion as we steered the rough course to completion. For the tangible production of this beautiful book and for sometimes daily personal support, I thank Ornament's designer Martie Tinsley Meyer who worked closely with me from the inception, artfully sandwiching it between magazine deadlines, and doing her best while adjusting to pregnancy, her newborn son and my own strong directives. Besides editorial support, I relied heavily on assistant editor Annie Ross for the book's complex appendices, for computer instruction and retrieval of archival material. As marketing manager, Stephanie Morris's preliminary work will soon result in even more challenging days, and we look forward to her calm efforts. Thank you to subscription managers Jitka Kotelenska and Peter Bertelsen for recording the book orders as well as responding so judiciously to customer queries. They have been well aided by office assistant Mary Suprise, who at seventy-six abashes us with her physical stamina. And thank you to Ornament's advertising manager Simona Trifunovic for maintaining a lively spirit and optimism. With us during much of the initial production were Lois Weis, Georgina Vukovic and Cynthia Cuadra. All Ornament staff members, whether present or past, have assisted in my professional and personal growth. While many have helped in this endeavor, any errors or omissions are ultimately my responsibility.

My beloved sister Margaret Liu, professor of English and Chinese at Northern Virginia Community College, took on at short notice proofing of the manuscript for clarity and grammar; I cannot thank her enough for sacrificing an all too short summer break. Jamey Allen assiduously read each chapter's manuscript for content and accuracy, engaging me in seemingly countless exchanges of viewpoints and helpful searches for literature, as well as compiling the glossary. He is my constant sounding board on all aspects of beads.

I have always stressed that bead research is best accomplished through cooperation, without which no informed work can proceed. Many have unselfishly helped with thoughtful conversations or access to research material. I especially thank my good friend Elizabeth Harris for her unstinting dedication to furthering bead research; I was often the recipient of this effort. The bead community has always been generous with providing me research material, but I must especially thank Ruth and John Picard and Rita Okrent. All the many others who have loaned me beads over the last twenty years are gratefully acknowledged in the captions. In my early years of working with beads, the late Gerald Fenstermaker was larger than life, full of boundless enthusiasm, energy and generosity. Our mutually busy professions do not permit much contact, but I always enjoy the reflective and insightful opinions of Lois Dubin.

CONTENTS

INTRODUCTION

The paradox of collecting is that very few write about this process; most just engage in collecting. And so it is with collecting beads. One cannot easily explain the enormous fascination of these perforated artifacts without seeing or acquiring a number of them, by which time their collectible attributes become obvious and the collector is hopelessly in love with beads. Glancing through the pages of this book is a better demonstration than any words. This contention is amplified later in this introduction, in a discussion of beads made by both unknown and known beadmakers who embody the beauty of these artifacts.

Thousands in America and around the world have succumbed to this collecting passion, spawning a bead movement which has been ongoing since the late 1960s. The steadily increasing variety and volume of beads imported into the United States was overwhelming for those who were in the throes; it was such an exhilarating period. But the obvious lack of information about our new interest was both stimulating and frustrating. Here were objects with an early association to our fundamental nature as humans, as simple beings who went on to develop complex societies and civilizations. From birth to burial, thousands of years later they remained as vivid testimony to our evolutionary changes, yet we knew almost nothing. Realizing that a more comprehensive forum was needed, a group of bead pioneers in Los Angeles formed the first society in 1975. Only shortly before, I had begun publication of *The Bead Journal* in 1974. (It was retitled *Ornament* to reflect its coverage of all ancient, ethnic and contemporary personal adornment in 1978.) The first issue of *The Bead Journal* was sent to only about three hundred people who sought reliable information and documentation.

Even though beads date from at least forty thousand years ago, they have been generally ignored by archaeologists and anthropologists until the last twenty years. Due in part to a bias against small objects, those not of precious materials, and ignorance, beads have been neglected and regarded as the small change of history. Yet the advent of beads coincides with the development of human society, assuming varying roles in a universal expression of religion, economics, politics, and art. These little perforated artifacts embody the skills, emotions and intellects of early humans, and these same manual and mental processes pertain to their use today. The most intimate of artifacts, virtually every bead is the product of human hands, often involving long, laborious processes. Thus it is not overstated by those who love beads that so much of who and what we are is revealed in them.

While academically trained scholars and specialists have made contributions to the research and documentation of beads, essentially self-trained laypeople educated in other fields, like Horace C. Beck and W.G.N. van der Sleen, became fascinated with beads and pendants and initiated independent investigations which have furnished much worthwhile data and information. Lois Dubin, a nationally recognized landscape architect, follows this tradition; in 1987 her monumental volume, *The History of Beads* was published by a prestigious company known for its books on art. Jamey D. Allen, Peter Francis, Jr. and I are all self-taught in bead technology and history. Though relatively few demonstrate scholarship in this manner, we and thousands of others share the common bonds of our dedication to beads and a quest for more knowledge. This is well reflected in today's bead movement, manifesting itself in a comprehensive fashion through national and international bead societies, journals and other publications, bead museums, research organizations, private funding for research, conferences, lectures, workshops, bazaars, the hundreds of marketplace sources for beads, and by the

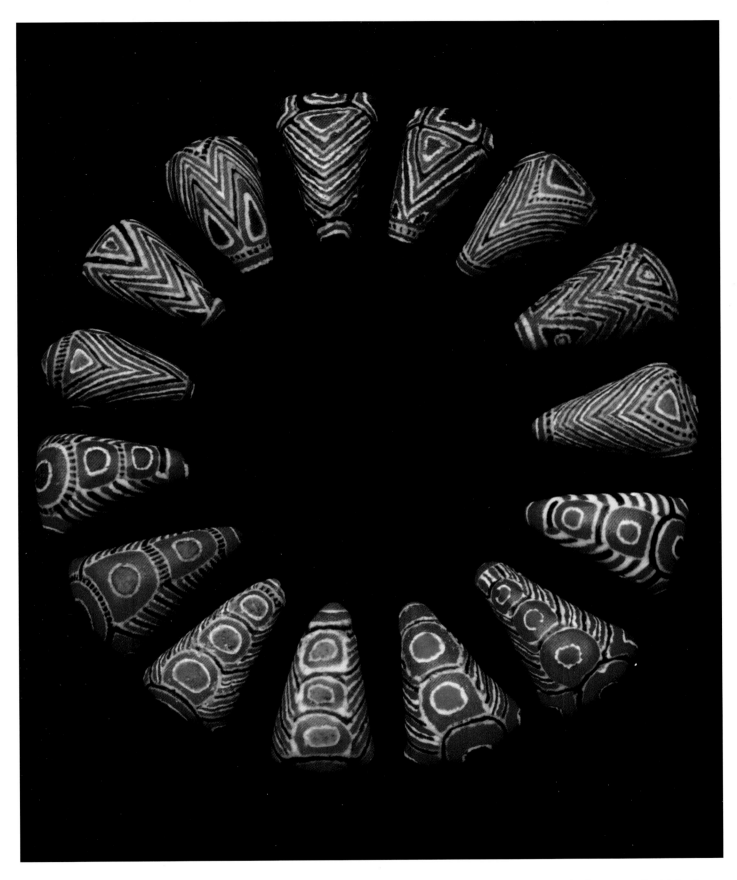

KIFFA POWDER GLASS ORNAMENTS Mauritanian women display great skill in making these marvelous pendants, among the highest form of bead art. Clarity of the colors results from finely crushed and cleaned glass powders. Ornaments show two predominant design motifs of the triangular polychrome type, with and without readily discernible circles or eye-forms, average length 2.5 cm, purchased 1986 in Nouakchatt, Mauritania. *Courtesy of Elizabeth J. Harris and Marie-Pierrette Pauchet.*

artists and others whose livings are derived from them.

The triangular Kiffa beads from Mauritania shown on the previous page represent one of the highest levels of artistic ability and ingenuity in beadmaking. These particular beads were primarily worn in women's hair and made by them, part of a considerable repertoire produced by the powder glass industry in this north-western African country. (Powder glass beadmaking is practiced primarily in the African countries of Mauritania, Ghana, Nigeria, and possibly Niger; in North America during the nineteenth century by Native Americans; during the Warring States period of ancient China as seen in composite beads of glaze and faience core; and in the twentieth century in Indonesia and Lebanon.) In Africa this manufacturing method may date back a few hundred years for West Africa and possibly to 1200 A.D. in Mauritania (Francis 1993), but others attribute it to only the nineteenth century (M.-J. and H. Opper, *pers. comm.* 1994). Techniques involving powdered glass were no doubt an indigenous response to how to make glass beads since these artisans lacked lampworking and other hot glass skills and tools. Mauritanian women, using the simplest of materials and tools (pulverized European glass beads, or fragments of them and bottle glass, pottery shards, sardine cans, twigs, steel needles, some gum arabic, and open fires), apply a wet-pack method to produce designs on glass beads that are as fine as those on Limoges enamel. Their skill and patience in applying, with extraordinary control, saliva-moistened powdered glass onto a glass core with the point of a sewing needle amazes all who have seen such delicate beads and pendants. Out of admiration, Western artists have tried their own versions in lampworked glass or polymer clay, but none begin to reach the beauty of Mauritanian powder glass ornaments. Although just a few years ago this Saharan art was predicted to be dying out, newer versions of Kiffa beads are still being made, but now mainly for export instead of only for internal consumption (M.-J. and H. Opper, *pers. comm.* 1994); others may be made in neighboring Mali. There may be even other sources for Kiffas (J. Busch, *pers. comm.* 1994).

There are many other unnamed or unknown artists in the bead world, but an increasing number of contemporary beadmakers are gaining recognition. The late Kyoyu Asao, perhaps the greatest glass beadmaker of our time, is a shining example. Completely self-taught in the research institute he established, Asao sensi mastered all the difficult techniques of lampworking, as well as traditional Japanese metal techniques, lapidary work, pottery, and skills in other media. Even when the tombodama shown here was photographically enlarged to the size of a grapefruit, each detail of the bead easily passed scrutiny. While earning his living by producing ornamented leather for manufacturing purses and zori, Asao replicated and reinterpreted the best features of traditional tombodama, many Venetian beads and ancient Chinese glass beads. Had he lived longer, Asao would no doubt have solved many more of the technical challenges of beads.

Within the last ten years a number of bead books have been published, although none have seriously traced the rise and development of the past twenty or so years since beads became so popular. Sadly, some of these publications are filled with misinformation and misattributions which will have damaging effects on bead enthusiasts, especially beginners. Because the worldwide trade in beads is conducted primarily by individuals or small businesses, no organization amasses comprehensive economic data on bead imports and exports, and much of the information is gathered verbally in bits and pieces or by printed ephemera, contributing to the difficulty of writing an overview. Clearly, serious and reliable information form the crucial underpinnings of the bead movement and reflect on its integrity and future healthy growth.

For my contribution to bead scholarship, I have relied and drawn on materials assembled since the earliest publishing days of *The Bead Journal,* as well as numerous articles written prior and since by many others. For more than two decades I have studied and written articles about beads and related artifacts while recording them photographically. As material was prepared for photography, measurements and technical data were notated as well as other information supplied by the owner. In this way, I saw and continue to view a great deal of material from both collectors and dealers.

In a series of research notebooks, now numbering almost forty, I have carefully recorded written and verbal information. This slow, cumulative process of gathering information, combined with extensive networking through all levels of the bead movement and my

CONTEMPORARY OJIME made by the late master Kyoyu Asao of Osaka, Japan. A superb craftsperson who exercised precise control in the making and placing of millefiori canes or mosaics, his total bead output totaled some five hundred. The glass bead is 1.9 cm high and was made in 1979. Patterned after Edo period tombodama, the ojime's perforation has been sized for the twin cords that are used as part of an inro ensemble.

consistently acquired bead study collection together formed the foundation for the book *Collectible Beads*. Some three years ago I began to plan for it, selecting from over thirty thousand slides drawn from the *Ornament* archives. When the original photography was judged no longer of sufficiently high quality and the material was still available, photographs were retaken.

Beads may be the most numerous of human artifacts, and any representative selection or sample is essentially a minute one. While I chose to include only beads and some pendants that were available on the marketplace within the past two decades, the array of beads presented here easily attests to the immense variety. Ancient, ethnographic and contemporary beads and necklaces are covered, and they have been organized according to the geographic area or time period from which they last originated. Thus the book covers Africa, China and Taiwan, Japan, Korea, India, Burma, the Himalayan Countries, Thailand, the Philippines, Indonesia, the Middle East and North Africa, Precolumbian Americas, and the Americas and Europe. For example, if certain Venetian glass beads were obtained from Africa, they would be discussed within that continent. But if similar specimens were never exported from the country of origin, they would be considered European. This convention is necessary since beads are extremely portable items that travel great distances. It is usually only possible to know their last destination with any degree of certainty.

Four chapters cover the very important, active areas of contemporary necklaces and artist-made beads, fakes and simulations, and of collecting, curating and studying beads. These chapters are not constrained by geographic or time periods.

The large numbers and types of more inexpensive beads that were produced primarily within the last twenty years are not reviewed, since many such beads are not considered collectibles. Perhaps in another era some of them will be collected. Many other perforated artifacts of interest to bead collectors, such as spindle whorls, seals, toggles, archer's rings, netsuke, Ethiopian crosses and rings, Agades cross pendants, broadwing pendants, celts, and contemporary beadwork (see Moss and Scherer 1992) are also not covered.

Prices have been included only within a historical context and no attempt is made to provide a current price guide since prices for the same specimens vary widely among dealers and according to where they are purchased. Local value means the same bead will often be priced differently according to location. In addition, short term fluctuations in supply, condition, rarity or perceived rarity are among many factors affecting wholesale and retail prices.

Even though the information age may seem omnipresent, the reality is quite different. Shrinking library budgets make it more difficult to access journals and specialized books, even for those who are part of the communications industry. Therefore, I have tried to make the extensive information in this book easy to obtain. The text provides more general information, while the captions contain specific details; many have references for further research. Information recorded in my notebooks are given as a personal communication (*pers. comm.*). Each chapter has a reference and bibliography section with listings of books or periodicals that are easy to acquire for additional information. Thus journals with wide distribution will be cited in preference to those of more limited availability, although the latter is included if an important reference is involved. Most references provide entry into the more select scientific literature.

While beads from many geographic areas and of varying vintages will remain available on the market, changes will also certainly occur. Many areas of the world are increasingly difficult to access, while others are being depleted of beads or have stricter sanctions against export of older cultural material. Still others are being opened due to the decrease of superpower tensions, more open market economies, and a need for Western currency. While some bead industries close, others are revived or developed, and the role of the artist beadmaker becomes increasingly more important.

It is imperative that our generation reflects positively on future generations of bead enthusiasts, and it is up to each of us to exercise moral and ethical behavior in collecting. This is a responsibility we must willingly assume as we seek to preserve the traditions and cultural heritages of countries all over the world.

GRANITE OR GNEISS BEADS AND GLASS SIMULATIONS The beads of the innermost strand, supposedly illegally excavated from Djenne, Mali, exhibit a matte surface and are among the smallest gneiss beads; some are ca. 2 cm long. Center bead in second strand is attributed to the Dogon; ca.10 cm long, well-polished, with a uniform perforation. Third strand from top has both Venetian and African glass imitations of gneiss; the latter possibly made in Mali. (See Liu 1988a, Opper and Opper 1989e). *Courtesy of Picard Collection and Elizabeth J. Harris.*

AFRICA

The recent popularity of beads in the West traces its origin to the enduring and powerful traditions of African peoples who have used them for ritual ceremonies and decorative purposes. Until the late twentieth century no other geographic area received such vast quantities of beads with foreign provenance or yielded as many different types of its own. During just the last few decades, Africa began supplying beads to the West, their abundant number and diverse array of colors, materials and shapes overwhelming and delighting those who came into contact with them. Bead collecting seemed to instantly arise and with it a fervor and passion that shows no sign of abating. While there is no determination of exactly when beads from Africa were initially imported to the United States and other Western countries, the late 1960s to early 1970s are the generally accepted dates of what included an unusually fertile period of political, racial, sexual, and economic movements. With feminists promulgating the dissolution of gender-based definitions, some males provided surprising visibility to beads or other jewelry by wearing them as a response to the traditional nature of dress. Inexpensive air fares made it possible for large numbers of young people to journey throughout the world, and Peace Corps volunteers, in particular, were exposed to products by Third World nations. Upon returning home those desiring a more enduring association with countries of former service as well as a livelihood began importing beads and other ornaments to the United States. Once these goods sustained a broader market, African runners or traders introduced much larger amounts into the United States and other Western countries, and continue to do so. While these small scale entrepreneurs have not limited themselves to work from Africa, their impact on the worldwide trading of African exports is integral to the changing history of beads.

AGATE AND JASPER PENDANTS Probably illegally excavated in Mali; longest is 3.8 cm. Scientific excavations conducted in the area of Djenne indicate it as the source of most ancient stone, bronze and glass beads from Mali. Except for some French reports on Niger Bend and lower Senegalese sites which are neolithic and not Indian in origin, almost nothing has been published. Other stone pendants from the area are more triangular, perforated through the top apex, and may have served as prototypes for later Indian carnelian pendants of similar shape.

My first purchases of African-made and European beads from Africa date from 1972, although by then I had encountered the so-called Goulimine beads from Morocco. Among the first beads imported from Africa and of interest to antiquity dealers because of their relationship to odd and curious money, they were no more than cylindrical Venetian millefiori beads brought to southern Morocco by Mauritanian traders (Picard and Picard 1987). Individual Goulimine beads initially commanded high prices of five dollars or much more, but dropped drastically as the flood of beads from Africa diluted their singularity. A typical strand ranged from four to eight dollars wholesale by the late 1970s; in Africa similar ones supposedly cost eighty-five cents in 1973. And yet as late as 1985 they could still be found selling for five dollars apiece in Moroccan souks (Gumpert 1985).

Misperception over what constitutes the unique is illustrated by just such a bead in a late 1970s trial where I appeared as an expert witness. A crucial element was the proper identification of a leather thong necklace strung with ostrich shell disks, African powder glass beads and a cylindrical Venetian millefiori.

AMAZONITE AND SCORZALITE BEADS These beads and pendants have been valued in northern Africa from antiquity. Scorzalite is much rarer and along with lapis are among the few blue stones used for beads. Blue and green were important symbolic colors. (See Opper and Opper 1990a). Beads are 5.2 cm and 2.7 cm long respectively, the latter from Mauritania. *Courtesy of Rita Okrent.*

AGATE AND CARNELIAN BEADS Made in Idar-Oberstein, Germany and imported from Africa in the early 1980s from Mali, Togo and Gambia; largest disk bead is 3.3 cm diameter. Normally brightly polished, with excellent grinding and rarely of the orange-red of Indian carnelian, the raw material is South American. The Czechs imitated a few of these shapes in glass. (See Liu 1987). *Courtesy of Rita Okrent.*

Whether due to my pretrial testimony, errors in the bead dealer's testimony or mistakes made by the criminologist in analyzing the necklace, the jury voted to acquit the suspect. The prosecution's bead dealer witness testified to the distinctiveness of the millefiori based on information transmitted via traders, popular heresay or inaccurate brochures. It was not a unique type, yet casting doubt on this point was extremely difficult since over five thousand Venetian bead patterns exist and more than one hundred thousand different beads are contained within European bead commission houses (Liu 1975c). The Picards' 1991 volume on millefiori beads shows almost three thousand specimens, and none matched the one in the trial. Almost two years after the trial I spotted a bead with an identical pattern but with an elbow shape in a Venetian millefiori bead collection offered for sale in Colorado.

Very little concrete data exists about the degree of movement of beads from Africa to the West and, to a much lesser extent, to Asia. Reports from the Department of Commerce during the height of the import boom to the United States did not even list bead imports from Africa as Third World imports filed under Form A were not subject to duty (J. Picard, *pers. comm.* 1993). However, one Arizona firm reportedly sold up to one hundred thousand dollars per day in beads from Africa for a period of eighteen to twenty-four months (J. Hengesbaugh, *pers. comm.* 1993).

The underlying reasons for the vast exports of material culture, such as beads and jewelry, from Africa and China to the West during the last two decades vary, but the result is the largest transfer of personal adornment in this century and perhaps in recorded history. In China, jewelry and dress have always been controlled by radical turnovers in political regimes (Liu 1984b). While Africa experiences various forms of warfare and drought-caused starvation, its bead exports are more likely due to acculturation and changing taste in personal decoration.

Through time, enormous quantities of beads

were exported to Africa by waves of East Asian Indians, Arabs, perhaps Chinese, and finally European merchants, who overwhelmed other traders by the numbers of beads they introduced. Francis (1992d) states that in 1831 imports into the Gold Coast were at their highest level with about four pounds of beads per person. While commerce was certainly not geographically uniform, West Africa's population, then some twenty to twenty-two million, would have made it the recipient of extremely large numbers of beads.

Paradoxically, few illustrations display beads being worn in this part of Africa, and in general, few ethnographic photographs portray bead usage throughout Africa. The Oppers (1990b) suggest examining early twentieth century postcards as a source of information on ornament styles. Kaplan (1993) further amplifies this postulate, although Geary (1991) cautions against relying on historical photographs for research. Francis (1992a) reported on the scarcity of visual documentation of beads while utilizing Karklins's survey of ethnographic photographs in several museums for an article regarding the erotic function of waist beads in Ghana.

Always worn by Ghanaian women of good taste, waist beads encircle the waist or are worn underneath skirts. The Oppers (1989b) recount similar customs in nearby Senegal among the Laobe women, who wore up to thirty or forty strands of waist beads, including shark vertebrae and various glass beads. Women from Mali, Chad and Sudan also wore them (Francis 1992a). Cole and Ross (1977) show three Krobo girls from Ghana during a Dipo ritual wearing possibly twenty strands of waist beads (all visible, as no skirts were worn), as well as ten strands of beads around the neck and bandoleer style across the shoulders. Although the photograph was taken in a ceremonial context rather than daily life, it demonstrates the extent to which beads were worn. Africans also wear beads above the elbow, below the knee and around the ankle. Cole believes that waist beads are the primary source of beads to the West from Ghana, with the influence of Christian missionaries and changing fashions rapidly diluting their importance for tribal use (Casady 1986 and H. Cole, *pers. comm.* 1993). The Oppers (1990b) mention the enormous quantities of French beads exported to this part of Africa since the 1950s, and undoubtedly some were worn as waist beads. Besides glass, stone and bone beads, palm nut shell and plastic disks were also worn around the waist.

While the fact that some waist beads are hidden from view partly accounts for the scarcity of beads in historic or ethnographic photographs, the books of Chesi (1977) and Fisher (1984) which emphasize jewelry indicate that surprisingly few Africans wore beads. Yet this relative lack of bead adornment, rather than actual, may be a result of incomplete coverage of the subject in the literature and symptomatic of cultural transformations in modern Africa. Certainly, a decade earlier in

ANTIQUE INDIAN-MADE AGATE AND CARNELIAN beads from Mali, with a few Venetian glass beads; largest tabular bead is 3.0 cm long. Some of the smaller beads look similar to those excavated in Mali. Because the outermost strand of tabular beads and some of the adjacent date-shaped beads are crude, it is likely they are lapidary products of Cambay, India, given the long dominance of Indians in the African agate bead trade. Compare the quality of stones, shapes, precision of lapidary work, and polish with those on page 15. (See Liu 1984c). *Courtesy of Picard Collection.*

AFRICAN-MADE BEADS Center clockwise are West African, primarily Ghanaian and possibly Nigerian powder glass beads, a disk-shaped powder glass coral simulation, 3.8 cm diameter; above it is a large cylindrical coral simulation 5.1 cm long. Others show the latest technique of fusing two halves (black bicone with blue equatorial line), a large cruciform decorated bead and ones with preformed components. There are also strands of ostrich and land snail shell disk beads (1.0 to 2.0 cm diameter), segmented terra cotta beads, an *Arca* shell pendant and its Czech glass copy, a terra cotta bead painted to resemble a millefiori, cylindrical and barrel gneiss beads of 9.8 cm long ($30 in 1983), a bauxite bead, Kirdi and Yoruba brass beads, East African aluminum beads, Mauritanian powder glass, and Bida wound glass. (See Liu 1980a, 1984d). *Courtesy of Stephen Cohn, Elizabeth J. Harris, Suzanne Miller, Rita Okrent, John Picard, Boyd W. Walker, and Patti Yeiter.*

Adamson's (1967) more detailed survey of Kenya, her photographs and paintings illustrating the book show people wearing many more beads.

Given that much of the African bead trade of the late twentieth century is based on African runners or traders and their informal relationships with Western or Asian merchants, the result is a network so extensive and a history so complicated that research either in Africa or the West has been minimal. At times contentious exchanges between African traders and Western bead merchants have marked their dealings; as early as 1974 bead dealers on the west coast of the United States felt that African traders were saturating and undercutting the market. Traders have been and continue to be victimized by both African and Western bead merchants (Koschnick, *pers. comm.* 1993).

A hardy and adventuresome lot, just their experiences in North America are fascinating. Arriving with huge cardboard cartons of beads, the first traders flew to various cities making deals with their customers in taxis which would wait hours as business was transacted. African traders were seen selling beads alongside their Native American counterparts in the historic plaza of Santa Fe, New Mexico. Still a prime component of the bead trade, these same runners, besides trading to the West, have visited Venice, Italy and Jablonec, Czechoslovakia (J. Picard, *pers. comm.* 1993).

Diamanti (1991) states that African traders buy the Picards' books and carry them back to Africa, using them "to spread the word about what beads American, Asian and European customers are looking for." These books also sell in France, Italy, Belgium, the Netherlands, Egypt, Australia, and Japan as well as North America, making it likely these areas have collectors interested in African beads. Diamanti (1991) also reports that her clients from Japan, Australia, Singapore, Indonesia, and Peru read the Picards' books.

It has been suggested that half of all beads in Africa have already been exported and while there will never be an objective way to confirm this estimate, certainly the number of beads traded is impressive. Michael Heide, a dealer and collector of African beads with an emphasis on chevrons, alone imported one hundred thousand strands with a wholesale value of approximately three hundred thousand dollars.

Western bead dealers have primarily concentrated on the countries of West Africa and Ethiopia and Kenya in East Africa for their trading activity. Francis (1992b-d, 1993a, b) and Steiner (1990) have discussed some aspects of the West African bead trade; Saitowitz (1993) and Kaufmann (1993) have covered the South African bead trade; and other brief accounts continue to appear in various bead newsletters. Karklins (1992) has identified glass beads in nineteenth century central East African trade. Apparently, the increasing flow of beads into the United States during the late 1980s and

early 1990s was sizable and unusual enough to stimulate commentary by both veteran bead collectors and dealers (Diamanti 1991, Gumpert 1989b). The Picards (1989) conjectured that the large influxes of seemingly new beads from Nigeria into the international market were drawn from former warehouse stock or even the actual sample cards of Sick & Co., since the geographic sources of the beads coincided with three former offices of this important bead distributing firm.

The critical importance of chronicling and studying the African trade needs to be stressed. Those who become interested in beads in the future will have an extremely confusing and nearly impossible to decipher mix of beads dating from late twentieth century trade. Because of rapidly changing participants, some of whom do not desire documentation, it is not likely we will ever have a coherent worldwide picture. Aside from the trade of beads from Africa to the Americas

MAURITANIAN POWDER GLASS BEADS AND PENDANTS The commonly called Kiffa bead may actually be made in the town of Kiffa or the towns of Oualata and Mederdra. Saliva-bound powdered glass is applied to indigenous and European bead matrices; green specimen, 1.0 cm diameter. (See Opper and Opper 1989a). *Courtesy of Elizabeth J. Harris, Rita Okrent and Patti Yeiter.*

BODOM BEADS are both controversial and highly valued by Ghanaians as well as by advanced collectors. Distinguished by a gray or black core; newer powder glass beads also exhibit this feature. The dark core may be due merely to the use of cheaper glass (K. Stanfield, *pers. comm.* 1992). With a diameter of ca. 3.5 cm, this bead is decorated with preformed elements. Even shell disk beads have been used as preformed elements. *Courtesy of Michael Heide.*

(Liu 1975b: United States, Central America), and to Asia (Japan, the Philippines and later to Indonesia and Thailand; Gumpert 1989), beads imported to the United States from West Africa have even been reexported to East Africa and back to West Africa (S. Cohn, *pers. comm.* 1990, J. Allen, *pers. comm.* 1993). Within the United States, African snail shell disk beads, copal and chevrons were sold or traded to Native Americans (L. Wataghani, *pers. comm.* 1972).

The now much more extensive network includes the exporting of beads to Africa from Europe and Asia, especially from India, with the reintroduction of China to the market. Examples of global diversity abound: a strand of Ghanaian powder glass beads bought in Thailand (E. Mann, *pers. comm.* 1985); *Arca* shell pendants (erroneously called hippo teeth) on necklaces from Singapore; an ancient Javanese millefiori bead strand in West Africa (J. Allen, *pers. comm.* 1993); and store prices for glass beads from Africa costing ten dollars each in Kyoto, Japan (D. Casady, *pers. comm.*

1979). A fascinating ancient Middle Eastern stone and faience bead necklace found in Oaxaca, Mexico (Davis 1975) is undoubtedly due to jet age trade. The Oppers (1990b) have observed contemporary Indian, Japanese and Chinese imports in their bead reconnaissance of West Africa; while privately published and thus of limited distribution, their survey covers neolithic to modern beads and also details important new information on the role of French bead manufacturers and exporters to West Africa following World War II.

A small but important portion of the African bead trade involves illegally excavated beads from the area of Djenne (Jenne) and Gao (Insoll 1994), Mali, and possibly other archaeological locations. Certain sites still yield a surprising number of surface finds (the Oppers found five hundred beads on one day; Gumpert 1989a), and beads were not uncommon on the beaches of Kenya, Tanzania and the nearby islands of Pemba and Zanzibar. Dubin (1987) speculates that bodies of water on that continent may well yield large

BODOM BEADS show characteristics that indicate possible European manufacture. The left specimen's decorations are made from preformed glass rods, some overlapping, ca. 3.9 cm diameter. Lamb (1976) has described inlays fired on pottery molds, yet it is hard to imagine how they would be applied. Even if bodoms are made by wet-forming, requiring an adhesive like saliva or gum arabic to hold the beads together prior to (Lamb 1972) and during firing, how are the rods bent and applied to unfired powder glass? The center illustration shows enlarged portions of an African-made bead and its fuzzy-edged decoration of powder glass. The sharp-edged decoration is most likely produced by trail decoration, clearly not with preformed elements. Both are decorated with cruciform designs, but one is probably of European manufacture. The right specimen is the same as the center right, showing lemon-yellow glass, trailed cruciform decoration (Picard and Picard 1989: bead 1323 shows a type of trailed cruciform decoration that may have served as a prototype for bodom beads), with black glass core, ca. 5 cm diameter. *Courtesy of Michael Heide.*

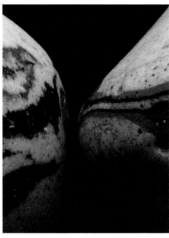

While the Krobo and other West African powder glass beadmakers were and are very skilled, the above two represent possible European bodom simulations. Such beads are marked by an outer yellow or lemon-yellow that is brighter than true African bodom, and have very smooth surfaces (the long wear on these old beads is one argument against European origin by E. Harris, *pers. comm.* 1991), trailed decorations, uniform perforations (versus out-of-round perforations in genuine bodom), and signs of being marvered (Liu 1991b). Some real bodoms have smooth surfaces but their decorations are not sharp-edged. These observations, based on the examination of less than a hundred bodom beads, need verification; in addition, because there are few good bodom collections further study is even more difficult. Since Europe is the source for the glass, elemental analysis may not be definitive. Collaboration between glass artists and bead researchers may help clarify this interesting problem.

CONTEMPORARY GHANAIAN KROBO POWDER GLASS BEADS Of a quality not commonly found on the market, these are well-made copies of Venetian beads with trailed or millefiori decorations, as well as copies of Islamic beads from Djenne (blue matrix beads with white eyes or the black beads with yellow stripes; see page 26). The bicones are made by fusing two shell halves. Stanfield (*pers. comm.* 1992) feels this method may be over sixty years old, as it was reportedly being used in the 1920s, but it is only recently that such fused beads have appeared on the market. Some beads are made from coarsely crushed old beads. Sizes range from 0.7 to 1.8 cm diameter. See Haigh (1991) for current bead fabrication in Ghana. *Courtesy of Kirk Stanfield.*

GHANAIAN POWDER GLASS BEADS of primarily adjagba types, many with cruciform decoration of powder glass and decoration from preformed elements, both indigenous and European, such as foreground bead with chevron fragments. Largest bead is ca. 5 cm long. Those with spiral lines have been twisted in the mold while glass was still viscous. Postfiring procedures, like grinding of bead ends so they fit well on a strand, are visible on many. Upper left bead is Venetian with trailed decoration. *Courtesy of Picard Collection.*

numbers, given historical accounts of bead offerings at water crossings. Dredging operations have revealed glass beads from the Columbia River in the northwest United States, making such means of recovery possible in Africa.

STONE

Ranging from hard quartz to soft bauxite, stone beads commonly consist of agates, carnelian, chalcedony, jasper, gneiss, diorite, and marble. Although difficult to differentiate from the post-neolithic (*see page 14*), very beautiful semi-precious neolithic hardstones—amazonite, the rare scorzalite and others—are the oldest found in northern Africa, from Egypt to Mauri-

tania (Opper and Opper 1990a). Mali is the largest source for ancient stone beads, including tabular ones and pendants (*see pages 14, 32*), which are reputedly drawn from the illegally excavated sites around Djenne and possibly Gao, as mentioned by the Oppers (1990b), who also state: "Taking beads from such burial sites has been practiced in Senegal and throughout West Africa for a very long time," (Opper and Opper 1989c). Some ancient tabular beads from Mali and elsewhere in Africa are similar in shape and material to those from Afghanistan, although much rarer in Africa than the Middle East.

Perhaps the most dramatic indigenous stones are ancient and contemporary gneiss or granite beads

(Opper and Opper 1989e). Best known are the large barrel granitic beads often attributed to the Dogon of Mali, but their beads may not be of modern manufacture since medieval or older sites yielding granitic beads are located here (*see pages 12, 45*). Much smaller barrel beads of duller finish have also been attributed to the illegal excavations from Djenne (*see page 12*). Even with limited published data on granitic beads, they must have been of sufficient economic importance for Europeans and for Africans to a lesser extent, to simulate them in glass (Liu 1988a). Venetians made mandrel wound glass copies while Africans used powder glass techniques (*see pages 12, 29*); Ghanaians made copies with glass crumbs or powder glass in clay molds. The Oppers' (1989e) supposition that simulations of gneiss composed of sintered crumbs of glass are made by Mauritanians living in western Mali is based on their observation that some glass fragments are derived from "medieval Islamic beads found at burial sites in and around the region of Djenne, Mali." Unlike the Venetians, these simulations produce irregular perfo-

rations due to the insertion of twigs into the crumbs prior to firing. This would confirm the existence of well-fused copies of granite beads as well as those with a granular appearance made from barely fused fragments, meaning that there are both African and European beads made from fragments of other beads (*see page 29*). These are erroneously called "end of the day beads" by dealers.

While it is not known how gneiss or granite beads were manufactured in Africa, detailed information exists on other indigenous hardstone beads. Lantana beads of cylindrical, barrel or other shapes were made in Ilorin, Nigeria from jasper, banded agates or chalcedony; O'Hear (1986) was the first to fully describe their manufacture and distribution and to illustrate them in color (*see pages 15, 29 for Idar-Oberstein examples similar in shape*). Laboriously chipped with small steel hammers and chisels into roughouts, these are drilled by tapping with a steel punch, taking three hours to reach a one inch depth. A necklace of eighteen beads required four days to a week for completion (not published in O'Hear's article but stated in origi-

GHANAIAN AND MAURITANIAN POWDER GLASS ORNAMENTS AND EXPERIMENTAL BEADS Upper left bead fragment with thin red outer cover over white core is coral simulation, 3.1 cm wide, possibly Nigerian; upper right is experimental powder glass made by Mathijs T. van Manen, with saliva-bound core rolled in red glass powder. The West African bead may have been made by a mold-less method. Kiffa bead and overfired experimental saliva-bound powder glass bead have similar well-fused surfaces (Liu 1984d). *Courtesy of Lois Dubin, Elizabeth J. Harris and Mathijs T. van Manen.*

nal manuscript), indicating why lantana beads have been so valued in Nigeria during the nineteenth and twentieth centuries.

Except for meerschaum, bauxite is the softest material used for beadmaking in Africa. The crude but attractive cylindrical or disk beads from West Africa are generally unfired and made from weathered and leached volcanic soils rich in aluminum or iron oxides. Not often documented photographically, Chesi (1977) shows an Ewe girl of Togo wearing a strand of these beads while participating in a voodoo ceremony (*see barrel bead on page 18*).

Collectors are more likely to come into contact with foreign stone beads than those of native origin because of the strong impact of successive waves of imports. The oldest trade presence in Africa is India (Francis 1982a), and it is not at all surprising that so many Indian agates and carnelians were among the beads imported from Africa (*see pages 17, 38, 39, 41*). The industry that produced them has been well studied (Francis 1982b, Kenoyer 1986). While capable of being as elegant as the slender and slightly

AFRICAN, CZECH AND VENETIAN CORAL SIMULATIONS Three beads have possible polyp scars; the two smallest are powder glass, made in West Africa, and show post-firing grinding; smallest is 1.6 cm long. The large fake coral bead on page 43 appears to defy credibility, but de Negri (1962) possibly shows just such a strand being worn by a rich Ibo woman. Middle specimen is Czech molded glass and has the most pronounced or exaggerated scars, a trait often seen in imitations. The curved bead with a black core is probably Venetian, 4.7 cm long. *Courtesy of Boyd W. Walker.*

BIDA BEADS represent the only extant wound bead industry in Africa. The glassmakers of Bida, Nigeria use bellows-fanned clay furnaces to make beads as well as bracelets. The raw material is probably European glass, although an indigenous black glass has also been used. Largest bead is ca. 2.0 cm long. (See Liu 1984b). *Courtesy of Elizabeth J. Harris.*

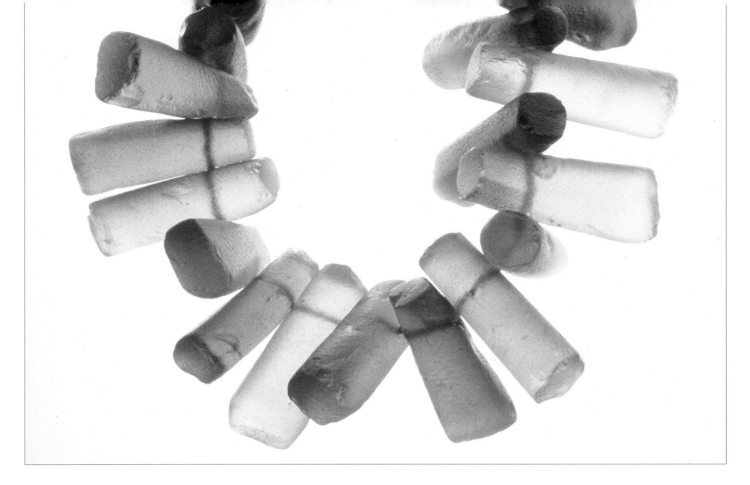

COLD-WORKED GLASS PENDANTS made from ground and drilled pieces of bottle glass, near Bida, Nigeria. The pendants or beads are ground except for portion of bottle where the walls and bottom meet; they are also drilled lengthwise, either straight through or from both ends; such beads are 2.0 cm long. Using European glass as a resource is not limited to Africans: Siberian Eskimos fashioned bottle glass into labrets and Native Americans used it for projectile points. Bottle glass is a major source of raw material for various West African glass beadmakers and for those in the Middle East. *Courtesy of Picard Collection.*

tapered carnelian barrel beads found at the ancient sites of Ur, Mohenjo Daro or in Afghanistan, most Cambay, India beads are crafted much less regularly and precisely than those made by European competitors who imitated and then succeeded them. Proportionately, there are more Indian agate and carnelian beads and pendants than those from Idar-Oberstein, Germany, even though Idar-Oberstein produced more than one hundred million perlen or wearable stone objects with perforations between circa 1830 to 1970-80, with a hiatus during World War II (Liu 1987). Besides the quality of work, the shapes and colors of most German ornaments in the African trade are markedly different, partly due to the Brazilian or Uruguayan agate used by Europeans versus native supplies in India (*see pages 15, 29, 38, 41, 47*); Germans also artificially colored agate while Indians only heat-treated stones for color enhancement (J. Allen, *pers. comm.* 1993).

Indicating imitation of the Indian stone bead industry, most Idar-Oberstein products refer to Indian terms for their names and shapes (Trebbin 1985), still it is difficult to match many items. Codrington (1932), in reference to European glass copies of Tibetan dZi or gZi beads, is often quoted regarding the "extreme astuteness of the Central European manufacturers who seem to control this trade in India. Their knowledge of anthropology is perhaps a little one-sided, but it is obviously detailed." His judgment places great weight on these bead salesmen's powers of anthropological observation, but that opinion is expressed in two sentences in an article less than a page in length.

Ebony samples of tower rings (Turmring, talhatana or talhakimt) were sent to Idar-Oberstein at the end of the nineteenth century to serve as models for agate versions, showing how closely these competitors monitored the market (A. Peth, *pers. comm.* 1986 in Liu 1987), and perhaps bolstering Codrington's assessment that representatives of European bead firms acted as economic anthropologists. But the precision faceting and polishing of Idar-Oberstein products as well as actual design alterations and stylizations brought about changes in form which made their products very different from Indian prototypes.

DJENNE, MALI is the source of most ancient and medieval beads from Africa. These fascinating strands are mostly glass, with a few stone and faience melon beads; some specimens are as large as 2.7 cm diameter. Glass beads include a Fustat fused rod example (center of outermost row), blue eye beads and spiral decorated ones that Francis (1992c) states are also of Fustat (Old Cairo) origin, and many other Islamic beads, both early and late. These arrived through the trans-Saharan trade, destroying the myth that Roman beads are among those found in Mali. Some are very similar to those previously identified as Ptolemaic, which may be the result of identification based on insufficient data. The impressed crumb beads are probably Hebron-made; the plain and twisted monochrome cane beads are similar to those associated with Nueva Cadiz beads in the New World (Harris 1982a, Liu 1978a, 1984e; see also Francis 1989, 1990a, Picard and Picard 1991). *Courtesy of Picard Collection.*

Photographs taken from the 1960s to 1980s of Africans adorned with beads or other ornaments apparently show many more German and Czech products than Indian, despite the numerical abundance of the latter in the African trade of the last two decades (Liu 1987). The derivation of designs is noted when comparing Indian and German tal-hakimt (*see page 41*), but the closest overall congruence comes with Czech glass imitations of German stone ornaments (*see pages 32, 33*). Though Idar-Oberstein was active in African trade since the nineteenth century and even after World War II (Trebbin 1985), these German stone ornaments did not appear regularly among African imports until the middle 1980s. They were shipped from Gambia, but most likely Mali and Senegal were the original sources. Among the most attractive and collectible beads from Africa, the agate ornaments were truly regal when worn with gold jewelry by the Peul women of Mali. The complete history of this phase of the stone-cutting industry in Idar-Oberstein may never be known; its own museum does not contain many examples of the African trade nor is it systematically organized (A. Peth, *pers. comm. 1986*).

SHELL

Encompassing ostrich eggs, giant land snails and marine shells, both uni- and bivalve, shell beads and ornaments are numerous and beautiful, providing wonderful surprises about human ingenuity and crafting. Among the oldest are disk beads made from ostrich egg shells, distinguished by spots on the outer surfaces of the shells, attractively colored and uniformly thick; those with smooth circumferences are most appealing. Laidler (1934) notes that many South Africans used disk beads, with specific sizes characteristic to each tribe (ranging from 0.5 to 2 centimeters in diameter). Those on the market do not vary this widely in size, in contrast to land snail (*Achatina sp.*) shell disk beads, which are sometimes confused with bird shell beads (*see page 18*). Van der Sleen (1973) has suggested that these disks are simulations of ostrich egg shell beads. It is difficult to conceive why, since the two beads are very different. Snail shell beads range from less than 0.5 to 2.5 centimeters in diameter, vary from white to brown and are not uniform in thickness due to variances in the shell sizes and in the thickness of various portions. Both are attractive beads, their neutral colors and uniformity make them excellent foils for more colorful beads in necklaces.

Relatively few marine shells are used as beads or pendants, but among them are some of the most beautiful and fascinating African ornaments. Perforated pecten shells from West Africa provide a good example, but nothing is known about these necklaces (*see page 47*). While the cowrie

STRANDS OF PRIMARILY VENETIAN POLYCHROME BEADS epitomize the attractive aspects of European glass beads from Africa. A few are neither Venetian nor trail decorated, including the possibly fake Czech chevron, Nueva Cadiz-like cane, African powder glass, and Venetian millefiori in the foreground strand, and a portion of a Venetian chevron in the second strand. Many are simulations of chevrons, visible in three of the strands. Largest polychrome shown is over 3.5 cm long, far exceeding the arbitrary size category for very large beads (Karklins 1982c: over 10 mm). Most of these beads are described in the Picards' volumes. *Courtesy of Picard Collection.*

NUEVA CADIZ CANE BEADS are well-known from the Americas (the thinner examples), and date from the mid-sixteenth to mid-seventeenth centuries; very few have been found in Africa. A strand of green and blue ones sold for $600 in 1988, but prices dropped in the 1990s when more were imported. African ones, probably of more recent vintage, exhibit greater widths (1.2 to 1.9 cm wide); some have been ground by collectors into faceted bicones. (See Harris 1982a, Liu 1978a, 1984e). *Courtesy of Beads of Paradise, Gerald B. Fenstermaker, Elizabeth J. Harris, and John Picard.*

may be considered the most common univalve shell used in adornment, it is rarely strung but mainly applied to surfaces, although Chesi (1977) shows strings of cowries worn bandoleer fashion by Ewe women. Various species of the *Conus* shell are perforated for stringing; they are the most important shells culturally and economically. In one form, the upper portions of the spire are cut off and probably ground

Called el bot min teffou (Fisher 1984), conus whorls are worn by Mauritanian women in their hair, often in long strands hanging down the temples; tresses are decorated at close intervals by beads, conus disks and numerous miniature glass or stone talhakimt. Shell disks are also strung on necklaces made of human hair, bearing many of the same elements used for hair styling (*see page 47*).

FOREIGN-MADE BEADS AND PENDANTS Starting center clockwise: the so-called Kano, which Francis (1990a) attributes to Hebron, followed by molded Czech beads, including a square clear bead (0.9 cm long) and a faceted agate imitation next to agate beads from Idar-Oberstein; ending with a claw simulation. Below it is an Indian carnelian bead, adjacent to a Czech chevron fake (note equatorial mold seam); just above may be a Czech vaseline bead. Above this bead are Venetian monochrome, trail decorated, and drawn beads, including a Nueva Cadiz-like square cane (8.2 cm long). There is also a Venetian gneiss imitation, and the larger example to its left is probably Mauritanian. The two blue beads with white eyes are Islamic. *Courtesy of Elizabeth J. Harris, Gary Hauser, Rita Okrent, Ann Maurice, Suzanne Miller, Picard Collection, Boyd W. Walker, and Liza Wataghani.*

down; then the two halves are strung together to form a bicone sphere, making a dramatic necklace (*see page 34*). Such arrangements also figured in Delarozière's (1985) book on Mauritanian beads. Among the most beautiful of shell ornaments, carved disks or basal whorls of conus shells are found in the greatest quantities in Mauritania (*see pages 34, 47*). There are even transposed examples in silver and plastic (J. Allen, *pers. comm. 1993*) whereby ornaments in one material are duplicated in another material but not for simulation purposes (Liu 1985a).

In East Africa, conus disks or whorls are also used but in a flatter form or cut as hemidisks. Functioning as currency in the former British Central Africa colony (now Malawi and Zimbabwe) and especially among Arab slavers, the conus whorls were destroyed by the British in the late nineteenth century (Liu 1975a). As a substitute, Czech porcelain copies were commissioned in 1892 after wood or metal tokens were rejected by the populace. The first porcelain copies had serial numbers on the reverse, and were followed by counterfeits without numbers.

Some porcelain copies were almost twice the diameter of the originals. Sometime later, probably in the late nineteenth or early twentieth centuries, Czechoslovakia made molded glass hemidisk imitations of conus shells in white or other colors that bore no resemblance to the real shell (*see pages 42, 49*). Some necklaces contain both real and imitation hemidisks, and it is readily apparent that no one would be fooled by the imitations. Carey (1986) shows some pre-1900 Zambian examples of conus hemidisks in ivory, and it is possible that these served as prototypes for Czech glass copies. There are also white and red plastic copies of the basal whorl that are just as unrealistic (*see page 42*). Yet masterpieces of simulation by the Czech are astounding for their accuracy, evidenced by those made of glass, the so-called hippo teeth. [There are no beads made from real hippo teeth (E. Harris and J. Allen, *pers. comm.* 1993), although hippo teeth are used as pendants in Zaire.]

CHEVRONS Called the aristocrat of beads (named Bakim-Mutum in Hausa), this magnificent strand dates to the sixteenth or seventeenth centuries. Mainly composed of seven layers, the largest ones are ca. 4.0 cm long. Other unusual chevrons include a fake made by trail decorating, considered to be possibly Czech by the Picards (1986); a seven layer bead ground down to five so that its outer layer is brick red, and green seven layer ones and five layer ones with alternating yellow and white stripes. (See Allen 1983a, b, 1984a, b). *Courtesy of Picard Collection.*

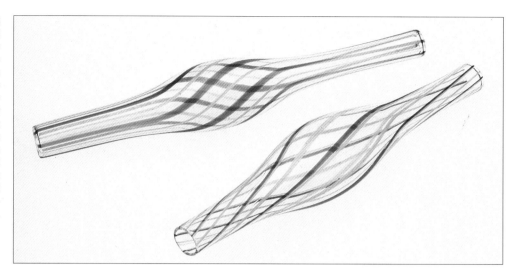

VENETIAN BLOWN GLASS BEADS probably from Nigeria, decorated with filigrana or retorte; lattimo or thin white and blue canes are twisted; the thin cylinders are blown in the center, 9.3 to 10.0 cm long. Once $75 each in 1988, price dropped to $5-9 in 1993. It is remarkable that these survive both transit to Africa and being worn. One such bead was shown on a strand from Benin at the Museum für Völkerkunde in Vienna; I identified it as Czech as it was strung with other Czech glass beads and coral (Liu 1982b), but this was probably incorrect. *Courtesy of Patti Yeiter.*

UNUSUAL CHEVRON BEADS from inner to outer layers: six layer specimen on the left has white, green, white, brick red, white, green glass; four layer specimen has red, black, white, green glass; and a very rare six layer bead has white, blue, white, yellow, white, blue glass. This specimen sold for $500 in 1983. Largest chevron is ca. 2.5 cm long. As an indication of the value placed on chevrons, $10,000 was paid by Michael Heide for a strand of twenty-four beads, of which five were chevrons, the largest 5.0 cm long. (See Fisher 1984: page 102; Picard and Picard 1986a). *Courtesy of Boyd W. Walker.*

The erroneously labeled hippo teeth are rectangles of thick shell, cut from either *Arca grandosa* or *A. senilis*, large bivalves with thick shells. Even though glass imitations were first detected in 1976 (Liu 1976b), it is not known how such beads were used and why they were important enough for Europeans to copy them (*see page 43*). Even now some writers do not know the identity of *Arca* shell pendants; in a recent book published in Britain, they were referred to as bone. Some geometric beads cut from *Arca* have European counterparts in porcelain (Liu 1980a), and these imitations are more sought after by collectors than the originals. Determining why products of the same Czech industry, and probably contemporaneously, differ so greatly in their realism is an important question. The reasonable explanation may be the difficulty of molding glass similar to an actual conus hemidisk with its deep, thin ridges, making it difficult to separate from

a mold and susceptible to breakage (*see page 42*).

Very small gastropod shells of the family Buccinidae or Columbellidae are perforated for stringing by having one or both ends ground off (*see pendant on Mauritanian necklace, page 47*). These may be prototypes for Venetian glass imitations, as shown in Picard and Picard (1989), and have been mistaken by bead experts, possibly even by Beck (1928: 30, figure 25 B.5), for Egyptian ornaments of Dynastic age. Other gastropod shells have been perforated for stringing, as illustrated in the structured necklace on page 49 or that shown by Chesi (1977).

ORGANIC MATERIALS
Included in this category are both organic substances (claw, horn, copal, or similar resins) and those largely inorganic but derived from or produced by living organisms (such as coral, teeth and bone).

Truly organic beads would include wood and scented paste made from ground vegetal matter. Scented beads are not shown or discussed here, but those of Africa are covered in a booklet by M.-J. Opper (1990); a number of other vegetal beads are discussed by the Oppers (1990b) in their survey of Senegal. Wood beads are very rare, although those worn by the Akamba consist of thin wooden rectangles with one or two perforations strung together into short necklaces. Masterpieces of

woodworking, these beads are supposedly made by fathers for their daughters' circumcisions (E. Mann, *pers. comm.* 1985: the necklaces have not been made for some thirty-five years; this tribe circumcises both sexes).

Except for Morocco, there are few coral beads from Africa on the market. Because of the importance of coral in court regalia of West Africa, it is not surprising to see such extensive imitations. There are mandrel wound glass beads probably from Bida, Ghanaian or Nigerian powder glass examples, some marked with pitting as occurs with real coral, others made in surprisingly large sizes, and a rare strand of painted terra cotta (*see pages 18, 23, 24, 43*). Even lantana or jasper beads may have substituted for coral; the Oba, for example, loaned lantana during the Festival of Corals (O'Hear 1986). Czech molded glass cylindrical beads also imitate larger branch coral (Liu 1980a), while thin red glass cane beads make excellent coral simulations, to the dismay of unwary tourists visiting the American Southwest. Czech molded toggle beads were common imitations of beads made from short branch coral; this type of imitation is also found in the Middle East and the Americas.

Pendants or beads derived from vertebrate animals are less numerous than those from shell but tend to be more dramatic in appearance. Claws and teeth

COMPARISON OF CZECH PENDANTS in upper photograph with ancient stone beads and triangular pendants (2 cm wide) from Mali, which may have served as prototypes for both Indian carnelian and later European stone and glass pendants of same shape, 2.0 to 2.5 cm wide. Lower photograph compares two strands from Mali with Czech claw and drop pendants (3.3, 2.5 cm long respectively) versus those of contemporary manufacture in Czechoslovakia, where prisoners supplied labor for some bead production (Liu 1987). Note glossy versus matte surfaces on drop pendants. *Courtesy of Vladislav Chvalina, Stephen Cohn, Elizabeth J. Harris, and Picard Collection.*

CZECH MOLDED PENDANTS FROM MALI began to be imported into the United States in the mid-1980s. The dazzling variety of shapes and colors produced similar excitement among collectors when Venetian beads were imported in the early 1970s. Strand contains a rare white tooth pendant; pendants range from 1.5 to 3.5 cm long. Although strung on monofilament, such necklaces may have been worn by the Peul, Fulani, or Bella of Mali. Some were also strung with Idar-Oberstein or Kiffa beads. *Courtesy of Stephen Cohn.*

of large predators like lions, leopards and crocodiles are used in structured necklaces, as are horns (*see pages 43, 45, 49*). Indigenous imitations of claws and teeth in bone as well as transpositions in brass, often result in stylized ornaments of great power. German simulations were made in carnelian, while the much more numerous Czech molded glass examples were made in a wide variety of colors, most of which bore no relationship to the prototype (*see pages 29, 32, 33*). Teeth were so highly valued that the Czechs molded glass imitations, which are rarer than real ones. Except for the unrealistic sheen of glass, anatomical features and colors are duplicated, equaling the *Arca* copies (*see page 43*). Unfortunately, no glass versions have been found on bead sample cards and no exact dating exists, although they cannot be older than late nineteenth to early twentieth centuries.

African bone beads are often made from fish (sharks and possibly bony fishes) or snake vertebrae, the latter considered most valuable. There are now

many new bone beads, probably made from camels, which are often stained to show various designs. When snake vertebrae are used for necklaces, they are usually ground smooth to varying degrees. Those that are almost round in cross section bear a close visual and functional relationship to molded Czech interlocking beads of glass, the most well-known being the snake bead (Liu 1976a). While these beads may have been inspired by actual snake vertebrae, their colors do not resemble snake bones. Interesting for their variety and modes of interlocking, these glass beads are also useful to contemporary necklace designers. Those designed to fit closely together function almost like thick chains, thus ornaments with large enough perforations or loops can be strung on a strand of interlocking glass beads. Actual snake necklaces are worn by the Luo and Kikuyu of Kenya, Dinka of Sudan and most likely other African peoples (Adamson 1967, Dubin 1987, Mack 1988). Snake vertebrae have also attracted contemporary

CARVED CONUS SHELL BEADS from Mauritania, where it is called koos according to the African runners, are excellent examples of the stunning beauty of simple shapes and graduated serial imagery, accentuated by contrast of carved conus disks. They are worn by Mauritanian women in their hair and on necklaces. While the stringing suggests an intact necklace, it has actually been strung by a dealer; shells range from 1.2 to 4.9 cm diameter. *Courtesy of Rita Okrent; now part of the Bead Museum Collection.*

CARVED CONUS DISKS from Morocco, although most likely from Mauritania originally, utilizing either simple straight cuts and grinds or hole drilling; 2.4 to 3.3 cm diameter; purchased in the middle 1970s. *Courtesy of Liza Wataghani.*

jewelers such as Dan Telleen who transposes sections of African snake necklaces into gold (Osburn 1992; *see page 185*).

Copal and amber beads are the most misunderstood and controversial of African organic materials (*see pages 34, 36, 40*). Often of imposing sizes, large numbers of beads labeled as amber or copal have been imported from Africa. Misinformation has been rampant from the start. Allen details his own experiences with so-called African amber and copal in his series on amber and its substitutes (1976a, b), wherein almost eighty bead samples that had been previously identified as amber or copal were carefully tested. Only seventeen percent were amber; five percent were recent resins such as copal, fifty-two percent were plastics of various types, and the balance was other materials such as horn. Naturally when the results were published, there was an uproar from dealers claiming that their copal business was ruined. At that time plastic copal was about one hundred dollars per strand while real copal was five to six times more expensive. (In 1990, genuine copal sold for three dollars per gram wholesale, making it one of the most expensive bead materials from Africa.) But given the short memory of customers and perhaps their desire to believe that these attractive beads were real, the furor over identity soon blew over. By 1985, such beads were selling from one hundred-fifty to one hundred-ninety dollars a strand wholesale. A well-known dealer reported that they were being sold to an Indian supply firm which then sold them to Zuni fetish carvers. As early as the middle 1970s, fetish (usually hummingbirds) and hishi necklaces made from plastic imitations of copal were appearing on the market (Allen 1976a: figure 23). While possibly merely an example of carvers exploring a new material, other copal beads were used as outrageous frauds; carved plastic beads of the reddish variety were being sold in Arizona as carved Tibetan amber, with the Ural mountains of Russia as the amber source (G. Liese, *pers. comm.* 1983; *see page 224*). These fantasies sold for five hundred to thirty-five hundred dollars a strand, with plain and carved beads combined, and hopefully few pur-

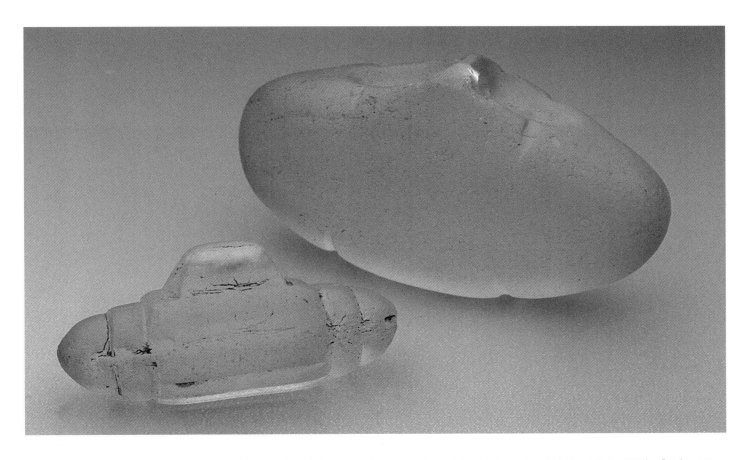

WELL-WORN CZECH MOLDED AMULETS that are probably based on Islamic rock crystal prototypes. These were often worn by Peul women in Mali and Upper Volta (Burkina Faso), sometimes in multiples, as shown by Chesi (1977: 172, 183). Their beauty has been enhanced by the effects of wear, turning stylized objects into abstractions, 2.5 to 3.6 cm wide; obtained in West Africa. *Courtesy of Ann Maurice.*

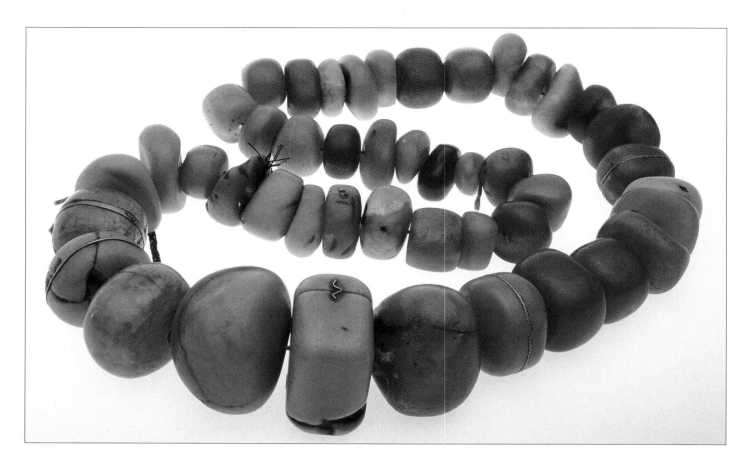

SUPERB STRAND OF COPAL AND AMBER supposedly from Morocco, maximum size is 5.8 cm wide; such strands are often found in Sudan. Real copal and amber are relatively rare in Africa and plastic imitations are rampant (see Allen 1976a, b). While light in weight, copal and amber are among the most expensive per unit weight. Note variety of bead shapes; these show a great deal of wear and repair, as evidenced by the wire used to tie broken beads together (like binding wire for soldering) or corrugated inserts for the same purpose. The repairs add a decorative beauty to the beads. *Courtesy of Wind River.*

AMBER BEADS from Mauritania, possibly of Baltic amber, with embedded caps of gilded copper, decorated with fragments of glass set in pitch. This form of square bead often has perforations in two axes; 4.0 to 4.2 cm long. *Courtesy of Rita Okrent.*

chasers were swindled. It is likely that plastic copies of copal were also used in Africa for carving other ornaments, such as the talhakimt displayed on page 40 where the hole in the middle of the broken piece matches the position of a bead perforation. It is highly probable that many European talhakimt copies were made from a plastic not too dissimilar from that used for the beads.

SYNTHETICS

Faience and ceramic or terra cotta beads belong to this category. Available faience are typically large melon beads associated with ancient glass and stone beads from Djenne, Mali (*see page 26*), which are most likely imports from the Middle East, although faience melons are widely distributed in time and location. Since Islamic glass beads are not uncommon in ancient sites from Mali, the Middle East is also the likely source for faience, as such beads were products of the early Islamic period (Francis 1989).

It is surprising that there are so few types of ceramic or terra cotta beads. Although difficult to prove, most spherical terra cotta beads in Africa are probably spindle whorls. Fisher (1984) shows that the Dogon occasionally incorporate clay whorls into fetish necklaces. The illustration on page 43 shows a rare strand of terra cotta beads painted to imitate coral. There are many contemporary Moroccan simulations of coral and copal in ceramic (*see pages 134, 220*). The most numerous true clay beads from Africa are thin, segmented cylinders from Mali; some call them Dogon (*see page 18*). Their exact origin and age are uncertain, but they have been dated to circa 1200-1500 A.D., although a thermo-luminescence test placed them at six hundred-fifty plus or minus ninety years (J. Picard, *pers. comm.* 1986). Found ceramic objects are sometimes strung on structured or intact African necklaces (*see page 49*), and now contemporary ceramic beads are made by a Kenyan workshop.

METAL

African metalsmiths are skilled in forging and fabricating beads and casting metal by the lost-wax method, or by much cruder means. Thus there are beads of gold, silver, brass, copper, iron, and aluminum; base metal beads are sometimes plated or washed in silver or gold, but they are of poor quality. Gold beads are rarely on the market, but silver ones are numerous and derive from Ethiopia and less often from the northwestern country of Mauritania. In Ethiopia beads are usually just sheets rolled into cylinders, while those from Mauritania utilize intricate repoussé and false granulation (*see page 36*). The best selling bead from Africa in terms of sheer volume is the humble Giryama, used in loincloths and made from a coil of thin copper or brass wire, which may be slightly flattened by forging (Liu 1990b). One dealer sold five hundred to one thousand strands a month, prompting him to encourage the tribe to reinstate their bead production (S. Cohn, *pers. comm.* 1990; at that time, strands were eight dollars apiece wholesale). They were immensely popular with Western designers and jewelry manufacturers who used them not only in necklaces but as fillers in earrings. The small copper beads were finished with silver and other metal platings.

Elsewhere in Kenya, the Borana and possibly other tribes make aluminum beads in a unique manner from old cooking pots or Volkswagen engine

MAURITANIAN NECKLACE detail with plastic imitation of copal, carnelian beads (including some plastic copies), Venetian polychromes, and indigenous fabricated silver beads. The silver beads are beautifully crafted repoussed halves soldered together; costing up to $25 each, 3.3 cm long maximum. A proportion of copies are now cast instead of fabricated from sheet silver. Some plastic copal copies are sleeved with metal, like those on page 36 which are probably real amber, indicating that copies are valued by Mauritanians. The trader believes that this necklace is over one hundred years old. (See Delarozière 1985). *Courtesy of Rita Okrent.*

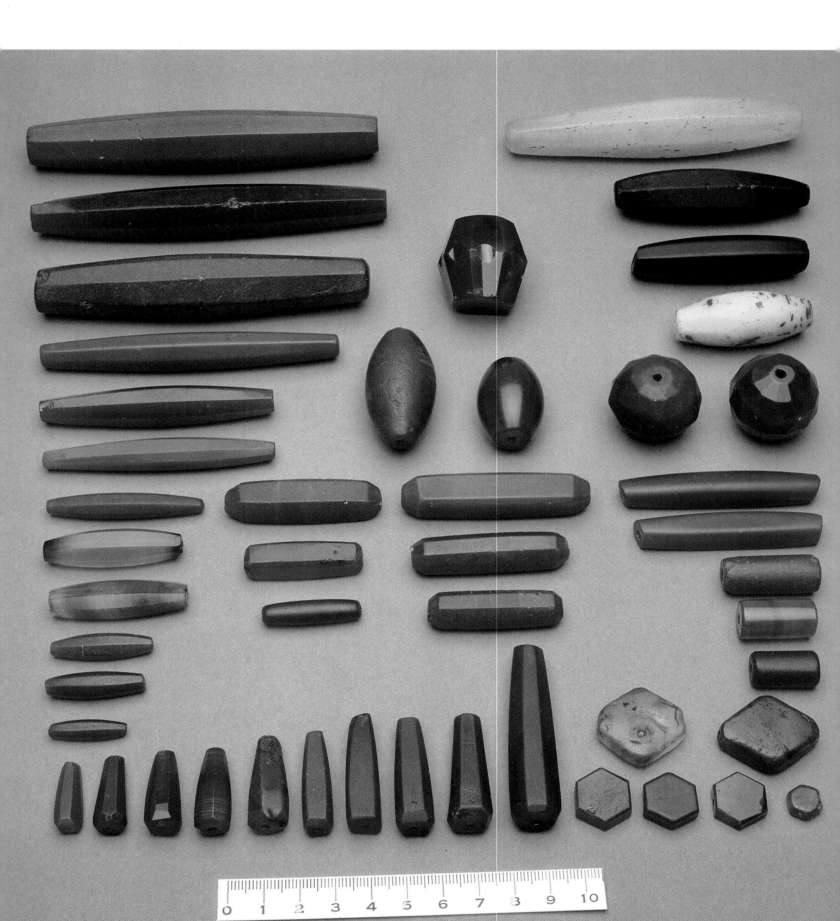

blocks. Furrows in the ground are supposedly used as molds for casting rods of aluminum, which are then cut and forged into square or faceted beads. Well-cast barrel beads with indented patterns may also be of native origin (*see page 18*). Probably cast aluminum beads are also found in Senegal, dating to 1925-1940 (Opper and Opper 1990b). The Kirdi and other non-Islamic peoples of northern Cameroon and northeast Nigeria lost-wax cast large and varied numbers of brass pendants and beads (Wente-Lukas 1977; *see pages 18, 50*). In West Africa, the Baule of the Ivory Coast cast extremely beautiful, intricate gold and brass beads of which only the latter are available. These sold for one hundred dollars a necklace in Africa ten years ago (J. Picard, *pers. comm.*

1983). Elsewhere in Africa, very large beads were cast from brass (the spherical, probably Yoruba one illustrated on page 18 is a small brass bead example).

GLASS

Due to the quantity of glass beads imported into Africa for so many years it is that continent's most important bead material. Now Africa's own glass beads, especially those of the powder glass industry, are experiencing a minor boom, although wound Bida glass beads are barely in production. The vast numbers and types of glass ornaments on this continent are bewildering unless one can categorize or sort them by origin. The oldest glass beads are Indian, followed by Islamic, then European, with the Chinese perhaps

CARNELIAN NECKLACE The striking, probably intact necklace is from Cambay, India, except for the two Czech glass beads. (See Liu 1984c, 1987). *Courtesy of Ricki Pecker. Opposite page:* CZECH GLASS SIMULATIONS OF CARNELIAN BEADS with a few Indian and Idar-Oberstein agate and carnelian beads interspersed for comparison. Czech molded glass has a duller surface than agate as glass is softer and wears faster in Africa's dusty environment. It is the source of these specimens except four from Morocco (a faceted Idar-Oberstein bead with equatorial notches, the agate barrel bead below it and faceted spherical beads in carnelian and glass). Czech glass simulations have faceted barrels (2.3 to 12.3 cm long) and date-shapes (left edge and along bottom); seventh specimen from left is a nearly transparent red glass, much less convincing as a carnelian substitute than the dense, almost opaque red-orange glass usually seen. These two colors may reflect chronological differences. The faceted barrels at top right are not carnelian copies; the Czech produced such shapes in many other colors. Versions from Cambay are on the bottom two rows, in a date-shape and as tabular beads. To differentiate between Czech, German and Indian stone and glass copies look at the precision of the shape, the surface finish or polish and the presence or absence of mold-lines. *Courtesy of Michael Heide.*

playing a quite limited role. Post World War II, the European imports returned as well as Indian, Japanese and now Chinese (*see page 29*). While Africa had its own glass bead industry in medieval times that lasted to possibly the eighteenth century, the only examples of indigenous glass beads found in the marketplace are the mandrel wound beads of Bida glassmakers and the powder glass beads of West Africa and Mauritania (*see pages 12, 23, 24*). The Bida industry continues while the West African portion thrives and the Mauritanian survives. Indo-Pacific or trade wind beads, which Francis (1990b) attributes to the Indian drawn glass bead industry, do not really figure among imported African beads, except among the many small monochrome glass beads from Mali. Part of the North African trans-Saharan trade carried on by Arabs, they may occur among the large number of bead types from illegal excavations at Djenne. Islamic and early European glass beads are found in strands from there (*see pages 26, 29*), and parallel ones found in Mauritania.

European manufactured glass beads from Africa are preponderant, with Venice, Italy possibly outnumbering those from Czechoslovakia (the current glass bead industry is in the Czech Republic). The photo-graphs in the Picards' seven volumes on West African trade beads indicate the vast numbers of types that have been manufactured: approximately 1,000 chevrons (of which some 500 are from the African trade), 345 tabular beads, 716 fancy beads, 1,797 white hearts, feather and eye beads, 1,470 Russian blues, faceted and fancy beads (about 560 of these are Bohemian or Czech), and 2,915 millefiori beads. These total over eighty-two hundred types, a minority of which are Czech; some are not from the African trade and possibly others are variations that are not really separate types. These numbers easily exceed the five thousand types estimated in early twentieth century bead catalogs (Liu 1975c). When collectors Michael Heide and Albert Summerfield planned a book in 1983 on wound, trail decorated European glass beads from the African trade, their personal collections held over two thousand types (*pers. comm. 1983*). While the numbers of wound European beads can be overwhelming, many examples have been illustrated in the Picards' books and other publications (*see page 28*). Drawn beads, like chevrons, are among the most treasured (*see pages 29, 30, 31*) exports from this continent, but others also amaze collectors; good examples are blown,

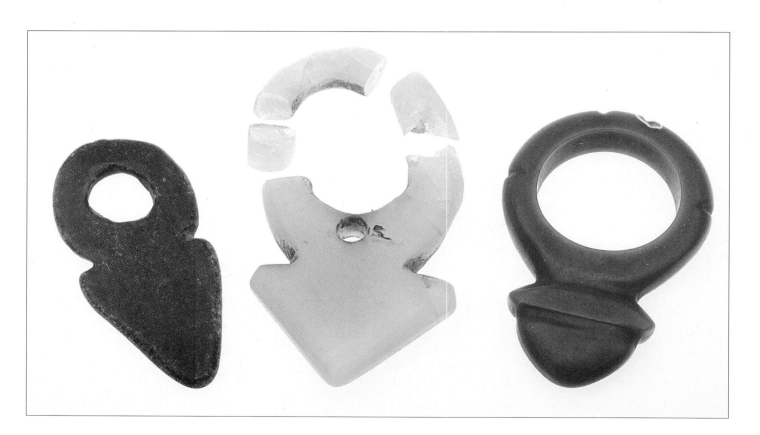

PLASTIC TALHAKIMT One is lucite, another carved from a simulated copal bead (note hole for perforation), made in North Africa; the plastic specimen on the right is a European import to North Africa, 4 cm long. *Courtesy of Jamey Allen, Elizabeth J. Harris and Liza Wataghani.*

CHALCEDONY/AGATE, GLASS AND PLASTIC TALHAKIMT *Clockwise from top center:* Made in India, Morocco, unknown European origin (some locally modified), Idar-Oberstein, and Czechoslovakia. Indian carnelians are similar to those collected in the Sudan, while plastic examples are from Morocco; the rounded agate tower ring and adjacent two talhakimt are from Germany, while the other Idar-Oberstein specimens and large molded Czech talhakimt were collected in Africa and small glass ones from Cairo. Size range is 1.7 to 7.5 cm long; used in North and Saharan Africa. (See Liu 1977, 1987). *Courtesy of Joel L. Malter, Niger Bend, Rita Okrent, A. Peth of the Museum of Idar-Oberstein, Peter W. Schienerl, and Liza Wataghani.*

probably Venetian beads which have survived long journeys to and from Africa (*see page 31*).

A fair number of Venetian and some Czech glass beads are now datable if they are types that can be matched to dated bead sample cards, sample books, or bead catalogs of the mid-nineteenth to early twentieth centuries (Francis 1988, Karklins 1982a, b). Based on an analysis of millefiori beads made for the African trade that were shown by the Picards (1991) from the Sick Collection, Francis (1991) has postulated that composite or bundled mosaic chips were used in millefiori beads primarily during the early decades of this century, while molded canes were used after World War I, thus enabling the astute

observer to date mosaic or millefiori beads. But Allen (*pers comm.* 1993) counters that the diagnostic difference may relate more to utilizing composite canes for beads made in homes, as Venetian beadmaking was often a cottage industry, versus factory molded canes. Allen states that "the Sick company utilized canes from homecraft industries early, and from factories later." Harris (1984b) has discussed Venetian beads from the African trade that may date to the 1950s.

However, in dating glass beads to similar ones of known or estimated age, it is important to recognize that a particular type may have been made before or after this time period, and may have been

CONUS SHELL BASAL WHORLS AND IMITATIONS in glass and plastic. Given the symbolic and cultural importance of the *Conus* shell in Africa, it is not surprising that so many ornaments are made from the real shell and its copies. Shown are two basal whorls, one used by the Akamba of Kenya as well as a plastic imitation from there (probably European; 4.1 to 4.5 cm diameter), and real and Czech glass imitation conus shell hemidisks (4.0 to 4.2 cm wide). The latter is the most common type of copy and is produced in a variety of colors (see page 38). These copies are not very realistic, in contrast to other Czech glass imitations. It is intriguing to consider why certain indigenous beads were imitated. For example, small blue cylindrical glass beads with grooved or scarred surfaces have been imitated by both Venetians (Harris 1982b) and the Czech, since they are highly valued in West Africa. Lamb calls them pseudo-seghi; if seghi or segi are equated with or related to the mysterious and elusive aggrey beads, then this copying is understandable. See other conus disks on pages 34, 47. *Courtesy of Stephen Cohn and Patti Yeiter.*

manufactured only on demand (Liu 1975c). Beads and other artifacts are also considered heirlooms throughout many cultures, compounding the problem of accurate dating.

Although much less numerous than Venetian wound beads, Czech molded glass beads and ornaments are often more interesting. At the apex of bead artisanship, Eastern Europeans were especially adept in imitating shell, teeth and stone ornaments made by native cultures or their fellow European competitors (*see pages 24, 29, 32, 33, 35, 38, 41, 42, 43, 47, 49*). Only Chinese simulations are comparable in skill.

Today the Czech glass bead industry is healthier than those of Venice and Germany, producing innumerable wound and molded types and reproducing many of the forms previously made for the earlier African trade (J. Picard, *pers. comm.* 1993). Some of these new beads are exported to Africa, where they are restrung and dipped in dirty solutions to simulate an aged effect. To differentiate new from old, glass surfaces must be closely examined to determine signs of wear, especially prevalent when beads are worn constantly in an environment where body oils combine with the abundant dust to make an abra-

LION'S TOOTH AND RARE CZECH
MOLDED GLASS COPY representing
the epitome of glass copies. Except
for sheen of the glass and some exaggerated features in the copy, their
appearances are nearly identical
(ca. 6.2 cm long). Real lions' teeth are
frequently strung with large chevrons.
Courtesy of Boyd W. Walker.

ARCA SHELL ORNAMENT AND ITS CZECH
GLASS VERSION, which is possibly even
better than the lion's tooth simulation.
Clues to the copy are the regular shape
and sides, plus its flat reverse, versus the
actual shell with its variation in shape and
concave reverse. Copies are very rare,
ranging from Senegal to the Cameroons
(Diamond 1978, Liu 1976b).

FAKE CORAL BEADS of
painted terra cotta and
powder glass (5.1 cm
long), both African-
made. *Courtesy of
Picard Collection
and Boyd W. Walker.*

SAMBURU OR RENDILLE NECKLACE One of the most structured and striking personal adornments from Kenya, these necklaces range from a few to as many as six tiers of ochred cloth, binding doum palm fibers, and supposedly consisted of elephant tail hairs when these animals were more numerous. Not actually circular, the necklace is 27.5 x 28.5 cm.; center beads are Venetian glass, like cornaline d'Aleppo. (See Adamson 1967: page 163; Dubin 1987: page 131; Fisher 1984: pages 38, 39). *Courtesy of Stephen Cohn.*

sive. While worn, beads rubbing or knocking against each other leave distinctive peck marks and raised trailed decorations or other surface features become rapidly ground down.

Aggrey and bodom glass beads of African origin constitute two of the more controversial issues of bead research; Francis, for one, has reviewed problems pertaining to their identification (1990c, 1993a). It may never be known if certain dichroic and corded glass beads are indeed the fabled akori or aggrey beads, given vague and changing descriptions in the literature (published as color photocopies in Opper and Opper 1990b). There have been heated and acerbic exchanges about the definition of bodom beads due mainly to misunderstandings between scholars seeking to establish identity through interpretation of previously published accounts versus those working with actual specimens (*see pages 20, 21, 22*). Controversy aside, bodom and other powder glass beads are among the most fascinating of glass beads, and their methods of production illustrate just how technical problems are resolved by craftspeople of various African cultures. While older powder glass beads may be more aesthetically appealing, newer ones reveal the changing nature of this energetic industry. For example, most Krobo powder glass beads are now made in two parts then fused together, and glass shells may be used instead of solid halves (K. Stanfield, *pers. comm.* 1992).

SAMBURU necklace detail showing one to two tiers with additional bead edging; 22.5 x 24 cm, $150 in 1988. *Courtesy of Patti Yeiter.*

LOBI NECKLACE FROM MALI Although restrung asymmetrically, the redesign may reflect the original. The striking components consist of gneiss beads (largest 6.5 cm long), leather mounted and incised possibly antelope horn (10.5 cm wide), feline claws, a nut, and Venetian, Czech or German glass beads. *Courtesy of Picard Collection.*

YORUBA NECKLACE from Nigeria. Multiple strands of small Venetian and Czech beads are strung through large European glass beads, making fringes at both ends of the necklace; each large bead has fertility ringlets. The necklace demonstrates the phenomenon of accumulation as well as the great skill of the Yoruba. White beads are 3.0 cm diameter; length is 164 cm. Some of the large monochrome glass beads from Nigeria are similar in appearance to Chinese glass beads in shape and inclusions. See Liu 1992b for complete view of this necklace as well as an outstanding Yoruba braided one. *Courtesy of Picard Collection.*

Some beads presently identified as bodom may actually be European copies of African powder glass beads; if true, they nicely demonstrate the clever abilities of these so-called economic bead-maker anthropologists (*see page 21*). Lamb (1972) shares this belief.

Women beadmakers within the Mauritanian powder glass industry must be especially encouraged to continue their superb craft, as they make remarkable beads. As maximum production is only three per day from a single beadmaker, beads are scarce (Gumpert 1990), but perhaps through steadily increasing interest in their beads, opportunities for change and innovation will be stimulated (Opper and Opper 1992). In contrast, the West African powder glass

industry is very active due to innovative methods such as forming beads from powder glass shells and the introduction of British ceramic colorants; some Kumasi villages now have approximately twenty bead ovens each (K. Stanfield, *pers. comm.* 1992).

Researchers with extensive field observation and collecting experience in West Africa will hopefully provide much needed information on these extraordinary African beads. The excavation of powder glass beads in a nineteenth century context from Elmina, Ghana (DeCorse 1989) is promising as the data obtained may help determine the origin and age of this industry in Africa. Francis (1990b) believes that powder glass beads are at

MAURITANIAN NECKLACE An intact specimen strung with human hair. Used by few Africans, this medium is much more common in Polynesia. Conus shell whorls and Idar-Oberstein carnelian talhakimt (ca. 3.0 cm long) are probably sewn onto the hair. Note that the openings have been edged with brass. The pendant is composed of indigenous brass beads tied together with Idar-Oberstein colored agate drop pendants, along with a copal imitation and a *Pusiostoma* shell. Similar elements are used in Mauritanian women's hair styles. (See Fisher 1984: pages 219-223). The Guedra dancers wear large numbers of shell disks, miniature European-made talhakimt and beads in their hair. *Courtesy of Elizabeth J. Harris.*

SHELL NECKLACE from Lomi, Togo, of pecten-like bivalves; possibly *Pecten* or *Chlamys*, mostly orange, a few purple, much like the colors of *Spondylus;* maximum size is 6.5 cm wide. It is not known how these shells were used, a dilemma with many ornaments from Africa, such as the rectangular *Arca* pendants shown on page 43. *Courtesy of Picard Collection.*

least three hundred years old and based on the oral history of some Ashanti-related peoples, their origin may be traced to western Sudan. Carey (1991) suggests that the cylindrical garden-roller beads of Zimbabwe may be powder glass, which would push this industry back to circa 1200 A.D. A tenth to twelfth century powder glass bead mold has been shown in Francis (1993a). Besides entirely indigenous beadmaking, various peoples alter European beads (Francis 1993b) as well as cold- and hotworking European glass into pendants (Liu 1984d; K. Stanfield *pers. comm.* 1994; *see page 25*). Most of these processes and other products of the powder glass industry result in opaque beads with rough surfaces, which are desirable qualities to the Ghanaians (B. Menzel, *pers. comm.* 1975).

AFRICAN NECKLACES

As stringing materials are impermanent, it is exceedingly difficult to determine whether a necklace's arrangement or structure is original and meaningful or has been altered prior to collection (Liu 1984a). To Westerners, many African necklaces in cultural context seem devoid of design, differing little from the way bead strands were typically offered for sale (certainly understandable with waist beads which are not worn structured), excepting some that may have been strung with precious objects like gold nuggets (see Cole and Ross 1977: figure 28, color plate XVII;

STRIPED ALLEY BEADS bought in Lomi, Togo, but probably from Nigeria, with a clear glass pendant (5.0 cm long) added, also from same source. Such giant Venetian beads, ca. 4.2 cm diameter, (possibly German because of their marble-making expertise, J. Allen *pers. comm.* 1993) can be made by a variety of techniques; the largest may be hot pinched, with characteristic bulge in the perforation. Very expensive, the beads sold for $150 each in Africa during the middle 1980s. (See Harris 1984a). *Courtesy of Picard Collection.*

ZAIRIAN NECKLACES The right necklace with crocodile teeth (largest ca. 8.0 cm long) and feline claws on Czech cylindrical and German annular beads is intact (Karklins 1993, Opper and Opper 1990b). The left necklace is assembled from components of two other necklaces, using Czech hemidisks, ceramic tops from sodas, probably *Aporrhais* shell pendant, and other Czech and Venetian glass beads. While not an intact necklace, it illustrates the common use of found objects in African jewelry. (See Liu 1990a). *Courtesy of Picard Collection.*

Garrard 1989: figures 103, 143). Other necklaces, like those composed of Baule lost-wax cast gold or brass beads, follow a patterning that a Western bead designer might also choose (see examples in Garrard 1989). There are numerous examples of highly structured necklaces, such as those from East African tribes—the Masai, Turkana, Rendille, Samburu, or further north, the Dinka (Dubin 1987, Fisher 1984). Of those necklaces that are structured upon the body, highly developed specimens do not appear for sale, since they may have to be partially destroyed or dismantled upon removal from the wearer. For example, collected neckpieces of mpooro engorio or palm fiber necklaces of the Rendille and Samburu are very elementary compared to highly stacked specimens seen in context (*see pages 44, 45*). In West Africa, some of the most interesting strung necklaces are found among the Dogon, Fulani, Peul, and Bella peoples. Only those from the Peul appear on the market in any numbers (*see page 33*). Some necklaces are beautiful due to the repetition and serial imagery of their elements, although it is difficult to discern if the components were actually so worn (*see pages 12, 17, 22, 25, 47*). A number of supposedly intact necklaces can be found in publications by Borel (1994), Brincard (1984), Harter (1992), Nourisson (1992), and van der Zwan (1985). A necklace of beads strung with leopards' teeth and miniature iron knives shown by Brincard may demonstrate transposition of usage, equating the functions of animal and human weapons or their role in amuletic functions (Schienerl 1979).

NIGERIAN NECKLACE intact, with indigenous elements strung on thin rawhide; the lost-wax cast bells are roughly graduated (maximum length 5.0 cm) with considerable variation in detail and crafting, due mainly to thickness of the wax rods; these functional bells have a very pleasant tone. Brass pendants are most likely made by the Kirdi or other non-Islamic people of the Mandara mountains bordering Nigeria and the Cameroons (Wente-Lukas 1977). Some bell pendants are not cleaned of the clay or charcoal investment left on the interior from casting. Others are cleaned and a small pebble is inserted through the opening, then the sides are pinched to retain it. The small cylindrical beads appear to be powder glass simulations of coral. *Courtesy of Picard Collection.*

When observing or commenting on African adornment, differences between the various cultural aesthetics and other stylistic characteristics must be appreciated, including the particular arrangement or sequence of elements, symmetry, center weighting, gradation, and rhythms (*see pages 30, 34, 36, 39, 46, 47, 48, 49, 50*). In East Africa, adornment tends to band and constrict males and to bulk and expand females (H. Cole, *pers. comm.* 1986). For West Africa, design criteria for necklaces differ and random clustering, not symmetry or balance, is important (H. Cole, *pers. comm.* 1977; *see page 45*). In some instances, change through time or accumulation are important aesthetic statements. Multiple ornaments on Masai, Samburu or Rendille women evoke a startling image. Within a single necklace, accumulation may be applied by the insertion of substrands or circlets to separate each bead (*see page 46*). Enhancing visual interest, the design focuses attention on individual beads (Liu 1984a).

Even though the relationship of scale or size to the importance of a bead or other perforated artifact has received little study, it has been observed that Africa produces or uses the most large beads. Cole (1974) has commented on the use of large beads as symbols of wealth and prestige in Ghanaian society. Excess, design redundancy, enlarged size, and scale are attributes of royal or chiefly jewelry in Ghana (Cole and Ross 1977). Found objects are also important in African adornment, as seen in examples by Fisher (1984) and the necklace illustrated on page 49. Beyond visible criteria, beads have protective spiritual qualities that Western collectors rarely confront. Cole (*pers. comm.* 1977) relates that among the Akan of Ghana beads are equated to portable shrines of minor gods or deities who cure headaches or prevent accidents while dancing.

Two decades after the first imports of beads from Africa to the West, this continent continues to be one of the best sources. Certainly prices have increased greatly, and the variety and numbers of bead types have decreased, but new discoveries constantly occur in the African trade as witnessed by the recent finding of large numbers of so-called Kano beads in Nigeria. Always relatively rare, the new finds of Hebron-made glass beads include types not previously seen. Unfortunately, these beads may come from illegal excavations. The looting of beads and other antiquities is very damaging to a country's cultural heritage and to knowingly collect from such a context is strongly discouraged. A wealth of material can be safely derived from legitimate sources.

SEMI-PRECIOUS BEADS AND PENDANTS Although cut with jigs, these beads still require a great deal of hand labor by a largely female work force, located primarily in the People's Republic of China. The stones include turquoise, jasper, carnelian, quartz crystal, rhodocrosite, hematine (synthetic hematite), obsidian, rose quartz, chalcedony, amazonite, colored agate, and onyx, ranging from 1.0 cm length to 4.2 cm diameter. *Courtesy of Abeada Corporation.*

CHINA AND TAIWAN

Ironically, the recognition of China, second to Africa as the most prolific source of beads, was limited to one short paragraph by van der Sleen (1973) who doubted that China even produced glass beads, a view supported by Woodward (1967) and by some serious collectors (Jenkins 1975). Beck (1928) showed only one Chinese bead in his widely utilized monograph on the classification and nomenclature of beads and pendants. Collectors in the United States though have long acknowledged the presence of Chinese glass beads given the history of fur and opium trading between the two countries and the religious activities of American missionaries in China. Examples demonstrating the early dispersion of Chinese glass beads have been shown in exhibitions large and small, with Crossroads of Continents: Cultures of Siberia and Alaska (Francis 1988) and Dragons in the New World: Native Americans and the China Trade (Liu 1985c) among the more notable. The Innua exhibition displayed glass beads as decoration for the seal floats, skin scrapers, labrets, utility boxes, and harpoon rests of the Bering Sea Eskimos. And within the permanent collection of the Museum of the American Indian, there are necklaces belonging to the Seminoles of the southeast United States who may have strung Chinese glass beads along with alligator teeth on these pieces (A. Taylor, *pers. comm.* 1985).

In the early 1970s as trade resumed with the People's Republic of China, the ensuing wave of jewelry imports comprised one of the largest influxes of foreign jewelry in this century; while not as widespread, historically complicated and closely observed as beads imported from Africa, it was nevertheless far reaching. Some Chinese necklaces reassembled specifically for the foreign market were originally shipped to Morocco and then imported into the United States during the late 1970s. (L. Wataghani, *pers. comm.* 1978).

However, unlike large scale exports of African personal adornment to the West based on both economic and social factors, China's primary impetus for exports was political revolution (Liu 1984). Changing governmental regimes radically affected Chinese jewelry and dress twice in this century, when the Manchus were overthrown in 1912 and then in 1949 after the Communists drove the Nationalists from the mainland. Each time the prevailing personal adornment was virtually banned and court regalia and jewelry of the populace and of many minorities were channeled through the new government as part of an ongoing tradition of recycling (Cammann 1979, J. Vollmer, *pers. comm.* 1983). Just how these vast amounts of jewelry were obtained may never be fully understood; sources have relayed tales of confiscation by collection centers located in interior provinces like Sichuan or of people selling their jewelry to government stores. Some minorities along the border provinces were treated more leniently, partly influenced by memories of the Long March through these areas and assistance provided to Communists by them (H. Wong, *pers. comm.* 1987).

The bulk of the exported jewelry consisted of early Qing to post-World War II vintage beads and ornaments, including numerous glass pieces. Glass bead production since resumption of trade with the West has been sizable, and with the addition of other materials like metal and stone, the growth of bead production is an expanding one in the world market. These new and antique ornaments from the Chinese mainland along with the large volume of contemporary stone and cloisonné

ANCIENT JADE AND OTHER HARDSTONE BEADS attributed to Han dynasty (1.1 to 3.0 cm lengths). Purchased recently in Hong Kong, stone beads of this vintage are rarely seen in private collections. *Courtesy of Naomi Lindstrom.*

beads from Taiwan and the substantial carved bead industry of Hong Kong (*see page 52*) make this Asian region a rich and diverse one for collectors.

In the middle 1970s, I began to research and write about Chinese beads, and in the 1980s about those from Taiwan. My primary motivation was to compensate for the lack of scholarship on Chinese beads, but having immigrated to the United States from China at an early age I was also interested in learning more about my heritage. Paradoxically, Chinese far better educated than I were equally unaware of the field; beads and other jewelry had received scant attention by Chinese scholars because they were considered to be minor arts. Western and Japanese scientists and scholars showed far more interest in personal adornment especially with regard to Chinese glass.

Some twenty years later we know much more about Chinese beads, mostly those made of glass. The first written account of Chinese glass beadmaking (Chu and Chu 1973) described anecdotal information from south China, near Canton: long bamboo reeds covered with clay slip were used as mandrels, onto which "threads of molten glass" were poured at intervals by one person, while two others held the ends and turned or twirled the bamboo presumably as glass was poured onto the mandrel. This technique may work, but glass cools or freezes extremely rapidly, and having three people do the work of one does not fit the basic frugality of the Chinese. The first accurate account to be documented by photographs is by Kan and myself (1984), showing glass beadmaking at a kiln in Boshan, northern China, now known to be a site long used for glassworking (Yi and Tu 1991). These kilns or furnaces for glass beadmaking are probably much closer to the type of equipment used since antiquity by glassworkers in most cultures. The use of lampworking equipment (burners using an unspecified mix of gas and air or diesel fuel and air) for Chinese glass bead and other ornament manufacture described by Sprague and An (1990) is undoubtedly a recent development, assisted by Czech technical help and possibly their equipment.

In the 1980s, Francis began researching various Asian bead industries, including those in China; his results reveal that glass and glass beadmaking have had a long but probably discontinuous history, perhaps dating to the first millennium B.C. (Francis 1986). Other Western scholars are studying Chinese glass, but not primarily glass ornaments (Dohrenwend 1980/81, Brown and Rabiner 1990). With the discovery of large amounts of glass artifacts from archaeological excavations initiated after the 1949 Revolution, Chinese scientists are now displaying more interest in their own glass history, especially its origin (Brill and Martin 1991). Perhaps the question of whether indigenous glass existed at that early time will now be more thoroughly revealed.

EARLY CHINESE GLASS

Even though ancient Chinese beads owned by collectors are limited and few, those made of glass or related materials are so spectacular they especially merit discussion. While some researchers believe that the Chinese made glass by approximately 1000 B.C. (Western Zhou), all beads analyzed from that time are closer to faience than glass, some of which are similar to faience beads from Iran or Afghanistan (Wang 1991, Zhang 1991, Fan and Zhou 1991). By the Warring States period (ca. 500 B.C.), there was an explosion of elaborate mosaic and horned compound eye beads as well as ones with less complex structures (Liu 1975c; *see pages 56, 57*).

Attention has been drawn to the so-called revolving eye of Chinese simple and compound eye beads, in contrast to Western eye beads whereby the eyes do not usually appear acentric (Liu 1975c). Blair (1951) made an elegant argument for this phenomenon based on Chinese design philosophy. But examination of numerous early Chinese eye beads evinces relatively few with this feature. The revolving eye's design appears to be more a product of eurocentric belief in a 'slanted' oriental eye, than of actuality.

STONE BEADS, PENDANT AND TOGGLES These are probably antique, although many such ornaments are still being made, except for toggles, the Chinese equivalent of Japanese netsuke, and considered highly collectible. Note lotus fruit toggle utilizing so-called skin of the stone as part of its design, often the case with Chinese carvings. Composed of agate, carnelian and serpentine, the beads range from 1.2 to 4.7 cm length. Paneled or lantern beads are frequently copied in glass. Winged objects are well-crafted stylizations of *Trapa*, an Asian aquatic plant that is cultivated worldwide and edible; these range from 1.4 to 3.9 cm wide. *Courtesy of Leekan Designs.*

COMPOSITE BEADS Normally exhibiting a thin layer of glaze over a core of glass faience, these replicas of Warring States or early Han beads were made in the People's Republic of China; sizes are 2.0 to 3.0 cm diameter. Many other terra cotta copies of ancient Chinese beads are currently on the market, as well as porcelain copies made in Taiwan. Fakes or replicas of ancient Thai, Indonesian and other Asian beads are being manufactured, usually in cooperation with government agencies, to reduce demand by tourists or collectors for the genuine articles (D. Ross, *pers. comm.* 1994). *Courtesy of Naomi Lindstrom.*

Some of these Chinese eye beads are among the most complex and best-crafted glass beads in the world (*see this page*). After the Warring States and possibly early Han periods, neither the complex flush nor horned eye beads appear again, evidently a stylistic anomaly in the history of Chinese personal adornment. Engle (1976) has raised the possibility of a Hurrian origin for glass in China based upon the rosette and cruciform motifs used on Chinese mosaic glass beads and the metal artifacts of these early Middle Eastern people.

With exotic materials like glass, the Chinese experienced cycles of importation and assimilation (C. Brown, *pers. comm.* 1992), yet the acceptance of ornaments such as those from the Warring States period appears to be of relatively short duration. If glass did not emerge in China until approximately 500 B.C., how did a nascent industry gain glassworking skills so quickly (possibly through foreign beadmakers), go on to develop their extremely well-crafted and elaborate beads and then essentially abandon this pinnacle of skill? Even the best contemporary Japanese glass beadmakers using modern technology were not able to replicate them (Ukai 1984).

Some of these early beads are definitely glass but others are a composite structure with glaze over

STRATIFIED HORNED COMPOUND GLASS EYE BEAD of the Warring States or Late Zhou period (473-256 B.C.). Among the most complex and well-made beads in the world, the specimen's colors have changed due to burial, but the structure is magnificent even though it has been repaired. It is hard to imagine how all the elements, probably made in a furnace or kiln, could have been assembled so precisely, especially since the bead is such an early one. These complex beads disappeared after the Warring States period. Note that the compound eyes are not acentric, as claimed by some researchers. The owner believes the horns were lapidary worked. Specimen was purchased from a European source, costing $1,000 in 1986; height 1.9 cm, perforation 0.8 cm diameter. *Courtesy of Albert Summerfield.*

a faience-like core (*see page 56*); if such beads date to later times of the early Han their duration would have been longer than elaborate glass ones. The chronological relationship between composite and glass beads, their respective classifications, the political or intellectual environment which permitted their presence, and reasons for the lack of further evolution of faience in China still need to be resolved (Liu 1975c). Dubin (1987: 156, plate 153) presents a figurine bead, possibly Warring States period or later, made entirely of faience, an example demonstrating the use of faience for other than bead cores. And Seligman and Beck (1938) show a late Zhou clay jar decorated with glass eye inlays, so apparently ceramic and glass technologies coexisted, although it is not known how faience fits into this relationship. With the question of faience in China largely ignored and the recent discovery of five faience collar beads among numerous glass beads in a Thai site dating from 900 B.C. to 800 A.D. suggest-

ing its existence elsewhere in Asia (Pilditch 1992), more sustained research is long overdue.

Early elemental analyses showed some glass beads to have a high barium and lead oxide content unknown to any other contemporaneous glass. No summary has been attempted of more recent analyses of Chinese faience and glass (Brill and Martin 1991), but it is obvious that these materials are more complex than previously understood. There are at least seven types of Chinese silicates and only one contains both lead and barium, three others have lead and three do not (Brill, Tong and Dohrenwend 1991). No uniformity exists within a given historic period as lead could be present or absent in both Han and Tang glasses (An 1991). Even within a very specific type of glass ornament like an ear spool, lead can be absent or present. However, the three types of glass containing lead overlap in usage from circa 500 B.C. to the 1900s, with a gap of about four hundred years. Francis (1990a,

GLASS EYE BEADS OF SQUARE SECTION may date from late Zhou or early Han; no other culture has made similar eye beads. They were possibly made by applying eyes to a wound bead, then marvered into four flat sides, sizes 1.25 to 1.9 cm high. These are remarkably preserved, in contrast to specimens in the Royal Ontario Museum, Toronto, Canada or the Field Museum of Natural History, Chicago, Illinois. *Courtesy of Naomi Lindstrom.*

PENDANTS FOR COUNTERWEIGHTS OF COURT NECKLACES consisting of glass simulations of jade and possibly aquamarine; one is a faceted quartz crystal. Note use of metal caps and lapidary work of drilling and wheel cutting on end specimen; maximum width is 2.0 cm. Court necklaces are difficult to adapt for Western tastes and are usually disassembled for the components. These examples are from reassembled court necklaces imported during the middle 1980s via a Chinese dealer known for the quality of his goods. *Courtesy of Rita Okrent.*

WOUND GLASS BEADS Even though crudely made, these beads show the wonderfully soft and variable colors of older Chinese glass; maximum diameter is 1.0 cm. *Courtesy of Elizabeth J. Harris.*

GLASS STRIPS AND BEADS from Boshan glass bead workshop in Shandong province, People's Republic of China. Instead of glass rods typically used by Western beadmakers, glass strips are bundled together; the pouring of strips may be less complex than the pulling of rods, also requiring less equipment. Strips range from 0.9 to 3.5 cm wide. *Courtesy of Leekan Designs.*

GLASS COUNTERWEIGHTS ON COURT NECKLACES showing best (bottom) to poorest crafting of stylized eternal knots; maximum width is 4.5 cm, $50 each in 1984. *Courtesy of Rita Okrent.*

1991a) has equated leaded glass in many Asian beads with Chinese manufacture, but caution must be exercised about attribution, since neither glassmaking sites nor specimens have been found on mainland China for some types identified as Chinese.

Polychrome beads of the Paiwan people, fake chevrons and others found in Southeast Asia are all trail decorated. Not historically widespread in Chinese glassworking, it is a technique rarely seen in extant Chinese beads and usually only in those with millefiori (*see pages 60, 61*). If beads decorated by combing and trail decorating were Chinese (*see pages 70, 71*), why did their makers almost totally abandon such a successful technique and its product?

Chemical analyses of Chinese beads have also revealed Chinese blue or purple, an analog to Egyptian blue (Brill, Barnes and Joel 1991), a finding that had been anticipated by Seligman and Beck (1938). Because Egyptian blue or kyanos was used for some Iranian and Afghani faience ornaments (Liu 1982c), discovery of its analog may provide clues to additional trade and technology exchanges between China and these countries. Chinese blue or purple consists of copper, barium and silicon oxides and has been found either as a coating on Han beads or as bars. (Such bars and possibly beads made from them were displayed and labeled as clay sticks of Tang vintage in the Field Museum of Natural History in Chicago, Illinois.) Other ancient Chinese ornaments are stylistically so distinct from those of the West that they are presumed to be Chinese, such as ear spools or erh-tang worn by women (previously called capstan beads, these are inserted into a hole in the ear lobe with beads and pendants hanging from the ear spool's perforation), and square beads with eyes on the corners (*see page 57*). Such square beads, while unique among eye beads of the ancient world and held in several museum collections, have elicited almost no commentary (Liu 1975c).

Of interest to scientists and collectors alike are ancient Chinese beads of the Western Zhou; eye beads of both composite structure or glass, they are probably derived from Western prototypes but then adapted by Chinese to their style, distinctive from any Western eye bead. These are usually spherical, occasionally cylindrical, all with eyes, ranging from simple to complex, both flush impressed and horned, with the latter type among the most spectacular. Some are extremely complex in both decoration and structure and show precise crafting (*see page 56*). Japanese craftspeople like the late Kyoyu Asao tried

GLASS BEADS VIEWED WITH TRANSILLUMINATION, showing large numbers of bubbles, clay inclusions and irregular outlines characteristic of many Chinese glass beads; longest is 1.9 cm; compare with page 58. *Courtesy of Pauline Lum.*

replicating them (*see page 11*); although very similar in appearance and crafting, Asao's were not as elaborate.

Access to ancient Chinese beads has been mainly through collectors living in China and with Chinese dealers from Hong Kong or Taiwan, although some beads appear on the market because of other foreign sources or auctions. Unfortunately, all these beads were probably the result of illegal excavations, both prior to World War II (Seligman and Beck 1938) and since the late 1980s, when economic and political conditions were unstable and these activities occurred. It is currently rumored that there are numerous beads stalls in the markets of Shanghai and Beijing from

COIL BEADS, a term coined by Francis (1990b) for wound beads where the windings of melted glass are often not fused. These beads are from Thailand (Akha) and Burma; the Ami of Taiwan use similar but larger beads (Liu 1983). Longest is 1.7 cm. *Courtesy of Elizabeth J. Harris and Elaine and Paul Lewis.*

CHINESE BEADS FROM THE MINORITIES TRADE These may have been made by the Boshan workshop in Shandong province, or possibly obtained from Thailand, Burma, or even border provinces like Yunnan; consisting of monochromes, crumb, melon, trailed, decorated with millefiori, and occasionally striped beads. Note the sunburst pattern of the millefiori, combined with irregular trailing, 0.9 to 2.1 cm diameter. *Courtesy of Hands of the Hills.*

which the Chinese themselves are collecting and that even the Bureau of Antiquity is buying from them (B. Wu, *pers. comm.* 1993). Fakes abound, and museum staffs are also making replicas not meant to be sold as genuine antiquities. (Among hundreds of ancient Chinese composite and glass beads that I have personally examined over time, the more recent purchases have included fakes.) Elaborate porcelain fakes of ancient beads are now being made by the Taiwanese (D. Ross, *pers. comm.* 1994). Hong Kong dealers have offered a number of composite beads and a few ancient glass ones, with prices ranging from one hundred-thirty to six hundred dollars each (P. Kan, *pers. comm.* 1989); among the buyers were Taiwanese and the Japanese, who have superb collections as seen in Yoshimizu (1989).

TAIWANESE GLASS BEADS

The glass beads of Taiwan's indigenous or aboriginal peoples have been prized since possibly the nineteenth century when the island was occupied by the Japanese. Japanese ethnographers have carefully studied some aboriginal groups, describing in detail their jewelry, including glass beads (Kano and Segawa 1956, Miyamoto 1957). These beads were often incorporated into traditional Japanese jewelry such as hairpins and obidama, or later by Taiwanese into rings or pendants; incorporation was also practiced in the Philippines with Kalinga tribal beads (Abellera 1981, Liu 1983; *see page 71*). Glass beads of aboriginal Formosans are perhaps even more difficult to collect than ancient Chinese ones as the supply of the aboriginals is finite versus the large number of still unexcavated ancient beads. At least four

LARGE GLASS BEADS like these are uncommon and made more carefully than smaller ones; some areas around the perforations are ground flat (two dark blue ones). Note residue of clay bead release in perforation; size range of spherical beads is 3.0 to 3.4 cm diameter. Yellow bead is blown, made recently in Boshan for the minority trade as an amber imitation, 5.1 cm diameter. These workshops' capability for making blown glass beads was unexpected; in general blown glass beads are rare in China. *Courtesy of Robin Atkins, Gerald B. Fenstermaker, Elizabeth J. Harris, and Liese Artifacts.*

IMPRESSED CRUMB BEADS purchased as Japanese ojime. Only right specimen is Japanese; it has a telltale countersunk perforation, regular outline and good quality glass versus Chinese version with clay inclusions, crumbs not flush, irregular outline, and poor quality glass, 1.8 to 1.9 cm diameter. Note that matrix colors and crumbs are similar yet differ. (See Liu 1982b).

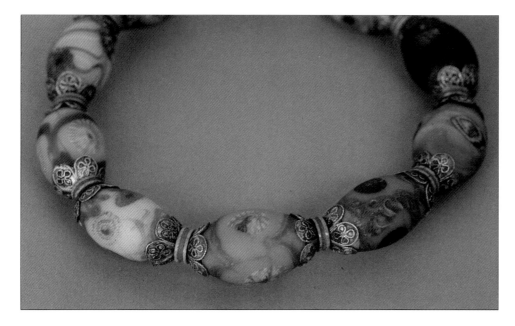

MATTE SURFACE MILLEFIORI BEADS are among the rarest Chinese beads; probably only half a dozen necklaces and bracelets, plus some loose beads are known. Most were bought in Hong Kong, some in Shanxi, although one strand was purchased in London. Those obtained in Hong Kong were accompanied by a certificate dating them to the eighteenth and nineteenth centuries, but they are more likely from the twentieth. Such beads did not appear on the market until the 1980s. Some collectors believe that these beads are Japanese while Allen's information that they were made by a Japanese-managed factory in China during World War II is plausible. The colors are within the range of Chinese glass and the sun-burst millefiori is exactly like that used on other Chinese beads (see page 60). Some trailed decorations are simpler than those on the more common glossy surface millefiori beads, but others are duplicates of common millefiori (see light blue specimen, center). In light of these similarities, the beads are probably Chinese especially since the sunburst millefiori has not been seen in glass beads known to be Japanese. Harris (1984a) has further described these beads. Individual beads cost $50 each in 1984; maximum length is ca. 2.4 cm. *Courtesy of Gabrielle Liese, The Bead Museum.*

RED OR ORANGE OVERLAID BEADS AND CRUMB BEADS are among the large quantities of glass beads (some probably drawn) imported from the People's Republic of China since the middle 1970s; these are middle 1980s imports. Due to the cost or difficulty of making red glass, solid red glass beads of any size are rare. Red or orange overlays white or yellow matrices; maximum diameter is ca. 1.8 cm. *Courtesy of Leekan Designs.*

RED BEAD ASSORTMENT illustrating elaborate measures taken to obtain this color; *from lower right, clockwise:* red paint over glass, blown glass with red paint on inside, probably plastic over glass, cased beads of red or orange over yellow or white cores; maximum length is 1.3 cm. *Courtesy of Rita Okrent and Elizabeth J. Harris. Lower left:* CARVED GLASS BEAD with dragon, probably partially formed before finished with lapidary techniques. This modern coral simulation is ca. 3.5 cm diameter. *Courtesy of Leekan Designs. Lower right:* HORNBILL BEAD flanked by glass simulations shows difference from prototype. There are hornbill beads without such elaborate carving. One glass copy is much poorer than the other; probably both are Chinese as no other culture made beads from the hornbill casque. Hornbill bead is 1.8 cm diameter. *Courtesy of Fred Chavez and Hugh Weiser.*

Taiwanese indigenous peoples wear beads, with those of the Paiwan being most notable (*see pages 70, 71*). Few Western collectors own these beads, and the best collections are either Taiwanese (Liu 1983) or Japanese (Yoshimizu 1989). Some beads are undeniably Chinese in origin and others appear to be Edo period tombodama (Dubin 1987: 240, figure 246), but the source of polychrome glass beads of the Paiwan and the Puyuma is still unresolved (Liu 1983). Beads similar to combed ones of the Paiwan have been found in Sarawak, Malaysia (Darmody 1987, Francis 1991a), Thailand (R. Liu, *pers. observation* 1994), excavated from Java (Francis 1992: ca. 1300-1500 A.D.), and possibly Iran (Fukai 1977: plate 49, bottom row).

CHINESE BEAD CHARACTERISTICS

Investing a tremendous amount of labor into each bead, the Chinese utilized a diversity and uniqueness of materials unlike other beadmakers. Also inspired by a large repertoire of images and motifs, they widely simulated other materials with their beads, which were commonly made with methods derived from other craft industries (Liu 1975b, 1980, 1984). Examples here show kingfisher feathers applied as a mosaic to a wood bead core or composition, hornbill casque carved into beads and simulated in glass, lapidary methods applied to glass ornaments which are frequently simulations of stone, intricate carvings of mundane or minute stone ornaments, and the beading of ornaments with seed beads, often in complex pat-

MOLDED AND CARVED GLASS ORNAMENTS with one carnelian example (flower, left side) for comparison; these include monkey pendants, perforated flat floral elements that are sewn onto clothing and a glass bi. The monkeys may have been used by Chinese minorities; sizes range from 2.3 cm diameter to 3.2 cm high. *Courtesy of Leekan Designs.*

terns (*see pages 55, 58, 62, 63, 66, 68, 69*). The larger beads on court necklaces for the emperor were supposedly hollowed for reducing their weight. One fluorite bead upon examination showed such hollowing (F. Ukai, *pers. comm.* 1993); it is the doubly perforated bead adjacent to the baluster bead on the counterweight, and demonstrates the amount of labor and care that can be expended on just a single bead. Extant court jewelry collections amply testify to such extravagance (Ch'in 1986, Liu and Liu 1982). Highly prized for their aroma, other beads carved from imported wood were stored in airtight lead boxes with wood shavings to prolong the fragrance (M. Liu, *pers. comm.* 1976).

The carving of pits, seeds and shells into beads is a notable aspect of Chinese ornaments (*see page 68*). When not made into intricate miniature sculpture, the surfaces are sometimes engraved with calligraphy almost microscopic in size. Lengthy Buddhist prayers may be encompassed within a few centimeters. Carved words are important for their meaning and sound, or for the beauty of the calligraphy, such as the carved rebuses or pictorial puns on beads that have been described by Bartholomew (1985, 1988a, b). Calligraphy performs a similar function for Islamic ornaments. Banes (1988-89) has presented a general account of Chinese beads, including their symbolism; this fascinating aspect has been covered additionally by Cammann (1962) and Fenstermaker and Williams (1979).

Some old collections of Chinese beads and necklaces contain wonderful examples of intricate work and labor expenditure. Joan Feast's collection dating from 1935 had ribbon-carved turquoise, pierced or painted porcelain, carved and heat treated quartzes, jade, lapis, dyed marble, howlite (a turquoise simulation which tends to fade), inside painted glass, carved glass (*see pages 58, 62*), cinnabar (*see page 67*), wood, gilded copper, enamel and cloisonné (*see page 65*), and possibly pressed amber beads and pendants.

Most beads from China were used on court necklaces, rosaries, fringes for other types of jewelry, toggles, and pendants (Liu 1975b). A fringe of hanging beads located on the front and back of metal hats, worn by high officials of the Ming Dynasty, is one example of a fairly atypical use of beads. Hairpins and personal toiletry articles such as moustache combs often employed beads and other perforated ornaments as dangles. Many other perforated artifacts were sewn onto articles of clothing, such as cloud collars or tippets, and on headdresses (Liu 1982a); while similar artifacts are seen on Chinese necklaces it is not known if the use is traditional.

Soon after resumption of trade with the People's Republic of China, collectors were overwhelmed by

DANGLES ASSEMBLED FOR EXPORT These pieces combine elements that were never actually used together, but are a means for acquiring unusual beads or elements. There are five real Tibetan dZi beads (three broken), a broken etched agate, a plastic dZi copy with organic inlay, two ceramic dZi, and four copies in glass. Longest dZi is ca. 3.0 cm. Note other beads, bi and eternal knots. *Courtesy of Overseas Trading Company.*

CLOISONNE AND ENAMEL BEADS are probably pre-World War II vintage and purchased in the United States during the middle 1970s. Made of copper, with varying degrees of finesse; best are the large tabular beads. Some display an openwork technique in which part of the surface is gilded; others are stamped and enameled (silver or blue tabular bead). Contemporary examples from the People's Republic of China or Taiwan can be readily differentiated from the ones shown. It is still not known how these were used, but some were joined for use as belt buckles. Sizes range from 1.9 to 5.1 cm long.

the quantity and quality of Chinese beads and jewelry flooding into the West. A fair number of older collectors had originally purchased beads from existing supplies in the United States, and these beads have provided a basis for comparison with newly arriving ones; for example, substantial amounts of glass ornaments may have been imported in the 1920s, evident from quantities represented in collections dating from that period (Liu 1984). After trade resumed, the best sources in the United States were usually from individual dealers and small firms that imported directly from China; native-speaking Chinese had an edge, especially when they bought in the large lots required by government agencies. The prices and selections were often better than those of the Far East, a disappointment to collectors who enjoyed combining travel and personally searching for beads. Dale (1981) reported on this aspect of

bead buying in South Asia and the Far East, while Eyster (1988) lists some Asian and Pacific bead stores.

The major auction houses in Hong Kong, London and other important Western cities are ongoing sources of fine beads and other perforated ornaments. For example, the Spink & Son Chinese jewelry and glass auctions of 1989 and 1991 in London offered fine quality beads, frequently rearranged for Western aethetics. Even ancient Chinese glass beads have been occasionally auctioned.

NATURAL INORGANICS

Stone is an abundant part of the natural inorganic bead materials. Ancient and antique stone beads and pendants remain available, but separating the genuine from a copy is difficult, especially since the copying of earlier prototypes was an accepted and established practice for at least the last thousand years (*see page*

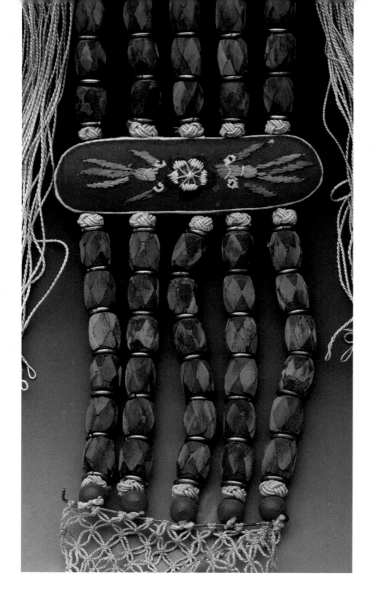

KINGFISHER FEATHER BEADS on a hanging ornament. Feather mosaics are glued onto a wood or composition core; the beads are 0.8 cm diameter. Note metal fillers; red beads are similar to those on page 62. Such antique feather beads are unique to the Chinese. *Courtesy of Overseas Trading Company.*

INTRICATELY PIERCED PENDANT AND BEADS comprise this antique necklace; the beads and gourd pendant are hollowed ivory or bone. Supposedly this form of carving was a specialty of the Cantonese industry. Contemporary workers are not apt to work at this level of crafting. *Courtesy of Overseas Trading Company.*

54). Use of traditional imagery pervades Chinese personal adornment yet today, and antique and more recent stone beads, pendants and toggles make most attractive ornaments. Their well-carved (a more accurate term is well-ground) shapes and excellent crafting are regarded as wonderful miniature sculptures (*see pages 55, 63*). As imitations and substitutions abound (Liu 1980), some simulations of semi-precious beads in glass are so good that professional jewelers and other authorities have misattributed them (Liu 1980), like the prominent department store in Texas that sold as jade a strand of twenty-three carved glass beads for twenty-three hundred dollars (J. Feast, *pers. comm.* 1980). There has also been idiosyncratic use of carving: Guatemalan and British Columbian jade scraps were cut into beads in Hong Kong during the late

1970s; at that time, some Western firms' primary business was jade paraphernalia for cocaine use. For contemporary jewelry designers, the semi-precious stones of Hong Kong, Taiwan and the People's Republic of China continue to be an indispensable part of their supply repertoire, with ever more shapes and materials (*see page 52*) providing diversity in designs.

SYNTHETIC INORGANICS

Clay, faience, ceramic, glass, and metals predominately make up the synthetic inorganic bead materials. Chinese beads of clay and faience are rarely found in the marketplace; those of ceramic, usually porcelain, are fairly common, although the quality is not good. Antique metal beads and pendants, abundant and highly collectible during the 1970s and 1980s (Liu 1984), have been superseded by large numbers of stamped and enameled beads and other perforated ornaments made from thin gauge gilded or plated base metals (Liu 1993), in contrast to the silver of older vintages. Cast copies of older beads and findings have been molded by Western firms to meet the demand for these desirable antique prototypes.

GLASS BEADS

Most Chinese glass ornaments available to collectors date from the nineteenth and twentieth centuries (late Qing dynasty, 1644 to 1911), with a very small portion of them from possibly a few hundred years earlier; even smaller amounts are ancient, and considerable numbers are from post-World War II production. While glassmaking in the Qing dynasty has been well-covered by Yang (1987, 1991), glass beadmaking itself has received little attention. Physical examination of Chinese glass beads, often called Peking or Canton glass, does not help determine where they were originally made. Boshan (Po-shan in older literature) in Shandong province is one of the better known Chinese glass bead-

making centers (Kan and Liu 1984). Workshops there have not only made glass ornaments but produced glass ingots and strips probably used elsewhere for reworking into glass objects, as in Beijing (Yang 1991). One workshop in this town was observed by Kan from 1983 to as recently as 1992 (*pers. comm.*), contrary to reports that it had concluded operation in 1990 (Sprague and An 1990). Once the workshop ceased exporting in the 1950s, the three to five middle-aged male workers began making beads primarily for Chinese minorities, a practice which continues with much of the product going to Yunnan and Thailand. Yunnan itself has a small glass bead workshop (P. Lewis, *pers. comm.* 1994). Guangzhou is another well-known bead manufacturing site. Francis (1990a) reports on other sites in Guizhou and Manchuria; the latter supposedly made beads for the Ainu of Japan. Yongzhou (near Shanghai) and Suzhou may have been other Qing glass bead producing locations (P. Kan, *pers. comm.* 1985-1986, Yang 1991*)*. During this period, Imperial workshops were making higher quality glass (Curtis 1991) and could also have made the better components of court necklaces, but

CINNABAR BEADS AND PENDANTS made in the People's Republic of China of mercuric sulfide lacquer built up in layers over a wood base, then template carved by machine on both sides; largest is 5.4 cm diameter. Carved cinnabar may date to the thirteenth century. Black derives from lampblack coloring the sap. *Courtesy of Abeada Corporation.*

COURT NECKLACE OF CARVED, PROBABLY PRUNE PITS AND LAPIDARY WORKED GLASS ORNAMENTS, which has likely been reassembled. Necklace consists of 108 beads, four large divider beads (Fu t'ou), a counterweight (44.0 cm long) with a balustrade bead and tabular or pancake-shaped bead (pei yün) and drop pendant (ta chu), as well as three counting strings worn two to the right, one to the left. Cammann (1979) states that fine glass was valued similar to lesser precious stones. This strand was bought in Beijing in the middle 1970s. *Courtesy of David K. Liu.*

FINIAL OF CORAL BEADS FOR MANDARIN OFFICIAL'S HAT The tiny beads are sewn in the shape of a Turk's knot. Both seed pearls and coral beads were used for finials; 2.3 cm diameter. The coral may have come from the Persian Gulf. *Courtesy of Dorothy J. Osakoda.*

proof is lacking. Currently, Boshan may be the only source of mandrel wound beads from China. Taiwan has glass beadmaking workshops, as evidenced by a strand of faceted blue cane beads examined in 1990 (G. Liese, *pers. comm.*), trail decorated glass beads by the Paiwan, and even glass seed beads.

A number of techniques observed at Boshan differ from Western methods and do not make sense unless viewed from a beadmaker's perspective. According to Kan (*pers. comm.* 1986), glass strips are made by pouring glass on stone or metal. Bubbles in the glass, considered almost diagnostic for Chinese glass beads, result from melting the glass strips together while making various colors (*see pages 58, 59*). One experienced American beadmaker surmised that these strips were dripped from a pot and then wheel rolled. Chinese beadmakers probably bundle the glass strips to help anneal the poor quality glass before it reaches the direct heat of the kiln's working fire (E. J. Johnson, *pers. comm.* 1989).

PORTION OF CORAL AND SILVER HAIRPIN (1.2 cm diameter) with dangle of seed pearls, coral and jade, including a tiny bat. Many types of beads and pendants are not used for necklaces. *Courtesy of Overseas Trading Company.*

Chinese glass beads of all types are treasured by collectors, from simple monochromes to the most elaborate millefiori (*see pages 58, 60, 61, 62, 64*). Chinese beads with millefiori designs, while not common are still being made, and normally with glossy finishes. A rare kind has a matte surface decorated with carefully trailed and millefiori designs, with the millefiori showing the similar sunburst design of more common ones (*see page 61*). Necklaces, bracelets and loose beads of this type are reputedly from one Hong Kong dealer with a Shanghai source that supplies from bead stock either confiscated by the Japanese or taken from a Japanese managed factory with Chinese labor that operated during World War II (J. Allen, *pers. comm.* 1981, 1993), although others have bought similar beads when visiting Xian. Altogether there are probably not more than half a dozen necklaces, bracelets and loose beads utilizing such millefiori in the United States; some were owned by a collector who flew to Hong Kong upon hearing of its avail-

ability. Harris (1984) and I (1985b) have further described these remarkable beads.

Although not all of these processes have been applied to Chinese glassworking, it has been heavily influenced by lapidary, carving, cloisonné, lacquerware, and metal techniques (C. Brown, *pers. comm.* 1992, Liu 1975c, 1985b), and many beads have been cold-worked after initial forming and/or overlay. Examination of imported Chinese glass jewelry shows that nearly every standard beadmaking technique has been used: mandrel winding (most common, including coiling, a term used by Francis 1990b; *see page 59*), cane, molding (second to winding), pressing (Harris 1983), hot pinching (Harris 1984b), and blowing (*see page 61*). Molding combined with lapidary methods was of paramount importance (*see pages 58, 63*). A full spectrum of decorations has been seen: overlay (*see page 62*), faceting or other lapidary work (*see page 62*), marvering (*see page 59*), impressed crumb and inlays (*see pages 60, 61, 64*), trailing (*see page 61*), millefiori (although in a peculiarly Chinese style, Harris 1984a),

NECKLACE OF CHAIN, JEWELRY COMPONENTS AND BEADS assembled for foreign sale; made of fine quality coral, turquoise, lapis (4.5 cm length), probably malachite beads, metal beads, caps, and fillers. *Courtesy of Dr. Bailey.*

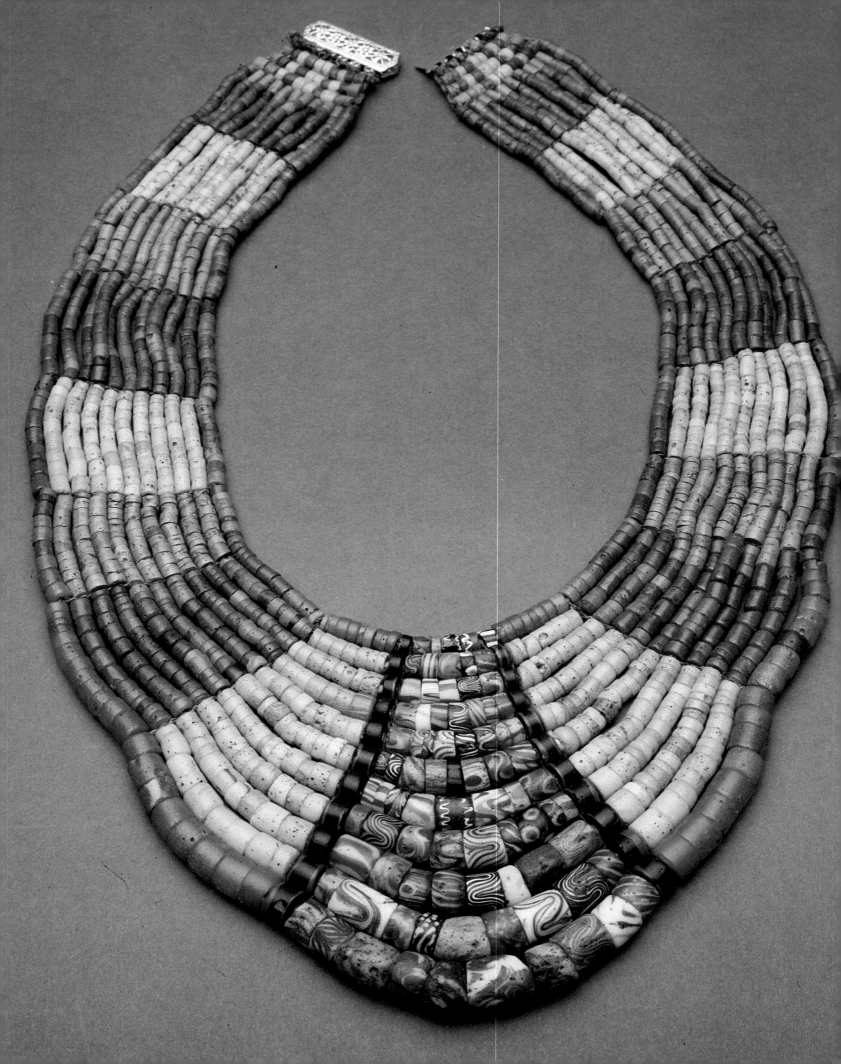

and filigrana or vetro a retorti (incorrectly called latti-cino). Yang (1991) describes more techniques, but these were not used for beads.

NATURAL ORGANICS

Chinese beads of natural organic origin are numerous, ranging from a notable use of carved seeds and corals (*see pages 62, 69;* old beads are being recarved in the People's Republic of China), to mollusk shells such as mother-of-pearl and freshwater pearls. A unique feature of Chinese pearl culture was the use of lead nuclei to form shapes like Buddhas. (Most Chinese pearls were non-nucleated until recently, but all other pearl industries use nuclei of shell origin.) Also used were bone, perhaps even snake vertebrae (M. Combs and B. Brandlein, *pers. comm. 1977),* walrus tusk, often dyed green to simulate jadeite or malachite, ivory (*see page 66),* hornbill casque

(*see page 62),* and amber. Beads of synthetic organics are made from reconstructed bone, ivory, wood, or incense dust. Cinnabar lacquer, formed from mixing the sap of a conifer with mercuric sulfide (Frankel 1993), is widely used for beads (usually in red and/or black colors; *see page 67)* and larger decorative objects.

A contemporary event of interest concerns dZi beads. For the last few years they have been in demand in Taiwan, which has had no traditional use of such beads. Supposedly, after the sole survivor of a vehicular accident was found to be wearing one, these Tibetan beads became quite popular (J. Carlsson, *pers. comm.* 1990). But an expatriate Tibetan has supplied another perhaps more appropriate version: the Taiwanese were told that by wearing dZi beads every day, their business would prosper (C. Blessing and H. Thalmann, *pers. comm.* 1994).

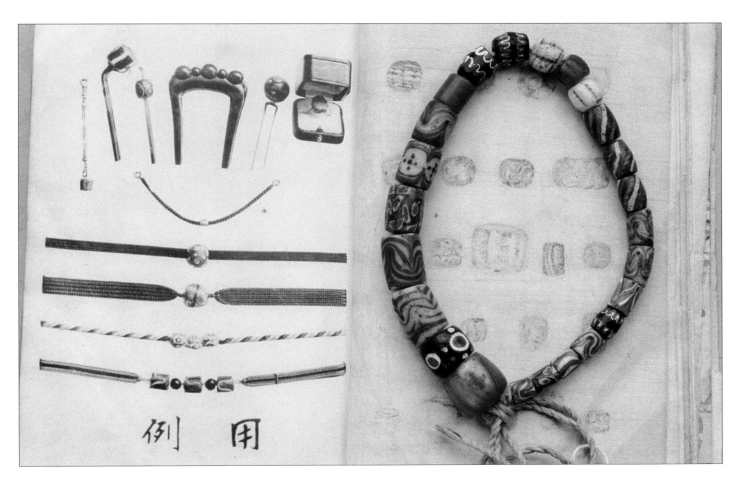

STRAND OF GLASS BEADS USED BY PAIWAN OF FORMOSA laid upon Japanese book published in Taipeh by the Aboriginal Shop circa 1920-28, showing use in traditional Japanese ornaments like hairpins and obidama. Bleeding colors underneath the beads are paintings of beads. The Paiwan gave female and male names to beads. Francis (1991, 1992) attributes the gold foil bead, the combed designs and chevron imitations as Chinese, although the latter are very similar to false chevrons in Indonesia and Africa (M. Heide, *pers. comm.* 1983). Melons are most likely Chinese. *Courtesy of Chung Collection. Opposite page:* RESTRUNG PAIWAN NECKLACE with center section containing valuable polychromes, similar to ones above. Two other similar necklaces are shown in Yoshimizu (1989), and one in Chen (1968), which has side strands near ends of the necklace, a feature also seen on a Formosan Bunun tribal necklace of shell (Chen 1978). (See Liu 1983, 1985a). *Courtesy of Donna Jacobs.*

JAPANESE LAMPWORKED GLASS BEADS depicting stylized fruits and vegetables in enticing colors and shapes. Some of the beads utilize crumb and glass powder for decoration. These fairly rare beads probably date from the 1950s, 1.2 to 1.9 cm long. *Courtesy of Ornamental Resources.*

JAPAN, INDIA, HIMALAYAN COUNTRIES, THAILAND, PHILIPPINES, AND INDONESIA

Although these geographic areas are grouped together partly for convenience, there are also significant relationships among them. In east Asia, the beads of Japan and Korea show similarities to each other, as well as to those of China. The beads of south Asia, Pakistan, India and her tribal areas, and the Himalayan countries (Nepal, Ladakh, Tibet, Bhutan) share common traits. Southeast Asia and island southeast Asia (the Philippines, Indonesia, Malaysia) can be grouped together as heirlooming of beads is common in this region. Sadly, the popularity of their ethnographic and ancient beads threatens the area's cultural heritage and the rapid acculturation and the looting of archaeological sites contribute to the depletion of their beads. Island southeast Asia also demonstrates the promising phenomenon of indigenous bead researchers conducting regional studies of their own beads such as Abellera (1981), Adhyatman and Arifin (1993) and Villegas (1983). In addition, many regions support considerable bead industries: Japan is now known for glass seed beads; India and Indonesia for glass (silver and gold bead manufacturing is another strong Indonesian jewelry industry); Thailand for metal; and the Philippines for beads made of natural products. The large array of new and old beads from this region makes them important to collectors, although the overall numbers are smaller than those from Africa or China.

KOREA AND JAPAN

Comma-shaped beads, called kogok or gokuk in Korea and magatama in Japan, are culturally and historically prominent pendants in both these countries, but only newer glass or stone versions are found on the market. Yoshimizu (1989) shows a fascinating necklace with a carnelian kogok as the center pendant, excavated in 1973 at Kyongju (Kwangju), Korea. Besides stone beads and the pendant, the necklace contains monochrome glass beads and an incredible glass bead with mosaic face and bird inlays. Of fine detail and realism, the millefiori images are distinct from those on Roman mosaic face beads. Individual image-bearing cane slices are marvered randomly onto the bead, instead of the orderly registers found in early and late Roman mosaic face beads. The closest parallel may be with mosaic beads bearing duck images, found in east Java (Adhyatman and

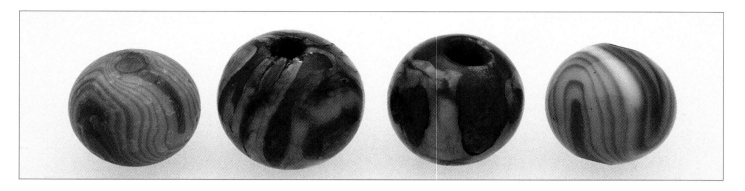

DYED WHALE MOLAR OJIME AND GLASS COPIES are unique to the Japanese. The beads are sometimes dyed green. The red colored beads are often incorrectly called crane's crest. These are 2.0 and 1.8 cm diameter respectively. *Courtesy of Fred Chavez and Naomi Lindstrom.*

SIMULATED CHEVRONS USED AS OJIME The left specimen is sleeved with a gold tube so cords will abrade less. Both beads are trail decorated; right bead is from Formosa, 1.6 to 1.7 cm diameter. Compare with those on pages 89 and 92, which are possibly of Asian and European origin. *Courtesy of Hugh Weiser.*

GLASS OJIME is a prime example of the beauty of Japanese glass beads. Countersunk perforation with a large and uniform diameter is diagnostic of Japanese beads used as ojime (Liu 1982b). It is likely of nineteenth or twentieth century vintage, 1.5 cm diameter. *Courtesy of Hugh Weiser.*

Arifin 1993), or an unpublished bead fragment with possible phoenix images from Afghanistan, now in the collection of The Bead Museum, Prescott, Arizona. These intriguing hints at other sources for mosaic beads need to be studied. No researcher has yet ventured a guess as to their origins.

While Francis (1985a, 1994) has surveyed the beads of Korea, few are available to collectors, nor has there been much contact with Korean beads. He has shown products of beadmakers trained in Japan when Korea was occupied by that country. These are mainly lampworked beads, including some that appear similar to the interlocking snake beads of Czechoslovakia. At the request of the Korean government, Howell traveled there in 1975 to advise them on how to start a glass bead industry (*pers. comm.* 1983). While his expertise was primarily in drawn beads, the bead sample cards Howell showed in 1983 from the

STRAND OF KOREAN BEADS including melon, oblates and coil beads, bought from a Seattle dealer. Beads bear resemblance to Chinese glass beads of similar shape, but have fewer bubbles and inclusions. A similar strand in the Bishop Museum, Honolulu, Hawaii is attributed to Korea. Largest bead is 2.2 cm diameter. *Courtesy of Albert Summerfield.*

MAGNIFICENT PIERCED AND ENGRAVED GOLD OJIME with a crab that has been possibly raised or repoussed from the inner surface. Only 2.8 cm high, it demonstrates the superb skills of Japanese ojime makers. The small scale does not diminish the aesthetic value. The perforation is sleeved to protect the hanging cords from abrasion. *Courtesy of Fred Chavez.*

Korean industry were chiefly lampworked beads, some very similar to so-called Peking glass beads and small gokuks. The similarities to Chinese beads may hinder identification in the future, as it has in the recent past. In over two decades of bead collecting, I have seen very few unequivocally Korean beads or pendants. Those displayed on this page are attributed to Korea, although they also fit the characteristics of Chinese glass beads; I have similar melon beads originally identified as Korean.

Japan is a major source of numerous types of beads sought by collectors, especially those that might have functioned as ojime, or slide fasteners on the netsuke-ojime-inro ensemble of feudal Japan. Ojime are among the most expensive beads; in 1979 one sold for about seventeen thousand dollars at a London auction. Ten years later, a quality ojime commanded twenty thousand dollars (R. Kinsey,

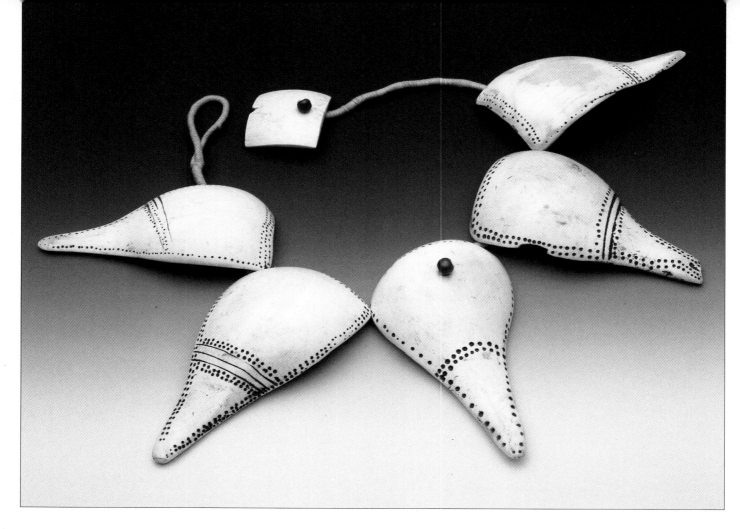

NAGA CHANK SHELL NECKLACE made from shell segments and decorated with dots and carnelian beads, possibly from Konyak Naga. Chank is a *Turbinella* species, not a conch. Whether segments are worn with the outside or inside of shell showing depends on the tribe (Jacobs *et al.* 1990). Necklace is possibly not intact. These sold from $300 to $400 wholesale in 1989. *Courtesy of Jackie Little.*

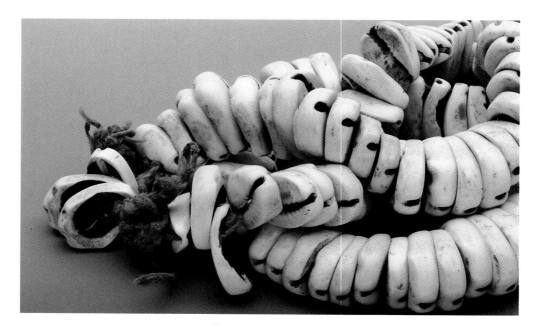

NAGA OR CHIN STRAND of cowrie shells that have been ground laterally, dorsally and ventrally. When strung these are very even in comparison to those that have not been ground; most cowries are sewn and not strung. Probably from Burma, each cowrie is about 2 cm long. (See Gabriel 1985). *Courtesy of Hands of the Hills.*

KONYAK NAGA NECKLACE with chank buttons as closures, bone spacers, glass beads of probably Indian origin, and cast brass pendants, purchased 1982 in India. These large necklaces hang low on the body. (See Gabriel 1985). *Courtesy of Hannelore Gabriel.*

pers. comm. 1989*)*. Recently, prices for high quality ojime have ranged from three to seven thousand dollars. This contrasts with about five thousand dollars for the current top price of Roman mosaic face beads. Any bead with a perforation large enough for double cords could have been used as ojime, and could be domestic or foreign in origin (Liu 1982b). Kinsey (1991) has discussed further differentiation of beads from ojime; his own collection numbers some two thousand. Some ojime are easily identified by material, crafting or whether they are sleeved (*see pages 74, 75*). Those not easily distinguished as ojime could have been considered just as desirable, since Edo period glass beads show high aesthetic merit, despite their often simple designs (*see page 74*). Like Chinese glass, some Japanese glass beads of the late seventeenth and early eighteenth centuries may exhibit crizzling if there is too much alkali flux in the glass. Glass beads with this deterioration tend to sweat drops of moisture on their surfaces when the

ambient humidity is above forty percent. This glass defect was introduced through Western glass formulae (C. Brown, *pers. comm.* 1992).

Post World War II, the Japanese glass bead industry produced many beautiful beads (*see page 72*), although it is currently oriented toward the production of precision glass seed beads that are sought by the large numbers of people engaged in beadwork. Fortunately some older products of the Japanese wound bead industry, such as foil or delicate fluted beads, are still available through Western bead dealers (Liu 1993a).

During the last decade and a half, Japan has produced a number of the world's master glass beadmakers. Many of their beads have been displayed in Yoshimizu (1989). Two of the greatest, Kyoyu Asao (*see page 11 and chapter eight*) and Kisao Iburi, have died. They not only made great strides in the reconstruction of ancient glass bead techniques, but were also artists (Liu 1986, Ukai 1980, 1984). In 1989, a

MOND MULTISTRAND NECKLACE of glass and brass beads; latter is 2.5 cm diameter and entire necklace is about 120 cm long, $150 in 1990. The lush colors, striking contrast with the glass and metal and dramatic volume of the multiple strands typify the best of Indian tribal designs; the simplicity is timeless. The massed effect of beads is also evident in Naga multistrand monochrome necklaces. *Courtesy of Art Expo.*

ANTIQUE INDIAN BEADS of gold washed silver, demonstrating the long tradition of that country's metalsmiths. Well crafted old beads like these are rare; largest is 5.3 cm high, 176 grams. *Courtesy of Art Expo.*

few years after his death, Asao's beads were selling for six hundred-sixty dollars each; prices for Iburi's work at a New York gallery were comparable prior to his death in 1993. Kenoyer (1993) reported prices of sixty to one thousand dollars for contemporary eye beads on a recent trip to Japan. By contrast, the highest price for a contemporary American glass bead was six hundred dollars in 1993. Whether Japanese craftspeople will continue to create quality beads remains a question, as beads are not an important item of personal adornment in that country. Artist-made glass beads may assume a position comparable to contemporary ojime, which are not worn, but frequently collected by foreigners and some Japanese. Interestingly, contemporary ojime are now carved by both native Japanese and Western artists.

INDIA AND THE HIMALAYAN COUNTRIES

India is such an important producer of glass and stone beads that anyone collecting beads from Africa, the Middle East or Asia will encounter them. It has long been assumed that some ancient stone beads found at Ur in Mesopotamia originated from the Indus Valley civilization (in modern Pakistan and India). Kenoyer (1993) has observed that ancient beads now brought out by Afghan refugees and antique dealers, which were looted from burials dating from 2000 to 3000 B.C., bear similarities to those of Ur, raising the possibility that additional sources supplied carnelian beads to Mesopotamia. The long, elegant carnelian bicones from the Indus Valley as well as those from Afghanistan and the Tairona of Precolumbian Colombia were all popular in the recent past, selling at five hundred dollars each.

Francis (1988) has thoroughly covered the beads of India, from those of natural products to ones made by the large glass bead industries of the northern and southern regions. While Indian beadmakers are quite active, it is only recently that their wares became collectible. Wound Indian glass beads of the 1970s and early 1980s were often large, garish and crude, traits shared by the beadmakers of Hyderabad, Pakistan

who left India after 1947 (Francis 1988). Czech bead-making expertise has been available to at least some portion of the northern Indian wound bead industry since 1940 (Francis 1988), but it was only in the 1980s that Indian lampwork and millefiori beads began making real progress. Among these were Indian face beads (Harris 1981, 1991, van der Made 1988), chevron beads (Picard and Picard 1993) and lampwork beads now being sold in America, Europe and Japan, and often confused with antique Venetian beads. Leong (*pers. comm.* 1993) reports that three best-sellers at a Japanese store were Indian glass beads, old workshirts and dishes from the United States. Peterson (*pers. comm.* 1994) reports that even Venetians are selling Indian glass beads, presumably as their own products.

Because India has so many ethnically diverse minorities, its jewelry is equally varied. Untracht (1988), an authority on Indian metalwork, has summarized the jewelry, including beads; those of metal reflect superb jewelry technique (Liu 1990b;

MIZORAM CARNELIAN STRANDS WITH AND WITHOUT PUMTEK BEADS One strand has Venetian glass beads. Largest carnelian bead has a 1.4 cm diameter, possibly of Indian or perhaps German origin. The Mizoram also wear amber, some fake. *Courtesy of Art Expo.*

TREATED AND ETCHED AGATES AND CARNELIANS from the Himalayan countries and the Middle East. The etched carnelians are most likely of Indian and Afghan origin and are desired collectibles. Among the natural banded agates (treated to accentuate banding) and etched agates are probably some from Middle Eastern sources. Note Chung dZi at the lower left, and upper right; latter is 11.9 cm long. *Courtesy of Robert Brundage.*

see page 78). Not often available, but imported by a few American dealers, are beads of various Indian tribal groups, such as those from Orissa and other states (see page 78).

The Naga possess India's most spectacular and prominent tribal jewelry. These hill peoples of northeast India and adjacent areas of Myanmar (Burma), renowned for their martial prowess and past head hunting practices, comprise some fifteen tribes (Jacobs, Macfarlane, Harrison, and Herle 1990). At least seven tribes wear beaded necklaces and belts, usually composed of large shell elements and beads, as well as glass and stone beads, brass pendants and wide spacers. The most prominent are worn by the Ao, Angami and Konyak (Barbier 1984, Jacobs et al. 1990; see pages 76, 77). The Angami made long shell beads from the columella of conch for their own use and for trade. Jacobs et al. (1990) show the process and tools for this manufacture. Naga jewelry started appearing in the United States in the late 1970s; its dramatic appearance and associated mythology created demand and high prices, the latter dropping by the middle 1980s. Access to outside material culture, rapid acculturation and conversion to Christianity (introduced by Indian Naga rebels in the middle 1970s, Jacobs et al. 1990), all contributed to the Nagas' relinquishment of their striking personal adornment.

Myanmar, part of which borders on Nagaland, also has tribes with interesting jewelry, such as the Chin (see page 76) and Kachin. Pumtek (Allen 1986), Burmese amber and intact necklaces of shells or mixed materials are not only collectible but technically challenging (Liu 1992a). Pumtek beads are important to the Chin; in the early twentieth century, the beads were supplied by villagers who were looting at the site of an old Pyu city (Francis 1994). When this source was exhausted, new beads with similar patterns were made of fossilized wood, in contrast to the opalized palm wood of the Pyu beads (Francis 1994); some may have been made with excavated bead blanks (J. Allen, pers. comm. 1993). Allen also feels these Mizo beads were inspired by and imitate etched agate beads; he has seen transitions between pumtek and real etched agate that came from Myanmar in 1988 (Allen 1990; see pages 79, 83).

The Himalayan area in south Asia is extremely rich in beads, more so since Tibetan refugees have moved into Nepal and other countries of the region. Beads are still very much a part of the religious and cultural lives of the inhabitants of Ladakh, Tibet,

TIBETAN PENDANT worn from the shoulder; three dZi are 1.8 cm long, of a type commonly worn on ornaments. Other components are Chinese jadeite carvings, jade elements and beads, pearls, real and imitation precious stone beads. *Courtesy of private collection.*

TWELVE EYED AGATE DZI BEAD with well executed designs and a translucent quality, 6.4 cm length. Analysis of perforation casts by Kenoyer has confirmed Allen's suspicion that this is a dZi bead copy made by Idar-Oberstein. Compare real stone dZi and this imitation in Liu 1982a. There are other stone, glass, bone, metal, and plastic fakes. *Courtesy of Art Expo.*

Nepal, and Bhutan. Coral, turquoise and amber beads have been the staples of this area, although agates and other hardstones also figure prominently in collectors' interests (*see this and opposite page*). American turquoise beads have been brought from the Tucson gem show for sale to Tibetans in Nepal (M. Maxwell, *pers. comm.* 1983), and Russians are now selling European amber in the Himalayas (C. Blessing, *pers. comm.* 1993).

It is the patterned agates, ranging from so-called etched or bleached carnelians to the famous dZi or gZi beads, that make Himalayan beads so well known to collectors (*see pages 80, 81, 83*). An Australian couple even bought a collection of these beads while they were living in New Guinea during 1983. Prior to 1980, no one had written about dZi beads in detail (Liu 1980a); since then, a vigorous debate has arisen. Articles on numerous additional patterns and fakes have been published (*see references and bibliography*), but people are still being deceived. An American woman in Venice paid about one thousand dollars for a sup-

posedly real dZi, and Tibetans in Lhasa were using fake dZi as loan collateral at Chinese banks (J. Carlsson, *pers. comm.* 1990). Many countries have made imitation dZi beads, ranging from ludicrous to excellent: India, China, Taiwan, Germany, Italy, and at least one other unidentified European country that used a dense plastic. Kenoyer and Allen, the former through examination of silicon casts of perforations, have confirmed that Idar-Oberstein made convincing agate copies of dZi beads (J. Allen, *pers. comm.* 1993; *see page 81*). Kenoyer believes the method of drilling perforations may be diagnostic for country of origin (J. Allen, *pers. comm.* 1994). Real dZi are revered in Tibet, where they are still extremely expensive; in 1975, a nine eyed dZi in Nepal was traded for forty-four hectares of land (J. Cline, *pers. comm.* 1970s). In the United States, prices for various dZi beads range up to more than eight thousand dollars. Weihreter (1988) and zu Windisch-Graetz (1981) have published excellent photographic documentations of Himalayan

CARNELIAN, TURQUOISE AND CORAL BEADS FROM THE HIMALAYAS show favored materials for personal adornment. The carnelian pendant or pemma-raka (4.9 cm wide) is strung with mother-of-pearl and melon beads. The turquoise nugget bead is Tibetan, as are the coral beads, which are fragments bound together with an asphalt-like material. This gives a matrix-like effect similar to turquoise, adding to the attractiveness of these beads along with the irregular contours. *Courtesy of Art Expo.*

BEADS FROM HIMALAYAN COUNTRIES WITH MANY DZI showing six eyed (3.1 cm long), Chung and other patterns, as well as coral, turquoise and amber beads. The eyed dZi is the most highly prized of those shown; recent prices in the United States for two to four eyed dZi range from $2,600 to $8,400. Note the small tyio strung as a bead, perforated beryl crystal and the molded, worn Chinese glass imitation of carved coral. Beads of natural substances vastly outnumber synthetic ones. *Courtesy of Robert Brundage.*

PUMTEK BEADS from Mizoram, India made from opalized wood, they superficially resemble etched or bleached agates or carnelians. Heirloomed by the Chin of Burma, no one has yet suggested how these patterns are applied onto the beads. New pumtek beads are also being made (See Allen 1986, 1990). Square, tabular beads are 2.7 cm long. *Courtesy of Art Expo and Michael Heide.*

UNIQUE TRUNCATED BICONE BEADS OF BAN CHIANG These beads range from deep blue to turquoise to greenish, with diameters of 1.2 to 2.5 cm. They are usually not devitrified nor refinished. Perforations are large, ranging from 1.0 to 1.2 cm diameters. No study on their origins has been undertaken. There are also fake ones of more translucent glass (D. and S. Dunning, *pers. comm.* 1990); those shown are 1.5 cm diameter.

BAN CHIANG BEADS Shown are characteristic bicones, disks of orange glass and cylindrical beads of stone and glass (7.5 cm long), the latter among the longest in Asia. Ban Chiang glass often has a greasy appearance. *Courtesy of Ken Klassen, Jackie Little and Sid Port.*

bead jewelry, including dZi beads shown as worn, similar to the chest ornament on page 81.

THAILAND

Beads from Ban Chiang and related cultures famous for pottery are perhaps the most well known beads from Thailand, consisting of distinctive assemblages of short bicones of green and blue glass, long cylindrical beads of the same color, disks of orange glass and associated carnelian, quartz crystal, and other hardstone beads (*see this page*; only the disks have been dated to 300 to 250 B.C.). The cylindrical glass beads rank among the longest of beads in Asia (Liu 1985b; *see this and opposite page*). There is even a very rare type of sharp pointed comma-shaped pendant reminiscent of magatama, which is contemporaneous with Ban Chiang bicones (Brown 1983, Francis 1985b). Indo-Pacific beads are also found in Thailand (Francis 1990e, Liu 1985a) and may even have been manufactured there (Francis 1990c). Other sites yield carnelian, agate and etched agate

QUARTZ, GLASS AND BRONZE BEADS possibly from Tak sites (Shaw 1985), some showing signs of decomposition from burial. Those most affected are the melon beads, while coil beads are in pristine condition. If these are Chinese, the fact may help in dating. *Courtesy of Jackie Little.*

BAN CHIANG CYLINDRICAL BEADS OF GLASS AND STONE, 16.0 and 8.9 cm long respectively. Glass beads are folded or rolled and are probably imitations of the stone ones; all have sloping ends. The stone bead shows evidence of string sawing on the ends; therefore, it is possibly not a hardstone. These cylindrical stone beads have been dated to between 880 B.C. and the middle third millennium (Francis 1985b). *Courtesy of Jackie Little and Bob Olson.*

beads (Glover *et al.* 1984). Tak hilltop burial sites yield glass and rock crystal beads (Shaw 1985) which are similar to those on this page. Like many other archaeological sites in Thailand, it was looted, so little information is available, a situation also relevant for Ban Chiang sites. Even faience and additional types of glass beads were found at a site that was occupied circa 900 B.C. to 800 A.D. (Pilditch 1992). Some glass beads resemble those of the Paiwan on Formosa but neither their source nor age is known. Chinese monochrome beads are sold in Thailand and the Philippines and attributed as beads excavated in the People's Republic of China (E. Mann, *pers. comm.* 1985), although Kessler (1992) was not able to find similar beads in Beijing's artifact markets.

Only heirloom glass beads of the Akha are of ethnographic origin, primarily Chinese and often made in Shandong workshops (see Liu 1992a). The Lewises (1984) thoroughly describe the ornaments of the Akha and the neighboring hill tribes, and Francis (1992b) has included illustrations of some of their

beads. Many beads from the Akha or other tribes who use beads in the vicinity of the Golden Triangle (Burma, Thailand, Laos, Yunnan) have reached the market only through the arduous collecting trips of dealers like Hands of the Hills. Here beads or ornaments are bought or traded without significant influence on the cultural heritage of these tribal or minority peoples as the relinquishing of goods is voluntary.

This is in sharp contrast to those beads obtained by the looting of archaeological sites in Southeast and island southeast Asia, especially Thailand, the Philippines and Indonesia. Beads were probably not the principal target of the looters, as ceramic pottery and gold jewelry are the primary antiquities offered in auction catalogs. Even though tomb or grave robbing is a phenomenon dating to ancient times and may even have acceptance in some cultures (*see chapter one*), there is no doubt that buying items from illegal excavations presents a major moral quandary. The collector or researcher desires to acquire new and unknown material so that it can be documented, since one never

PHILIPPINE SHELL NECKLACE (palagapang) of the Ifugao, northern Luzon. Strung on braided rattan and incised, these trapazoidal plaques of mother-of-pearl are probably from the gold-lipped pearl oyster, often seen whole in New Guinean adornment. Most plaques are undecorated and worn by both sexes "tied closely around the neck to form a fan of gleaming light on the wearer's chest" (Ellis 1981). Jewelry made of mother-of-pearl and other shells, as well as hornbill, was worn in striking ways by a number of Luzon tribes. *Courtesy of Jackie Little.*

KALINGA HEIRLOOM BEADS, northern Luzon, Philippines; on top row are onyx beads probably from Idar-Oberstein and glass imitations. To the right is a Czech or Bohemian glass copy of a carnelian bead, next to which is a melon bead that is probably Chinese. The monochromes and polychromes are most likely European but the trail decorated chevron is not. Its core is white, cased by cobalt blue, with red and white trailings. Beads are 1.2 to 4.8 cm long. *Courtesy of Benjamin Abellera.*

SHELL, STONE, GLASS, AND METAL BEAD NECKLACE from the Philippines, either from the Bontoc or the Ifugao of Luzon. The large cylindrical beads with double perforations could be either giant clam, *Tridacna* or white limestone; largest is 6.6 cm long. Francis (1992b) feels most are stone and have been cut by the Bontoc. There are also some Czech imitations, presumably of glass. Other stone beads in this necklace consist of carnelian, onyx and possibly glass imitations of the latter. The glass beads are Venetian trail decorated and chevrons, along with small metal beads. In the Philippines, metal beads are often intricate and beautifully made but overlooked because of their small size. Note there are thin spacers with double perforations flanking each shell bead. These spacers are possibly horn, which is widely used for beads in the Philippines; such beads are often a golden red color. *Courtesy of Jackie Little.*

knows if they will be available again. One rationalizes that the damage has already been done to the site and that the beads will certainly be bought by someone else. But an individual's refusal to purchase looted beads will not stop the practice, only a concerted effort might, along with help from local officials. In addition, where poverty is rampant, alternative economic incentives must be offered.

THE PHILIPPINES

The Philippine archipelago has been the crossroads for many cultures, religions and sea traders, and it is rich in beads found in archaeological and ethnographic origins. Because of the abundance of gold jewelry and beads in archaeological sites, gold ornaments are probably the cause of most looting, with glass and stone beads a byproduct (Stark 1992, Villegas 1983). Of the excavated material, Indo-Pacific glass beads, Chinese coil beads (Francis 1990a) and hardstone beads are the majority. Here the destructive effects of looting are ameliorated somewhat by the maintenance of a type bead collection by the Philippine National Museum. Begun by American archaeologist Robert Fox, it has been continued by Rey Santiago since Fox's death (Francis 1990a, 1991b). This type collection will provide a record of the

islands' beads and continue to grow in usefulness. Such practices should be emulated by countries where beads are important to their cultural history.

Filipina bead collectors and traders are among the most numerous for any Asian country. I have encountered few who sold ancient or ethnographic beads in the United States, although contemporary beads from there are often on the market. In 1975, a woman dealer visited me, bringing strands of glass beads supposedly from the Philippines but actually more similar to those imported from Africa (Liu 1985a: figures 2, 10). Among types found in both areas are the so-called Ming beads, white glass Venetian wound beads with blue trail decorated squiggles. Much valued by the Kalinga, to whom it was worth the equivalent of a small pig (Abellera 1981), this is an example of local value, an important factor in determining the desirability and value of beads. Perhaps the difference in perception of value may lie partly in misattribution, as the Ming bead is regarded in the Philippines as a porcelain bead from Syria (Abellera 1981, Villegas 1983).

Besides the Kalinga (*see opposite page*), the Ifugao, Gad-dang, and Bontoc all value heirloom beads (Abellera 1981, Francis 1990a, 1992b, 1993b). The Bontoc are among those who wear snake vertebrae as beads,

CONTEMPORARY GRANULATED SILVER BEADS from Bali, Indonesia; largest is 3.6 cm long. Some are partially oxidized and some have sleeved perforations. All are well made, part of a considerable silver and gold Indonesian jewelry industry which also produces high karat granulated gold beads. *Courtesy of Art Expo.*

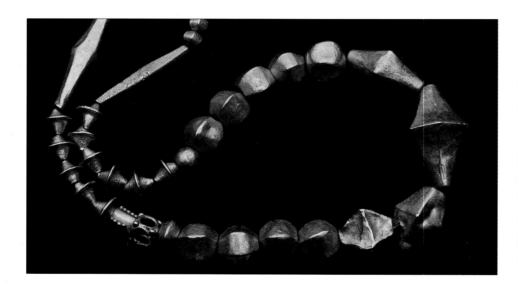

STRAND OF ANCIENT GOLD BEADS from east Java, Indonesia circa twelfth to fourteenth centuries. Made primarily of sheet gold, with some granulation, this strand weighs 24.2 grams; longest bead is 2.2 cm; auctioned in 1992, with an estimate of $600. Many gold beads and other gold jewelry of similar vintage were in this major Singapore auction (Stark 1992). *Courtesy of Andy Ng.*

in the form of handbands; only two tribes in Africa, possibly the Jaleno of New Guinea, some Native Americans, and possibly some Chinese also engage in this practice. Shell spacers and beads of *Tridacna,* the giant clam, are used by the Bontoc (*see page 87*). Other shell pendants, especially various oysters, are a dramatic part of Philippine adornment, as well as in the South Pacific (*see page 86*). On some strands, such as the Bontoc necklace, one notes the use of small metal beads; these are usually silver, low karat gold or gold washed silver (Liu 1985a: figure 12). Exquisitely made, their vintage is

medieval or colonial (Villegas 1983: table 4).

As to the age of most Philippine heirloom beads, Francis (1990a) postulates that they are no more than one hundred-fifty years old, in contrast to Sarawak, Malaysia, where some heirloom beads are a thousand years old. This difference is attributed to more trading activity with Malaysians, who may have supplied the early Islamic beads of Sarawak. In the Philippines, a longer period of burying the dead with their beads may have prevented them from being heirloomed.

Carnelian and onyx beads of heirloom origin

HEIRLOOM BEADS FROM KALIMANTAN, INDONESIA with one bone bicone among the glass ones. The glass beads include monochrome oblate and melon which may be Chinese, two barrel beads similar to those Francis (1992c) labels Let beads, valued by the Kelabit; possibly made by Chinese living in Java. Those with retorte or trailed decorations are usually assumed to be Venetian, although some may have other origins. Of the chevrons, one is possibly a molded five layer cane bead, two are simulations. Blue cases a white core; others (not shown) are all black (chevrons 0.8 to 1.0 cm long). Although labeled by some as Chinese, more information is needed. *Courtesy of Andy Ng.*

ANCIENT FACETED BICONE WITH NEW EXAMPLE, former from Java, considered by Adhyatman and Arifin (1993) to be made by Indo-Pacific beadmakers. The new one is from the active beadmakers in the vicinity of Surabaya, Java; it has a ground finish and a drilled perforation versus folded or rolled for the excavated specimen, 2.8 and 2.3 cm respectively. *Courtesy of Elizabeth J. Harris and Gabrielle Liese.*

appear to be German, although a number are not as regular and may be Indian. Often mixed with real stone beads are Czech or Bohemian glass imitations. None of the glass beads are manufactured domestically (Francis 1990a), with the oldest of Indian origin, although some of the Indo-Pacific beads may have also been made elsewhere in Southeast Asia (Francis 1990c, e). Newer beads are Venetian and Czech. Those made by the Prosser method may come from yet another European country. While some beads may be Middle Eastern, too many have been erroneously labeled Syrian or Egyptian (see Villegas 1983: 34-35).

Many other glass beads have been attributed to the Chinese; the monochromes appear to fit the characteristics of Chinese beads. The Pang-o of the Ifugao, which is a type of gold foil bead found only in the Philippines and dates from the fifteenth to sixteenth centuries, is also declared Chinese because of its high lead content (Francis 1993b). Francis has identified other glass beads as Chinese, such as trail decorated imitations of chevrons, although caution is needed until more information is available. Once attribution has appeared in print, it is often difficult to correct.

EAST JAVA MILLEFIORI GLASS BEADS of the more common patterns and colors. All except for the green one have straight perforations, 1.7 to 2.4 cm diameter. Those with mosaic canes of yellow, red, white, and blue are most similar to ones from the Middle East. All have been ground to some degree with emery paper. The white and blue one in the foreground has resin in the missing portions. The glass of the yellow and green bead to the far left is most susceptible to devitrification. Most Jatim beads (term for Jawa = Java, Timur = East, Adhyatman, *pers. comm.* 1994) have only a thin coating of canes over a monochrome core. *Courtesy of Michael Carr and John Strusinski.*

COMBED EAST JAVA BEADS, right specimen is one of the rare ones that have not been sanded, like the adjacent one (2.75 to 2.8 cm high). Jatim beads came on the market in the middle 1980s. They were selling for $15 to $35 each for the more common types; monochrome ones were much cheaper. The highest asking prices were $1,200 to $1,600 each, but those beads actually sold for $600 to $800 each (J. Allen, *pers. comm.* 1994). Not all monochrome beads from Indonesia are considered Jatim, as there are large Indo-Pacific beads, as well as later Chinese ones. *Courtesy of Cynthia Boeck and Richard Stamm.*

INDONESIA

Indonesia is the most interesting part of island southeast Asia for bead collectors. This large archipelago has not only ancient glass beads that are intriguing as to origins and methods of manufacture, but also heirloom beads of varied ages and origins and a nascent glass bead industry which mimics many heirloom beads.

The recent publication of Adhyatman and Arifin's (1993) book on Indonesian beads is of great assistance in documenting this rich heritage. While errors exist in the work due to a lack of communication with other bead researchers and the difficulty in accessing bead literature, such studies are a welcome sign that Indonesians and others are recognizing the importance of all aspects of their cultural heritage. (Ulrich Beck, a former resident of Indonesia, has put his own excellent collection of beads from Indonesia on display in a private museum and gallery in Albufeira, Portugal.) When comparing what is available in Indonesia with what has been exported to the West or Japan, it is evident that American imports

MANDREL WOUND SIMULATION OF EAST JAVA MOSAIC BEAD AND PROTOTYPE (note resin restoration around the perforation); the new bead is a product of the Javanese glass bead industry, 2.5 cm diameter. The mosaic canes are imitated by trail decoration, then the bead is ground to copy the similar surface of looted beads from which corroded glass has been removed. Due to the beadmaker's secrecy, it is not known exactly where the bead was made, although there are many beadmakers around Surabaya. *Courtesy of Michael Carr and Elizabeth J. Harris.*

are a representational sample, although much limited in range.

Only stone, metal and glass beads, along with some animal teeth and claws, have been offered on the marketplace; glazed ceramic beads are rarely encountered. The most common stone beads are carnelian, often faceted; undoubtedly most are Indian, although Francis (1993a) has described an ancient as well as several contemporary stone industries in Sumatra. Idar-Oberstein carnelians and Czech glass imitations are found in heirloom assemblages (Liu 1985a). Fossil and limestone beads and their possible glass imitations have interested collectors (*see page 222*). Metal beads include gold washed silver beads or gold beads (*see page 88*) of ancient or ethnographic origins; such gold beads of the eighth to fourteenth centuries are exceedingly numerous (Stark 1992). Although Adhyatman and Arifin (1993) have cited foreign collectors' interest in beads as the reason for tomb looting in Indonesia, the richness of the gold jewelry might also have had an important contributory role. There is now a thriving jewelry industry

GOLD JAVANESE EAR ORNAMENT set with a possibly glass cabochon and striped Indo-Pacific bead in claw mounts, most likely pre-1400 A.D. Mounting of beads in metal jewelry is still practiced in Taiwan and in the Philippines. Bead is 0.6 cm diameter. *Courtesy of Andy Ng.*

that produces beautiful granulated silver (*see page 88*) and high karat gold beads.

Indonesia's glass beads are the most exciting. Indo-Pacific beads, which are widely distributed from east Africa to Japan (Francis 1990c), are valued as heirlooms and known as mutisalah. This term encompasses both drawn Indo-Pacific beads and coil beads; the latter are wound and attributed to the Chinese (Francis 1991a). Both are monochrome,

GLASS BEADS FROM IRIAN JAYA (the Indonesian portion of New Guinea) are most likely Chinese, although few such beads have ever been found in the People's Republic of China. These beads are supposedly used in bride purchases. There are now copies of melon beads from Java. Longest cylinder is 3.5 cm. *Courtesy of Andy Ng.*

but the drawn mutisalah always bears a matte surface. Adhyatman and Arifin (1993) also attribute some striped beads as Indo-Pacific (*see page 91*) and call other opaque or clear faceted bicones by-products of this industry (*see page 89*).

From Java come the largest glass beads in Asia (others being Ban Chiang cylinders and possibly melon beads of the Ainu), these reach up to five centimeters in length. Monochrome or polychrome, east Javanese beads are distinguished by a thin layer of mosaic canes or preformed stripes over a monochrome core (J. Allen, *pers. comm.* 1994). In a few specimens the canes extend throughout (Liu 1986b: figure 6). Francis (1991a) has classified Javanese beads into two main types, depending on the degree of fusion of the core and the type of perforation (*see pages 90, 91*). These Javanese beads appeared on the market in the middle 1980s; almost all are refinished with emery paper to remove the devitrified surface, resulting from burial in moist dolmen graves primarily of eastern Java (*see page 90*). Some oblates are even reground to different shapes (such as melons and faceted bicones) or have missing portions filled with resin. Eventually all resin beads, cement fakes or contemporary glass imitations in trailed glass appeared on the market (Adhyatman and Arifin 1993, Liu 1986b, 1992b). Monochrome blue glass beads with trailed bird and sunburst designs are

VENETIAN POLYCHROME BEADS AND IMITATION CHEVRON BEADS, probably from Kalimantan; while the beads of the outer strand are often identified as Venetian, some patterns are also shown in an illustration of the valuable Lukut Sekala beads (Chin 1984). Inner strand consists entirely of black chevron copies; largest is 0.8 cm long. These are middle 1980s imports. *Courtesy of Andy Ng.*

other famous ancient beads from Indonesia. In very rare instances, birds and millefiori occur on the same bead. There are at least five different styles of birds (Adhyatman and Arifin 1993), possibly contemporaneous with other ancient glass beads from Java. Fakes have been made of bird beads and now are available in many new versions (*see page 225*).

Some mosaic patterns of Javanese beads are identical to Persian ones of the first to third centuries, although the canes extend to the perforation in beads from the Middle East (Fukai 1977: plate 47, second row from top). A few Javanese mosaic beads are similar if not identical to Paluan millefiori beads that are used as money (Ritzenthaler 1954: Palua in Micronesia is about fifteen hundred miles from Java). Previously labeled as Majapahit, these Javanese monochrome and polychrome beads are probably made in the Sriwijaya kingdom, dating from the ninth to tenth centuries (Adhyatman, *pers. comm.* 1994). Stamm (*pers. comm.* 1987) has seen small to large clumps of glass in coconut groves in Java, possible indication of glassworking sites. It has not yet been determined if the mosaic canes were imported from the Middle East, locally made or a combination. Indeed, no one has published on what methods were used to make the various types of Javanese beads, although Allen (*pers. comm.* 1993) has advanced the theory that they were hot-pinched.

Undoubtedly ancient Javanese beads were strung and worn in necklaces, but there are two other more interesting uses. Some contemporaneous gold Javanese jewelry, including pendants and rings, used striped beads as jewels (Liu 1986b: figures 1, 2; *see page 91*). This unusual use is also practiced by the Japanese and Taiwanese with Paiwan beads, and in the Philippines with Kalinga beads. In addition Javanese millefiori beads are supposedly used to cover the eyes, nose, ears, mouth, navel, and genitals of corpses (A. Ng, *pers. comm.* 1986), similar to placing jade artifacts such as cicadas on the dead of ancient China (Liu 1986b).

Beads from Indonesia of ethnographic or heirloom origin are equally fascinating: Chinese monochromes occur in a wide variety of shapes, especially from Irian Jaya (*see pages 89, 92, 94*); those purported to be Chinese, such as imitation chevrons (*see page 89*); Venetian and Czech beads (*see pages 89, 92, 94*); the enigmatic mulberry and twisted square beads, possibly Dutch (Karklins 1987; *see this page*), and native-made glass, including powder glass beads (Francis 1992c). Real and imitation

MULBERRY, TWISTED SQUARE OR PENTAGONAL AND MELON BEADS from Sumatra, Indonesia, 0.7 to 1.2 cm long. Dating from the seventeenth to nineteenth centuries, their origin is unknown, although some attribute to the Netherlands. *Courtesy of Andy Ng.*

chevrons of all types abound (*see pages 89, 92; compare with those used as ojime on page 74*).

According to Adhyatman and Arifin, various glass beads have been imported into Indonesia; Indian millefiori and trail decorated, possibly Egyptian eye beads (1993), Chinese monochromes, and certainly European and African beads from Africa. The authors report that much faking occurs, with striped Javanese beads made of cement, ancient monochromes apparently decorated with recycled modern Japanese beads, various bird bead imitations, and new copies being made by the Javanese glass bead industry (*see pages 89, 91*).

A Javanese wound bead industry started in 1982, first in central Java, where an Indonesian learned the craft from a Pakistani glassworker in 1972 (Adhyatman and Arifin 1993), a circumstance explaining why many modern glass beads in Java are similar in color and design to those from south Asia. At least some are cottage industries, such as at Plumbon Gambang, where recycled bottle glass is melted in clay containers and then worked at a brick furnace heated by a blowtorch, possibly using gasoline pressurized by a bicycle pump (Adhyatman and Arifin 1993, S. Schriver, *pers. comm.* 1994). Mosaic canes made from Japanese seed beads are used to decorate these wound beads, which are glossy or matte, depending on the beadmakers. Short cane pendants are even made in the glassworking village around Surabya (S. Schriver, *pers. comm.* 1994).

MALAYSIA
Sarawak, the Malaysian portion of Borneo, is famous for its precious heirloom beads, some of

NECKLACE FROM KALIMANTAN Supposedly intact and with magical powers, it is strung on nylon monofilament. Pendant consists of cast bell, glass seed and polychrome beads, plant seeds. Chinese coins, small bells and feline teeth (possibly civet) are strung with a mix of Chinese, Venetian, Czech, and locally made glass beads, including some Indonesian powder glass. Green eye beads are 1.5 cm long. *Courtesy of Don Bierlich.*

A PROBABLE SHAMAN'S NECKLACE FROM BORNEO showing portion with center pendant consisting of joined boar's tusks, bear canines, unidentified claws, upper jaw of lizard, wood carvings, Chinese blue glass beads, and carnelian Idar-Oberstein bead. The diversity of the materials emphasizes the richness of beads on this island. *Courtesy of The Bead Shop.*

which are old and were worth thirty-seven hundred dollars per bead in 1988 (Francis 1992b, c, 1994). Some Islamic glass beads from the Middle East look similar to mosaic beads from east Java; chequer beads also occur there (Chin 1984). But the Lukut Sekala of the Kayan, which are small "black or dark blue lampwound beads with flattened ends and four rosettes in white, amber and yellow on the sides and one at each end" (Francis 1992b), are visually more similar to Venetian beads found in Indonesia (*see page 92*).

Few beads reach collectors except for those who visit Sarawak or live there, and are not likely to because of their value to natives. Beads from Kalimantan, the Indonesian part of Borneo, have

been exported to the West in limited numbers (*see page 89*). There is considerable overlap in beads from Borneo, except for the early Islamic types and those most valued, the Lukut Sekala (Chin 1984). The small sample of beads from Sarawak that I have studied is more varied than beads found in Kalimantan, perhaps due to sampling errors.

Like most areas with a thriving bead industry, Indonesia is worth watching. Since the 1980s, numerous developments have included restoration, faking, imitation, and innovation. Because many new beads are now destined for the heirloom market, the Indonesian industry may mature and produce notable beads of its own design.

LENTICULAR OR RHOMBOID AGATE BEADS transilluminated to emphasize the beauty of their colors and shapes. Dating possibly from the third millennium, agate beads of this quality originate from Afghanistan. Doubly tapered bead at lower edge is 3.0 cm long. *Courtesy of Anahita Gallery.*

MIDDLE EAST AND NORTH AFRICA

Home to our earliest civilizations, the Middle East developed the most important bead technologies of stone, glazed stone, faience, and glass. Also the oldest source for beads as well as a center of conflict for millennia, its boundaries are sometimes confusing—the area has been confined to the eastern Mediterranean, inclusive of countries from Egypt to Iran, but often more widely defined to encompass southwestern Asia to northeastern Africa, including Libya to Afghanistan or Morocco to Pakistan. And because North African jewelry is closely related to that of the Middle East, the Magreb countries of Algeria, Morocco and Tunisia fit within the region's larger parameters for personal adornment.

Given that the world's great civilizations attract so much attention from archaeologists, there is proportionately more bead research, including excavation site reports and specific studies. Yet it is difficult to utilize many of them for comparison with actual specimens: archaeological literature contains few color illustrations, and simple line drawings customarily represent beads—even good photographs are not common. Van der Sleen's drawings with their poor rendering and incorrect perspective are almost indecipherable. Pleasant exceptions are Beck's articles illustrated with photographs by his daughter and accurate line drawings and occasional watercolor paintings provided by his wife (Westlake 1976).

Contemporary bead industries located here are neither greatly important to bead collectors nor economically significant. Glass beadmakers are found in Turkey, Egypt, Hebron, Pakistan, and possibly Afghanistan to a minor extent, while a transplanted Prosser industry recently began in Morocco (Francis 1979c, 1994, Harris 1993, Küçükerman 1988; *see pages 127, 135*). Faience or beadmaking of simulated faience may still be ongoing in Iran and Egypt respectively (Francis 1994). Stone beads are currently made in Pakistan and Afghanistan (Kenoyer 1992), and metal beads in Yemen and the Maghreb, but very few are seen in the West except those from Morocco (*see pages 133, 134*). There is faking of ancient glass ornaments in Lebanon and Syria and simulating of coral, copal and amber in Morocco (Dale 1978, Ross 1991; *see pages 134, 220, 223*). Far more ethnographic than contemporary beads exist in collections from the Middle East. This is especially true for Afghanistan, Egypt, Iran, Morocco, and Turkey (*see page 126*).

Origins of ancient beads from the Middle East are often unknown or deliberately misattributed. Afghanistan, Egypt, Iran, and Turkey were major sources of ancient beads during the last two decades, with Lebanon, Syria, Iraq, Pakistan, and Tunisia playing lesser roles in the marketplace. Dale (1982) describes in detail a large cache of third millennium beads from Syria; the discussions with dealers from Damascus are especially interesting. Syria is still a source of ancient beads; a collection of glass ones were imported as recently as 1993.

Armed conflicts over the last twenty years have been especially destructive to the cultural heritage of Afghanistan, Lebanon and Iraq. Raschka

RHOMBOID HARDSTONE BEADS from Afghanistan, probably from the third millennium. The larger bead is made of agate and the smaller one is fossilized coral, 6.0 cm long. Patterns nicely harmonize with the shape of these fine quality beads. *Courtesy of Anahita Gallery and Jim LaFortune.*

DOUBLE AXE OR BUTTERFLY BEAD This large serpentine bead tapers to a fine thinness and the perforations run through two protruding nacelle-like structures. Also made in obsidian and carnelian, this form is complex and must have been difficult for ancient beadmakers to shape. Possibly dating from 6000 to 7000 B.C., it is 6.3 cm long and imported from Israel. The specimen from Turkey on page 120 is an unidentified green stone. *Courtesy of Rita Okrent.*

(1994) chronicles the looting of Lebanon during the recent civil war, whereby bulldozers and hydraulic excavators were used to "search for gold jewelry and antiquities". Dealing in antiquities is now illegal in Lebanon. In the continuing Afghanistan civil war, archaeological sites and graves are also being bull-dozed, with the recovered artifacts, much of it third millennium material, going to Kabul and from there to Peshawar, Pakistan (M. Kenoyer, *pers. comm.* 1994). Westlake (1993) reports on the looting of Iraqi museums during the Persian Gulf War, and lists of stolen antiquities, including beads and necklaces, have been published. Even in countries not now at war, much illegal digging occurs, some jointly sponsored by collectors and dealers, as in the Caspian Sea region of Iran during the 1970s.

Consequently, some of the largest bead collections in the world belong to Middle Eastern antiquities dealers. One Iranian dealer had a conservative estimate of over one million ethnographic and ancient Persian beads in his New York loft during the 1970s. A Palestinian dealer stated he had the largest bead collection from that area: his Jerusalem shop grossed six million dollars in 1984. Many ancient Middle or Near Eastern beads illustrated in Dubin (1987) were from the collection of antiquities dealer Henry Anavian.

Grave robbing has had a long history in the Middle East, witnessed by the looting of Egyptian Dynastic tombs and comparable burials in antiquity. Still, given today's use of mechanized construction equipment or rampant digging by hand as in Mali (Insoll 1994), the current scale of illicit unearthing is alarming. There are practically no means of suppression now. In the middle 1970s, all legal antiquities exports from Afghanistan required clearance from the Kabul Museum; yet, except for those of clay, beads were never confiscated (K. FitzGibbon, *pers. comm.* 1977).

In the past, beads from legal excavations were not always deposited entirely with the institution or museum excavating or the host country; some went to the sponsor's collection or to contributors (Dale 1981). Also, until after World War II, the purchase of antiquities was not illegal in much of the Middle East, so older collections were acquired legally, or at least from legal sources. Thus beads from this region can be of questionable or illegal origin and smuggling to Western countries still occurs, whereupon the material is redistributed. For example, in the middle 1970s, Munich was the primary outlet for Turkish antiquities (J. Malter, *pers. comm.* 1977).

A small portion of beads on the market are perforated artifacts deaccessioned by museums, such as ten lots of ancient beads, including Phoenician face pendants and Roman face beads, from the St. Louis Art Museum auctioned by Sotheby's in 1985. Occasionally, major collections have been auctioned to benefit museums, like the sale of the Thomas Barlow Walker collection at Sotheby's (Anonymous 1972). Auctions are still the venue whereby many ancient beads and large quantities of jewelry reach the market (Anonymous 1985, 1986, Content 1992, Green 1993). Besides attracting a knowledgeable clientele that can afford their prices, auctions provide buyers with provenance and a degree of respectability for the artifact; the latter aspect is especially important if an item is under scrutiny. Most antiquity galleries carried some quantities of beads during the 1970s and 1980s. While a small number of importers and runners, usually refugees, also brought beads to the West, none dealt in amounts comparable to those of the African runners—almost five hundred strands were offered once, in this instance from Turkey in 1975.

During the late 1970s even the stores of major museums sold jewelry made from genuine ancient Egyptian faience beads. One museum curator's limited expertise resulted in the purchase of Venetian beads as ancient Egyptian by a prominent New York museum: in embarrassment, there were attempts to hide the unfortunate mistake, instead of using the incident for heuristic value.

While ancient Middle Eastern and North African beadmaking materials were perhaps no more diverse than those of other locations, highly developed faience and glass industries produced a vast and varied

AFGHANISTAN STONE AND SHELL BEADS of agate, carnelian, quartz crystal, breccia, possibly opalcite, hematite (signet seal), lapis lazuli, unidentified stone (red and tan barrel bead with diagonal bands), and shell; sizes range from 0.8 to 6.7 cm long. The long bicone carnelian bead was coveted for its beauty and crafting. Note the lapis lazuli spacer, perforated small quartz crystal pendant and shell pendant virtually identical to stone ones of the Tairona (see page 152). These beads and pendants date from neolithic to possibly Islamic vintage (the faceted carnelian ornaments). *Courtesy of Anahita Gallery and Jim LaFortune.*

LAPIS LAZULI FROM AFGHANISTAN with a few carnelian beads interspersed. These are probably ancient, but exact dating is unknown. Cylindrical and round tabular beads are traditional shapes; the latter are generally a centimeter in diameter. Kenoyer (1992) has described contemporary lapis beadmaking. *Courtesy of Anahita Gallery.*

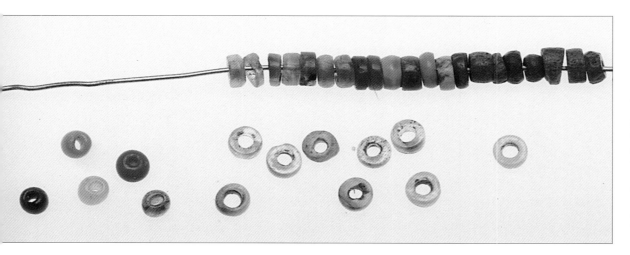

ANCIENT STONE MICRO-BEADS COMPARED WITH VENETIAN GLASS SEED BEADS at far left. Stone microbeads are from neolithic Afghanistan and somewhat larger than the glass beads, averaging 0.11 cm in diameter. In 1985, these Afghani stone beads sold for about $50 per inch or $1 to $1.50 each. Composed of carnelian, turquoise and lapis, these are a little larger than Harappan microbeads, the smallest in the world. *Courtesy of Anahita Gallery and Bethune Gibson.*

assemblage, in addition to a unique use of glazed stones for beads, pendants and amulets (*see page 102*). Evidence from the New Kingdom in Egypt shows that glass technology was also applied to faience as the two industries were then contemporaneous (Vandiver 1982). Powdered glass was added to faience bodies or used as inlay. Stone was the other important material, with shell, materials of organic origin and metal playing minor roles in bead collections. Because the sources of many beads from the Middle East are vague, it is even more difficult to specify country of origin. Ethnographic necklaces have been available from the Middle East in larger numbers than those from other geographic areas covered in this book, but their authenticity also is frequently uncertain.

STONE

The astonishing array of stone beads from this region ranges from the precisely formed products of Idar-Oberstein to the beautiful, soft shapes of neolithic workshops. The oldest stone beads available to collectors are mostly from the third millennium, although some may date to the sixth or seventh millennium. None can match ancient Afghanistan for the beauty and the ability of their beadmakers to exploit the intrinsic qualities of precious and mundane stones (Liu 1983d, Dubin 1987: plate 6). Precious minerals of antiquity were lapis lazuli, turquoise, carnelian and other agates, and rock crystal, and all were used in Afghanistan, especially in lenticular or rhomboid form (*see pages 96, 98, 99, 100*). This shape is distributed throughout the Middle East, with the oldest dating to approximately 7000 B.C. from Turkey. Lenticular beads were also found in Egypt, Mesopotamia, Iran, Syria, southern Turkmenia, and Afghanistan. Beads from the royal cemetery at Ur and at Tepe Hissar, Iran are comparable in quality to those from Afghanistan. A great many stone bead types used by the royalty at Ur had identical counterparts in gold.

Ancient cultures of Afghanistan were equally adroit in turning drab-colored porphry, limestone, fossiliferous limestone, conglomerate and other softer rocks into barrel or lenticular beads of great beauty (Liu 1983d: figure 7). These were distinguished by fine forms, finishes and the use of textures or patterns to best advantage (*see cover and page 98*). Surprisingly, the exploitation of interestingly patterned stones and rocks for ornaments does not appear to have occurred

ANCIENT IRANIAN ETCHED CARNELIAN BEAD bearing human images; one register shows five figures, some resembling women. The lapidary work is poor, but the features are well-etched, 4.6 cm long. This unique bead is probably not a very clever fraud since the expertise for such faking is lacking in the Middle East. No other etched bead with human images is known to exist. (See Davis-Kimball and Liu 1981). *Courtesy of Joel L. Malter.*

GLAZED CHALCEDONY PANEL BEAD from Afghanistan showing crude lapidary work, 3.4 cm long. The glaze is worn away except on the panel and incised lines or depressions. Similar ones in Iran date to the Sassanian period. Francis (1994) suggests these date from 200 to 600 A.D., or as late as 1300 A.D. *Courtesy of Kate FitzGibbon and Andy Hale.*

elsewhere. The excavations at Ur reveal what beads royalty preferred (Liu 1984b), but there is no information on who wore these aesthetically more interesting beads of common materials. Lenticular and rhomboid beads were used in necklaces, a number of which are displayed in museums. These were also used as dangles on Mesopotamian dress or toggle pins, functionally comparable to the topo pins of highland Bolivians (Liu 1979).

Beadmaking using lapis lazuli is still practiced (Kenoyer 1992), so perhaps replicas made by contemporary craftspeople will relieve the pressure on collecting ancient beads. Some four years ago, new lapis beads, interspersed with ancient carnelian ones, were represented as completely ancient (J. Allen, *pers. comm.* 1994). Lapis and, to a lesser degree, turquoise were much valued beadmaking materials on the Iranian plateau in the third millennium. Its trade and technology have been well detailed by Tosi (1974) and others. Much less is known about hardstone beadmaking, that is, beads above Mohs

ANCIENT BEADS AND PENDANTS FROM COMMON BEAD MATERIALS OF THE MIDDLE EAST *Left to right*: Pierced shell, quoit bead or ring made from conus shell, amber beads consolidated with liquid nylon then polished; alabaster with circle dot motif, mother-of-pearl, steatite beads, faceted jet, white hardstone, hematite bead and pendant (2.4 cm long), bronze beads, molded lead beads, one with exposed ceramic core; glass beads and pendants, Iranian and Egyptian faience beads, including broken crumb bead.

BEADS FROM MARLIK, IRAN possibly dating to the first or second millennium, and described as frit by Negahban (1964). When not corroded, like the center bead of the middle row, they are very glassy and show trail decorations. Glass would be a more accurate attribution. Average diameter is 1.2 cm. *Courtesy of Henry Anavian.*

scale of five to seven. But within the last decade and a half, the coupling of the scanning electron microscope and silicone impressions of bead perforations have provided a great deal of new information about the drilling and manufacture of beads (Gwinnett and Gorelick 1991).

Other notable demonstrations of beadmaking in this region bear mentioning. As early as the sixth to seventh millennium, a peculiar form known as the double axe or butterfly bead was fashioned of serpentine, obsidian, carnelian, and other hardstones (*see pages 98, 120*). The cross section of these beads is as thin as lenticular beads, complicated by the protruding cylindrical portions that carries the ends of the perforations, and much like the complex curves of an airplane's nacelles merging with the wing. By perhaps 1000 to 2000 B.C., agate was shaped like a wide, flat V, into the so-called leech bead; those at Ur were capped with gold (Dubin 1987: plate 12), while later ones were not, enabling their entire beautiful form to be visible. (*One is shown both on the cover and title page*). Perforations were drilled from the ends of the V, meeting in the center, which might be no more than five millimeters thick. If perfor-

ations were drilled into a rough blank rather than the finished bead, there was less risk of breakage after the expenditure of so much labor. Beads sold on the market are mainly from Iran or Afghanistan, although they have been found as far afield as Taxila, India, dating from 300 to 700 B.C. (Beck 1941).

Also found in Afghanistan, the Indus Valley and Mesopotamia are the long, slender and elegantly tapered barrel or bicone beads of carnelian and other agates (*see page 98*). If a long carnelian bicone had its provenance as Ur of ancient Mesopotamia, then the price would have been one thousand dollars, double the usual amount (G. Dale, *pers. comm.* 1982); these Middle Eastern bicones were also used as drug paraphernalia. At the other end of the size spectrum, hardstone microbeads of fine crafting are also found in Afghanistan (*see page 100*). Comparable in size to the smallest glass seed beads of industrial Europe, they are just slightly larger than extruded Harappan microbeads of talc and kaolinite. The latter Indus Valley beads are only about one millimeter in external diameter and may rank as the smallest beads in the world (Liu 1985b).

Well known to collectors and archaeologists

ANCIENT IRANIAN FAIENCE, CARNELIAN AND BRONZE BEADS Note the cylindrical and hand-modeled faience beads and amulets and the deep blue color of those on each side of the gadrooned vase pendant on middle strand. Many beads have multiple perforations. Round pendant has 2.0 cm diameter. *Courtesy of Margaret Moore.*

FAIENCE BEADS FROM IRAN, SYRIA, AFGHANISTAN, POSSIBLY EUROPE, EGYPT, AND HARAPPA *Clockwise from left:* Iranian strands of cylindrical and hand-formed beads; bead with multiple perforations (preceded by bright blue disk bead), 0.8 cm long; two disk beads and spherical bead (1.2 cm diameter) are Syrian, third millennium; those encircled by cylindrical bead strand are Afghani, note rich blue of kyanos beads; doughnut-shaped bead with glaze is 1.65 cm diameter; adjacent melon beads may be European, 1.5 to 1.8 cm diameter; Egyptian cylinder (longest is 2.9 cm; Egyptian faience industry produced larger beads than other Middle Eastern industries) and disk beads with thick glazes; Harappan spherical beads. *Courtesy of Anahita Gallery, Antiquities International, Mark Kenoyer, and Rita Okrent.*

alike, etched carnelian and agate beads are widely distributed from the Indus Valley (modern Pakistan and India) to Afghanistan, Iran, Iraq (ancient Mesopotamia), and the Arabian coast (During-Caspers 1971, Francis 1980a; *see page 99*). And dZi or related etched agate beads are found mainly in Tibet and the Himalayan countries. Most etched carnelians and agates bear only geometric designs, but one bead with human figures was recovered in the area between Hasanlu and Marlik in Iran. Purchased for five hundred dollars in 1980 (J. Davis-Kimball, *pers. comm.*), it is either a clever fraud or a unique and extremely rare specimen (Davis-Kimball and Liu 1981; *see page 101*). The iconography suggests proto-Elamite or Elamite origin and the etching is very convincing. At this point in our technology, it may not be possible to arrive at an answer, although the likelihood of a fake is fairly minimal since this type of fraud requires considerable expertise.

Whether Morocco and other Maghreb countries are included in the Middle East or North Africa, the source of beautiful stone beads is frequently Morocco. Here, as in Egypt and Mauritania, amazonite is

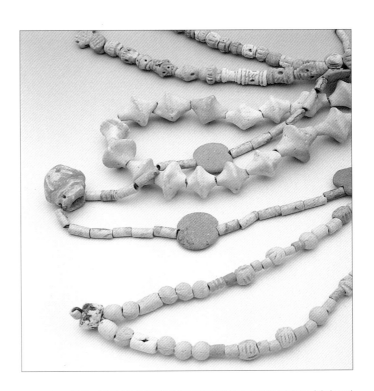

IRANIAN AND AFGHANI FAIENCE BEADS The bright blue Afghani tabular beads are 1.3 cm diameter. An interesting variety of complex shapes is shown on the top strand from Iran. *Courtesy of Anahita Gallery and Antiquities International.*

CONTEMPORARY FAIENCE BEADS AND AMULETS by Carol Strick, and broken spacers and bead by Virginia Curran. Curran's work was made in the 1950s, while Strick's pieces date from 1979. Large spherical blue bead by Curran is typical of those made with Egyptian paste. Rolling the beads and press molding the amulets, as well as hand-modeling the floral pendant, Strick has practiced most techniques available to ancient Egyptian faience workers, such as marbleizing and bicolor faience. She has simulated Egyptian gold foiling of faience by electroplating with gold. Sizes range from 0.3 to 4.0 cm. *Courtesy of Virginia Curran and Carol Strick.*

ANCIENT EGYPTIAN DISK, CYLINDER, SEGMENTED, BICONE, AND SPHERICAL BEADS, as well as a faience spacer, probably dating from Eighteenth Dynasty or later. The spacer is made from six cylinder beads joined by slurry, 2.3 cm wide. Even with this small sample, the delicacy of Egyptian faience, demonstrated by the large, thin flat disk bead and brilliance and thickness of the glazes are readily apparent. Bright blue or turquoise is usually provided by copper oxides, dark blue by cobalt oxides, green by a mixture of iron and copper oxides, and purples and blacks by manganese oxides (Kaczmarczyk and Hedges 1983).

greatly valued (*see page 128*). Large amazonite beads are more common in Morocco and Mauritania than Egypt, where smaller drop-shaped beads of this green feldspar are preferred. Except for metal jewelry, I have rarely seen any beads from Algeria or Tunisia offered for sale, although Allen (*pers. comm.* 1994) saw Tunisian coral for sale in the 1970s.

pose; if so, their wide distribution in both time and geographically is understandable (*see page 105*).

Other amulets are difficult to identify and attribute, such as some rock crystal, faience and bronze ones with four cusps that may represent stylized human molars. These amulets also serve as excellent examples of the phenomenon of trans-

EGYPTIAN FAIENCE AMULETS *Clockwise from lower left corner:* Eighteenth Dynasty bicolor lotus bud amulet with suspension loop in red, and joined by slurry to main body prior to firing, Sekmet or bastet, Apis bull, cornflower pendant, papyrus sceptre, Taurt, and two Udjat or Eye of Horus. At least two amulets are Eighteenth Dynasty, others date later. All are molded and hand-finished; the sizes range from 1.1 to 2.9 cm long.

With the great emphasis on amulets since antiquity, these ornaments abound in nearly all materials but particularly stone and faience. Because of its funerary practices and well established stone, faience and glass industries, Egypt has more amulets than anywhere else in this region. A glance at Andrews (1994) demonstrates the variety. Amulets from Iran, Turkey, Afghanistan, and Syria have all been on the market. Beads also served an amuletic function in many of these civilizations. Eisen (1930) suggested that melon beads served just such a pur-

position (Liu 1985a; *see page 108*). But Philistine stone altars of 700 B.C. for burning incense also have four horns (Gitin 1992), so it is possible these amulets are stylized miniatures of such altars. Dubin (1987) has identified one in stone as an altar bead. The marble twin-headed pendant on page 109 suggests a pre-Hittite or Hittite double image motif bearing the characteristic circle dot decoration but, again, this is merely informed speculation. Some amulets are easier to attribute, such as the wonderfully animated quartz crystal fish or dolphin of

SCARABS OF FIRED TERRA COTTA, FAIENCE, CARNELIAN, STEATITE, AND GLAZED HARDSTONE The most numerous Egyptian amulets are scarabs. Hieroglyphics are on the reverse of the multiple, molded scarabs (2.2 cm high). The two large ones are glazed steatite, with no visible remnant of glazing; green one is faience. Note the carved hardstone scarabs in carnelian (0.75 cm long) and glazed chalcedony, with glaze partially flaked off.

ANCIENT AMULETS, POSSIBLY PORTRAYING TEETH in quartz crystal, faience, and bronze; faience specimen is 0.6 cm square. Closely resembling each other, these demonstrate the phenomenon of transposition whereby a desired form is transposed into another medium but is not meant as an imitation. While they look like stylized molars, the amulets may actually represent four-horned stone altars for burning incense (Gitin 1992); Dubin identifies one as an altar bead (1987: no. 364). *Courtesy of Joel L. Malter and Rita Okrent.*

Roman vintage (*see page 111*).

These examples illustrate the importance of seeking information—merely collecting beads and pendants is rather meaningless. But it is not just ancient material that must be so treated: all perforated artifacts should be accorded attention and respect. Ethnographic and contemporary materials are obviously easier to research, since there is the prospect that the buyer or collector can directly interview the seller or maker. Yet this is often not possible without a great deal of effort. Even then, previous owners may know nothing or little about their acquisitions. If the buyer is interested and possesses the requisite language skills, the amount of worthwhile data is increased, as in the case of Moroccan jewelry bought over twenty years ago by a French-speaking dealer (Liu and Wataghani 1975; *see page 128*).

GLAZED STONE

An important but small part of Middle Eastern ornaments, glazed stones fortunately are relatively easy to identify. Glazing is the immediate predecessor to faience and was applied to both soft and hardstones, ranging from steatite or soapstone to quartz crystal (Beck 1931a, b, 1935, Liu 1975b). Glazing was commonly used in Egyptian ornaments and also found in Mesopotamia and the Indus Valley. Interestingly, glazing and faience were related industries in the Indus Valley and Mesopotamia, whereas glazing, faience and glass were all produced in Egypt, sometimes contemporaneously. The most frequently found examples of glazed steatite are Egyptian scarabs, where most traces of the original blue or green glaze are usually worn away or removed by the effects of burial, leaving a tan-colored, hard matrix, although Petrie (1972) states that black steatite was also glazed (*see opposite page*). Occasionally the colored glaze can be detected within inscribed lines. A proof of glazing is the hardness, whereby the softness of soapstone (Mohs hardness of one) is transformed during the dehydration of firing to between five and a half to seven on the Mohs scale, hard enough to scratch glass. With burnt or painted steatite, the increase in hardness is much less (Beck 1931). Some hardstone scarabs also may have been glazed (*see opposite page*). Steatite and talc are the softest materials used for beads in this area, although talc beads were never glazed. Some neolithic talc beads look like a four-sided staircase. Of glazed hardstone beads, the most common are paneled

THOTH AMULETS comparing finely crafted and degraded Egyptian examples (Liu 1987a: 1.9 to 2.2 cm high). Petrie (1972) shows at least ten versions of this god of writing and knowledge.

POSSIBLY PRE-HITTITE AMULET WITH TWIN HEADS in limestone, with circle dot motif. The small but powerful image is 3.3 cm high. *Courtesy of Lost Cities.*

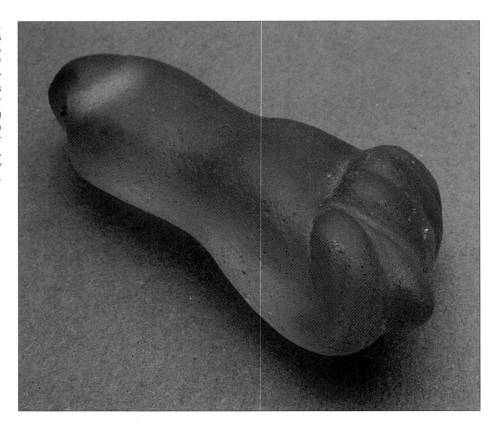

beads of chalcedony from Iran, possibly of Sassanian origin, 300 to 400 A.D. (Anonymous 1974; *see page 102*). Usually the previously thick blue glazing was reduced to only a remnant; the obvious objective was to turn a white or colorless material into the desired blue color. It is unknown whether glazed paneled beads imitate the blue of lapis or turquoise or both, the only blue minerals available to the ancient beadmaker. Much rarer is the so-called imitation tooth bead from Nineveh, described by Beck (1935), consisting of a pointed piece of quartz topped by a cap of faience and pierced for stringing. Two chipped specimens are shown in Liu (1975b: figure 1). There is a tendency for faience to separate from the quartz portion, as the bonding is not as strong as it is with glaze to stone.

FAIENCE

The first synthetic material, faience was used almost entirely for non-utilitarian objects, much of it for personal adornment. It was developed primarily in the advanced ancient civilizations of Egypt, Mesopotamia and the Indus Valley, and the Aegean to a lesser degree. Europeans may have made distinctive faience beads during the second millennium instead of importing them from the Mycenaeans (Newton and Renfrew 1970). Dayton's (1993) startling claim that Mycenaean cobalt blue glass also may have a European origin possibly supports a similar origin for faience. Apparently all early faience and glass colored by cobalt were derived from cobalt-bearing silver ores from Saxony (Dayton 1993). Faience also may have played a minor role in China during the Warring States and Western Zhou periods of 500 B.C. to 1000 B.C., as it formed the core of composite beads of glaze and glass powder, and other plain beads composed entirely of faience. A faience figurine bead or amulet from China dating from 400 to 500 B.C. (Dubin 1987: plate 153) is further proof of faience production in China. Faience may have been made in other Asian cultures, as beads of this material have been found in Thailand (Pilditch 1992).

This siliceous self-glazing ceramic dating to the middle fourth millennium is possibly still in

LATE ROMAN OR BYZANTINE QUARTZ CRYSTAL PORPOISE
OR FISH, more likely the latter as the anatomy is incorrect
for a marine mammal, 3.5 cm long. If it is Byzantine, the
fish may represent a Christian theme or motif. Romans and
Greeks frequently used the porpoise in their ornaments.
Courtesy of Joel L. Malter.

ANCIENT GLASS BEADS AND GLASSWARE
FROM AFGHANISTAN The beads are
primarily Islamic and were produced
for nearly seven hundred years, ending
about 1300 A.D. No comprehensive
study of Islamic glass beads has been
undertaken. *Courtesy of Anahita Gallery.*

production, but only in Egypt and Iran and by a few
Western craftspeople. Contemporary glazed clay and
steatite beads from Egypt look superficially like faience
but are really only simulations (Liu 1980). Carol Strick,
a highly skilled contemporary faience beadmaker,
recently quit production, but her work, particularly
the replicated broadcollars, is impressive even by
ancient Egyptian standards (Liu 1981). Tom Holland
has fused hot glass to faience in his beads, a technique
not previously attempted (Liu 1994).

Research on faience has been renewed, with
much of the analyses performed on beads from
Egypt and the Indus Valley (Kaczmarczyk and Hedges
1983, Kenoyer 1994). Kaczmarczyk and Hedges have
performed some analytical comparisons of Egyptian
versus Mesopotamian, Minoan and Mycenaean
faience and glass. Faience ornaments from Afghanistan and Iran have received little attention or the
results are not yet published, even from a descriptive and stylistic standpoint, while those from the
Aegean have been the subject of a monograph
(Foster 1979, Liu 1982b).

Considerable confusion surrounds the terminology for faience and related substances. True
faience refers to tin-glazed earthenware such as
maiolica or majolica, made since the late medieval
period at Faenza in northern Italy (Liu 1975b). But
because of its broad usage among archaeologists
and for lack of a better term, faience is also associated with objects having a siliceous core of finely
powdered quartz grains loosely cemented together,
covered by a colored surface glaze. Most researchers
use the word faience, although a few prefer glazed
composition or composition. In older literature and
even current auction catalogs incorrect designations
like glazed gypsum, steatite and limestone, frit,
vitreous paste, porcelain, polished shell, and glass
paste have been used for faience.

Ancient frit or Egyptian blue is a crystalline
silicate of copper and calcium used for molding
jewelry and as pigment. Supposedly a dull dark blue
to almost black color, it was shown by Dayton and
Dayton (1978) that Egyptian blue "can be a wide
variety of natural and manufactured substances",
most of which are not Egyptian in origin. Among
pigments confused with Egyptian blue is blue frit,
which the Daytons equate with the kyanos of Greek
domain. Foster (1979) extensively discussed faience
terminology and did not agree with the Daytons'
interpretation. Two color illustrations of beads made
with kyanos from Ur and Alalakh, a Hittite site of

1500 B.C., are shown by Dayton and Dayton (1978: plate 20, 1 and 2). These beads, not a very dark blue, are nearly identical to some imported from Afghanistan and Iran (*see page 105*). Superficially, kyanos beads do not appear very different from Mycenaean molded glass spacers, which may explain why this term is interpreted as glass paste in ancient Greek texts. Kyanos or Egyptian blue beads were never glazed and extant specimens appear dull and chalky, possibly due to the corrosive effect of burial; their color throughout is homogeneous. Non-Egyptian faience beads and ornaments are not usually sought by collectors, but beads of kyanos illustrate how seemingly mundane and inexpensive beads may be historically important.

Although Egyptian faience beads have been imported by the kilo during the last two decades, relatively few bead collectors are interested in faience ornaments. One importer brought five kilos of Egyptian faience to the United States in 1976, of which only about twenty-five percent was the coveted turquoise blue; the beads were made into jewelry or loosely sold in small packets at forty-five dollars per ounce. In 1977, Egyptian faience disk beads were offered at one thousand dollars per kilo but found no buyers (J. Malter, *pers. comm.* 1977). This lack of interest was reflected in the few imports of faience to the West Coast appearing in United States customs records. For those of good quality, prices were much higher: such as sixty-five to one hundred-seventy dollars each for faience amulets purchased in 1972 in Vancouver, Canada, and fifty dollars per eighteen inches of well-glazed turquoise blue Egyptian cylindrical faience beads in New York City during 1974. Currently there is very little Egyptian faience for sale, especially of better quality, except at auction. Faience from Iran and Afghanistan was usually very reasonable but only imported by a few dealers. While faience beads from Egypt, Iran, Afghanistan, and a few from Syria have been available on the marketplace, only those from Egypt have had any real acceptance, and usually as jewelry. Perhaps lack of sales will slow looting in these countries.

This technically and historically important material for beads has not been collected by many enthusiasts. The small size, relative drabness of many faience beads and amulets, delicate nature, and high cost of good Egyptian faience may be inhibiting.

ANCIENT GLASS BEADS FROM TURKEY showing pitting and remnants of layering or iridescence; the bicone is 2.6 cm diameter. Depressions protect iridescence from dislodging by handling or wear. Iridescence is prized for its rainbow-like colors, the result of interference effects and not pigmentation. Attributed to 800 B.C., their vintage actually may be Islamic. *Courtesy of Joel L. Malter.*

BROKEN GLASS EYE BEAD from ancient Egypt, showing stratified eyes built of layers, 1.3 cm diameter. Much of the exterior glass is devitrified and colorless, so interior shows original color and condition of the glass. *Courtesy of Jamey Allen and Rita Okrent.*

ANCIENT STRATIFIED EYE BEAD from Syria; the placement and color of eyes is similar to the top bead, 1.6 cm diameter, dating from 300 to 800 B.C. Eisen (1916) believes that certain glass colors are diagnostic of age. *Courtesy of Rita Okrent.*

CONTEMPORARY STRATIFIED EYE BEAD OF PYREX GLASS was made by Lewis Wilson. Modern eyebeads are easily distinguished from ancient ones. This one has a 2.4 cm diameter. *Courtesy of Lewis Wilson.*

The fear of purchasing fakes may also play a part. Criteria such as these contrasts with the generally high esteem accorded to Egyptian faience artifacts in the antiquities market, especially amulets.

FAIENCE GLAZING AND MANUFACTURING

The glazing and manufacture of Egyptian faience have been thoroughly studied by Vandiver (1982, 1983a) using physical examination, analyses and replication. Faience is glazed in three ways, the simplest is a water-based slurry of the glaze that is poured, dipped or brushed on the faience body. The most common method is mixing water soluble salts into the faience body; these salts effloresce or wick out on the surface during evaporation. The thicker the efflorescence layer, the thicker the glaze, so it is desirable to have as low humidity as possible during the process. Since the glaze covers the body by itself, the term self-glazing has been applied to faience. In the third method, the body is placed into a glazing powder and fired; that portion of the powder in contact with the body glazes it. This method is called cementation and is also considered a self-glazing process. Large, so-called donkey beads from Qom, Iran were glazed by this process.

Seeking the most effective formula for contemporary faience, Strick once took an extensive trip through the Middle East carrying enough faience mixture for seven stops: Khartoum, Cairo, Luxor, Tehran, Qom, Jerusalem, and Tel Aviv (Liu 1981). The intention was to test the effect of local climate on the performance of the same glazing formula. At each locale, either slabs or beads of faience were prepared from the mix, dried, and then wrapped for firing upon return. The formula worked only in Jerusalem, apparently the driest of the cities during the time of year she visited. Presumably enough efflorescence was produced in this city to result in glazing. So it is not surprising that faience production coincides with areas that are hot and dry.

Vandiver's research (1982, 1983a) showed that in a four thousand year progression from Predynastic periods (circa 4000 B.C.) to the Later periods (circa 30 A.D.), faience workers employed more and more techniques as they refined their control and became more productive under factory-like conditions. Manufacturing methods of a faience body included modeling a core for grinding, molding on a form, forming on a core, pressing into open face molds,

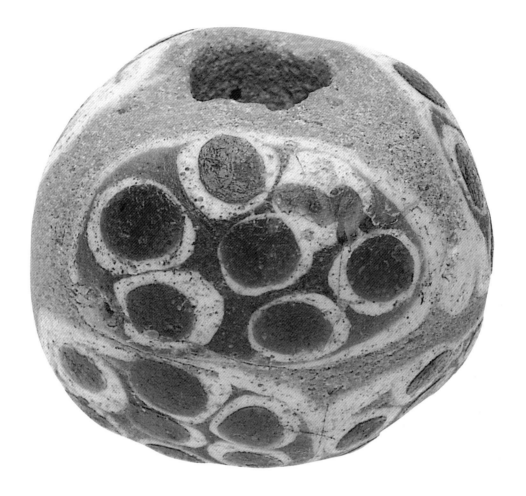

joining of molded parts with quartz slurry, surface grinding, and possibly throwing. Decorating techniques included marbleizing, layering, painting with a colored quartz slurry, incising, inlaying, resisting, and painting with a pigment wash. During the New Kingdom, powder glass was added to the body or as an inlay to extend the color range of faience (Vandiver 1982: table 1). During this time, especially at Amarna, the use of terra cotta molds for mass manufacturing of faience ornaments was widespread (Liu and Content 1979). Some state that these open face molds were sundried, others feel they were fired (Dayton and Dayton 1978, Nicholson 1993). Many press molded ornaments had disk beads joined to them by a slurry, usually of contrasting color (*see page 107*). If disk beads were placed on the top and bottom of these molded pendants, they could then be

used to make Amarna period floral broadcollars, which were the easiest to string because of their double suspension loops (Scott and Liu 1979).

Not all these techniques were applied to faience ornaments, but Strick's beads and pendants utilize most of the methods (*see page 106*). Her amulets were also largely press molded, substituting plaster for the terra cotta used by ancient Egyptians. In addition, the Egyptian practice of gold foiling faience was emulated in electroplated faience beads. Her self taught replication of nearly all Egyptian techniques of faience making and ability to maintain a high aesthetic standard were truly remarkable: an excellent example of the juxtaposition of art and science.

Faience was initially used as an inexpensive substitute for precious or valued minerals like turquoise, lapis and malachite, with techniques probably derived

ANCIENT COMPOUND EYE BEAD FROM TURKEY While the eye bead has devitrified to some degree, it is structurally intact, although the color has probably changed. The stone-like appearance of the matrix confuses accurate identification by inexperienced collectors. This specimen has seven groups of compound eyes, 2.3 cm diameter. *Courtesy of Joel L. Malter.*

AMPHORA OR JUG PENDANT FROM SYRIA with beautiful lampworked latticework, 2.3 cm high. With no perforation, it was probably strung by the handle; see page 225 for conglomerate. *Courtesy of Rita Okrent.*

from stone technology (Vandiver 1982). Then faience workers realized the material's versatility and greatly expanded their repertoire of manufacturing and decorative processes. They excelled at both mass produced items and individual pieces of great beauty. Examples include openwork ornaments in the form of beads, spacers and rings from approximately 1500 to 750 B.C., such as those shown in Riefstahl (1968) or Andrews (1990). These Egyptian ornaments were probably made from a combination of molding, joining with a quartz slurry and detailing by hand. Many finer amulets are treated in the same fashion (*see pages 107, 109*). Such faience beads or ornaments were no longer merely a substitute for stone beads and amulets but a unique and innovative miniature art.

Besides Egyptian faience, collectors have had access only to Iranian, Afghani and a limited sample of Syrian faience (*see page 105*). Indus Valley faience has never been on the marketplace, although some private individuals have collections. One Pakistani teacher built an important collection merely through surface finds (Kenoyer 1993). Some Afghani material may contain Indus Valley faience but remains unstudied. Besides coarse-grained faience that is similar to Egyptian and Mesopotamian, the Indus Valley civilization produced a unique compact type of talcum-fine grains of colored glass and quartz (Kenoyer 1994). Since a certain proportion of Iranian and Afghani faience is visually identical to kyanos, the faience of these areas may be of considerable antiquity and do not all date to the late period, which was an earlier assumption of mine (Liu 1982b). The earliest occurrence of this material in Iran is the fourth millennium, but most of the available faience beads may be Parthian and Sassanian circa 250 B.C. to 640 A.D., with some as late as Nishapur, circa 900 to 1200 A.D. Marlik yielded interesting cylindrical beads regarded as frit by Negahban (1964: first to second millennium). When not corroded, the trailed decoration and matrix are very glassy, so they may represent an early glass (*see page 103*). Even the few Syrian faience beads are probably from the third millennium and originate from the same site as described by Dale (1982).

Faience from Afghanistan is rarely studied and superficially resembles Iranian, although the sample is presently too small for meaningful comparison (*see page 105*). Large amounts of faience were exported to the West from northwest Iran after World War II, as illegal excavations started. The impact among bead collectors has been minimal;

PHOENICIAN MASK PENDANT The face was probably originally white, eyes and other features cobalt blue, as were the coiled hair and beard. Dating from 200 to 350 B.C., the pendant is a type C III (Seefried 1982), devitrified and 6.2 cm high. *Courtesy of Joel L. Malter.*

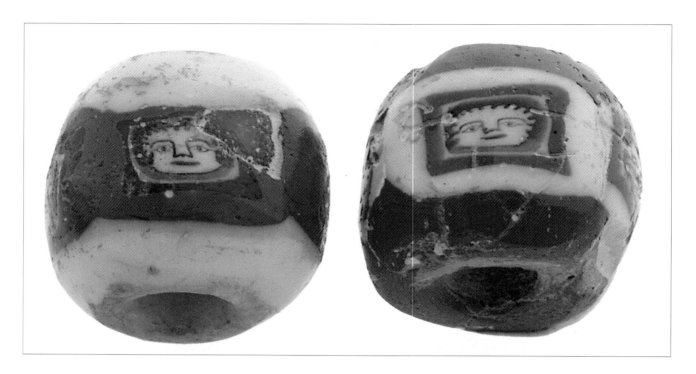

ROMAN MOSAIC FACE BEADS of early type, dating from circa 100 B.C. to 100 A.D. These have been so highly reground that one mosaic cane is partially broken; both are 1.25 cm diameter. Essentially similar except for the reversal of matrix and register colors, the face canes are also alike, suggesting they are from the same workshop. There are four faces on each bead. They averaged $60 each when bought at auction in 1962.

COMPARISON OF IMAGE TYPES ON MOSAIC FACE BEADS showing the two most common face canes: one is the head only; the other shows a woman with flowing hair wearing a necklace. Of twenty-eight face beads in Yoshimizu (1989), half were face alone, six were the necklace type, and the balance were other facial images. It is not known whether these types represent chronological differences.

I would not have been aware of the wide assortment of extant bead shapes except for the receipt of a study collection through the generosity of antiquities dealer Henry Anavian. Both traditional shapes such as melon beads and ones very different from other Middle Eastern bead forms were present in the collection (Liu 1982b). While some molding was used, most shapes appeared to have been hand-formed and incising was the primary means of decoration. Many irregular shapes are difficult to describe, contributing to the inadequacy of both written and pictorial descriptions of faience jewelry components from the Near East.

In contrast to the well preserved, thick and brilliant glazes found on most Egyptian faience, it is rare to find remnants of glaze on Iranian or Afghani faience beads. Glossy glaze was found on only a few small beads, most are matte but not colorless as the matrix is often colored, instead of the white found in the majority of Egyptian faience. Perhaps this is due to kyanos which is uniformly colored from the surface to the interior. Although corrosive soil conditions can account for the stripping of glazes from most recovered specimens, the original condition of Iranian glazes probably differed fundamentally from Egyptian faience. They may not have attained the thickness or brilliance of the latter, and examples of glassy faience of Iranian origin have not been found, while this condition is fairly common in Egyptian faience. Except for rare bicolor beads of cobalt blue and turquoise, there are no other polychrome faience beads from Iran.

The shapes of Iranian amulets are more abstract than those from Egypt (Liu 1982b: figure 6). Some molded Sassanian amulets, most likely based on Roman prototypes, have been excavated by Sono and Fukai (1968). Consisting of gadrooned vase pendants and penis and scrotum amulets, both are widely distributed in the Middle East. Many of the

ROMAN MOSAIC FACE BEAD with five panels showing a woman wearing a necklace, 1.35 cm high; the dating is the same as beads on opposite page. Only moderately weathered, it has not been reground or repolished. The bead was priced at over $5,000 in 1992 (Liu 1992d). *Courtesy of Lost Cities.*

STRAND OF MIXED VINTAGE BEADS from Turkey, ranging from possibly 6000 B.C. to modern Europe. The stone butterfly bead (upper left, 2.6 cm long) is the oldest and the Czech and Venetian glass beads are modern. Similar mixtures of ancient and modern beads have been seen in other areas, like the Czech molded amulet inserted with ancient stone pendants in Mali, as displayed on page 14. Visible are stone, glass, metal, jet, and clay beads and pendants. Note large turquoise-colored Islamic glass bead, bronze pendant, gadrooned clay bead, and faceted Islamic stone and jet beads. Spindle whorls were once strung on this strand. *Courtesy of Joel L. Malter.*

ISLAMIC COMBED GLASS BEAD
from Syria, showing beautiful
crafting, 2.2 cm high. Fukai dates
a similar Iranian bead from
300 to 400 B.C. (1977: plate 49).
Courtesy of Rita Okrent.

ISLAMIC TRAIL DECORATED AND FOLDED GLASS BEADS from Syria with dragged decoration. The upright cylinder is 4.5 cm long and folded bead is 4.6 cm long. Kolbas's survey (1983), which does not appear to cover beads, dates dark and light green glass colors from 700 to 1100 A.D. *Courtesy of Rita Okrent.*

beads are marked by multiple perforations, but it is not clear whether these are decorative or meant to function in complex stringing arrangements. The presence of faience spacers suggests that Iranian necklaces may have had elaborate designs.

Many Iranian faience beads sold on the market have short, relatively large diameter cylindrical beads: if only exposed to these, one might form a skewed impression of the diversity of Iran's faience industry, which may be ongoing in Qom. The problem of having limited samples of the beads of any one region or culture is obviously not limited to the Middle East.

GLASS

This close relative of glaze and faience is undoubtedly the favorite and most abundant material among bead collectors. Numerically there may be more beads in other materials, but a preference among

dealers and collectors for glass has made it the most prominent, a position also enjoyed by glass among contemporary beads.

Few contemporary glass beads come from the Middle East and are confined to large and fairly crude transparent, translucent and opaque beads from Cairo and Hebron, to an active furnace-wound industry in Turkey whose beadmakers emigrated from Hebron, and the nascent Prosser industry in Morocco (*see pages 127, 135*). Pakistan also has glass beadmakers, but their work is rarely collected. The transplanted Uzbekistan glass beadmakers of Herat, Afghanistan may no longer be working, given the years of civil war in that country (Francis 1994).

Glass beads of ethnographic origin are common in the Middle East, as it was a rich trading ground for all countries making glass beads since colonial times. Francis (1979a, b, 1980a, b, 1981a, b, 1982) has partially surveyed the beads of various Middle Eastern countries, but no one has systematically researched them. Beads can be found by most European glass beadmakers, dominated by the Venetians and Czech (*see page 126*). Even Chinese glass beads have been found here (Liu 1975a). Some imported strands of ancient beads have been interspersed with modern European glass beads, and sometimes are deliberately misrepresented as ancient (*see chapter nine*).

The Middle East is the prime source of ancient glass beads, with Afghanistan, Turkey, Iran, Syria, Egypt, and Israel as the main suppliers to the market. The extent of trade from any region varies with political unrest, military conflict and laws on trading antiquities. For example, in the middle 1970s Turkey passed a mandatory sentence of one to five years for smuggling antiquities or new gold artifacts, an action which immediately suppressed trade on the open market. Until the 1970s, Egyptian beads were often available, now only older collections are sold at auction. The Per-neb auction (Green 1993) offered materials gathered by a Swiss collector in Egypt from the 1920s to 1940s. A faience and glass collection of this quality and magnitude probably will not be available again.

It is difficult to ascertain the true sources of beads. Suppliers and dealers are often reluctant to disclose information and do not know or may supply false origins. In addition, the original source and the country from which the beads are exported may not coincide. A further complication is that many bead types were widely distributed geographically and used for a long time. Older beads often are considered more desirable, so there was a tendency to attribute greater age to them. We now know that many glass beads from this region are no older than the Islamic period. Like the situation with African runners, most bead buyers are more concerned with the actual purchase rather than gaining historical information.

Because of political unrest and military conflict in the Middle East, the bead trade has decreased. Only a few people visit Egypt, Syria and Israel on a regular basis to search for beads, in contrast to the activity of the 1970s and 1980s. This is particularly ironic, since

PTOLEMAIC OR ROMAN PERIOD MOSAIC AND MILLEFIORI GLASS BEADS from Egypt and Syria, and probably elsewhere in the Middle East. These are among the most attractive glass beads, especially those with red caps (spherical bead is 1.25 cm diameter). The cylindrical beads are often made by rolling a sheet of fused millefiori rods, not by marvering rods onto a core. *Courtesy of Rita Okrent.*

bead prices are now much more elevated and the overall number of collectors is much larger.

The most famous ancient glass ornaments from the Middle East are Phoenician mask pendants and Roman mosaic face beads, dating respectively from approximately 700 B.C. to 50 A.D. and from 100 B.C. to 500 A.D. (Seefried 1982, Stout 1986). Bead collectors have always been fascinated with human faces on glass, ranging from Phoenician to contem-

utilizing a type of plastic are amazingly good. Some Venetians have attempted faking Phoenician mask pendants by using a combination of an ancient glass bead as a core, coupled with contemporary glass components (*see chapter nine*). Replicated Phoenician core-formed pendants have been shown in Tait (1991). Recent indications from observations at the Bead Expo '94 in Santa Fe, New Mexico, point to faked mask pendants from elsewhere in

STRAND OF ROMAN BEADS of primarily glass, in fairly stable condition. There is one carnelian Egyptian cornflower or lotus seed pendant in upper right corner. Clear glass bulla (round disk with attached loop) is 1.2 cm wide. The strand was purchased at an antique show for $600 in 1993. *Courtesy of Jackie Little.*

porary. Other ornaments bearing facial images include molded single and double faces in the round, Venetian mosaic beads with faces and East Indian beads with faces. Contemporary mosaic face beads were revived in the United States by Brian Kerkvliet only a few years ago and in Japan by some of their glass beadmakers (Liu 1976, 1989a, Yoshimizu 1989; *see chapter eight*). Patty and Dinah Hulet are also skilled in making mosaic face canes. Crude attempts in Syria to fake Roman mosaic face beads and other ancient glass beads have been reported (Dale 1978). In fact, some recent Syrian reconstructions of other kinds of ancient beads

the Middle East. Venetian replicas of Phoenician pendants are currently available from importers. Japanese glass beadmakers have also core-formed and lampworked their versions of Phoenician ornaments (Yoshimizu 1989).

Made from core-formed glass, Phoenician mask pendants and beads usually portray bearded males (*see page 117*); animals are also represented, and occasionally female and male genitalia. Male genitalia, popular subjects for amulets or pendants, are made in glass and faience in a number of cultures (Liu 1983a). Eastern Mediterranean polychrome glass phallus

PTOLEMAIC OR ROMAN PERIOD GLASS BEADS from Egypt, and probably contemporaneous with one another. The same shapes are made in monochromatic or striped glass. Yellow, yellow-green and yellow-brown are the primary colors, with a few having a third color. Solid colors capped by yellow are called date beads; largest is 1.65 cm long.

amulets are quite amusing, resembling the Kilroy graffiti of the 1940s (Green 1993: numbers 174, 175).

There are about thirty subtypes of Phoenician pendants, depending on the classification system; they range from Europe to Sudan and as far east as the Black Sea (Haevernick 1977, Seefried 1982, Tatton-Brown 1981). In a study of Phoenician mask pendants and beads, Seefried examined over six hundred specimens from approximately one hundred-twenty sites in about nineteen geographical or cultural areas, probably a record of thoroughness for any single bead or pendant type. Without having seen the complete range of styles and types of Phoenician pendants and beads, a collector could easily be fooled by fakes. In addition, the glass is often devitrified to some degree, so that there is difficulty even in identifying the material. For example, the original colors of the glass of the mask pendant shown on page 117 was probably white for the face, cobalt blue for the facial features, yellow for the four applied dabs near the temple; the curls

CHECKER OR CHEQUER GLASS BEAD Contemporaneous with early and late Roman mosaic face beads, this specimen, 2.2 cm long and probably dating from 100 B.C. to 100 A. D., is a type rarely found in private collections. Checker glass was generally used in Viking glass beads of 800 to 1000 A.D. When found in the Middle East, checker glass is often corroded; the one from Turkey on page 121 has been consolidated with liquid nylon. *Courtesy of Lost Cities.*

SANDWICH GOLD-GLASS BEADS from Egypt; longest is 1.7 cm. Constricted clear tubes sandwich gold foil, although analysis frequently reveals no gold. The beads are often late Roman but also made in other cultures and localities, possibly even Asia; some consider the collars as characteristically Indian. (See Spaer 1993 for review of gold-glass beads.)

which were cobalt blue are now almost colorless. Such ornaments were never inexpensive and currently cost a great deal. Prices vary depending on size, type and condition: in 1974, $200; 1976, $65 to $95; 1977, $450; 1979, $150; 1980, $750; 1985, $415 each in a lot of ten; 1993, $5,700 to $12,500 each. Recent high auction prices for Phoenician mask pendants were for unremarkable specimens. The example shown in this chapter was given to a street musician as a tip, whereupon he sold it to an antiquities dealer for seven hundred-fifty dollars (J. Malter, *pers. comm.* 1980).

While Phoenician glass pendants are well represented in Japanese collections and virtually every antiquities auction carries some examples, they are in very few bead collections. The larger type C pendants, showing males with coiled hair and beards, are among the most elaborate glass ornaments.

Roman mosaic face beads, usually less garish and grotesque, show fascinating crafting and variations. Spherical beads and flat circular or square plaques are the most common. Square plaques may be no more than mosaic cane sliced and perforated, or the cane

VENETIAN GLASS BEADS from Egypt with squiggle trailed designs, showing the variety of European beads with this type of decoration; sizes range from 1.0 to 2.0 cm long. The large bead at the upper left is probably Islamic. *Courtesy of Rita Okrent.*

embedded in a monochrome matrix. Spherical beads have face canes in a register circling the equator in a band, interspersed with monochrome, patterned or chequer glass. Beads decorated with chequer patterns are often associated with face beads (Stout 1986). Some beads have face plaques touching each other. Later face beads have three parallel registers, always decorated with chequer glass. Others have round face canes embedded randomly. Rarer mosaic ornaments are shaped like spindle whorls, barrel beads, drop pendants, or vases (Green 1993, Liu 1976). The culture that made the intricate mosaic face and duck bead discovered in Korea remains a mystery (Yoshimizu 1989).

Each feature of the mosaic face bead varies considerably, especially the face canes themselves (Alekseeva 1971, Dubin 1987, Stawiarska 1985, Stout 1986, Tempelmann-Maczynska 1985, Yoshimizu 1989). Face beads are a fraction of the size of large Phoenician mask pendants, and the plaques bearing the faces are only 0.5 to 0.9 centimeters wide. They are distributed from northern Europe to the Black Sea, as well as Italy and Egypt (Stout 1986). Roman face beads may be found in more areas, but those with datable contexts are few.

Since ancient mosaic face beads have never been comprehensively studied, one can make personal discoveries while contributing to bead research. For those who love the acquisition of knowledge, finding information is as satisfying as obtaining additional beads for collections. There is no plausible estimate of the numbers of extant Roman face beads and pendants. A thorough search of auction catalogs would show how many may have been available in the marketplace. Those bought in the Middle East and those described in the literature may comprise only a minority of the extant bead population. In just three auctions from the last two decades, twenty mosaic face plaque beads and ninety-six spherical mosaic face beads have been offered (Anonymous 1972, 1985, Green 1993). Some people collect only Roman face beads; one bought approximately thirty in Beirut (J. Malter, *pers. comm.* 1977).

Closest to a systematic study of mosaic face beads was Stout's (1986) survey of early and late period beads which placed emphasis on very rare, late Roman face beads. Only eighteen such beads have been found,

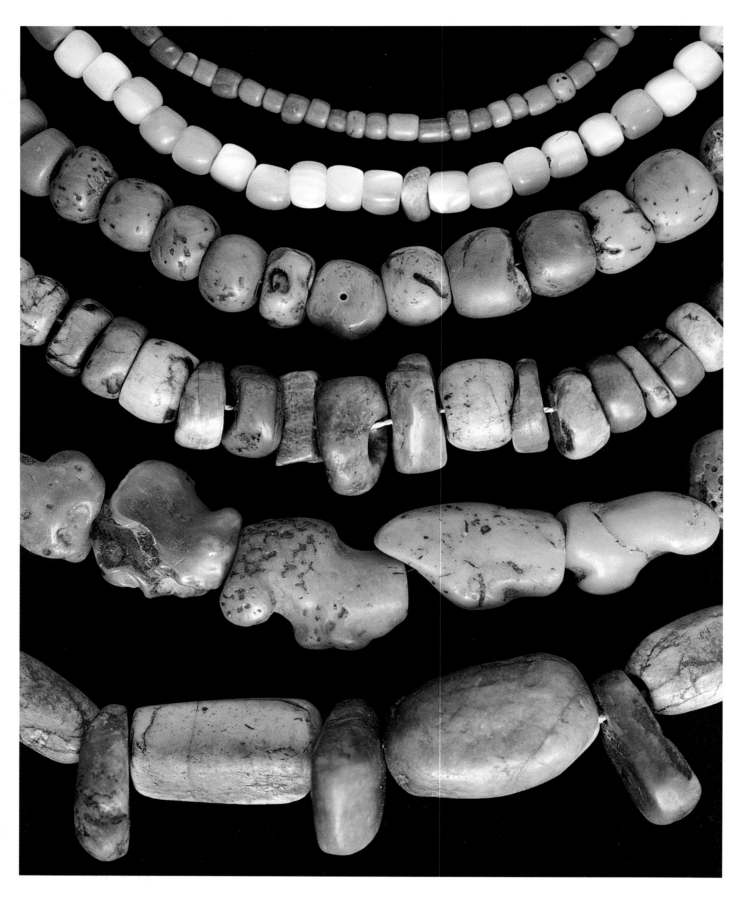

CORAL, MOTHER-OF-PEARL AND AMAZONITE BEADS from Morocco; beads of this quality are now rare. *Top to bottom:* Short tubular or disk beads of coral, mother-of-pearl, coral barrel, amazonite disk beads, beads made from large pieces of branch coral, and rough cylindrical beads and drop pendants of amazonite. Shown slightly larger than actual sizes. *Courtesy of Liza Wataghani.*

undoubtedly dwarfed by the larger numbers of early face beads of the first century B.C. The latter may attain a count of at least the low thousands.

This estimate is based on a mosaic face bead being amenable to large scale production. Once a face cane is made and drawn, numerous beads can be easily made. Judging from the many shapes onto which mosaic face plaques are applied, it is apparent that such mosaic slices are valued, in appreciation of the difficulty of making a face cane. The styles are distinctive, so it may be possible to distinguish between the work of different glass beadmakers and perhaps segregate face beads according to the original workshop. Muzzy (1993) describes how Brian Kerkvliet makes a face cane, while Yoshimizu (1989) shows how a Japanese beadmaker, probably the late Kisao Iburi, made his version.

Like other buried ancient glass, many mosaic face beads show corrosive effects. If the resulting iridescence does not flake easily, it is still considered desirable (Liu 1986; *see page 113*). But Roman face beads do not generally display this type of corrosion; they usually devitrify, losing color in the process. Because of the value placed on face beads, corroded specimens are often sanded with emery paper to remove surface layers of devitrified glass. Some refinishings are subtle and well done, while other specimens are sanded too much and polished too highly. Canes bearing faces are often ground so thinly that portions break off. One can see varying degrees of this restoration on page 118. The specimen on page 119 is barely touched, as are many on page 236.

The effects of burial often change the appearance of ancient glass so much that it is misattributed. Recently, half a tabular glass bead with three face plaques was misidentified as inlaid stone in a London antiquities catalog. Phoenician mask pendants are not subject to regrinding with emery paper, perhaps due to the difficulty of sanding their complex features.

Like mask pendants, Roman face beads have risen dramatically in price, and like other collectibles, price varies greatly with quality, knowledge of the buyer and the rarity or perceived rarity at time of sale. In 1972 when a friend and I successfully bid for a necklace with face beads, they averaged sixty dollars each. During the same year at Sotheby Parke Bernet, a buyer paid three hundred-fifty dollars each. Prices during the last two decades consisted of: 1973, $125 wholesale, in Egypt; 1977, $1,600 offered for six face beads; 1979, plaque and spherical beads

MOROCCAN ORNAMENTS used by the Aït Atta; composed of coral, amber, copal and its simulations, wood and glass beads, shells including conus, and plastic talhakimt, approximately 24 cm long. The ornaments are worn near the temples, draped from women's hair. *Courtesy of James Jereb.*

at $125 to $175 each, while a New York dealer charged $250; 1985, two lots at auction averaging between $84 to $173 each; 1992, $5,250 retail for one bead; and 1993, $3,000 to $5,000 each, and thirty bought for $1,150 each of good to excellent quality, or $350 each for seven of lesser grade; 1994, $1,000 for two plaque beads, $930 for a plaque and a bulla. This overview of prices strongly suggests that buying at auction is still advantageous, even if few offer Roman face beads. Auction material is often strung with intervening filler beads to render it more wearable: including the purchase of extraneous beads, the per unit cost of face beads is still lower than buying them separately.

The variety of other glass ornaments from the Middle East is vast, but availability is more limited. Beads offered at auction and in the stocks of antiquities dealers in the 1970s, and possibly early 1980s, were often Egyptian. Now, Afghanistan via Pakistan may be the largest supplier, with much less coming from Turkey, Iran or Syria. Because of the uncertainty of the source, beads sold from any of these areas are usually labeled ancient Near Eastern.

Egyptian glass beads include striped or monochrome beads of various shapes capped with yellow, and often called date beads. They are undeniably Ptolemaic or Roman (*see page 125*), although Goldstein (1979) dates similar beads of blue and yellow glass to circa 1400 B.C. Long drop pendants of glass, with counterparts in faience, are certainly Egyptian,

MOROCCAN NECKLACE from Ajoud region, Aït baha tribe; consisting of beads of coral, amber, copal and its simulations, amazonite, silver pendants and amulets, glass, conus and *Pusiostema* shells (also used in Mauritania); strung on wool, 38 cm long. *Courtesy of James Jereb.*

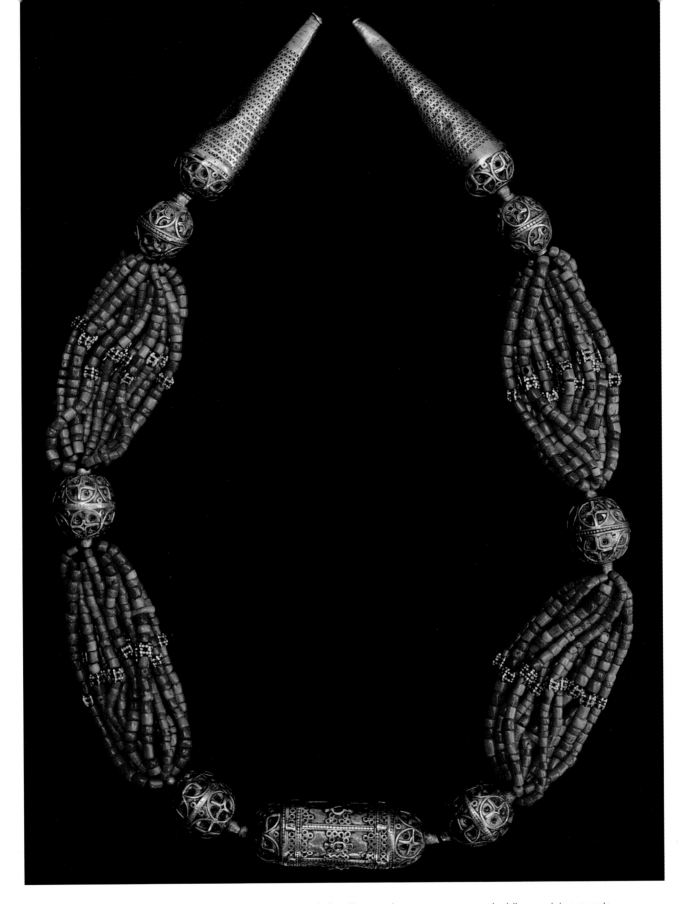

AQD MIRJAN NECKLACE FROM YEMEN Worn by women during the marriage ceremony and while receiving guests after giving birth, this necklace consists of sixteen strands of coral beads with five-sided tut beads in the middle of each, made from soldered silver granules. The intricate spherical silver beads are called jauz; the cylindrical center bead, heikal (7.3 cm long); and the cone-shaped ones, mismar. Mismar means a nail, which because of its sharp steel structure, will function as a needle or sword against evil spirits (Kennedy 1979). Uniform, dark-colored coral is preferred for this necklace, with the number of strands ranging from twelve to fourteen. *Courtesy of Sylvia Kennedy.*

SILVER AND STONE JEWELRY FROM AFGHANISTAN against an ikat background. Afghanistan is the source of many ethnographic and ancient beads. Shown are tabular and other carnelian beads from India. In the center, the multistrand of coral, silver and shell beads is actually a headdress ornament from the Teke and Kirghiz peoples. *Courtesy of Anahita Gallery.*

and possibly Eighteenth Dynasty (Liu 1980: figure 5). Fused rod beads from Fustat dating to 900 A.D. are another distinctive Egyptian bead (Francis 1989). Many other glass beads and pendants also come from Egypt and are widely distributed. A good example is the Roman millefiori bead with red caps, in spherical or cylindrical shapes; many have been found in Egypt and other Middle Eastern countries (*see page 123*).

Increasing acknowledgment that numerous Middle Eastern glass beads date to the Islamic period is of great importance to bead collectors, since there is a tendency to attribute early dates to all beads from this region (Dubin 1987, Francis 1989, 1990). Many glass beads from Afghanistan, Turkey and Syria shown here date from approximately 600 to 1300 A.D. (*see pages 112, 113, 120, 121, 122*). There have been no major studies on Islamic glass beads, although one is presumably underway. The color chronology of Islamic glass

by Kolbas (1983) may help in dating. No doubt Venetians were heavily influenced by Islamic glass, especially with regard to mosaic and millefiori beads. Roman glass possibly also provided prototypes. Being Islamic does not decrease market value; good quality glass beads sell for hundreds of dollars each in America but less than half if purchased in lots at auction in England (Anonymous 1994, Green 1993).

Ancient glass eye beads have always been favored by collectors, and these abound in the Middle East, dating from approximately 800 B.C. to 100 A.D. Dubin (1987) points out the presence of both stratified and mosaic rod eyes in beads (*see pages 114, 115*). Small tabular eyebeads also occur in this region, dated by Goldstein (1979) to the Eighteenth Dynasty (circa 1300 to 1550 B.C.). Some well known types of eye beads found in Europe, such as orange-yellow glass with stratified blue and white eyes, also occur in the Middle East (Venclova 1983; *see page 158*). They are occasionally offered at auction

NECKLACE FROM ETHIOPIA composed of smaller beads of soldered granules, and larger hollow beads from domed sheet metal halves soldered together; largest is 4.0 cm diameter. Wires and die-formed elements are applied onto the surfaces. The beads are usually attributed to Saudi Arabia and Yemen (Liu 1984c), but since Ethiopia is separated only by the Red Sea, it is likely these are imports. The beads are also made of silver or silver-plated copper. *Courtesy of Wind River.*

CONTEMPORARY MOROCCAN BEADS of glass simulations of coral and metal beads, plastic copal, metal beads, and ceramic imitations of coral and metal beads; largest ceramic bead is 4.0 cm long. Compare these strands with the ethnographic necklaces, ornaments and authentic coral on pages 128 to 130. *Courtesy of Liza Wataghani.*

CONTEMPORARY PROSSER BEADS made in Morocco using old Czech equipment now that Prosser beads are no longer being produced in the Czech Republic. Note the variety of these molded bead shapes; largest is 0.8 cm diameter. *Courtesy of Elizabeth J. Harris.*

for reasonable prices, considering their importance in bead history (Anonymous 1986).

Amphora or jug beads and pendants are not uncommon in the Middle East and often the handles are broken off or re-glued from a different specimen. They can be simple in construction or have a delicate lattice surrounding the lower portion of the jug (*see page 116*). A jug pendant with beautiful iridescence in my study collection was carefully glued to the lower half of a latticework jug. I thought it was genuine until Derek Content pointed out the cyanoacrylic glue joining the two portions (*see page 225*). This type of marriage or conglomerate can fool even experienced bead researchers.

Perhaps powder glass beads bound together with resin are more insidious. When genuine ancient glass beads are strung with these matte beads, collectors have accepted them as ancient. The more brightly colored ones would not fool many, but duller beads are more deceiving (*see page 222*).

Although only very small numbers of ancient Middle Eastern glass ornaments have been discussed, this large geographic area remains fascinating to those who love antiquity. The Roman glass fica shown on page 110 is a good example. A clenched fist with a bent thumb emerging between the first and second fingers immediately signals a derogatory gesture in many past and modern cultures, especially in the Americas (Kelly 1977). Sexual in connotation, it serves to protect against the evil eye. Many examples may exist (Hansmann and Kriss-Rettenbeck 1977), but in glass I am aware of only the Roman specimen and one related to San Pedro Quiatoni pendants.

CONTEMPORARY EGYPTIAN WOOD BEAD from Cairo, inlaid with wood and mother-of-pearl; purchased in 1979, 4.5 cm long. Except for rosaries, wood beads are not common. *Courtesy of Elizabeth J. Harris.*

OTHER MATERIALS

Because of the predominance of stone, faience and glass beads in the Middle East, those of other materials are given less attention. Organic materials for beads include shell, coral, amber, copal and its simulations, bone, and wood. Synthetics include terra cotta and metal, such as gold, silver, bronze, copper, and lead.

Shell was enormously important to most regions with access to the sea but is relatively minor to bead collectors. Although important ethnographically, almost no shell beads are found in a contemporary context. Ethnographic material includes conus shells, especially as carved disks, chank or conch for the small flat tabular beads, beads made from sections of the collumella in Afghanistan necklaces, and mother-of-pearl beads and pendants (*see page 132*). In antiquity, shells were sometimes perforated and used whole or cut into rings, often called quoit beads. Some of the largest ancient shell beads, made from the collumella of a conch-like gastropod, occur in Mesopotamia (Liu 1979). David S. Rees, who specializes in ancient shell and bone ornaments, has published numerous papers on these materials in archaeological literature. Coral is especially important in ethnographic necklaces, with Morocco as a major source (Fisher 1984, Jereb 1989; *see pages 128 to 132*).

Current and older coral simulations in glass and plastic are common (*see pages 134, 221*). Ancient amber beads exist, but exactly where in the marketplace they were found is unknown (*see page 102*). Called tomb amber in the trade, the beads are always badly crazed on the surface and subject to disintegration. Beads of amber, copal and their imitations are strung on ethnographic necklaces throughout the Middle East, presenting substantial problems in identification, and new types of fakes have been introduced (*see pages 129, 134, 220*). Ancient bone beads are found on some dealers' strands, as well as a few of ethnographic origin, but these types are found in very few collections (*see page 137*). Of synthetics like terra cotta, I have seen only one ancient gadrooned or rayed specimen possibly made of this material (*see page 120*). There are many bone and terra cotta spindle whorls, but few served as beads in antiquity. Only ethnographic and contemporary wood beads exist (*see this page*).

Metal beads and pendants are accorded prominence far beyond their importance in bead history because of the attention paid by archaeologists and art historians to items made from precious metal. Both ancient gold and silver beads and pendants are on the market, especially at auctions, but buyers should be cautious of the attribution attached to them (Content 1992). Ancient bronze, possibly copper and lead ornaments and beads also come from the Middle East (*see page 103*); those made of base metal are rarely faked. Ethnographic silver and base metal ornaments are very common and much better documented than those in other materials because of the interest in collectible and wearable jewelry (Brosh 1987, Camps-Fabrer 1990, Hasson 1987, Quillard 1979). Few metal components are actually beads, most being outside the purview of bead and perforated artifact collectors (*see page 130*).

NECKLACES

Few intact ancient necklaces are found outside of Egypt, and I am not aware of any intact ancient necklace on the marketplace. Many ethnographic necklaces from Morocco, Algeria, Saudi Arabia, Yemen, and Afghanistan have been available (*see pages 129 to 132*). As with any strung necklace, it is extremely difficult to determine if it is intact or reconstructed. Nothing is wrong with the latter if reconstruction is accurate and based on good documentation. Because there have been a number of reliable ethnographic studies of personal adornment in the Middle East, descriptive and pictorial data are available for many types of traditional necklaces. The combining of real and simulated material on the same necklace does not necessarily negate its authenticity.

The Middle East remains an important area for collectors; however, with the exception of ancient beads from old collections and those of contemporary and ethnographic origin, collectors must realize that the beads were most likely acquired by questionable or illegal means. All countries have laws against archaeological looting, but the incentive or means to enforce such laws may be lacking. Bead collectors and researchers will have to weigh the satisfaction of acquisition against the damage to the cultural heritage of other countries.

NURISTAN BONE BEADS FROM AFGHANISTAN made from drilled leg bones, using perhaps a small mammal or large bird. Beads are decorated with incised designs; sizes range from 7.3 to 9.8 cm long. Bone beads are uncommon in ethnographic jewelry. *Courtesy of Anahita Gallery.*

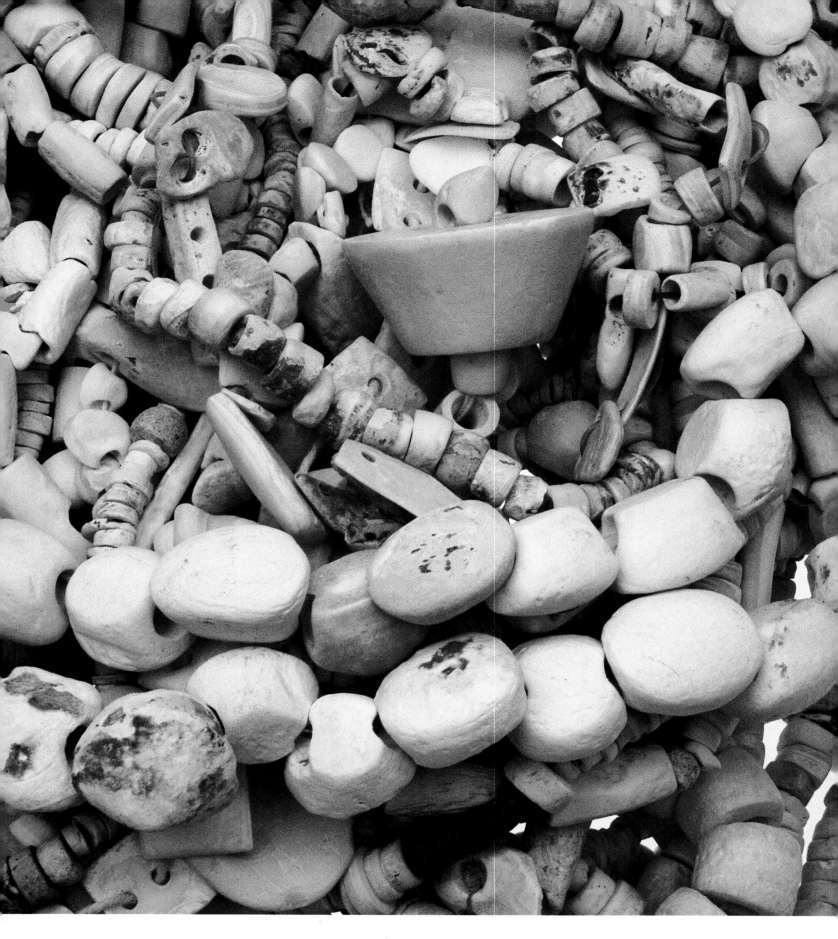

SINU SHELL BEADS AND PENDANTS from Colombia. The multiplicity of forms includes spacers, bullet and button shapes and thin squares with perforations on their flat surfaces. Mixed among the shells are a few stone beads. It is not known whether the large truncated cone bead functioned as a spindle whorl; top center specimen is 2.7 cm diameter. The Sinú culture dates from circa 600 to 1600 A.D. *Courtesy of Ken Klassen.*

PRECOLUMBIAN AMERICAS

The best study of bead and pendant jewelry from the Precolumbian Americas is still Jernigan's book published in 1978 on the prehistoric Southwest of the United States. Ancient craftspeople, their tools and methods were so thoroughly analyzed that the technical solutions and reasoning processes of these beadmakers have never been more comprehensively illuminated. The bead materials of the prehistoric Southwest were daunting to work—Jernigan estimates that it took an hour just to drill six softstone beads, and a cache of a hundred thousand such beads found near Tucson would have required "eight to ten man-years of labor." For Mesoamerican and South American cultures which employed large numbers of jade and hardstone beads, the techniques were even more challenging due to the hardness of the raw materials (Mirambell 1968). Because almost all research has focused on precious metal jewelry and large jades, literature on precolumbian beads is generally scarce with the exception of articles on the prehistoric Chumash of coastal California (King 1981, Liu 1983) and some site reports (see Gessler 1988 for Uhle; Mason 1936, Lothrop 1937).

Imparting a warmly tactile quality, beads from the Precolumbian Americas are enormously appealing. Many were obtained before the enactment of legal sanctions regarding the means of acquisition and the exporting of artifacts to Western countries, but virtually all derive from the looting of archaeological sites and surface finds. Almost all beads on the market in the last few decades originated from Peru, Colombia,

Costa Rica, and Mexico, with a very small minority from Panama and Ecuador. Beads and other perforated artifacts from Peru constitute the greatest portion on the marketplace, with some of the larger Peruvian bead collections maintained by collectors living in that country. Now legal imports are limited to just a few South American countries known not to have many antiquities. Most countries involved in antiquities trading have shown little interest in beads compared to larger artifacts or those made of precious metals. Beads were also considered secondary by the huaqueros or guaqueros of Colombia and their counterparts in other Latin American countries who concentrated on gold artifacts (Kessler and Kessler 1978). They also sold archaeological material to local Indians, such as the Goajiro, who bought Tairona artifacts (Mason 1936). Lothrop (1950) described the excavation of Panamanian graves of the Veraguas region by guaqueros, with gold artifacts as their primary goal.

Fortunately, relatively few collectors buy precolumbian beads, and current collections are not likely to be representative samples of the extant beads of any culture, with the possible exception of Peruvian or Colombian collections. Beads from either prehistoric or historic Americas are not shown in Yoshimizu (1989), which is surprising, as Japanese collectors are normally quite systematic (unless stone and shell beads were excluded from the scope of the book). In North America, there are probably more collectors of prehistoric artifacts than beads of the

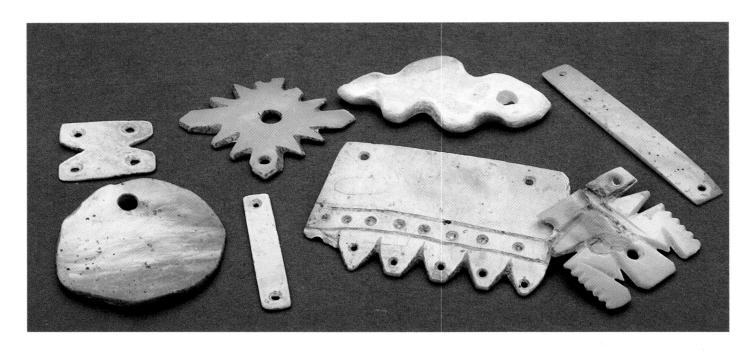

MOTHER-OF-PEARL ORNAMENTS from Bahia culture, Ecuador. Most are only between 1.0 and 2.0 mm thick; largest is 3.5 cm long. Possibly too fragile for necklaces, these may have been sewn onto clothing. *Courtesy of Alexander Hirtz.*

SPONDYLUS AND MOTHER-OF-PEARL BEADS and spacers, primarily from Peru. The round bead with four bosses (2.0 cm diameter) is possibly Ecuadorian. Many of the flat ornaments are drilled through the edge and one side. Note the brilliant orange-red color of the spondylus (thorny oyster). Once containing inlays, the purple-colored oyster beads have faded significantly. *Courtesy of Geraldo Roca.*

same period, although Jernigan (1978) states that large amounts of prehistoric Southwestern jewelry are contained within private collections. Interestingly, privately owned jade (actually jadeite) beads and pendants in North America appear to belong mostly to antiquity dealers, such as Edward Merrin Gallery or the Andre Emmerich Gallery of New York City (see Dubin 1987). Most bead collections seem to have only greenstone or metadiorite beads, not jade ones (*see pages 144, 145*). Sotheby's in New York

ancient ornaments to tourists. The best Costa Rican beads in San José were supposedly sold by a shoe store owner (B. Hill, *pers. comm.* 1988). A few fulltime dealers in precolumbian artifacts sell beads as a minor portion of their businesses; others occasionally bring in small quantities of ornaments when they visit the United States or import them, such as the Los Angeles travel agency which once traded in Nueva Cádiz and other Peruvian beads.

CLASSIC TIAHUANACO-WARI BEADS portraying stylized, possibly feline heads shown in profile, circa 700 to 1000 A.D. The inlays consist of mother-of-pearl, orange and purple spondylus and unidentified greenstone. Each rectangular bead has two parallel perforations and is 4 cm high. *Courtesy of Gessler Collection.*

City has held numerous auctions of precolumbian art, which have included a number of bead necklaces (Anonymous 1981). Some precolumbian ornaments have always been found in antique or antiquities stores in the west and southwest United States, such as Santa Fe, New Mexico. Mound Builder pendants, Mesoamerican and Southwest Mimbres shell beads (at twenty-five dollars per strand) were sold there during the early 1970s. There were and still might be dealers in Central and South America who sold

Of the beads and pendants that have survived burial, relatively few materials have been used. The pueblo beadmakers of arid prehistoric Southwest made seed and wood beads and pendants (Jernigan 1978), so it is not unexpected that similar perishable materials would have been used for personal adornment in the moist areas of the Americas, where they would not survive burial. Climatic conditions and the form of burial are vital to the preservation of archaeological material. For example, mummy bundle burials of the dry north

QUILLACINGA BIRDFORM AMBER BEADS from Colombia. Prehispanic amber artifacts are rare; the resin or amber's reddish color may result from burial, and the surfaces are often badly crazed. Eyes are visible on some of these stylized birds, ca. 1.8 cm long. The Quillacinga also made amber human figure beads as well as larger functional ocarina. *Courtesy of Ken Klassen.*

coast of Peru have often yielded fragments of necklaces where even the stringing is intact, providing pertinent evidence of the complexity of their necklace designs (Gessler 1988, Liu 1983). In neighboring Ecuador to the north, the much more humid coastal climate has destroyed most organic archaeological material and not even fragmentary necklaces remain. Yet detailed terra cotta statuary of the Jama-Coaque and the less well fashioned La Tolita or Tumaco clay figures display a wealth of elaborate necklaces (Liu 1992c). The Kesslers (1986) show a necklace which matches those on Jama-Coaque figures. Although many necklace arrangements, even complete specimens, have survived from the prehistoric Southwest, none attain the elaborate stringing of Peruvian necklaces. Among the Moche (Donnan 1993), neckware achieved structural complexity comparable to Egyptian broadcollars. A Chimu bib of *Spondylus*, the thorny oyster, and stone disk beads with figural images is even more elaborate (Dubin 1987: figure 266). This is less a North-South dichotomy than an illustration of the difference between the personal adornment of commoners in southwest North America and the ritual dress worn by the elite of South America.

At the time of European contact, some explorers chronicled Native American adornment (Francis 1984, Kelly 1992). Amazing quantities of beads worn by some Panamanians were described by Wafer during the late 1600s (in Kessler and Kessler 1988); both sexes had up to three and four hundred strands of beads around their necks. Women wore between fifteen and thirty pounds or more, and men double those amounts.

Intact and fragmentary necklaces and jewelry illustrated on murals, reliefs (Jernigan 1978), statues and figurines, and ceramic vessels (Liu 1983: figures 10-45, 52-55) provide some information regarding the usage of beads. Such sources though present difficulties and endanger the ability to make accurate interpretations; for example, the limited number of study samples bias toward those prehispanic cultures which produced visible and surviving representations of jewelry, such as those from the Maya and Veracruz regions of Mexico. Cultures known to have made most of the jewelry elements, and also developed elaborate stringing arrangements, such as Peru, are not represented since their terra cotta figures do not depict many necklaces.

Another approach to answering intriguing questions about ancient personal adornment can be assisted by the expertise of other professionals. By studying specialized necklace components and their perforations, the experienced necklace designer can provide insights regarding how unusual necklace forms were originally strung. Bead spacers, with up to eight perforations (*see pages 156, 157*), elements permitting stringing in two axes (*see page 151*) and perforations drilled at the edges of necklace components allowed the precolumbian craftsperson to display versatility and complexity in designing (Liu 1983). At times even simple beads were used ingeniously, as in the employment of disk beads strung vertically to function essentially as spacers (Liu 1983: figure 46, a Peruvian north coast necklace fragment). A nearly intact necklace shown in Rowe (1984: plate 25) beautifully demonstrates the use of disk beads as spacers.

Some necklaces modeled on prehispanic statues or votive figures are puzzling. Small but accurately sculpted Maya figurines from Jaina often portray necklaces with giant beads cascading down the chest in two parallel dangles. Examination of large greenstone beads does not indicate how such a structure would have been strung since the dangles would have to connect at some point. It would mean that some of these large beads would need perforations in two axes so that they could be strung as dangles and also attach to the adjacent parallel strand.

Museum personnel and other scholars have reconstructed necklaces based on reasoned conjecture (see references in Liu 1983), but unfortunately the majority of reconstructions lack validity. Many interesting necklaces are shown in Mujica Gallo (1959), but these reconstructions may not be representations of actual necklace forms. Treviño de Sáenz (1947) like-

SINU OR QUILLACINGA AMULET of a quadruped; other amulets from the same area portray fish, butterflies and crocodiles, ranging from 1.5 to 4.9 cm long. In reflected light, this resin amulet is a light yellow. *Courtesy of Ken Klassen.*

MAYAN JADEITE BEADS The assorted shapes in a fine apple-green color have been highly polished; largest is 1.8 cm diameter. Even though large spherical or cylindrical jade beads are usually seen, small beads may have been more numerous. As a rare and precious commodity, any small piece of jade would have been used by the Maya, unlike Costa Rica where the material was more abundant. *Courtesy of Noma Copley and Edward Merrin Gallery.*

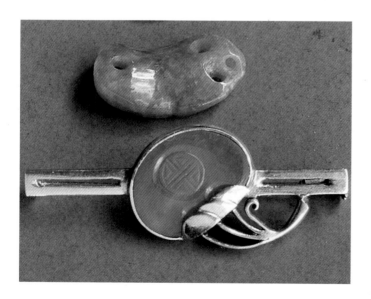

MAYAN AND CHINESE JADEITE showing the similarity of color. China also has nephrite jade, which is rarely found in Prehispanic Americas. Pre-World War II Chinese gold and jade brooch is 3.9 cm long. *Courtesy of Noma Copley, Edward Merrin Gallery and Mary Liu.*

wise displays many Peruvian necklaces of archaeological and ethnographic origin, but information on how they were reconstructed is again lacking. Based on her husband's collection, Treviño's book does show the extent of a Peruvian private collection. Some experts say they can distinguish contemporary from precolumbian stringing by the way elements are used (J. Jones, *pers. comm.* 1988).

MATERIALS

The shells of marine molluscs are perhaps the most common bead material, closely followed by those of stone, although the larger sizes of stone beads may mean they are more numerous by volume. Terra cotta beads are not common, although many collectors mistake spindle whorls for beads, and such tools are often made of clay (Liu 1978, 1984). Peru, Colombia, Ecuador, and Mexico have metal beads and pendants, as did the Mound Builders. Amber and resin ornaments are rare in the Precolumbian Americas, known only in Colombia. The Dominican Republic is one of the world's largest sources of amber, but none date from a prehistoric context. Bone beads are uncommon, but teeth are more common than bone.

SHELL BEADS AND PENDANTS

For the precolumbian jewelrymaker, shell was an important raw material, often imported over long distances by land and sea. Prehistoric Southwest pueblo peoples followed well known routes to the Gulf of California and also traded for abalone shell from coastal California (Jernigan 1978). Among the shells were those of *Spondylus,* the thorny oyster; this mollusc was of even greater importance to Prehispanic South America where it had religious significance (Liu 1992c) and was traded by sea routes north and south from Ecuador. The bright orange-reds and

purples of this bivalve are probably the strongest colors in the shell bead palette (*see pages 140, 141*). The bright orange of *Spondylus princeps* is often mistaken for coral, but no precious coral was available on the Pacific coast. Cylindrical beads made from spondylus can reach four centimeters, so the material was not used just for small disk beads. The desirability of the thorny oyster persists in contemporary Southwest jewelry.

Other than the thorny oyster and some mother-of-pearl, most extant precolumbian shell beads and pendants are usually devoid of color (*see pages 138, 140*). The lack of color is partly due to decomposition from burial and shell abrasion whereby surface layers of color are ground off. Many shell components are surprisingly large, probably originating from the horse conch (genus

GREENSTONE AND POSSIBLY JADEITE BEADS from Mexico. While some of the beads might resemble spindle whorls, their biconical perforations would prevent a spindle from firmly settling. Beads with large grains are probably metadiorite; others, lacking the large grain effect and showing a higher polish, are possibly jade. Large spherical bead is 2.7 cm diameter. The largest greenstone bead that I have measured is 4.3 cm long, and is proportionately much smaller than those depicted on Mayan ceramics. *Courtesy of Annette Bird.*

TAIRONA QUARTZ CRYSTAL BEAD with biconical drilling (5.8 cm long) and strung with small spondylus disks. This frosted bead would not be considered vivo. Other Colombian quartz beads are quite clear and up to 2.0 cm in diameter, with amazingly smooth perforations. The prehispanic bead industry must have been well organized in order to produce the enormous numbers of shell disk beads needed to make their necklaces. *Courtesy of Ken Klassen.*

Strombus). This marine shell is often used for spherical beads, since few other bivalves have sufficient thickness. Some Sinú square section beads are up to seventeen centimeters long. Other long shell beads include those made from the columella of *Kelletia* by the Chumash (King 1981).

Colombia's Sinú culture has yielded enormous numbers and types of shell beads (*see page 138*). Some resemble spindle whorls; others are bullet-shaped, somewhat like the carnelian and claystone Tairona beads, but without a concave end. Many look similar to buttons, but are drilled like a bead. Such pointed beads with a truncated base are also made in crystal by the Tairona, indicating that certain shapes had wide popularity (Kessler and Kessler 1978: figure 4). Cylindrical, disk (some of considerable size and thickness, which may be attributed to the Quillacinga, a tribe in the southern Nariño region) and flat beads, spacers and tabular pendants are all found. If sufficiently large samples were studied, undoubtedly many other forms would be uncovered. Little is known about most precolumbian beads, and descriptive assemblages have yet to be compiled. If Sinú bead shapes are contrasted with those of the prehistoric Southwest, one sees that South Americans used shell much more extravagantly compared to pueblo cultures where it was scarce. This relationship between working method and abundance of raw material is also seen in Costa Rican versus Mayan jadeworking.

Most shell beads are Peruvian, the majority consisting of disks, required in large numbers for the construction of complex bibs and pectorals as well as for less elaborate necklaces (Gessler 1988). By analyzing burials, Donnan and Mackey (1978) provide information on the distribution of beads in Moche graves. Cylinders, spheres and crude barrels are all common, although Peruvian beads are generally much smaller than those of Ecuador and Colombia. In fact, some of the smallest beads in the precolumbian world come from Peru, perhaps due to the use of miniaturized beads in jewelry (Donnan 1993) or on votive figurines and dolls (McEwan and van de Guchte 1992). More complex shell beads are also found, such as the fetish-like animals shown in Gessler (1988), Liu (1991) and on page 140. Numerous

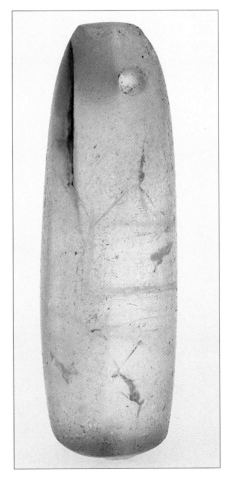

TAIRONA BEADS AND PENDANTS
of quartz crystal and carnelian, composed primarily of tapering pendants
with cone-shaped ends in various sizes.
The crystal pendants range from ca.
1.0 to 2.0 cm in length. Tairona beadmakers, especially when working hardstones, demonstrated expert technical
skill; no other precolumbian culture
compares with their precision in the
shaping of beads. Even though the
Tairona were superb goldworkers, their
beadmakers employed no metal tools
in the lapidary process, instead they
used "drilling, pecking, sawing, incising and gouging to shape and perfo-
rate beads and pendants" (Kessler
and Kessler 1978). Drills of hollow and
solid wood and bamboo were probably used in conjunction with quartz
sand as an abrasive (Kessler and
Kessler 1978). The Tairona culture
flourished from circa 600 to 1600 A.D.
Courtesy of Ken Klassen.

TAIRONA BEADS WITH FLARED ENDS in carnelian and quartz crystal, ranging from 5.5 to 9.0 cm long. The flared ends of the hardstone beads make the lapidary work a tour de force; these are even more difficult to fashion than the long tapering barrel beads of ancient Sumer and the Indus Valley. *Courtesy of Ken Klassen.*

TAIRONA QUARTZ CRYSTAL PENDANT, 6.4 cm long. These are quite rare in com-parison to ones with cone or bullet-shaped ends. *Courtesy of Ken Klassen.*

HARDSTONE AND SOFTSTONE BEADS probably from Colombia and Peru, including agate, carnelian, jasper, and softer stones. There are two perforations on one side of the button-like bead, merging into a single perforation on the reverse. *Courtesy of Geraldo Roca.*

BEADS OF GREEN AND BLUE MINERALS from South America, including turquoise, lapis and sodalite, 0.8 to 3.2 cm long. As in other ancient cultures, these colors are favored and symbolically important.

stylized forms exist, some of animals made from mother-of-pearl, which were often inlaid, although most have fallen out leaving depressions (*see page 140*). The Tiahuanaco-Wari culture of Peru produced elaborate shell inlay beads that are masterpieces, probably deriving their designs from contemporaneous textiles (Gessler 1988; *see page 141*). Even common beads are often the result of much handwork, like the round mother-of-pearl bead with four raised bosses on page 140. The much thinner mother-of-pearl beads from Ecuador have complex outlines and notches as well as drilled decorations (*see page 140, top*). Some

appear to be pushing the limits of this brittle material; perhaps as a result of its fragility, these beads were possibly sewn onto clothing.

Segments were cut from conch shells so beads would nestle closely together, forming a continuous band; such necklaces are found in Colombia and Panama, and probably other prehispanic cultures if interpretations from statuary can be verified (Kessler and Kessler 1978, 1988, Liu 1983). Besides large conch beads, the Tairona of Colombia have other large shell beads and pendants, including some that represent warriors or chiefs, and animals or animal parts such as pelicans and teeth (Kessler and Kessler 1978). Amulets of frogs, a popular motif, can be found in shell, stone and metal, illustrating the phenomenon of transposition (Liu 1985b; *see page 152*). Two types of Tairona stone pendants, respectively called Y and V shape (Mason 1936), are suggestive of stylized frogs. Because of widespread use of the frog motif among South American Indians (Wassén 1934) and the similarity of Tairona frog imagery to these pendants, such a comparison is logical. The Kesslers (1978: figure 16) included these forms and others as examples of stylized frog amulets. Afghanistan also has Y-shaped shell amulets. Panama has large shell imitations of boar teeth and shell frogs (Kessler and Kessler 1988), but few collectors have gained access to this country's beads. Carnelian and agate have been worked in ancient Panama for

TAIRONA AND SINU AMULETS Demonstrating the skill of ancient craftspeople, these mostly stylized animals in stone and shell portray a quadruped, birds and a stingray. It is not known what the bent hardstone amulet represents. Like those from the prehistoric Southwest, these amulets are both three dimensional and flat. The double shell birds are reminiscent of twin bird amulets found among the Inuit. The slate stingray is Sinú and 4.3 cm long. *Courtesy of Ken Klassen.*

PRECOLUMBIAN HARDSTONE AND SOFTSTONE BEADS from South America. Of less commonly used stones, the three cylindrical beads and greyish tapering square bead are hardstones, possibly bloodstone; the longest red cylindrical bead is similar to catlinite, 7.6 cm long. The slate spacer showing two perforations and the circle and dot decoration is widespread in Peru, 0.9 cm long. Most beads found in collections are made of ordinary and easily recognizable minerals and stones. *Courtesy of Geraldo Roca.*

NECKLACE OF TAIRONA AND PERUVIAN COMPONENTS with typical Tairona gusano or grub amulets, miniature carnelian broadwing pendants (1.8 to 2.0 cm wide), Y-shaped pendant (3.8 cm long), and cone-shaped crystal pendant. Those of Peruvian origin include the shell bird with inlaid eyes and animal amulets, although the one of shell is probably Tairona. The carnelian and crystal beads are from Colombia, and turquoise and other elements from Peru. The necklace is not based on a prototype. *Courtesy of Ken Klassen.*

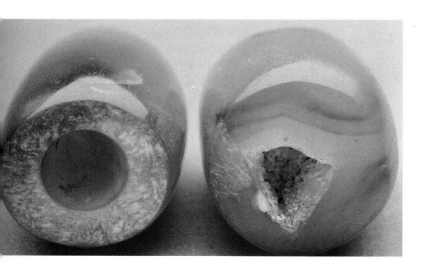

PANAMANIAN CARNELIAN BEADS Note the high polish, biconical drilling and how the geode's cavity was utilized for the perforation, 1.5 cm diameter. *Courtesy of Ken Klassen.*

beads and broadwing pendants. Among the carnelian beads found with these pendants was one which used the geode's cavity for the perforation (*see this page*).

STONE BEADS AND PENDANTS

Of all precolumbian stone beads or pendants only those of jade (jadeite) or similar hardstones have attracted the attention of archaeologists and art historians. Coverage of jade beads is scanty with celts predominating. Some researchers specialize in precolumbian jade (Balser 1980, Easby 1968, Lange 1993) and precolumbian jewelry (Jones 1988), while Keverne (1991) has surveyed jade worldwide. Few jadeite beads are known to exist in private bead collections or museum holdings. Most greenstone beads are metadiorite and some are possibly serpentine while Easby (1968) considers jadeite, diopside-jadeite and chloromelanite as jade in Meso-american contexts (*see page 145*). Mexico, especially the state of Guerrero, is the source of many green-stone beads. Aside from greenstone, many nonde-script stones were used for beads, including merely water worn pebbles with no color (*see page 228*). This situation exists throughout Mesoamerica, but stones in shades of green appear to be favored. Besides the spectacular large spherical or cylindrical Mayan jade beads (Dubin 1987) and necklaces of spherical beads and jaguar claw simulations (Jones 1988), it is likely that many jadeite beads are small and irregularly shaped to take advantage of every scrap of this precious material (*see page 144*). Some of the apple-green form resemble the jadeite that is considered so desirable by contemporary Chinese (*see page 144*). Another important source for jade is Costa Rica, where the winged and bar pendants and cylindrical beads with animal carvings are outstanding (Dubin 1987, Easby 1968). Bar pen-dants are among the largest extant beads (Liu 1985c), and the large beads with attached animals are probably the most elaborate. The beads on page 153 also have attached animals but are a pale version compared to those of jade.

Carnelian, agate and rock crystal are far more important hardstones than jade in prehis-panic ornaments in terms of sheer numbers and beauty. The Tairona culture of Colombia has been the primary source, yielding beautiful beads and amulets in these materials (Kessler and Kessler 1978). Tairona craftspeople were preeminent in the working of hardstone in South America, although rarely using jade. Softer stones like slate, serpen-tine, claystone, and steatite were also used for beads. Necklaces are represented on their ceramic effigy vessels and burial urns, but no intact exam-ples have ever been found (Kessler and Kessler 1978, Labbé 1986). Bracelets and necklaces obtained from a Kagaba-Arhuaco shaman offer some information on how the Tairona used beads and components, since this Colombian native used primarily archaeological materials in his stringing arrangements (Mason 1936: plates clix-clxiii). Most reconstructed necklaces do not follow the designs portrayed on ceramic vessels or those illustrated in Mason (1936; *see opposite page*).

TAIRONA CARNELIAN PENDANTS Labeled as having pointed bases by Mason (1936), these appear to be more bullet-shaped. Of the five existing variations, the ones shown have a flat top with a large perforation and two lateral perforations, which enable stringing through two axes. The pendants are considered muerte due to their dull surfaces; average length is ca 3.0 cm. *Courtesy of Ken Klassen.*

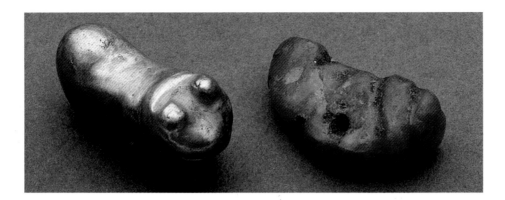

TRANSPOSITIONS OF GUSANO OR GRUB AMULETS made from carnelian and hammered gold. Carnelian amulets, which are the most commonly found, occur in many sizes. This example is 2.0 cm long. *Courtesy of Ken Klassen.*

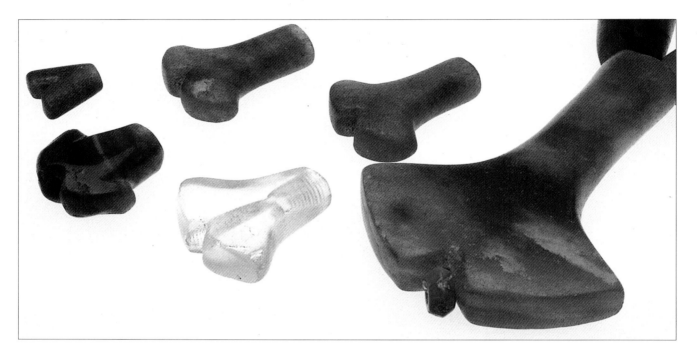

TAIRONA PENDANTS in carnelian and quartz crystal. The smallest is a V-shaped pendant, ca. 1.0 cm long; the rest are Y-shaped pendants. Note that the Y-shaped pendant next to the V-shaped one is notched and looks more like a stylized frog (also see below). Pleasing abstractions and unlike other prehistoric frog pendants, they may represent tree frogs versus other types of frogs or toads. *Courtesy of Ken Klassen.*

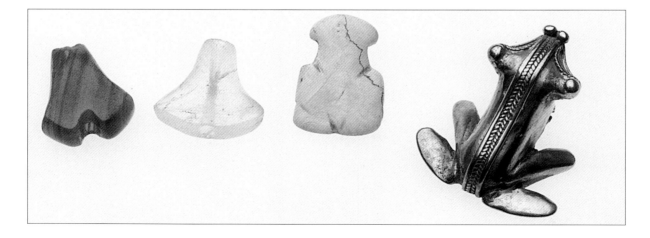

TAIRONA FROG AMULETS of cast gold, shell, quartz crystal, and carnelian; gold specimen is 3.7 cm long. Note that Y-shaped amulets are similar to those made from shell, except that the eyes have been deleted. *Courtesy of Ken Klassen.*

The Tairona's superior skills are reflected in the precise shaping of beads and pendants and the sculpting of naturalistic or stylized amulets. Gusano or the grub of insects is a form that is not evident in amulets or pendants of other prehispanic cultures in the Americas (*see page 150*). The gusano form was also transposed in gold (*see opposite page*). Among the most amazing Tairona beads and pendants are four pebbles that have been simply ground on their upper and front surfaces, leaving the bottom and sides minimally worked. Pierced at the front bevel, these suggest insects or scarabs (Liu 1989: figure 1).

beads of carnelian, agate, jasper, or rock crystal, elegantly made cylindrical beads with flared ends are reminiscent of similar long bicones without flaring ends from ancient Ur or the Indus Valley (*see page 147*). Tairona beads were also reputedly employed for cocaine use in contemporary times. A convenient form, its beauty and high cost, and possibly its country of origin have all contributed to the mystique and desirability of this bead.

There also are interesting pendants made of carnelian, agate and rock crystal. The bullet-shaped carnelian pendants on page 151, also found in ceramic,

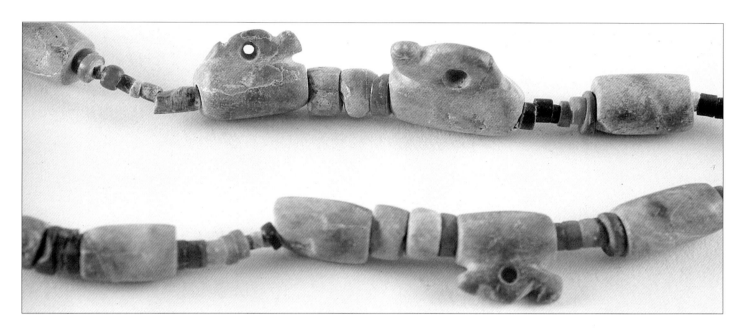

COSTA RICAN CARVED ANIMALS that have been strung with stone and shell beads. The dimensions, which were not recorded, are fairly small. While there is no comparison in terms of materials or skills, the concept of these beads is similar to the elaborately carved jade shown in Easby (1968). Few prehispanic cultures made asymmetrical beads. *Courtesy of Ken Klassen.*

Such simple and elegant ornaments display the sophistication of the Tairona. The carvers display equal skill with softer materials, as in the zoomorphic amulets on page 149.

The degree of polish and intensity of color greatly determine the value of Tairona beads and amulets: those that have been highly polished are considered vivo or live, while beads with a dull finish and muted colors are considered muerte or dead (*see pages 146, 147, 150, 151, 152*). The Kesslers (1978) have commented upon this concept, and dealers price according to such a standard. Vivo hardstone beads are now increasingly difficult to obtain.

In addition to spherical, diskoid and cylindrical

have a large perforation at the top or flat portion and lateral perforations on the sides. On some necklaces imported from Colombia, the pendants were strung in two axes, laterally as in conventional beads or pendants, and vertically, enabling two parallel strands to be joined. This practice may have been utilized by the Tairona for more complex stringing. Other pendants, made in either carnelian or rock crystal, have only lateral perforations (*see page 147*). Simple cylindrical pendants, pierced laterally at the top, are made of quartz crystal (*see page 147*). The Quillacinga or Nariño also worked obsidian for this pendant type, some reaching at least seven centimeters in length.

MULTISTRANDS OF CERAMIC DISK BEADS
The beads are often labeled as Sinú, but the Kesslers (1978) state that they derive from an older beadmaking tradition on the north coast of Colombia. Some of the dark beads may be stone. While the stringing is contemporary, the beads may have been worn similarly in precolumbian times, judging from the way South American Indians wear beads today. The simple twisting of the multiple strands adds to the volume and attractiveness. As skin oils absorb into the clay, the beads take on a deeper color. Modeled by Jeannette Muñoz. *Courtesy of Geraldo Roca.*

Hardstone beads and unperforated bead blanks are used as foundation offerings by the Kogi, present day descendants of the Tairona. Supposedly a bead is deposited for each woman and child, and blind blanks for the men (Kessler and Kessler 1978). Beads or bead blanks as offerings may have been practiced by the Tairona.

Many other stones in perforated prehispanic artifacts are more difficult to identify. Lapis, sodalite and turquoise were used as well as a number of other green stones. Hardstones include jasper, agates and bloodstone. Catlinite-like beads are found in precolumbian contexts, and a much drabber slate was used to great advantage by Peruvian north coast beadmakers (Liu 1989). They worked it with great vitality, making a number of stylized geometric animals and other shapes, often with two or more parallel perforations (*see page 156*). Intact necklace fragments shown by Gessler (1988) demonstrate how such elements linked two or more parallel bead strands. The prehistoric Peruvian beadstringer was often just as likely to increase the volume of the necklace strands by threading through ordinary disk beads (Gessler 1988), indicating that a paucity of spacers does not necessarily mean a lack of complexity. But the abundance of stone spacers among Peruvian bead components and of metal spacers in both Peruvian and Tairona contexts point to the importance of such devices to the precolumbian necklace maker (*see page 157*). In fact, large copper spacers were vital to the construction of complex Moche collars as the broad rows of beads could not easily be held in position without these narrow but strong spacers (Donnan 1993).

AMBER, RESIN AND COPAL
Amber is so rarely found in archaeological objects of the Americas that its existence has been questioned (Mason 1936). We now know that leguminous trees of the genus *Hymenaea* were widespread in the Caribbean, Mexico and Central and South America (Armstrong 1993). The resin is known as Central American copal and some of the subterranean resin in Chiapas, Mexico, the Dominican Republic, and portions of Colombia and Brazil may have been transformed into amber. If so, this material is undoubtedly the source for amber ornaments of archaeological origin in Colombia. Small disk beads may be either Quillacinga or from other Nariño tribes, and Quillacinga amber birdform and human figure beads, as well as ocarinas in amber,

have been attributed to the Karchi (*see page 142*). These bird beads are delightful abstractions, many having incised eyes, with the perforation located at the lower part of the body. The Quillacinga or Sinú made other resin or amber pendants of a light yellow color, ranging from relatively flat fish and butterflies to three dimensional quadrupeds (Liu 1992a, crocodile; *see page 143*) or tiny human figures. Mason (1936) reported on amber beads and simple pendants, none of which were representational. Ecuador also has small disk beads of resin or amber, possibly from the Karchi culture.

BONE, TEETH AND CLAWS

Beads and pendants of bone and teeth are found in all precolumbian cultures (Fogelman 1991, Jernigan 1978, Kessler and Kessler 1978, 1988, Lothrop 1937, Mason 1936), but they are not usually offered on the marketplace. Powerful amulets like teeth and claws were often transposed in other materials in prehistoric contexts (Lothrop 1937). I have encountered

only Peruvian tubular beads made from the hollow bones of birds, some stained light green by their proximity to copper during burial.

TERRA COTTA

Given the enormous numbers and ritual importance of ceramic vessels and other similar wares in prehispanic cultures, surprisingly few ornaments are made from this material. Numerous spindle whorls, some small and highly decorated, could have served an ornamental role as well as a functional purpose in spinning (Liu 1978). Many precolumbian necklaces offered for sale have whorls functioning as beads or pendants; others are composed almost entirely of whorls. The most abundant ceramic bead is the sharp-edged disk, attributed to the Sinú, but the Kesslers (1978) believe these are actually from Cartegena Maracaibo on the north coast of Colombia. Thermoluminescence tests show that they are approximately seven hundred years old. As multistrands,

MOLDED AND INCISED TERRA COTTA COATIMUNDIS AND HUMANS AS COATIMUNDIS from Manteño culture of Ecuador, 1.9 to 3.5 cm long, circa 500 to 1500 A.D. The amulets have lateral perforations, although the largest also shows remnants of perforations on the broken ears. The Manteño also produced remarkable clay whorls, among the most highly developed in the Americas. *Courtesy of Alexander Hirtz.*

PERUVIAN SLATE, POSSIBLY STEATITE AND BONE SPACERS that have been decorated with the dot and circle motif, probably from the north coast. The close spacing of the perforations indicates that only small beads were used with the spacers, 2.2 cm wide. The stones have biconical perforations, and the bone has a straight through bore; (see McGuire 1896 for drilling techniques). *Courtesy of Main Street Gallery.*

SINU OR TAIRONA GOLD BEADS made by lost-wax casting, a method whereby a model is built with flattened strips of beeswax then invested in a mixture of clay and charcoal. When the wax is burned out of the mold, molten gold is poured into the resulting void. The goldsmith's skill was considerable, both in the design of the graceful coils and casting of openwork structures. Largest bead is 0.9 cm long. *Courtesy of Ken Klassen.*

the effect of the beads is extremely attractive (*see page 154*). The Tairona also used ceramic spacers (Kessler and Kessler 1978) and made ceramic versions of their bullet-shaped pendants. Detailed and animated molded ceramic pendants of coatimundi were made in Ecuador (*see page 155*); even older ceramic pendants of stylized humans from the Valdivia culture of this country exist, although few have been seen. To the north, in Mexico, one finds beads and miniature clay figurines that are perforated, but these ornaments are rarely found in collections.

METAL

Because of the bias toward artifacts of precious metals, there have been numerous publications, conferences and exhibitions on precolumbian metalwork (Benson 1979, Bray 1978, Plazas 1986, Tushingham, Day and Rosshandler 1976, Tushingham, Franklin and Toogood 1979), although beads and pendants of gold, silver or tumbaga constitute just a minor portion of any coverage. Most precious metal ornaments are from Peru or Colombia, although tiny, beautiful soldered beads have been found in Ecuador (Orchard 1975). Those from Peru are generally formed from sheet and soldered. Allen (*pers. comm.* 1994) has viewed some in private collections, but they are rarely on the market. Six of eleven cultural regions of Prehispanic Colombia produced metal beads or pendants, and most of these were cast. A minority were hammered over a stone matrix, rolled or soldered.

Colombia is the largest source of metal beads. Given its prominence in crafting and aesthetics, its metal ornaments are among the most beautiful and varied (*see page 156, this page*). Colombian lost-wax cast beads have an abstract fluidity and simplicity appealing to the contemporary aesthetic. Some castings that might be considered pendants because of their singular delicacy and skillful quality may have been used as beads in graduated sizes. For example, the gold frog on page 152 was used in this manner on several necklaces shown in Bray (1978). The functional beauty of Tairona cast spacers or spacer pendants is also outstanding (*see this page*). Some have up to twelve perforations in a space of twelve centimeters (Bray 1978: number 293). These necklace components used in concert with other Tairona beads provided prehispanic craftspeople with superb materials for designing beautiful works of personal adornment.

A TAIRONA GOLD SPACER with six perforations, made by the lost-wax method. The two heads probably represent jaguars; the spacer is 2.2 cm wide. Small beads like the spondylus disks work well with the spacer. Similar ones have flanges coming out of the head (see Bray 1978: numbers 294, 295). Specimens exist with up to twelve perforations. Most of the prehispanic cultures of Colombia were highly skilled in goldsmithing, especially in casting. *Courtesy of Ken Klassen.*

STRATIFIED FLUSH BLUE AND WHITE EYE BEADS are widely distributed in central and southeastern Europe as well as portions of the Middle East; about fifty variants are known to exist (Venclova 1983). The examples date from 600 to 400 B.C. and are found as late as tenth century A.D. In the sixth and seventh centuries A.D., fragments were also used as amulets. Some of these beads are nearly pristine, others are corroded; note how the bead's condition greatly affects the color, ranging from almost orange to yellow. Devitrification may have changed the color of the eyes from blue to nearly brown, as seen in one bead. Perforations can reach 1.0 cm diameter.

RINGPERLEN or ring beads are found in the United Kingdom and the continent, particularly European Celtic sites, and may date to the late La Tene period of the last two centuries B.C. (Venclova 1972). These are translucent green to almost clear when transilluminated, 1.56 to 2.08 cm diameter. The condition of the glass is excellent, perhaps reflecting burial in a relatively moisture-free environment. All the beads on this page were bought through European auctions.

THE AMERICAS
AND EUROPE

Beads and other forms of personal adornment were made in Europe by the Cro-Magnons some forty thousand years ago (White 1993). Given that long history, the dense populations and proximity of ancient cultures to one another, the continent is rich with archaeological sites and regional museums. Many recovered beads originate from authorized excavations, but accidental discoveries and intentional looting also occur. For example, portions of Guido's book (1978) pertaining to the provenance of glass beads found in the British Isles list accidental finds as well as many in private collections. Partly due to stricter adherence to laws governing cultural heritage, less archaeological looting seems to have taken place in Europe compared to the Americas.

Few ancient European beads have appeared on the market, except occasionally through major auction houses located primarily in the United Kingdom and the continent. (Of the five times that I bid in European auctions, beads from Europe were offered just once (*see opposite page*). Described as eastern Mediterranean, only an old tag attached to the beads provided a clue to their actual origin.) Auctions are an important source for collectors who live in Europe even though the material may not derive from their own continent, such as the 1993 Christie's auction in London of the Per-neb Collection, which possibly represented the single largest offering of Egyptian, eastern Mediterranean, Islamic, and Roman glass and faience ornaments of this century.

Of the beads primarily from private Japanese collections described by Yoshimizu (1989), few are ancient European, and this fact seems telling: those shown were often represented by museum collections. While evidence is scanty and the conclusion speculative, apparently no private bead collections contain significant numbers of ancient European beads, and perhaps collectors of ancient artifacts pertaining to their native cultures, in both Europe and the Americas, do not overlap with bead collectors. For both bead and ancient artifact collectors, antique, ethnographic, Western or gun shows, auctions, and coin conventions (more likely to take place in the United States than Europe) are the common arenas for satisfying their special interests. Many museums in the United Kingdom and the continent have bead holdings, and numerous academic publications on beads are available in Europe, making it unlikely that the collecting public is unaware of its own beads.

Currently, beads on the European marketplace that have not been imported are largely from the nineteenth and twentieth centuries, although in the Netherlands many sixteenth to seventeenth century glass beads have been found—they were so numerous that decorative gardens were laid out with dredged glass beads (Karklins 1985a, van der Made 1978). Some of these beads have reached collectors. St. Eustatius in the Netherlands Antilles island chain yielded bead assemblages similar to those of Amsterdam but of eighteenth to nineteenth century vintage (Karklins and Barka 1989). Faceted

GIACOMUZZI VENETIAN BEAD SAMPLE BOOK, one of four tiers, all varying slightly in size; the beads date from 1852 to 1870. The sample book was found at a garage sale in the middle 1980s by Gloria and Charles Arquette who donated it to The Bead Museum in Prescott, Arizona. The Murano firm of Fratelli Giacomuzzi fu Angelo issued the book. *Courtesy of Gloria and Charles Arquette.*

pentagonal glass beads are a type occasionally offered to collectors visiting the island, although they may not be Dutch since no beads were produced there after the seventeenth century (Karklins 1974).

No specific information exists on the numbers manufactured for home consumption in Europe, but the continent was probably the recipient of numerous Venetian, Czech or Bohemian as well as some French, German and a few English beads. The extent of this trade can be traced through Venetian exports to Belgium, France and the United Kingdom in 1938, 1949 and 1954 (Francis 1988). Home consumption was also influenced by major archaeological events such as the discovery of Tutankhamen's tomb, resulting in a wave of Tutmania which included the production of Egyptian-themed beads and pendants (Opper and Opper 1994; *see page 162*).

Tomalin (*pers. comm.* 1994) indicates that large numbers of Venetian millefiori and trailed rosebud types can be found in the United Kingdom and Europe, many from the 1920s. In addition, England did not experience a flood of African imports; since the 1920s, many firms imported beads from Czechoslovakia; and during the 1960s, Indian glass beads were the fastest expanding import. Indian glass beads were also prominent on the American market during that period but produced little lasting effect as these were not considered collectibles; at most just a few specimens were kept for documentation. A number of American firms also imported beads from the Czechs and Venetians on a longterm basis, especially those located in the famous bead district of New York City.

The bead situation differs in each European country and in the United States. Since few collectors or researchers have bothered to systematically follow the bead marketplace, no relevant information has been published and is not likely to be forthcoming in detail.

VENETIAN LAMPWORK MANDREL
WOUND BEADS made in 1977 by
Luigina Cicogna, a fifth generation
member of the Visnooi family of
beadmakers. The beads are made
on thin, bare copper wires, unlike
the thick metal rods coated with
bead release used by most United
States beadmakers. A standard
Venetian practice was to dissolve
copper in acid thus releasing the
beads. Presumably, the smaller perforation from this method is an
advantage. The scale marks are
millimeters and centimeters.
Courtesy of Luigina Cicogna.

VENETIAN MILLEFIORI
BEADS with unusual shapes
and glossy finishes, 1.4 to
5.2 cm long, from the 1920s
to 1930s. Considerable skill
was used in marvering or
pressing, and forms may
have been used for shap-
ing. These configurations
are rarely seen in millefiori
beads used in the colonial
trade. Except for oval or
tabular beads, the majority
from West Africa are cylindrical; square ones are not
found in the Picards' volumes. The pattern on the
long teardrop pendant
was seen on some beads
from Africa (Picard and
Picard 1991: number 334).
Why were these wonder-
ful shapes not used more?
Was it due to cost, taste or
difficulty in manufacture?

CONTEMPORARY VENETIAN
LAMPWORK BEAD with fine
trail decorating, both raised
and flush. Raised decora-
tions are usually abraded
in Venetian beads from
Africa. The bead is matte
finished by acid etching; the
Czechs achieve the same
effect through tumbling.
*Courtesy of Picard
African Imports.*

CZECH MOLDED GLASS PENDANTS with Egyptian themes, from the late 1920 and 1930s; enamel or paint accentuates the molded details, 4.7 to 5.2 cm long. *Courtesy of Ornamental Resources.*

EUROPEAN SOURCES

Italy, the Czech Republic and parts of Germany and France continue to produce beads (*see pages 161, 162, 163*). As a consequence of changing world economies, the glass bead industry of Italy experiences rigorous competition from Czechs and Asians. Also, parts of the German and expatriate Czech glass industry face bankruptcy. Now, for example, German bead press tongs and glass rods for making pressed beads are exported to America (G. Darveaux, *pers. comm.* 1994; *see opposite page*), whereas previously the German industry did not sell tools or equipment to others. Jargstorf (1991, 1993) has covered the German and Bohemian bead industries.

Indian glass beads have improved to the extent that they are much more accepted in bead markets and are even sold in Venice. In the past, Italy would import glass from Eastern Europe, apply a simple procedure, then sell it as its own production; this practice may have extended to beads. The increased competitiveness of Indian glass beads is ironic, since Italian and Czech beadmakers reportedly coached the Indians in their glassworking skills (Gumpert 1989).

No one knows how the surviving French bead manufacturers will fare, although their specialized market caters to the high fashion industry which

CONTEMPORARY LAMPWORK CZECH BEADS with trail decorations, some with goldstone, 1.5 to 3.1 cm long. Studies comparing Venetian and Czech lampworking techniques have not been conducted. *Courtesy of Picard African Imports.*

CZECH MOLDED GLASS BEADS from the 1950s or earlier, ranging from 0.4 to 2.0 cm long. Some of the larger translucent beads imitate copal, others are types found in worldwide trade. The photograph was slightly overexposed to emphasize the attractive transparent colors. Some are toggles or interlock. *Courtesy of Laguna Beadline.*

may insulate them (Opper and Opper 1991; *see page 165*). Some French beads were labeled as Venetian or sold to the Venetians, such as glass simulations of matrix turquoise, but whether these practices will continue is uncertain (H. Opper, *pers. comm.* 1993). Similarly, the health of the once active Idar-Oberstein stone bead industry is unknown as it is facing competition from Asian beadmakers. The German industry was very successful in overseas markets until after World War II (Trebbin 1985) and has continued to make high quality semi-precious stone beads (*see page 164*). Individual European artists make glass beads, but the number is small compared to those made by their peers in the United States.

Venice is the principal source of old warehouse stock so eagerly sought by both bead dealers and collectors. The Picards have discovered old canes for red chevron beads, from which twelve thousand chevron beads were made by Moretti female workers who took about seven seconds for the grinding of each small chevron (J. Allen, *pers. comm.* 1992, J. Picard, *pers.*

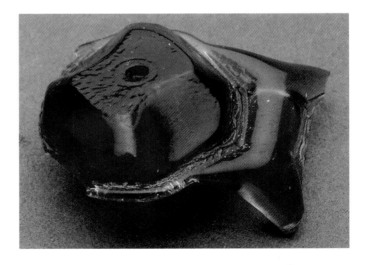

MOLDED BEAD SLUG showing excess glass or flash that flows from a mold when a preheated rod is pressed; bead is about 1.1 cm wide. Chill marks on top of the bead result from rapid cooling when hot glass contacts the brass mold. When the bead slug cools, excess glass is removed, then the bead is tumbled in a wooden drum to remove the mold seams. Sifting separates the excess glass, which is recycled. *Courtesy of Murray Winagura.*

comm. 1988). The Picards also found large canes similar to the much smaller Nueva Cádiz Plain beads that were prominent in early Americas trade; this demonstrates that these later, larger versions were Venetian (pre-World War II stock; *see page 28*). One such cane bead, shown on a sample card from the Pitt Rivers Museum, was labeled Trade beads for Central Africa (Springett and Springett 1987). Incredibly, some have suggested that these complex canes were manufactured in Africa (Polhemus in Smith and Good 1982).

With the recent closing of the Società Veneziana Conterie a Murano, its old stock and some sample cards were sold to various American dealers. Most of the Conterie's sample cards are being kept for an Italian museum. Old bead sample cards are normally scarce; in 1987, some were offered for almost five thousand dollars in Venice (*see page 160*).

Knowledgeable collectors appreciate the importance of Venice in the production of glass beads, as evidenced by the illustrated books on Venetian beads from Africa and elsewhere by the Picards, as well as Marascutto and Stainer (1991) on the fabulous De Gasperi collection of Venetian beads. While impressive

BEADS AND DOMED DRYHEAD SPECIMEN of Paragon agate, cut in Idar-Oberstein; largest bead is 1.6 cm diameter. In the middle 1980s, the firm selling these beads used Hong Kong and German beadmakers, reserving the best material for cutting in Germany. Now, most semi-precious stone beads are cut in Hong Kong, Taiwan, the People's Republic of China, and India. *Courtesy of Jan Daggett.*

ROUSSELET BEADS of enamel and glass over a copper sphere, 1.5 to 1.9 cm diameter. Louis Rousselet was a French beadmaker who operated in the period between the world wars (Opper and Opper 1991). Mostly unknown, these and other French beads would be sought by collectors if sources were available. *Courtesy of Gabrielle Liese.*

165

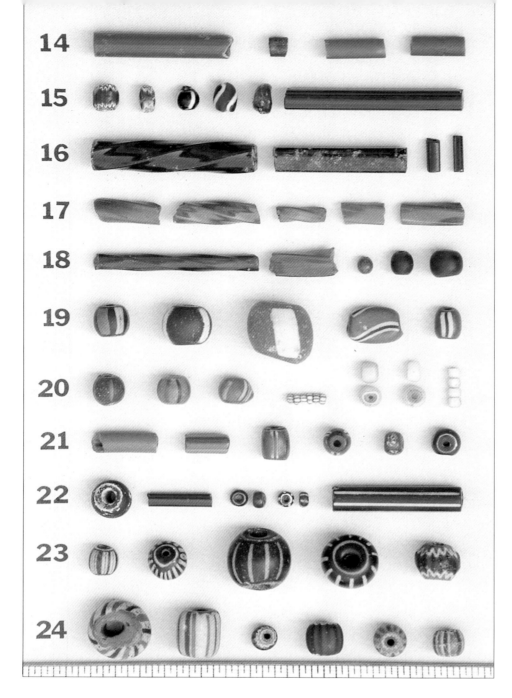

NUEVA CADIZ AND ASSOCI-
ATED BEADS from Plate II of
Harris (1982). The first three
rows show Nueva Cádiz,
some chevrons and a few
other beads from Peru usually accompanying them.
Two very rare specimens on
the right of the first row are
Nueva Cádiz from Africa.
These small diameter beads
should not be mistaken for
the much larger and later
cane beads from Venice
that have been found in
Africa and in old original
factory stocks. Nueva Cádiz
beads from South America
have reached collectors in
some numbers. The other
beads are from a Susque-
hanna site in Pennsylvania
where Nueva Cádiz beads
are also found, including
a number of other cane
beads dating as early as
the sixteenth century. Such
beads are accessible to few
bead collectors: I was able
to obtain only a few specimens for my study collection
through G.B. Fenstermaker.
Longest bead is 4.6 cm,
right specimen on second
line from top. The largest
spherical bead is only 1.6
cm diameter, demonstrat-
ing how small beads were
at that time compared to
current glass trade beads.
Metric scale is used for
measurement. *Courtesy
of Gerald B. Fenstermaker
and Elizabeth J. Harris.*

bead collections and bead or antiquity stores are located in Venice, relatively few collectors have successfully bought from these sources, unless they had connections to local glassworkers or bead factories. While Venetian face beads exist in private Italian collections, they are rarely found in the African trade. One American collector has seen only five in twenty years (J. Curry, *pers. comm.* 1993), although other Americans living in Mali during the late 1980s were able to buy these beads for ten cents each (Sharlach 1992).

Others have discovered old factory stocks elsewhere, such as eighty-eight kilos of glass beads and status cards from the Salvadori factory in France

(J. Hengesbaugh, *pers. comm.* 1993). Status cards are historically interesting, as they record individual bead runs, note sizes and weights, where beads were stored, and peculiarities or adjustments to the glass ingredients.

Czech bead factories appear to have successfully adapted to current market conditions, even though certain manufacturing processes are being eliminated, like the production of Prosser beads (Harris 1993). This could mean that the unique chain or snake beads, which may imitate snake vertebrae, will no longer be available, although Harris (1993) reports that Czech beadmaking equipment in Morocco is making a variety of Prosser beads for export. Picard

Imports provided some Czech factories with examples of glass beads from the African trade; those beads with extant molds are again being produced (*pers. comm.* 1993), and the resulting work is of good quality and inexpensive. However, pressed bead factories are still off limits to Western customers who are only admitted to lampwork facilities. These factories produce excellent beads, although collectors are less familiar with them (*see page 162*). Examination of sample books, of which there are at least twenty examples, reveals that the beads differ from those in the African trade. Like their Venetian counterparts, Czech lampwork beadmakers are women (J. Picard, *pers. comm.* 1994); women also predominate among contemporary glass beadmakers in the United States. In the Czech Republic and Neugablonz, Germany, men apparently operate the heavier pressed beadmaking equipment. With the end of the Cold War and the release of political prisoners, the Czech bead industry lost thirty percent of its production (S. Hopper, *pers. comm.* 1993). Presumably, more will be learned about the Czech beadmaking industry as communication and access improves. Chvalina and Valessi's brief overview lecture at the Bead Expo '94 held in Santa Fe, New Mexico showed the variety of Bohemian beadmaking with its use of glass, ceramics, wood, and plastic. They stated that extensive travel by Czech agents to Russia later resulted in the so-called Russian cane beads involvement in the fur trade between Americans and Russians. New research by the Picards (*pers. comm.* 1995) on the now defunct Bapterosses bead factory of France shows that it produced molded beads almost identical to the Czech; these included snake beads, imitation conus and glass lion's teeth.

THE AMERICAS

Beginning with the first European explorers, the long history of looting in the Americas continues today. Although rampant archaeological looting occurs in Central and South America, North America is not immune. Schoolcraft (1853 in Morlot 1992) reported on the extensive unearthing of the Beverly ossuaries for artifacts of personal adornment, including beads. Ceramic pot hunters are still active in many areas of the United States, and a significant number of people collect Native American artifacts, although many of these are only surface finds. Miller (in Seaman 1946) has described a Northwest site popularly known as The Bead Patch where numerous beads and other artifacts were screened from the soil. The degree of overlap between artifact and bead collectors in the United States is not known. Publications like *Indian-Artifact* display few beads or pendants in the editorial and advertising sections.

Amateur archaeologists have also engaged in excavating (Converse 1976; *see page 167*); Gerald B. Fenstermaker (1974a, b, 1976a, b, c, d, 1977a, b, 1978) was active in Pennsylvania and produced many booklets with illustrated charts of bead assem-

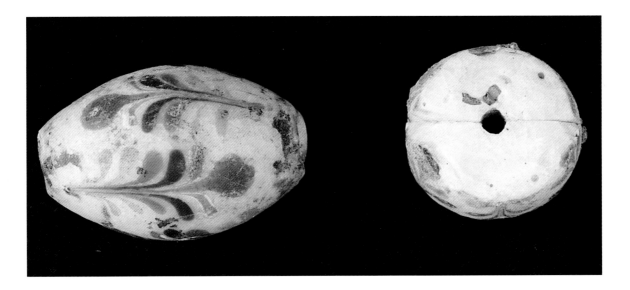

TRAIL DECORATED LAMPWORK VENETIAN BEADS excavated some forty years ago from possible Nez Perce site which yielded glass (1.7 cm length) and shell beads, elk teeth and mammal bone pendants. Bead patterns used by Native Americans are sought by collectors. *Courtesy of R. Willard.*

STRAND OF BEADS FROM VICINITY OF LAKE ONTARIO, supposedly excavated from a Native American campsite located on a beach, circa 1837. This strand is puzzling because it contains many aventurine and foil beads in pristine condition, and the bead types do not coincide with those seen in the fur trade. One family, beginning with a great grandfather, has maintained its ownership; the present owner has had the strand for over fifty years. *Courtesy of Erma Brown.*

blages from many areas of North and South America (*see page 166*). Since few previous academic bead articles contained full color illustrations, these booklets are useful in providing a general overview of regional bead assemblages. Fogelman's booklet (1991) and accompanying bead poster from the northeast United States is one of the more ambitious publications; the beads displayed in the poster are purchased and borrowed specimens. Glass beads from the Northeast and the East Coast are generally older than those from the West; much information on this topic is available from Hayes (1983). Most American historical archaeologists are primarily interested in beads from this continent.

Of course, many beads are not from found, screened or excavated sources. Heirloom beads and necklaces are infrequently seen and sometimes their attributed age cannot be verified (*see this and opposite page*), and many beads were imported to the Americas through the opium, tea and fur trades. Francis (1984a, b, 1985, 1986) has written extensively on American trade beads. Unexpected similarities are sometimes found in beads traded to North America and elsewhere. Chinese yellow glass melon beads quite similar to those found in Irian Jaya have also been seen in the Americas (Fenstermaker 1976a, from the Northwest; Francis 1985: figure 8). Southwest trading posts have been sources for beads—the so-called Hubbell beads from Ganado are controversial as it may be impossible to resolve which Czech glass imitations of turquoise qualify for this label, if any.

Americans are especially interested in beads of the fur trade; some collectors with large collections have donated them to museums, like John Weida's

168

contribution to the Jackson Hole Museum in Wyoming. Collections of trade beads of similar vintage are present in many museums, but very few have been studied. The 1971 publication of Sorenson's article on glass trade beads in *Arizona Highways* attracted a great deal of attention, but not all the beads shown could be verified as having been used by Native Americans; his and Le Roy's earlier article in 1968 is a much more reliable bead source. These articles coincided with the advent of the first import boom of European beads from Africa, so misattributions have perhaps occurred. While some of the same styles of Venetian and Czech glass beads were exported to the Americas, Africa and other areas of the world, the characteristics of bead wear or abrasion may be distinctive. Trailed decorations on North American trade beads wear much less than those from Africa, but this is not an absolute. The surface wear of beads is an interesting problem for study. As the popularity of dressing as mountain men and attendance at black powder meets and rendezvous increases, the misattribution of glass beads continues; the situation is not helped by the poor quality of articles written for this audience (Allen 1993). As many as twenty thousand participants may be interested in

trade beads used during the fur trade, but it is not likely that most beads collected by these groups were actually used by Native Americans.

While not significantly found in collections, there are a number of beads of organic origin or produced from living organisms. The materials include seeds (Armstrong 1991), amber (from Chiapas, Mexico and the Dominican Republic, Armstrong 1993), bone (snake vertebrae are used by the Seri and Cherokee as beads; in the collection of the Museum of Man, San Diego, California), and wampum, of which only modern examples are available (Wilcox 1976).

Except for those of precolumbian vintage, relatively few beads from Central or South America are collected. Other than Nueva Cádiz cane beads (*see page 28*) and early chevrons from the sixteenth century Spanish colonial trade (Harris 1982, Smith and Good 1982), almost all other beads are from ethnographic sources. Kelly (1992) has exhaustively detailed beads dating from the conquest of Mexico, which also include the above types. The origin of the intriguing glass pendant beads of San Pedro Quiatoni is still not known, although they are probably European, possibly dating from the six-

HEIRLOOM NECKLACE given to the owners by a great aunt via a grandmother; the beads were bought from the Hudson's Bay Company. The faceted barrel cane bead is about 3.5 cm long. Many of the so-called Russian beads from Northwestern America are a deep ultramarine color, but these beads and the cornaline d'Aleppo fit within assemblages from that part of the country (Harris 1985). *Courtesy of Nancy and Walt Seifried.*

INTACT NECKLACE from Otavalo Valley, northeast Ecuador, primarily of cornaline d'Aleppo (ventimilla), silver beads, Venetian polychromes, and unknown blue, possibly molded glass beads. The necklace was obtained almost thirty years ago. As in Guatemala, silver beads and coins are also used in Ecuadorian necklaces. *Courtesy of Alan White.*

teenth to eighteenth centuries (Cordry 1975, Dubin 1987, Johnson 1975a). Many subtypes and variations remain to be studied (Davis 1975). The most common beads from Central and South America are Venetian and Czech glass, with cornaline d'Aleppo as the most common (Johnson 1975b, 1976, Kelly and Johnson 1979). The beads became so popular that the supply was depleted; a California bead dealer then sold whitehearts to Guatemala, as well as vaseline beads, all imported to America from Africa (S. Cohn, *pers. comm.* 1990). In the 1970s, Guatemala was also the source of high quality silver beads and intact necklaces or chachales. Necklaces in their original form, including those from San Pedro Quiatoni, also came from Mexico but were never numerous (Cuadra 1993; *see this and opposite page*). The ones from Ecuador are even more rare (*see this page*).

There are questions regarding whether the glassworks of Puebla, Mexico ever made beads. A short lived glass bead factory in Mexico, near Guadalajara, was operated by the Merles of Oregon. From 1986 to 1989, Paloma Beads produced cane beads similar to so-called Russian beads of the Northwest trade but

NECKLACE OF SAN PEDRO QUIATONI PENDANTS and coral and Venetian glass beads. This piece might be reconstructed, but the types of beads fit assemblages usual to these necklaces. The glass pendants are excellent examples, showing why the necklaces are sought by collectors; longest is ca. 6.2 cm. The source of these ornaments is not known. *Courtesy of Federico.*

MIXE NECKLACE from Oaxaca, Mexico, containing Venetian, Czech and possibly Chinese glass beads; necklace diameter is 29 cm. The ribbons add color to the nearly white necklace. These intact ethnographic neckpieces are rarely found anywhere in the Americas. Note that similar white beads are strung on the Ecuadorian necklace shown on the previous page. *Courtesy of Folk Art International.*

with a clear layer to differentiate them from old ones. This feature prevented the output from being misrepresented. Similar beads made in Taiwan did not have this marker layer. Recently, old Russian blues sold from two to five thousand dollars per strand (J. Allen, *pers. comm.* 1993). Hopper (*pers. comm.* 1992, 1994) reported that a Czech operates a pressed glass bead factory near Monterrey, Nuevo León; the glass rods are imported into Mexico.

BEAD SOURCES IN THE AMERICAS

Surface finds, screening, dredging, and excavating have all yielded beads, some of which reached bead collectors, even though relatively few have North American beads in their collections. Some material was offered for sale near the recovery sites. Others were sold at events like the American Indian and Western Relic shows; while glass trade beads were most actively traded, precolumbian, Northwest,

Central Valley, Chumash, and African beads were also available. Throughout the United States, many antique and coin stores or the odd and curious money dealers carry Native American artifacts, and beads from China or the fur trade are occasionally offered. Even though serious interest in beads existed by the late 1970s to early 1980s, business transactions in these perforated artifacts always seemed quite minor. Later, as bead stores proliferated, very few carried much in the way of beads from the Americas. (Given my interest in beads and pendants from the prehistoric Southwest, I only twice saw any for sale, even though ceramics from the same cultures have been frequently available.) Importers or runners usually had the largest inventory in beads from Central or South America and were more aggressive in selling these wares, since the proceeds of each trip financed the next or paid off the current one; traders also went directly to clients whose collecting interests were known.

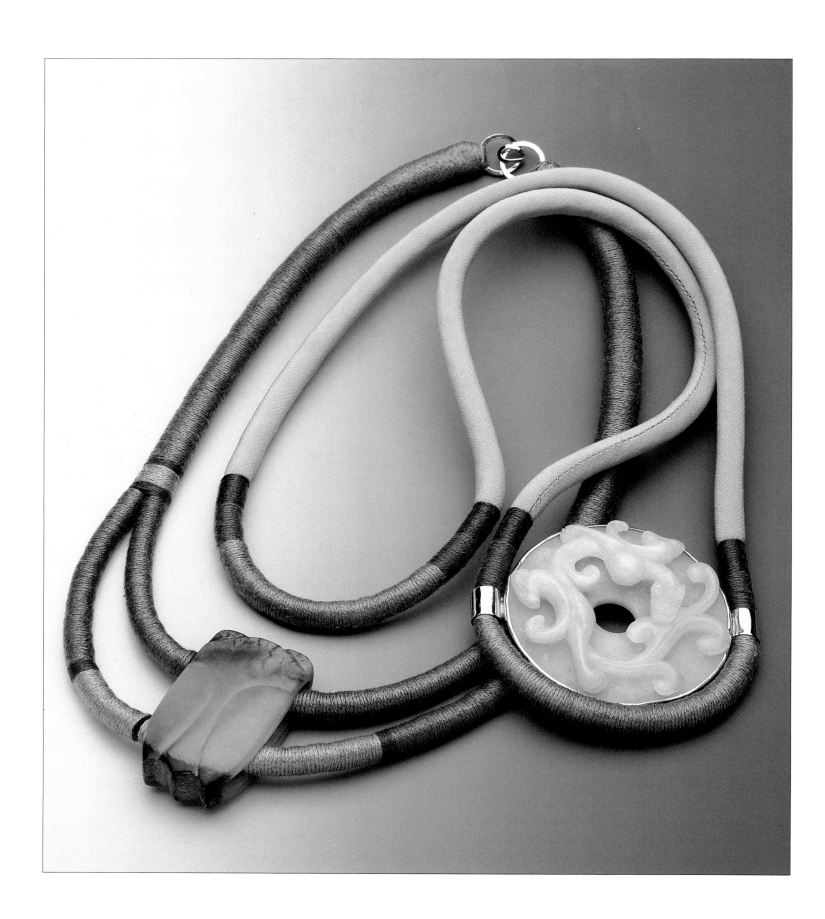

CONTEMPORARY NECKLACES

The most glorious aspects of beads are revealed in necklaces, whether they are presented simply or in diverse abundance. If beads constitute the most numerous human artifact, then necklaces must be the most popular form of personal adornment, even though such prevalence is unlikely to be proven since necklace structure deteriorates upon burial and the worldwide distribution of beads makes its study difficult. Except for those cultures which favored rigid metal torques, such as the Celts or certain Southeast Asian hill tribes, the strung necklace has been widely used; it is also the easiest and most convenient form to assemble. In Roman times though, beads were usually linked by wire rather than string or cord. And Egyptian broad-collars and the elaborate collars of certain ancient Peruvian cultures were made by processes function-ally closer to fiber techniques than stringing (Scott and Liu 1981, Donnan 1993). Other precolumbian cultures also made elaborate necklaces, some of which may have employed techniques similar to weaving (Liu 1983b).

Within the last two decades, the strung necklace has flourished along with the popularity of beads. While some collectors acquire individual beads or merely string together specimen bead collections for convenience in handling, others are attracted to wearing beads as adornment, stringing them in ways that display their beauty and make a strong aesthetic statement. As collectors increasingly wear or make necklaces, some choose beads from only one cultural area or medium, others mix both materials and cultures.

Although pearls, precious and semi-precious stone beads were held in high esteem during recent centuries, neckware in this century has used pri-marily metalworking techniques that required no strings or chains. Yet the strung necklace is often the most comfortable to wear, conforming nicely to the complex planes at the intersection of the neck and shoulder. In addition, wearing precious metal, diamond, or colored gemstone and pearl jewelry is riskier than those composed of beads wherein the value is not readily apparent.

Researchers should know how to design and string, otherwise the nuances of diverse materials and the shapes and functions of beads are missed or misinterpreted. How a bead or other perforated artifact hangs and where its center of gravity is located are small but important matters contribut-ing to successful design that are determined by trial and error. Visual, tactile, auditory, and occasion-ally olfactory aspects of beads are better under-stood and appreciated when actually worn. Scale,

PAT TSENG Antique cicada and bi strung on silk-wrapped cords subtly reflect the colors of the jade. By doubling the cords through the pendant, the cicada (5.0 cm long) necklace gains volume. The bi's circular form (5.8 cm diameter) determines both the shape of the necklace and its mounting. Gold clasps and mounting are by the artist. *Courtesy of Pat Tseng.*

PAT TSENG Forming a dramatic pendant, a Chinese jade archer's ring has been combined with an antique jade cylindrical bead and celt (ca 7.5 cm long), all bound by only fiber techniques, 1993. *Courtesy of Pat Tseng.*

proportion, interaction between necklace and skin or clothing, and the play of light on components are not fully comprehended unless one actually works with jewelry. Photographing necklaces also aids in illuminating design considerations.

Jamey Allen and Elizabeth J. Harris are both bead researchers who have designed for many years. Harris was one of the earliest to incorporate metal techniques, while Allen has spanned many areas, including beadwork, macramé and polymer. I currently work on necklace stringing or design only when a particular problem is being researched, such as making findings for beads as pendants (Liu 1993; *see page 203*).

So many excellent designers have made necklaces during the previous two decades that it is not possible to cover them all. Presented here are those working in mixed media with or without metalwork, ceramic, glass, polymer or other plastics, and soft or woven necklaces. With one exception, beadwork necklaces have been omitted; these have been thoroughly covered by Moss and Scherer (1992).

There are almost as many working in mixed media and metal as those using only mixed media. (Metal refers here to metal components actually made by the designer or custom made for them.) These two categories have the largest number of practitioners, followed by those working in glass. Even more artists may be stringing necklaces of their own glass beads, but many are novices at necklace designing. In fact, how to utilize contemporary artist-made beads remains a major problem for glassworkers. Others who specialize in a particular medium are faced with the similar challenge of integrating their work into jewelry. For enamelists, it is the problem of incorporating metalwork and enameling into a seamless whole. For glass beadmakers, it is utilizing their beads so that each has visual focus yet still contributes to the unity of the necklace. At the same time, many contemporary artist-made glass beads are large and heavy and that factor must be kept in mind. A heavy weight around the neck not only quickly decreases comfort, but muscle aches and circulation problems soon follow.

Interestingly, in cultures where the wearing of beads has not been a strong tradition, such as Japan, the beads of their contemporary makers do not appear to have been strung into necklaces. Thus, one does not see Kyoyo Asao's or Kisao Iburi's beads, or those of other talented Japanese beadmakers, used in personal adornment, even though stores catered to the Japanese market for necklaces both in the United States and Japan (Liu 1984a).

Having an appropriate showcase for one's work is paramount; no matter how talented, designers cannot maintain much of a career if there is no market. Almost all the designers covered here have sold or exhibited necklaces in a commercial establishment, gallery or home. The jewelry department at Brentano's bookstore in Beverly Hills once fulfilled that role for me and several other designers. Julie: Artisans' Gallery in New York City and Obiko in San Francisco have long promoted wearables. Besides boutiques, galleries and museum stores, trunk shows are a viable marketplace, whereby a designer visits a department store with a large inventory for brief periods, while the store provides advertising and occasionally models (Liu 1983c). In the middle 1970s, Ruth Frank's circuit included I. Magnin in Los Angeles and Saks Fifth Avenue in San Francisco and New York City. Some designers held as many as ten to twenty such promotions per year. In this way, they were able to present their work directly to the client, increase sales (many of them repeats), get feedback from the market through both customers and salespeople, make contacts with potential buyers, and obtain exposure. The artist rather than a salesperson who may not be familiar with the material or concept is often the best person at presentations. The appeal of buying directly from the artist undoubtedly contributed to many sales. Other successful markets have been trade shows, bead bazaars and conferences and home shows (Liu 1982, 1985c, 1991). Home shows have proved to be a very good venue for designers if appropriate arrangements, including security, are provided; for example, in 1981, twenty-two hundred customers attended the two days of one Los Angeles designer's home show.

During the past two decades, a lack of well made clasps has been largely alleviated by imports from Asia, especially Sri Lanka and Indonesia; most of them derived from the classic S-hook (Liu 1983a). Some designs are developed by importers, but others are frankly knockoffs. A most notable clasp was the intelligently designed and executed multistrand clasp used by Angela Cummings in her spectacular stone necklaces for Tiffany (Benesh 1981). One clasp was subtly

PAT TSENG Necklace of antique jade bi (5.8 cm diameter) set in fourteen karat gold, strung on silk-wrapped cord. As the neck places tension on the cord, pulling it away from the gold mount, an interesting negative space is created between the bi and model's body. *Model: Jitka Kotelenska. Courtesy of Pat Tseng.*

curved so that it would easily engage and lie on the back of the neck without irritation; other imitations often lacked these refinements.

Clasps are important necklace components and can mean not only the difference between functional success or failure but complement or detract from the overall aesthetic statement. The ideal clasp possesses strength, simplicity and ease of fastening and unfastening. Besides its obvious purpose, the clasp and its associated findings should provide a measure of safety by opening when too much pressure is applied; thus if a necklace is entangled, it gives before injuring the wearer (Liu 1974). Yet the method of stringing should be such that the beads themselves will not break loose.

All too often clasp design is neglected, but it is the single element that causes one to cease using a necklace and consequently stop buying from a particular designer. Many designers now appreciate a clasp's importance, and some feature it as a design element or as their signature. Designers should be able to work metal or collaborate with someone who can. By fabricating clasps or findings, they can greatly expand their options, including adapting a variety of small artifacts into clasps, clasp-pendants or pendants (Liu 1974, 1979, 1983a, 1984c).

Despite numerous workshops currently providing instruction on nearly every aspect of necklace making, few deal with teaching the designer how to make clasps or other findings that require basic metal

RITA OKRENT Strung with Venetian and Czech glass beads from Africa, the choker's simple construction of brightly colored beads makes an appealing effect, 1993. The triangular shape of the Czech molded imitation of a conus hemidisk (4.9 cm wide) complements the face. Sterling silver clasp is imported. *Courtesy of Rita Okrent.*

RITA OKRENT The engraved brass Tuareg tcherot is 8.8 cm wide, mounted in copper and strung with large diameter land snail shell disks (2.3 cm), Venetian glass beads, brass beads, and sterling silver clasp, 1989. A tcherot is worn as an amulet and contains verses from the Koran. Dramatic when worn, the large shell beads function as a ruff around the neck. Plain disk beads are attractive components, but their tendency to pull at the hairs on the back of the neck is a drawback; the movement of the closely stacked disks snags or entangles the hair. Designers test and redesign in order to avoid such problems. (See Applegate 1989.) *Courtesy of Rita Okrent.*

techniques, like soldering. While we are usually eager to embrace every new technique, material or tool, continually expanding one's mental and manual skills are also important considerations. Acquisition of a skillbase is a lifelong process, not something to be acquired or discarded depending on the prevailing fashion. New Zealand carver Stephen Myhre is one artist who has articulately expressed the concept and importance of possessing fundamental skills (1987).

In the 1970s, there was a dearth of information on necklace stringing techniques and only a few elementary booklets existed (Anonymous 1975, Butts 1971). In the 1980s and 1990s, this situation changed with the publication of a slew of booklets on stringing, or larger books on beads with portions on necklace making (Champion 1985, Coles and Budwig 1990, Gosselink 1990, Poris 1984, 1989, Tomalin 1988, Virchick 1989, Wilson 1985). The most comprehensive works were by Poris (1989) and Tomalin (1988). A new magazine, *Bead & Button,* contains articles on making necklaces (Waltz 1994). Recent publications describe specialized techniques, such as Helen Banes's widely taught technique of tapestry needleweaving (Fitzgerald and Banes 1993), or the use of wire in necklaces and other jewelry (Drew-Wilkinson and Hayes 1993). *Ornament* initiated a series of master classes, such as articles based on fancy knotting by accomplished necklace designer Judith Ubick (Cuadra 1993a, b). With some exceptions, . the publications provide only rudimentary necklace design and fabrication. Few deal with concepts or methods of incorporating metal techniques so that one can make a more formal statement or increase design options; more attention must be paid to the basics of good design with proportion, scale, balance, rhythm, emphasis, variety, and unity (D. Fitzgerald, *pers. comm.* 1993).

Because of a strung necklace's flexibility, the shape is determined by the diameter of the wearer's neck, length of the necklace, type of string or cord, and weight of the strung material, whether bead, pendant or both (Liu 1985a). Because of the interplay between weight and tension, the

JUDITH UBICK Necklace tassel composed of a cascade of beads hanging from an antique Chinese cloisonné bead which dangles from a macramé loop located underneath the jaw of an antique Chinese ivory dragon, 7.0 cm long, 1993. The rich array of Chinese beads and components includes silver, carnelian, amber, ivory, bone, and jade or other hardstone carvings, as well as a miniature toothbrush. Many of the beads are capped in silver. *Courtesy of Judith Ubick.*

JUDITH UBICK Necklace of freshwater pearls, jade beads, gilded Thai metal beads, and
Chinese jade prayer wheel pendant attached by square knot braids, 1993. Multiple strands
are threaded into the jade beads adjacent to the gilded ones; the stringing probably
required subtracting or adding of threads, depending on the size of the perforation.
Model: Dora Johnson. Courtesy of Judith Ubick.

FUMIKO UKAI Chinese pottery shard mounted in silver (8.5 cm wide) with contemporary tumbled turquoise, Chinese glass beads and Ukai's signature cast silver clasp, 1990. Sometimes the silver or bronze bar portion of the clasp bearing her name is combined with a bi. The two rows of beads are held in position by macramé knots and visually more interesting as a result. The beads repeat the colors of the glazes. (See Hamaker 1990). *Courtesy of Fumiko Ukai.*

lower contour of the necklace always falls in an arc, unless the pendant is heavy enough to pull the arc to a point. Otherwise complex stringing, sewing or weaving methods are used to alter the form, as in the construction of Egyptian faience broadcollars (Scott and Liu 1981). One alternative is to use the pendant shape to change the curve, as in Pat Tseng's elegant solution on page 175. Mary Jane Gilcrease and Kathlean Gahagan use long, curved prefabricated silver cones to alter the contours of strung necklaces, either toward the apex or at the neck. Glassworker Ann Miller (*pers. comm.* 1994) slumps cane beads into symmetrical curves to serve a similar

function, as well as helping to visually isolate the beads. Betsy and Dudley Giberson used long cane beads in a like manner. Jane Booth (1975), a pioneer in glass beadmaking, used Pyrex rod in similar ways, as solid neckrings for glass jewelry. Colored Pyrex tubing of her own formulation has been used by Phyllis Clarke as necklace components (Liu 1993).

I have long advocated the use of metal tubing in necklaces and findings (Liu 1979, 1985a). One can vary the circular contour of a strung necklace by using metal tubing to form the structural elements of the neckpiece, as well as findings that alter the basic shape. Tubing neckrings can be considered a system of articulated elements held together by tension provided by the stringing material. By carefully bending the tubing, the articulations permit a degree of adjustment to the wearer's body while maintaining a more formal design than is possible with strung necklaces, yet without excessive weight. These are provided by soldering tubing to metal beads or caps which reduces friction at points of contact with beads or other elements strung on the tubing neckring (Liu 1979, 1985a). In addition, many articulations are cupped so that the bead or artifact is held in place yet free to swivel, thus maintaining alignment. But there are drawbacks, beading needles must be made that are long enough to thread through the length of the tubing and its articulations. Threading the long needles through curved tubing, the small holes and the soldered on beads calls for a great deal of luck.

In addition to its structural role, uniform metal tubing provides a good foil for the presentation of single or multiple beads. The eye is drawn to isolated bead specimens, resolving the problem of visual clashes between adjacent beads. As with specimen bead collecting, the use of only a few beads conserves increasingly scarce material culture that are under pressure from collecting or commerce. Finally, open or closed V-shapes made from tubing can alter the basic shapes of strung necklaces, giving more structure or integrity, and adding dynamic focal points (*see page 184*). My fabrication of such findings or elements was inspired in part by Jacqueline Lillie's tubing or V-shaped clasps that are integral to her meticulously executed necklaces of beaded

FUMIKO UKAI There is knotting between the jade archer's ring and Chinese glass beads and the choker is finished with macramé, 1982. Probably of pre-World War II vintage, the glass beads (3.0 cm diameter) also come in other lovely colors. Note how they nestle into the ring, and that the ring portion of the clasp is a similar color of jade. Archer's rings are among the most popular Chinese artifacts used by necklace designers. *Courtesy of Fumiko Ukai.*

elements and beads. Nancy Aillery's ingenious system of tubing connectors and decorative clasps are a neat solution to providing flexibility by using manufactured elements (Liu 1989a).

Strung necklaces can take most any form or shape, from a single bead on a cord to complex multi-strands woven together. In fact, the single bead necklace is often the most personal of adornments, frequently serving an amuletic function. Using a single contemporary glass bead is a similar concept, although finding the appropriate mode of presentation is difficult (Liu 1993; *see page 203*). Tomalin (1988) has discussed necklace lengths: choker (40 cm/16 inches), princess (45 cm/18 inches), matinée (65 cm/26 inches), and opera (90 cm/36 inches).

Any necklace shorter than 60 cm/23 3/4 inches requires a clasp, whereas anything longer can slide over the head; 80 cm/32 inches goes twice around the neck if a clasp is provided (86 cm/34 inches requiring no clasp), while 120 cm/48 inches with clasp will go four times around the neck. I favor necklaces that do not reach lower than the bosom and prefer even shorter lengths. Longer necklaces tend to draw attention away from the face or neck. Since any striking necklace attracts attention, this strategy may be compromised sometimes. Neckware hanging lower than the waist often exposes the components to increased risk of damage, as the necklace tends to have more movement.

Designers need to take into account scale and proportion, and how their work fits different-sized wearers. These aspects are readily apparent when a

NATALIA JOSCA Ancient Egyptian faience disk beads and quadruple Udjat faience pendant (3.2 cm wide as set) are combined with eighteen and twenty-two karat gold bezel, beads, terminals, and clasps, 1991. The fine level of crafting enables these ancient beads and amulet to be safely worn in a contemporary setting. In her first three years of jewelrymaking, Josca completed over a hundred pieces. *Courtesy of Natalia Josca.*

MICHAEL WINSTEN Multiple strands of lapis beads, interspersed with granulated gold disks set with lapis or turquoise, electrum and twenty-two karat gold, surface-colored and depletion-gilded, 1989. From Afghanistan, the beads have been hand ground and polished by Winsten. Loops on reverse of disks hold beads in place. Center disk with 3.7 cm diameter is set with eight-pointed star of Ishtar. The clasp reflects the overall motif. *Courtesy of Michael Winsten.*

necklace does not work well on a model. Except for custom or commissioned pieces, jewelers are apt to adjust work according to their own bodies. Clients who match the designer's size are lucky. Interestingly, shorter necklaces tend to be more adaptable to people of different stature. Perhaps this is due to the relative consistency of head and neck proportions, even if overall body size varies greatly.

Some designers attempt to compensate for differences in body parameters affecting how well a necklace fits: the diameter of the neck and shoulder region and the size of the bosom, especially for females. These are usually chains attached to one side of the clasp so the necklace can be lengthened, but except for designers like Nöel Michelsen, few have devised solutions for shortening a necklace.

How well a necklace, or any piece of jewelry, projects is another important consideration. Many neckpieces are not interesting unless the details are seen, such as granulation; others attract the eye at a distance. Factors at play are the piece's mass, how it contrasts with skin and clothing, whether any elements interact with light thus throwing off reflections, and if the piece moves attractively on the wearer. Physics tends to suppress or accentuate the movement of a piece. This latter feature was vitally important to Native Americans, many African cultures and certain nomadic groups.

Necklace designers, like other contemporary jewelers, have not been sufficiently studied to

ROBERT K. LIU Necklace of coconut shell disks, Venetian glass disks, cornaline d'Aleppo beads, copper clasp, and tubing pendant (1.9 cm), 1985. The beads nestle within the metal tubing, inside of which is plastic tubing to protect the cord from the sharpness of the fabricated pendant.

develop a comprehensive overview. Dubin (1987) featured some twentieth century American and European designers of bead necklaces. Of the ninety designers discussed in this chapter, most developed their skills independently, as no academic institutions provided classes in this subject.

In the United States, Ramona Solberg, a practicing jeweler since the 1950s, has played a pivotal role in the growth and development of Northwest jewelers (Benesh 1989; *see page 186*). Her openness to many sources of inspiration, materials and techniques such as integration of beads and metal are already evident in an early book she wrote (Solberg 1972). While not a student of Solberg but belonging to her mutually supportive group, Kiff Slemmons (1977) has had a long attraction to beads, stating that "The problem in using old beads in contemporary jewelry is twofold: how to maintain the integrity of the beads and how to combine them with metal to make something new." Flora Book, a student of Solberg as well as of Mary Lee Hu, has continued this tradition of working metal and beads, although she fabricates all components (Benesh 1994).

Many others from across the country have also used metalwork and beads. Laurel Burch of San Francisco, one of the earliest to make necklaces in this way now has a successful line of commercial jewelry and decorative accessories. Elizabeth J. Harris used metal with beads early on. While her creative necklaces did not utilize many beads, Leslie Correll combined beads along with metalwork (Liu 1976b).

Pat Tseng uniquely blends metalwork and fabric (Bullis 1993; *see pages 172, 175*). While contrary to her general design philosophy of not combining artifacts and metal, in those instances where metal is used, it is appropriate. The object or artifact is firmly held by the metal and the gold defines and gives form to the piece. When Tseng's necklace with a bi set in gold is worn, the molding of the necklace to the circumference of the neck provides tension and pulls the fabric cord away from the metal mounting, introducing dynamic negative spaces that greatly add to the visual interest (*see page 175*).

Tabra Tunoa's successful jewelry lines include necklaces employing metalwork: one combines leather, silver cones and strung glass beads (Bullis 1992a: page 39), while the other uses soldered silver links for holding glass beads and silver elements. Both are good solutions for commercially produced necklaces, as their construction methods make them more formal than stringing, and reduce the risk of cord breakage. Heyoehkah Merrifield, who makes copious use of Native American and other cultural iconography in imagery rich necklaces, combines academic jewelry training with attention to detail in stringing (Liu 1987c). Annette Bird ranks among those who attained a high degree of success in home sales of her mixed media necklaces, although now she prefers cast and fabricated elements with beads (Prichett 1990). During Bird's sales in the 1970s, most necklaces cost twelve to fifteen dollars, with none more than one hundred dollars. Her latest pendants are human figures carved from *Arca* shell beads from Africa (*pers. comm.* 1994). Arlene Gellman-Levine has integrated metal components from Middle Eastern jewelry to give her necklaces form and structure (Jackson 1989).

Some of the most interesting necklaces have been collaborations. In fact, Collaboration, a 1980s

DAN TELLEEN Necklace of African snake vertebrae (1.2 cm wide) beads and cast replicas in gold, 1991. In order for the gold replicas to articulate like snake vertebrae, they had to be cast very accurately. Telleen has essentially engaged in modern day transposition, whereby a desired form is changed into another medium, but not for imitation; a technique practiced in antiquity and in tribal cultures (Liu 1985b). *Courtesy of Dan Telleen.*

JANE COURSIN Necklace is made of Taxco silver beads, Chinese turquoise beads, malachite bi, commercially produced silver beads; and sister hook clasp made from silver and brass Taxco key chains, 1993. Center bead is 3.2 cm diameter. The square silver beads nestle well with the round beads, changing their shapes, aided by the bi. Adapting a commercial product for jewelry adds a custom look to the piece. *Courtesy of Carolyn L. E. Benesh.*

RAMONA SOLBERG Forged and fabricated silver, opalescent glass and moonstone beads from Africa and India are combined with bezel-set moonstones. The Czech glass beads and Indian stone beads are so similar that there is a mutual synergy which enhances the beauty of each. Using seemingly simple metal techniques, primarily forging and soldering, Solberg produces sturdy and sophisticated necklaces. Declaring herself the Henry Ford of jewelry (Benesh 1989), her work is as straightforward and forceful as her personality. The strength, simplicity and beauty of her direct methods mirror those found in the ethnic jewelry that she admires. *Courtesy of Ramona Solberg.*

association of Lucia Antonelli, Martin Kilmer and Laura Popenoe, combined enameling, electroforming, beadwork, and innovative stringing to produce neckpieces of great complexity and power (Benesh 1983; *see this page*). Antonelli and Kilmer functioned as a team both before and after Collaboration (Liu 1986b), but now all three work independently.

Judith Ubick, known for her strung necklaces and teaching (Cuadra 1993a, b, Goebel 1978), has collaborated with jeweler Ann Quisty and metalsmith Robin Casady. In the past, the collaboration also included metalsmith Susan Kingsley (Liu 1981c). These joint efforts enabled Ubick to integrate metalwork into neckpieces. Other partners include Mary and Doug Hancock, who combine extensive metal ornaments with beads (Hancock and Hancock 1991), and Karen and Jim Hill. Karen makes glass beads and ornaments while Jim electroforms mountings and other necklace elements for the glass (*pers. comm.* 1993).

Kulicke-Stark Academy of Jewelry Art, now Jewelry Arts Institute, was another recognizable influence on designers who applied ancient techniques such as granulation (Liu 1976a). Jewelers working in this vein, such as Natalia Josca and Michael Winsten, are often called neoclassical; they have introduced a high level of ancient metalworking skills into strung necklaces, evoking the essence of antiquity with a twentieth century functionality (Hamaker 1991, Ebbinghouse 1989; *see pages 182, 183*). Metal and stone bead necklaces made by Breon O'Casey of England suggest antiquity but do not utilize specific ancient techniques; they are more a denial of modern technology (Brownrigg 1985, Goldberg 1987).

Other European jewelers have used beads in sophisticated ways: Wendy Ramshaw of England and Jacqueline Lillie of Austria are the most well known (Dale 1984, Ross 1991). Ramshaw has used beads as a thin, linear painting, adding or subtracting enameled, tubular beads of different colors (Liu 1981b), as well as geometric ceramic beads of her own design made by Wedgwood. Lillie ingeniously uses seed beads, often covering a bead core with the tiny beads, combined with beautifully designed and crafted clasps. Beatrice Rouge (Béatrice De) of Switzerland combines lush beads with mineral rough pendants. Some German jewelers make neckwear of striking simplicity, such as Klaus Dietz and Gabrielle Späth (Weiner 1992), Kurt Kubick, Ulrike Weyrich, and

COLLABORATION BY LUCIA ANTONELLI, MARTIN KILMER AND LAURA POPENOE A cloisonné enamel pendant, set with electroforming (6.5 x 8.5 cm), is strung on five bundles of twelve strands each of antique French copper seed beads, glass beads, and Biwa pearls. (See Benesh 1983). *Model: Angela Daniel. Courtesy of Collaboration.*

Marietta Sailer-Schiestl. These jewelers use antique beads, such as Sailer-Schiestl's Venetian millefiori, or have semi-precious stones cut into beads of their own design. The work of these German jewelers is usually seen only in advertisements in *Art Aurea,* their national design magazine.

In this country, many jewelers who are primarily metalsmiths have made bead necklaces with innovative techniques: Robert Ebendorf, David Freda, William Harper, Ivy Ross, Dan Telleen (*see page 185*), Jeff Wise, and Jan Yager. Ebendorf's beads of laminate or newspaper have drawn much attention (Blauer 1990, DiNoto 1985). David Freda, as much a naturalist as metalsmith, fashions beads in the form of newly hatched snakes and their eggshells (Dubin 1987), while Harper, Kay Whitcomb and James Carter have made necklaces of cloisonné beads. The signature metal pillowform beads and perforated pebbles of Jan Yager (Blauer 1987) are strung on metal chain but do not clump together at the apex due to clever design. A stop is soldered onto each chain necklace, so the strung elements maintain spacing. Jeff Wise has fabricated intricate beads of metal and semi-precious stones (Benesh 1990). Valerie and Benny Aldrich have adapted inlaid stones set in bezels as beads (Liu 1994b).

Mixed media tends to be material driven which makes it hard to characterize. While some designers work only with material from a particular culture, others use whatever is available. This is certainly the practical course, as supply sources or a client's interest can change. What remains constant with good designers is the quality of their design, materials and construction. These necklaces are also sometimes much more ambiguous as to origin. Although successful designers are often copied, it is difficult to pinpoint influences or trends. While there have been many designers of note, few works are instantly recognizable, such as Susan Green's fiber neckpieces or those of the late Rose Garfunkle, whose designs were sparse and elegant and accompanied by her signature knotted sennit or handcrochet knot (Liu 1983c).

Many designers started making necklaces during the first bead boom of the late 1960s to 1970s, continuing into the 1980s: Jamey Allen, Masha Archer, Annette Bird, Irena Corwin, Ruth Frank, Rose Garfunkle, Elizabeth J. Harris, Frances Mazarov, and Sharon Read. Most are still working; this is a field where many designers are now middle-aged or older. The late Agnes Stewart started her necklace

PARROT PEARLS Ceramic tubing arcs have been strung on ribbon ties, 1979. Low-fired, sometimes several times, they were either under or overglazed. One production difficulty is preventing warpage during firing, since the rainbow effect requires close-fitting arcs. Some warping occurred in this example. The primary colors, contrasted by flexible ribbons of differing colors, make a festive and magical effect. The necklace works best when it is worn close to the face with the ribbons carefully tied, suggesting a broadcollar. Otherwise the loose tubing arcs behave like an unruly bib, looking worse the lower the necklace is worn. Ribbon Rainbow was definitely a grand experiment. In 1979, it sold for $100. Many other necklaces in their line were fine uses of ceramics, mixing bright colors and complex and dimensional forms that had a fairy tale quality to them. "The jewelry reflects an optimistic attitude and invariably makes one feel delighted, as if a happy, long-forgotten dream had been recalled" (Benesh 1983). *Courtesy of Parrot Pearls.*

NEWCOMB COMPANY The necklace has ten strands of minute, subtly gradated cylindrical beads, 1986. At least twenty different shades of color were used and up to fifty steps were involved in production. One can see the resemblance to hishi, to which Newcomb was attracted. Matching earring made with same beads. *Model: Jeannette Muñoz. Courtesy of Newcomb Company.*

career at eighty-seven (Diamanti 1991), while well known bead collector and designer Dorothy Gerrity worked into her eighties (Hamaker 1990).

A number have made consistently fine work, including Susan Green, Rita Okrent, Judith Ubick, and Fumiko Ukai. All initially from California, they benefited from the area's acceptance of unorthodox adornment, had access to high quality material, or worked within the nurturing environment of Obiko. Sandra Sakata (Bullis 1992a), Obiko's owner, encourages jewelers and wearable art designers to create together, promoting more vigorous work, as well as giving them bicoastal exposure through her boutique at Bergdorf-Goodman in New York City. Eileen Coyne, an American designer living in England, was also promoted by Obiko (Bullis 1992a, Dale 1983).

Ukai restricts herself primarily to antique Chinese and Tibetan materials, creating necklaces of great simplicity and dignity, usually finished with macramé (*see pages 180, 181*). Because of the large scale of the few components in her designs, Ukai's pieces tend to be dramatic. The eye is forced to focus carefully on each part of the necklace. Hamaker (1990) points out, "As she continued to refine her designs, a color course that focused on grouping colors around the seasons of the year surprisingly transformed her approach to jewelrymaking, and became an important organizing principle in her necklaces." Ukai solved a basic problem of bead necklace design by defining and clarifying its statement with a diverse collection of beads. Besides one-of-a-kind necklaces, she produces a commercial line, which can also be worn as a lariat; two can be joined together to make a longer necklace. This type of versatility also has been practiced by Nöel Michelsen, who makes a necklace that converts to a choker by removing one portion which can then be worn as a bracelet; the longer necklace can also be worn as a belt (*pers. comm.* 1984). Her use of buttons as clasps makes this type of convertibility both practical and aesthetically pleasing.

Asian elements are prominent motifs in Judith Ubick's jewelry, although she works with nearly any bead or artifact of high quality. Asymmetry and cascading dangles are two hallmarks but only a small part of her repertoire (*see page 178*). Many pieces involve intricate knotting in order to utilize a variety of beads or artifacts that may not be amenable to simple stringing, (Cuadra 1993a, b; *see page 179*). Fancy knots are also structural elements holding the necklaces together over time and providing an effective and decorative method for securing components that are difficult to incorporate, such as Chinese bi (Cuadra 1993a). Ubick, like any good designer who works beyond straightforward stringing, excels at problem solving.

Rita Okrent is more diverse in her use of materials and stringing methods, often resorting to decorative chain. Among her favorites are beads from Africa and the Middle East, especially those that are antique or ancient (*see pages 176, 177*). While some of her most striking designs have been asymmetrical, the more simple neck-laces are just as powerful and effective. For example, a simple choker that uses a triangular Czech hemidisk as a pendant or focal point effectively changes the shape of the necklace from the usual semicircle to a pointed apex, mirroring or accentuating the facial contour of the wearer. Okrent frequently incorporates small beads, resulting in necklaces with subtle rhythms in the interactions of various metal, glass or faience beads. For many people the process of acquiring beads, attributing and designing with them are all part of the experience, perhaps more so for Okrent, because of her extensive travels to the Middle East in the quest for materials.

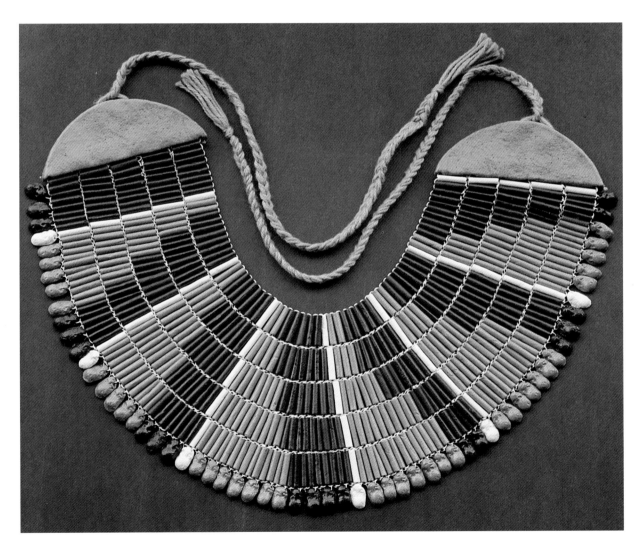

CAROL STRICK The broadcollar of Egyptian faience is strung authentically; only the terminals are modified, primarily to improve comfort, 1981. The cylindrical beads are strung vertically, with one row of amulets as edging. Strick used beads of the same length, unlike many Dynastic broadcollars, which used varying lengths and structures. (See Scott and Liu 1979). *Courtesy of Carol Strick.*

CARA CRONINGER Polyester resin teeth (longest tooth is 9.0 cm) and spherical beads are strung on multiple strands of cord and knotted between each bead, with the balance of the cords as ties, 1992. The beads are carved from cast blocks of resin with a hammer and chisel (Greenbaum 1992). *Courtesy of Cara Croninger.*

Susan Green's necklaces have always been unique in design concept and execution, and many pieces are truly timeless. Starting with early work (Liu 1977), she emphasized those portions of the piece in contact with the neck. Leather or wrapped fiber in flat bands is combined with lush cascades of small beads, in neckpieces that are either open or closed in the front. Some portion of her jewelry is clasped, using a comfortable universal finding of her design, which also serves to terminate the fiberwork. Green's unmistakable work is dramatic in appearance, comfortable to wear and kind to the body.

A few contemporary necklace makers are known for their use of materials from specific cultural areas or for staying within certain regional styles: Rhodia Mann, Phyllis Woods, Geraldo Roca, Nance Lopez, and Barbara Zusman. Living and working in Kenya, Mann nevertheless travels widely for her components but is most comfortable with African materials (Blauer 1986). Her work is simple, direct and lush through the use of short multiple strands. Woods utilizes manufacturing resources of various countries, but many of her strongest necklaces are composed primarily of African beads (Liu 1981a). The small, humble Giryama copper or brass coiled wire beads function like a chain in some of her most effective necklaces, helping to accentuate the sprinkling of larger glass and metal beads or elements sparsely scattered among the wire beads. Peruvian Geraldo Roca specializes in necklaces of precolumbian beads and elements from his native country, as well as Ecuador and Colombia (Liu 1983b). Because of the small sizes of many beads from these countries, multiple strands, often twisted, are used by Roca to provide mass and visual texture (*see page 154*). It is difficult to know whether Roca takes inspiration from precolumbian designs. Some supposedly period designs, such as those in Mujica Gallo (1959), while appearing very interesting and modern in structure, are not possible to verify as to authenticity.

Those living and working in the Southwest cannot help but be influenced by the local culture, as have Lopez and Zusman (Osburn 1992a, b). Lopez's treasure necklaces are a type that developed within the past decades in the Southwest, possibly influenced by Native American neckware incorporating carved fetishes, trade beads, pierced coins and elements derived from crosses. Zusman's work is in a similar vein, even including the Navajo wrapping on the back of the necklaces. Of course, both Lopez and Zusman incorporate other beads and perforated artifacts from the current worldwide trade in such material.

Some designers are so diverse that their work is hard to characterize. Besides integrating beads into leather belts and bags, Pat Smiley makes strung necklaces, of which the most interesting involve the seamless melding of stringing and beadwork. One striking piece incorporates a realistic beaded snake. Cloth doll designer Barbara Evans also fits this category. Having made cloth bead necklaces and leis with three dimensional dolls, she has now turned to wonderful sculptural figures of trade beads from Africa, which also comprise the body of the necklaces. Using telephone wire for armatures, these figurative necklaces demonstrate her considerable craft capabilities (*see page 203*).

Finally, in the category of those using mixed media, two designers who have achieved considerable commercial success are David Navarro (Liu 1983c) and Kai Yin Lo (Kennedy 1983a). Navarro and his signature lariat necklace were prominent during the 1980s and he continues to work, having his designs executed by his stepdaughter (S. Green, *pers. comm.* 1994). Lo of Hong Kong almost defined the field of Asian necklaces, having early access to Chinese antique jewelry components, as well as the considerable stone-cutting and metalworking resources of Hong Kong. Connections with Christian Dior, Guy Laroche, Givenchy, Hanae Mori, Bill Blass, and Geoffrey Beene have accorded Lo international status (Kennedy 1983a). Full page color advertisements in *Arts of Asia* have featured her jewelry, chronicling changes in material and styles with availability and preferences. In the middle 1980s, Lo had three lines: fashion, which ranged from twenty-five to fifteen hundred dollars, boutique from seventy-five to twenty thousand dollars, and one-of-a-kind, which started at two hundred-fifty dollars. Other designers also apportion their jewelry accordingly.

Ceramic beads were enormously popular in the late 1960s to 1970s and many designers made necklaces with them. So-called Egyptian paste was used by some craftspeople to make faience beads, but only Carol Strick used authentic formulations resulting

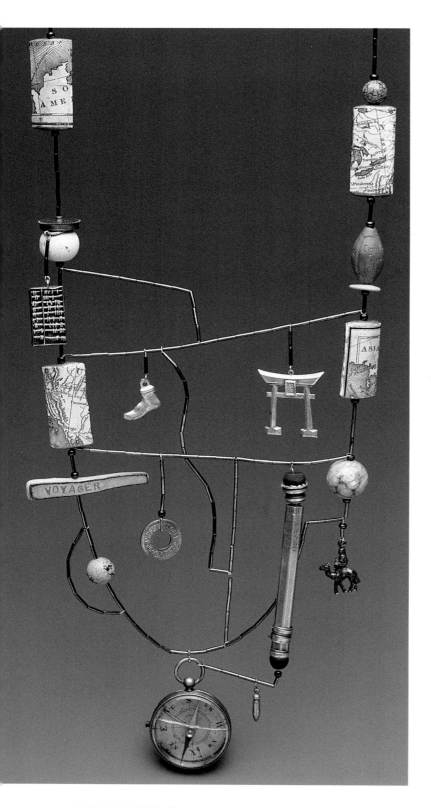

TORY HUGHES Necklace of reproduced and painted old maps, mechanical pencil with calender, antique French compass, Chinese abacus, Japanese silver tori gate, Chinese carved peach pit bead, and other artifacts, 84 cm long, 1989. In this emotion-laden piece, the physical volume is increased by artifacts interconnected through cylindrical metal beads that direct the viewer's vision. (See Hamaker 1989). *Courtesy of Tory Hughes.*

from her research. This led to a career in reproducing faience necklaces for the Metropolitan Museum of Art and the Boston Museum of Fine Arts, during which she made over half a million faience beads (Liu 1981d). In addition, she has made over a hundred broadcollars in traditional Dynastic styles, with only some modification of the terminals in order to make them more comfortable (*see page 191*). The fabrication of components and the stringing of each broadcollar took over a week. Although Strick has stopped working with this self-glazing ceramic, no one has surpassed her authenticity or productivity.

Other ceramic beads and jewelry were low-fired, using press-molded or slipcast processes. The most well known firm was Parrot Pearls which is no longer in business, although one partner continues to make ceramic jewelry. They produced an enormous variety of necklace designs, many of which were wonderfully innovative (Benesh 1979). Some were multistranded and terminated like broadcollars (*see page 189*), or consisted of naturalistic three dimensional elements strung into narrative scenes. The three partners' design skills and the ability of their staff to translate designs into production placed them at the forefront of ceramic jewelry.

Working on a much smaller scale were Cathy and Lloyd Glasson of Art Necko, who produced carefully made clay beads and pendants, of which the Egyptian and botanical theme necklaces are classical in simplicity and appeal (Liu 1980a). Their beads and pendants were often so exacting in shape and consistency that some craft show judges supposed that they were machine-made. This ironic aspect of handcrafted materials often occurs. The porcelain floral necklaces of Linda van der Linde (Liu 1983b) are among earlier pieces with this effect. Joyce Whitaker evocatively sculpts women's heads with coordinated beads in ceramic; these are then integrated into large macramé collars of considerable intricacy by Sauny Dils (Liu 1980b). The reverse of the centerpieces are inscribed with phrases or poems chosen by Whitaker, thus combining image and verse.

One of the most interesting ceramic necklace designers was Dorothy Feibleman, an American living in England, perhaps better known for her ceramic vessels of laminated and millefiori techniques (Liu 1987d). Her jewelry combines porcelain and Parian beads or elements with high karat gold

194

TORY HUGHES Various scarabs or substitutes join two parallel strands, nicely formalized by dentalia shells, 1989. Center scarab is handmade of South American beetle wings and an old beetle from a Victorian stickpin, along with polymer, gold foil, bronzing powder; other scarabs are made from found elements: an older scarab, an old bronze turtle, Victorian scarabs, old iridescent glass, vintage porcelain beads, brass plumb bobs and washers, 44 cm long. *Courtesy of Tory Hughes.*

PIER VOULKOS Necklace of polymer beads, drop and leaf pendants; the latter are attached by plastic-coated telephone wire of various colors, 1993. Leaves are 3.3 cm long, made with a cane technique. The large millefiori bead is split in half, with an embedded brass screw clasp, an ingenious solution for hiding the clasp. The appeal lies in the necklace's serial imagery enhanced by the patterned layers. *Courtesy of Pier Voulkos.*

beads and findings made by her. The components are closely integrated into the designs, a rarity among those making ceramic jewelry. These factors, combined with an attention to detail and a high level of skill, result in refined and often lush necklaces, suggestive of Egyptian Dynastic work. The spacers used in her necklaces, an example of her precision, have metal tubing soldered within them, so that the stringing material will not rub against sharp edges. Another clever design entails using a hinged clasp that can be moved along the sides of the necklace, thereby making

it almost any length desired, with the portions behind the clasp hanging down the back. Sufficient slack was incorporated into the foxtail-strung necklace to allow movement of the clasps anywhere along the single strand of beads around the neck. Feibleman was professionally trained as a potter but self taught in jewelry. Her words are as enlightening as her work. "Lamination in ceramics is similar to caning in glass, rosette making in wood for guitars, sushi or strudel making . . . I use water where a glass worker would use heat. I use slip where a wood worker would use glue" (Liu 1987d).

Newcomb Company perhaps carried ceramic jewelry to its furthest point of development. Composed of Howard Newcomb and Alice Scherer, theirs was a partnership between producer and organizer. By mechanizing beadmaking processes via ingenious machines of his design, Newcomb was able to offer a large line of porcelain beads that varied subtly in color gradations, so that a necklace consisted of up to twenty different shades (Benesh 1986; *see page 190*). The small sizes of the cylindrical beads meant that large numbers were required for each necklace; by 1986, one machine had cut ten to twenty million beads out of clay slabs, punching out twenty-four beads in each pass across the slab. Most other cylindrical ceramic beadmakers employ extruders. Newcomb also made beautiful lentil beads in graduated shades, as well as large hollow beads that were slipcast and tumbled. Terminations and clasps were cast or fabricated in sterling silver by Newcomb, who also did the difficult assembly, which was

facilitated by Scherer's organization of the inventories into timesaving arrangements. Lentil and big bead necklaces were usually short. Shapes, colors and finishes all added to their attractiveness and appeal. Newcomb now makes porcelain chevron beads of innovative shapes and designs, as well as molded ornaments (Liu 1992).

More people now make beads from polymer than possibly any other medium. Roche's book (1991) provided an important focus for this material, even though the use of polymer for beads and jewelry in the United States was then less than a decade old. Not only did practitioners learn techniques, they were shown the importance of design. Thus necklaces of polymer beads or ornaments are much more sophisticated than those of glass. Obviously the latter is more difficult to work, so the glassworker has less latitude. Pier Voulkos is one of the earliest and the best, possessing a wonderful sense of color and design. She lets the material speak for itself; the best pieces are exuberant,

CITY ZEN CANE The flat surfaces of the polymer beads display the technique of using graduated hues of specific base colors to achieve an illusion of depth and dimensionality. Vibrancy and movement in the beads result from opposing colors (Roche 1991). Necklace made by Steven Ford and David Forlano of City Zen Cane; pendants are 1.5 to 2.5 cm wide, 1991. *Courtesy of City Zen Cane.*

seemingly layered in colors and forms. A formative teacher, Kathleen Dustin brings a more narrative and lighthearted touch to her necklaces of clothed and nude women (Dustin 1988). Jamey Allen explores this material as if undertaking research, making necklaces that might fool archaeologists into believing he has uncovered hoards of ancient glass beads (Allen 1989). His necklaces are as much objects for contemplative study as for enjoyment.

Other masters of visual sleight of hand in this material are Steven Ford and David Forlano of City Zen Cane and Tory Hughes. City Zen Cane's earlier necklaces of geometric beads give the illusion of three dimensional space (Ross 1991; *see page 197*), while their new techniques

result in work that resembles miniature mosaic tile and ikat fabric. Tory Hughes expertly simulates many natural materials in polymer (Cuadra 1993c, 1994; *see page 219*), but she also speaks with a powerful artistic voice in other polymer necklaces (Hamaker 1989; *see pages 194, 195*). Besides polyvinyl chloride, other plastics have been used for necklaces; Cara Croninger has worked for some two decades in acrylic and polyester resins, making bright, luminous beads and pendants that often elicit strong sentiments in the wearer (Greenbaum 1992; *see page 192*).

Helen Banes's tapestry needleweavings are perhaps the most widely known fiber necklaces (Fitzgerald 1991, Fitzgerald and Banes 1993). Banes has taught this technique to many, including her pupil and coauthor Diane Fitzgerald. While many

JANE BOOTH Choker of clear Pyrex beads and pendants, hand-fabricated, sterling silver double hook clasp; strung on nylon monofilament, 37.0 cm wide, 1975. The necessity of using transparent stringing material is obvious with clear glass. Note the play of light on all parts of this neckpiece, further enhanced by air bubbles in the pendants. Other designers do not seem to use cylindrical beads vertically, as Booth has, resulting in a structure rarely seen in chokers. (See Booth 1975). *Courtesy of Jane Booth.*

HELGA SEIMEL Necklace of lampworked cone pendants is made with coiled rods cold-joined to the base plates made by the same technique; largest is 4.1 cm diameter. The necklaces of this German glassworker are carefully designed, facilitated by her making all the components. (See Hopper 1994). *Courtesy of Helga Seimel.*

artists include macramé in their necklaces, Barbara Natoli Witt (Benesh 1985) uses this method most extensively and complexly, in conjunction with precolumbian, Egyptian, Chinese, and other cultural artifacts. The late Tina Johnson DePuy used macramé as accents for necklaces that frequently incorporated Inuit artifacts (Liu 1990). She was one of many memorable artists making bead necklaces.

Among the pioneers of glass bead design, Jane Booth stands out with her beautifully conceived integrations of metal and glass (*see page 198*). Trained in metalworking by Arline Fisch but self taught in glassworking, Booth used primarily Pyrex for her lampworked beads and ornaments, although she was also one of the first to experiment with

powder glass beads in soft glasses (Booth 1975). Silver findings and necklace components are usually cold-joined, including socket joints, couplings, linkages, hinges, and clasps. With the riot of colors in current glass beads, Booth's use of Pyrex solid glass torques, both plain and shaped, is an approach designers might consider as a refreshing contrast.

Cane beadmakers constituted the largest group of necklace makers until the renaissance of lamp or flameworked beads; they also had the longest tenure, beginning with Betsy and Dudley Giberson. With tumbled and acid-etched beads made by Dudley, the necklaces are among the most elegant, aided by effective photographs of the pieces being worn. These muted cane beads provide very pleasing serial imagery, enlivened by larger or asym-

LAURA POPENOE Necklace of cast glass beads and elements, small commercial glass beads, electroformed metal beads, and beads from Africa; the clasp is a bone or ivory toggle and brass, copper and silver ring, 1990. The cast bi in foreground is 3.5 cm diameter; some of the beads may be additionally enameled. (See Liu 1989b). *Courtesy of Joan Ross Blaedel and Laura Popenoe.*

metric beads in the center portions of the necklaces or curved canes as the focal point. Long canes of neutral colors are often used as foils for the more colorful beads (*pers. comm.* 1993). Dudley Giberson no longer pulls canes or makes necklaces with them, having shifted to glassworking equipment and kiln-made beads.

Tom André, Elisabeth Cary and Rick Bernstein of Penrose Beads, Denise Bloch and Kerry Feldman of Fineline Studios, Lucy Bergamini of Vitriesse Glass, and Werick and Bloomberg have long made necklaces of cane beads. André has over two decades of experience with hot glass and is one of the few to have used pendants cut from sectors of carefully composed and blown glass vases (Cuadra 1991). Using cane beads pulled by André and his associates, his sister Sue assembles the beads and hand-faceted pendants into necklaces. Carefully cut cane beads are bonded to the perforations of the pendant with Loctite, so that there is a graceful transition between the pendant and the rest of the necklace (*see page 201*). This type of detail is often overlooked by designers and spoils the center of attention.

Cary also uses necklace components made from vessels, in her case flashed glass cut from sheet glass derived from slumped vessels made in her and her partner's studio. Their cane beads, commercial beads and flashed glass and metal components are all used in necklaces. The colorful flat glass elements are cold-joined, a technique which considerably expands her design vocabulary (Liu 1987b).

Denise Bloch and Kerry Feldman were active early on with their cane bead necklaces and among those who first participated in glass jewelry shows (Kennedy and Liu 1985, Liu 1987a); their necklaces incorporated hot-pinched beads. Lucy Bergamini makes both loose beads and necklace designs which employ soldered silver links onto which glass beads are strung. The large patterned cane slices and the smaller freely moving beads on the metal links add

TOM ANDRE Necklace of cane, metal beads and faceted pendant (10.5 cm long) cut from vessel, 1991. Glass components are made in his studio, with assembly by Sue André, his sister. Blowing of glass vessel is made in conjunction with Greg Englesby. Note beveled beads bonded to pendant, smoothing transition to necklace. *Courtesy of Tom André.*

JANE NYHUS Necklace of fumed cane, commercial glass and metal beads, together with aluminum tubes wrapped with filigreed cotton woven with iridescent cellophane ribbon, 1985. The glass cane, by Norman Courtney, is cut so the satin-covered button fits into end of cane. *Courtesy of Jane Nyhus.*

both movement and mass, as well as reducing breakage. Rings or square links of silver wire strung with beads function similarly to the accumulation phenomenon seen in Yoruba necklaces with more attention focused on these parts of the necklace. After the death of Judith Werick, her mother Angie Werick continued making the necklaces, while Joel Bloomberg made the cane beads. Previously, their necklaces also employed metal elements (Kennedy and Liu 1985). Jane Nyhus of Nyhus Designs produced tightly integrated necklaces, usually of curved cane segments or hot-pinched canes (made by Norman Courtney), often fumed, metal beads and fabric-wrapped

aluminum tubing; these pieces are still among the best designed glass jewelry (Kennedy 1985b; *see this page*).

Many glass beadmakers are using powder glass for pendants and beads, such as Nancy Goodenough, Donna Milliron and Nancy Potek. Laura Popenoe designs necklaces using her electroformed metal beads and cast glass beads and ornaments, which are ground, fire polished, and vibratory tumbled for a final finish (*see page 200*). Such a necklace demonstrates the beauty of cast glass, with its assortment of bead shapes and textures, imparting the illusion of softness upon the hard glass through the tumbling process.

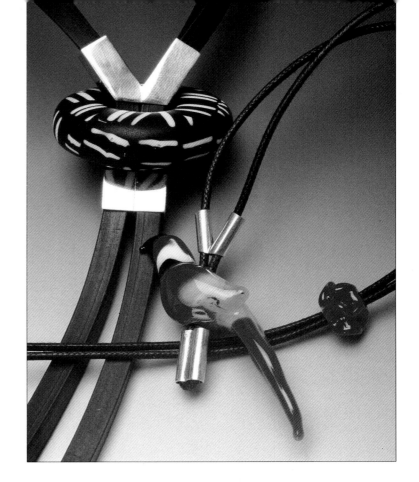

Certain of the cast glass beads are also enameled, with up to five firings. Popenoe has also etched and engraved glass beads (Liu 1989b).

Numerous lampworkers now make their own necklaces and some designers, such as Diane Fitzgerald (Casady 1994), are also incorporating the work of these beadmakers. Because of the vibrant nature of most contemporary lamp or flamework beads, they are the most difficult for a bead necklace designer to utilize successfully. The colors, shapes and large sizes of artist-made beads seem to shout for attention, and a necklace consisting of only such beads is hard to look at. Jane Booth (1975) astutely noted that the characteristics of ancient glass beads that we love, such as the irregularities of color and texture, were not present when they were made. Only the effects of age and burial brought out their beauty. Perhaps this is why new beads that are tumbled or acid-etched appear more attractive than those with shiny, glossy surfaces.

Some craftspeople have overcome this problem by design. German beadmaker Helga Seimel makes short necklaces and often graduates the elements and inserts with neutral beads to give some relief, so that their striking attributes are fully visible but not visually overwhelming (*see page 199*). In other neckpieces, only a few bold beads or elements are used. Inara Knight has used the same approach in some of her work, especially important when dichroic glass is a prominent component.

The pool of talented glass beadmakers will continue to grow, but artists need to resolve the difficult problem of presenting their work in wearable form; merely stringing beads together is inadequate. Perhaps some capable designers or jewelers will find solutions, whether beads are presented as single pendants or as multiples, so that the overall aesthetics of the necklace matches the quality of the components.

PHYLLIS CLARKE AND MOLLY VAUGHAN HASKINS Bead pendants and glass ornaments are kiln-fired or lampworked glass; brass or silver tubing findings made by Robert K. Liu. Haskins provided square rubber gasket for the cord, and Clarke used braided leather cord. Clarke's slide bead functions as an ojime. The findings are 1.2 to 1.5 cm long. *Courtesy of Phyllis Clarke and Molly Vaughan Haskins.*

BARBARA EVANS The beads are primarily from Africa, incorporating a pendant or focal point of a bead figure, strung on telephone wire. Figure is 11.4 cm wide, 1993. Evans imparts considerable animation and vitality into her bead figure necklaces. *Courtesy of Barbara Evans.*

CONTEMPORARY BEADS

The history of beads has been distinguished by anonymity, and only within the late twentieth century have beadmakers received attention. For every craftsperson or artist who is recognized, there are hundreds or even thousands who remain unnoticed—individual artistic distinction is a luxury limited primarily to Western and other well-developed countries. While perhaps Japanese ojime makers have received the lengthiest period of recognition, it was long after the end of World War II that ojime collecting actually became popular in Japan, spurred by Western interest (Kinsey 1991; *see pages 74, 75, 215*). Most Western beadmakers known for their high aesthetics have been primarily jewelers who make beads as components for their work, such as Jean Stark (Kennedy and Liu 1983), Robert Ebendorf, Stuart Golder, and Jan Yager. Just since the 1980s have beadmakers, not jewelers, been applauded for their art, starting with the late Kyoyu Asao, one of the greatest beadmakers of our time (Liu 1986, Ukai 1980, 1984; *see pages 11, 207*). When polymer as a media became enormously popular, many new craftspeople gained prominence (Roche 1991). Then at the beginning of the 1990s, which marked a renaissance of lampworking, glass beadmaking began its meteoric rise; a rebirth clearly evident at the Second International Bead Conference in Washington, D. C. (Liu 1991). Glass cane beadmaking has been practiced in the United States for over two decades, but the expensive equipment necessary for the technique has restricted its practice to a few studio artists (Liu 1990). Polymer and glass continue to be the most popular beadmaking materials, with ceramics a distant third, although this medium has enjoyed acceptance from the 1960s.

A major reason for the dominance of new media and techniques is the speed and ease with which they can be disseminated via workshops. Polymer and lampworked glass are not new; polymer has been available in Europe for about four decades and lampworking dates to the middle fifteenth century in Venice. The discovery of polymer by American craftspeople for use in jewelry, and later, the increase in lampworking, were both possible through a large nationwide network of individuals who shared their knowledge by workshops at the community level, not through academic circles as in the past. Shops, private organizations and craft schools are the main sponsors of these workshops, providing a means of acquiring information through fee payment, rather than course prerequisites. Retail shops are especially active locations, hosting between ten to forty classes a month, with numerous instructors. Interested members of the public can quickly acquire an impressive

CONTEMPORARY AMERICAN GLASS BEADS AND PENDANTS, except for Japanese tombodama in front by the late Kyoyu Asao, 1.9 cm high. All ornaments range from 0.85 to 4.0 cm diameter, dating from the middle 1980s to 1993. *Top row, left to right:* Tom André, cane beads; James Smircich, goddess; Elisabeth Cary, frosted cane beads; Fineline Studios, small frosted and yellow cane. *Second row:* Patricia Frantz, foil bead with knobs; Molly Vaughan Haskins, cross-shaped kiln bead; Lewis Wilson, Pyrex dragon. *Third row:* Phyllis Clarke, cat bead; Michael Barley, pink dichroic; Cay Dickey, blue dichroic. *Fourth row:* Art Seymour, green chevron; Heron Glass, diskoid chevron; Brian Kerkvliet, lampwork with mosaic face cane; Patricia Sage, eye bead.

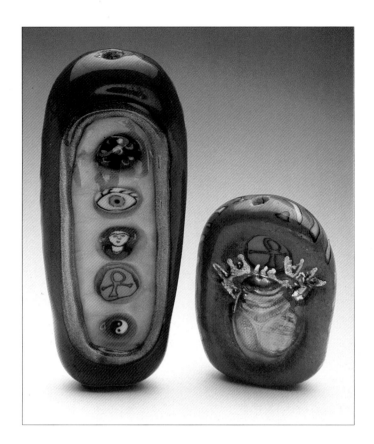

BRIAN KERKVLIET Beads from a six piece Egyptian-themed ensemble include a cartouche bead with a Ushabti on the reverse and five encased murrine and millefiori mosaics on the front, 6.1 cm height, as well as a scarab bead with four mosaics on the reverse, 3.6 cm height. Kerkvliet began making mosaic canes in 1985; he also produces larger sculptural pieces, some incorporating neon gas.

BRIAN KERKVLIET The mosaic cane slices include preformed eye and mouth canes used to form the more complicated murrines, such as faces. Note that the eye and mouth are used in the two sizes of pulled face canes at the top right; the mouth cane is 0.75 cm wide, while the smallest female face cane is only 0.6 cm wide. All Kerkvliet's mosaic canes are worked at the glory hole; these date from 1989.

KYOYU ASAO The cold-bundled composite canes and mosaic slices have been meticulously crafted. The sides of each slice have been ground to shape; the red one is 0.9 x 0.7 x 0.106 cm. Asao's inventory comprised thousands of slices, canes and fili-grana or retorte, carefully coded and stored with demonstrations of their appearance when melted into a glass matrix.

repertoire of techniques that can be integrated into their own work. Those with a sense of aesthetics, design and style, and capable of incorporating the appropriate techniques benefit the most.

While there are now thousands of contemporary beads in the marketplace, those makers known to the collecting public are comparatively few. Malcolm Logan of England makes beads from bonding diverse materials like leather, wood, shell, and recycled ivory. Gary Hauser builds enlarged interpretations of glass trade beads in various inlaid and laminated woods. Few artists make metal beads that are not incorporated with other jewelry components; however, Carol Webb uses innovative metal techniques to produce beads with the elegance of modern ojime. Copper and silver are eutectically bonded, then designs are etched into the silver with ferric chloride; beads are fabricated from this sheet, then sandblasted (*see page 215*). In addition, Carrie Adell's metal touchstones are

essentially beads richly decorated with traditional Japanese metal techniques and Barbara Minor's enamel beads are usually worn as single pendants, or occasionally as multiples.

Kenoyer (1992) is one of the few to give credit to individual Third World beadmakers working in stone, such as Mullah Ashur of Afghanistan who makes them from lapis lazuli. In the United States, other than Native Americans, few have utilized stone; Foreman (1978) was an exception. Germany, the People's Republic of China, Hong Kong, and Taiwan have important stone and bead carving industries, but none of their beadmakers have gained individual recognition, although those who use their products have received acclaim, such as Klaus Dietz and Gabriele Späth (Weiner 1992).

Synthetic materials are the principal media for contemporary beadmakers. Faience, the first synthetic made almost exclusively for decorative

KYOYU ASAO The ancient Chinese replica is decorated with single and multiple stratified eyes, with and without millefiori canes, 2.2 cm high; made in middle 1980s. Some other interpretations of Warring States or Zhou beads also required a great deal of work. Just one eye of his beads took twenty steps (Ukai 1984: figure 2); others required eight steps for each of the bead's nine eyes. Tom Holland is the only beadmaker currently working in a similar manner.

PATRICIA FRANTZ Lampworked and horned eye beads demonstrate her mastery of flameworking; gold foil bead is 2.4 cm long.

PATRICIA FRANTZ The aquarium bead shows Frantz's versatile use of glass. The bead is 3.75 cm high, made in 1993.

purposes, now has few practitioners. Carol Strick (Liu 1981; *see chapters four, seven*) recently ceased working in this self-glazing medium, even though she was almost a faience industry by herself. Glass artist Tom Holland also favors the material, so there is hope that this beautiful and versatile medium will not disappear. Besides making glass and faience beads, Holland is the only person known to combine the two media by other than inlay (Liu 1994). Other ceramics are still used by a number of beadmakers; many like Cathy Glasson of Art Necko (who now also makes polymer beads) and Diane Briegleb have used clay especially well. There are both traditional ceramic beadmakers, like Doyle Lane and Barnard Jones, as well as those who employ innovative mechanical techniques, such as Howard Newcomb (Liu 1992; *see chapter seven and page 216*). Galina Rein portrays miniature communities in her porcelain beads (*see page 217*). And Janel Jacobson carves exquisite porcelain ojime of plants and animals.

Polymer or polyvinyl chloride is perhaps the most important new beadmaking material of this century. Long available as a modeling medium, it was discovered by American jewelers and beadmakers

CAY DICKEY Known for her baroque dichroic beads, Dickey started making glass beads before many of those currently working in the field. The knobbed bead is 1.65 cm high.

ALICE F. ZIMMERMAN The dichroic glass beads range from 1.3 to 3.3 cm high. Author of an instructional book on glass beadmaking, Zimmerman also has made several videos on the subject.

MICHAEL BARLEY New to beadmaking, Barley uses dichroic and foils delicately, casing the dichroic for a spectral effect. The beads exhibit unusual shapes and precision. The lampworked beads range from 3.0 to 3.6 cm high, from 1993. All dichroic glass now contains metallic coatings.

ANTIQUE AND CONTEMPORARY VENETIAN BEADS AND BLOWN BEAD BY KRIS PETERSON made with a miniature blowpipe at the furnace (ca. 2.5 cm high); red bead with retorte is also by Peterson. Venetian beads range from 0.8 to 3.5 cm high. The yellow chevron was collected by Venetian beadmaker Sergio Tiozzo.

only in the 1980s. Pier Voulkos was among the first to recognize the beadmaking potential of this plastic and its ability to mimic glass in certain techniques (*see chapter seven*), although others, like Tory Hughes, have worked for a longer time with the material (J. Allen, *pers. comm.* 1994). Inspired by Voulkos's beads (Roche 1991), Kathleen Dustin became an influential teacher of polymer craft (Dustin 1989). With publication of *The New Clay* by Nan Roche, those working with polymer not only obtained inspiration, but also historical perspective through the skillful insertion of glass beads as prototypes for many of the examples shown. Brimming with techniques, the book also extols design principles lacking in much of today's glass beadmaking. Some beadmakers such as Jamey Allen have continued to explore polymer's capabilities to replicate ancient glassworking techniques (1989; *see page 218*), or Tory Hughes who uses polymer to simulate both natural and synthetic substances (Cuadra 1993b, 1994, Ross 1991; *see pages 218, 219*). Cynthia Toops utilizes the material in new ways, inlaying thousands of tiny rods as mosaics. A reflection of its increasing popularity, a national

DONALD SCHNEIDER The Pyrex tube bead dates to earlier production, when color was confined to the area under the clear lenses (3.7 cm long); now tubes are cased with many more colors and canes, yet still remain light in appearance.

TOM BOYLAN The borosilicate beads demonstrate Boylan's mastery of the colors and patterns of hard glass. The clear lenses of the center bead seem to act like portholes into a miniature fantasy world. Largest bead is 3.3 cm high, dating from 1991.

LEWIS WILSON The double dragon borosilicate or Pyrex bead is made in three parts. The dragons are kept in an annealing oven until they can be fused onto the finished central portion. Widely known as Wilson's signature, his dragon beads range from 3.5 to 4.2 cm high. This one was made in 1993.

guild publishes POLYinforMER, an excellent newsletter, and several books are in preparation.

The use of glass, the most important and attractive beadmaking material since antiquity, has proliferated among contemporary workers. While most people regard glass beads as factory products, in reality they have been mostly a cottage industry for small workshops or home sites; thus its return to the studios and workshops of individual Western artists has reestablished a long tradition in glassworking.

Historically, glass beadmaking most likely took place at a furnace or kiln, whereas contemporary Western beadmakers or those from developed countries use various gas torches which employ air and gas mixtures. European and American lampworkers tend to use torches placed at a horizontal or oblique angle, while their Japanese counterparts use a vertical torch, often with accompanying rests for the mandrel and

glass rod (Ukai 1980, Yoshimizu 1989). Torch furniture may have a pronounced effect on the precision of beadmaking and result in less fatigue for the artist. Additional factors such as orientation of the flame angles and presence or absence of a refractory shield to retain the heat from the torch may also have meaningful consequences. East Germans used a glass bangle kiln similar in appearance to that used by Chinese for beadmaking, which is probably closer to ancient beadmaking kilns (S. Hopper, *pers. comm.* 1993, Kan and Liu 1984). Interestingly, Dudley Giberson, a pioneer American cane beadmaker, has designed a small glass beadmaking kiln fueled by propane, using modern refractory materials. Meant for lampworking beads, this kiln may have a significant impact since it provides a different working environment compared to the prevailing use of torches (*pers. comm.* 1993, 1994, Liu 1994). Bead-

MOLLY VAUGHAN HASKINS These kiln formed ornaments are made with strips and sheets of Wasser glass; some have been previously decorated by lampworking. Possibly due to the unique way in which Wasser glass is made and its low melting temperature, Haskins is able to obtain saturated colors and unique shapes. Her methods require a long period of tumbling to achieve the final finish and form. Paper or ceramic tapes are used for making perforations. Upper pendant is 3.7 cm wide. Haskins's designs and intricate techniques produce striking results (see Ross 1994).

makers in Plumbon Gambang, Indonesia, combine a gas or liquid fuel torch probably with sheet asbestos in a lampworking furnace, also with a support for the glass rod (Adhyatman and Arifin 1993: figure 151). Because of the large role played by neuromuscular skills, variously called muscle memory or body knowledge by beadmakers, equipment setup must be conducive to long periods of both precise and relaxed work. With today's glass beadmakers drawing from the ranks of non-glass workers, stained or slumped glassmakers, there is probably not enough awareness of the physical demands, a realization important to those desiring an injury-free career.

At present, a pressing need exists for an overview of the techniques in this field, like that provided by Roche (1991) for polymer. Resources now available include a short instructional book on glass beadmaking (Zimmerman 1993), several books in preparation, a number of videos by Goertz and Mast, Reynolds and Dickey, Wilson, and Zimmerman, and a national Society of Glass Beadmakers. Despite a great deal of talent, innovation and energy among Western glass beadmakers, problems still remain. Possessing a compulsion to make beads, many glass artists have not seriously considered how their production can be used. The continual increase in overall size and complexity of artist-made glass beads makes them difficult to incorporate into necklaces. Too many striking beads placed together results in visual confusion and design problems. Attempts to use single beads as pendants to provide visual isolation are also problematic, as most glass beadmakers lack metalworking skills necessary for the fabrication of findings that give design integrity to beads used as pendants (Liu 1993). Heddan and Chutz cap their glass beads with repoussed metal, incorporating a design element that mitigates the visual effect of colorful glass. Some like Karen and Jim Hill have tried resolving the integration of glass and metal by electroforming settings around glass. No doubt a number of contemporary beads bought as collectibles or miniature sculptures are never worn, in which case concerns about size and compatibility are not applicable.

Due to the speed at which new ideas, techniques and designs spread through the glass beadmaking community by publications, workshops, conferences, and bazaars, a disturbing trend of too many glassworkers seizing on the same concept may occur, such as aquarium beads. These beads of a fish cased in clear glass were originally inspired by beads similar to the Japanese one shown in *The History of Beads* by Lois

ART SEYMOUR AND HERON GLASS These beads represent classical and non-traditional renditions of chevrons. The disk, ribbed, two large, the black, red and white, and small turquoise, yellow and brown beads are by Seymour, and rank among the best in the world. They are primarily five-layered, 2.95 to 4.4 cm long. The diskoid chevron with yellow, the black and white, and all-cane chevrons are by Mary Mullaney and Ralph Mossman of Heron Glass; many of their chevrons exhibit a clear center core, 0.75 to 2.4 cm diameters. Surprisingly, transparent color does not seem to have been used previously on any of the some one thousand types of extant chevrons.

Dubin (1987: figure 166); much more elaborate ones were then made by Northwest artists such as Brian Kerkvliet (Muzzy 1993) who inspired many others nationwide. Imitation is flattering, but artists need to express their individuality; perhaps looking at ancient and ethnographic glass beads is a better source of inspiration than following the work of peers.

Currently there are bewildering numbers of people working in glass who are nearly impossible to track; these can be divided into cane and lamp or flameworkers, with the latter employing soft or borosilicate glasses. Many are versed in both glass types. Among cane beadmakers, some also use optical molds, usually to produce chevron beads. A much smaller number use a kiln and soft glasses, either slumping with sheet glass, sometimes combined with lampworking, or using molds and powdered glass. Technically, none apply the pate de verre technique, since dry molds are now utilized. A very few make

blown beads, sometimes with the aid of a furnace. Venetian and Czech beadmakers are also active in this area, as their blown beads are now available in bead stores.

Cane beadmakers are in the minority, with Dudley Giberson having made beads the longest in this field, although he now produces wound and mosaic beads in a kiln or furnace of his own design. Others continuing to make cane beads are Tom André, Joel Bloomberg, Fineline Studios (Denise Bloch and Kerry Feldman), Olive Glass (Corrie Haight and Lark Dalton), Penrose Design (Elisabeth Cary), and Vitriesse Glass (Lucy Bergamini). Until the 1980s, cane beads of soft glass were almost the only American-made glass beads; their simplicity, bright and sparkling colors provide excellent materials for jewelry design (Kennedy and Liu 1985, Liu 1987, 1990; *see page 204*).

The most surprising aspect of the renaissance of glass beadmaking has been the American production

of chevron beads, long regarded as the aristocrat of glass beads and the domain of the Venetians. Bead admirers cannot help but notice the beauty of the antique and contemporary chevrons in the Picards' 1993 volume. Art Seymour was the first to make chevrons in the United States; those making such beads include Heron Glass and others (*see pages 204, 213*). Starting in the late 1980s, Seymour now has made about two hundred-fifty varieties, adding some thirty to fifty each year. Chevrons are distinguished from other cane beads by the use of optical molds and the grinding required to bring out the design's beauty. It is during grinding that chevrons come to life and their dynamic nature is revealed. Seymour's chevrons are rough, medium and fine ground; only small ones are tumbled. His canes are pulled twice a year in the spring and autumn, requiring twenty hour days and three pots of glass (A. Seymour, *pers. comm.* 1993; *see pages 204, 213*). Some chevrons are still produced in Venice; perhaps the worldwide interest in beads will also spark a revival there (*see page 210*).

Pyrex or borosilicate glasses are the earliest types used by American craftspeople, probably due to the influence of John Burton. The pioneer of glass beadmaking in the United States is certainly Jane Booth, who not only made clear and colored hard glass beads but designed sophisticated metal fittings for her necklaces (Booth 1975; *see page 198*). Her varied and ingenious methods for integrating metal and glass are

ELLIE BURKE The blown glass bead is decorated by trailing and melting on shards, creating a beautifully textured surface. Most of these processes were probably finished prior to blowing, 3.4 cm diameter. Relatively few American beadmakers use blowing now, although Venetian and Czech blown beads are currently on the market. Burke comes from a long background of scientific and novelty glassmaking (Searle 1992).

PHYLLIS CLARKE Even though photographically enlarged, the stances and sculptural shapes of the cats easily communicate the accuracy and delicacy of the glass feline portrayals. Maximum size is only 2.9 cm long. Her other mammals, birds and fishes are characterized by the same finesse, masking the experience and dexterity Clarke possesses for freehand torch work.

CAROL WEBB Appearing elegantly simple, Webb's metal beads actually involve a great deal of technique. Copper and either fine or sterling silver are eutectically bonded, sometimes involving three layers, such as the bead of copper over twenty-two karat gold which is over sterling silver (left bead, 1.6 cm diameter). The designs are photo-etched; then the bead halves are domed, soldered and finished with sandblasting. All perforations are sleeved, like ojime. Center bead is copper over fine silver, 2.2 cm diameter. Most metal beads now on the market involving hand work are foreign-made.

invaluable models for contemporary glass beadmakers.

A surprising number of artists currently use borosilicates exclusively (possibly six to twelve beadmakers in the United States) or else augment their work in soft glasses with hard glasses. Tom Boylan and Donald Schneider rank among those most skilled in working borosilicates, with the latter using both tubing and rod (*see page 210*). Kevin O'Grady also makes beads of hard glass, but he is better known for his distinctive glass bracelets (his brother George is a soft glass beadmaker).

Those using both hard and soft glasses include Phyllis Clarke, Tom Holland, Shari Hopper, James Smircich, and Lewis Wilson. Known for his dramatic dragon bead in borosilicate, Wilson is active in the production of beadmaking videos and promotion of glass beadmaking (*see page 211*). The greater strength of borosilicate versus soda glass is offset by its more limited and less brilliant color palette, as well as cost factors. While clear Pyrex is only four dollar per pound, Northstar's red rod is ten times more expensive (L. Wilson, *pers. comm.* 1993). More intricate and delicate features can be obtained by hard glass beadmakers, since most breaks usually can be repaired by refusing, not possible with soft glasses. In addition, the high

TOMIZO SARATANI A leading Japanese ojime maker working in lacquer, Saratani made these wonderfully realistic ants from black lacquer over a clear lacquer ground on an amber core. Numerous coats of clear lacquer, with intervening polishing, are necessary before the core is ready for painting on the lacquer designs (Kinsey 1987). This ojime was made in the late 1980s, 1.6 cm diameter.

working temperatures allow for such decorative techniques as direct flame deposition using nuggets of placer gold (M. and J. Capel, *pers. comm.* 1994, Liu 1994).

Besides the production of chevrons in this country, the other remarkable phenomenon in glassworking is renewed mosaic face canemaking. Manufactured primarily in the Middle East during antiquity, then revived by Venetians and lately used by Indians, such canes were first made in the United States by Brian Kerkvliet during the late 1980s (Liu 1989). Using the hot cased or hot strip technique at the glory hole or furnace, Kerkvliet has firmly reestablished mosaic face and other cane methods. In contrast, the late Kyoyu Asao made mosaics by the cold-bundled composite cane method (Liu 1986; *see page 206*). Initially a strong influence among Northwest glassworkers, Kerkvliet's fame has now spread throughout the country (*see page 206*). Dinah and Patty Hulet also make beads with detailed face canes, presumably by the hot strip method. Art Seymour met a woman pulling face canes in Red Lodge, Montana (*pers. comm.* 1993), so this technique is spreading.

A few glass beadmakers now make blown beads;

Kris Peterson blows beads when in Venice, where she has access to a furnace (*see page 210*). Others such as Phyllis Clarke make blown beads by offhand techniques on the torch; Shari Hopper uses neon or borosilicate tubes for blowing beads. Ellie Burke also blows beads (*see page 214*).

Kiln workers are in the minority; most cast glass frit or powder in molds, quite similar to the lost-wax technique for metals. These include Sara Creekmore, Shari Hopper, Donna Milliron, Nancy Goodenough, Laura Popenoe (*see page 200*), and Nancy Potek.

Molly Vaughan Haskins of Laughing Glass is the only one who slumps previously lampworked strips and sheets of Wasser glass in the kiln. Adhesives hold the components together prior to firing, and dams prevent unwanted flow; the raw slumped pieces are then tumbled for long periods, resulting in finished ornaments that are unlike any others in their shapes and brilliant colors (Ross 1994; *see page 212*). Haskins's vision and technical prowess truly transform glass in unique ways befitting twentieth century sensibilities.

The largest group of current glass beadmakers employs a torch and soft glass to make lamp or flame-

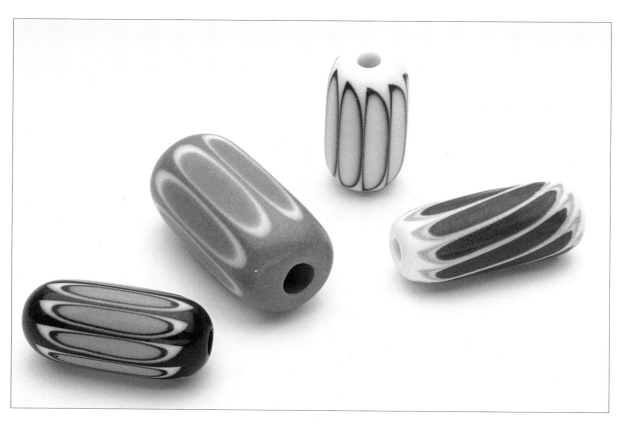

HOWARD NEWCOMB Made by proprietary processes, the porcelain chevrons involve up to five layers; these range from 2.1 to 3.1 cm long. Assisted by ingenious mechanical devices of his own invention, Newcomb once made up to two million cylindrical ceramic beads per year (Benesh 1986).

DOYLE LANE These low-fired ceramic beads are made in a variety of shapes, sizes and glazes, with the crackle, crawled and double glazes especially attractive, 2.4 to 3.4 cm diameter. Lane's beads express an appealing quality about glazed ceramics, the effect akin to wearing miniature pots.

worked beads, the technique probably used most in the past. The most memorable of this group was the late Kyoyu Asao (Liu 1986, Ukai 1980, 1984; *see pages 206, 207*). The late Kisao Iburi may have reached a similar excellence had he lived longer. Asao was ahead of his time, performing at a level not fully appreciated by those who had access to his beads, since the difficulties of glass beadmaking were not readily understood in the 1980s. There are other talented beadmakers in Japan, as evidenced by photographs of contemporary beads in Yoshimizu's book (1989), but Western knowledge of that country's crafts is limited.

With a multi-talented ability to handle different glasses and techniques, Phyllis Clarke creates masterful sculptural beads. Deceptively simple miniatures of fish, birds and mammals belie an extensive knowledge of animal morphology and behavior (*see page 214*). These are Zen-like sketches in glass, accurate yet aesthetically realized portrayals contrary to the cartoon versions made by other beadmakers.

A host of other talented flameworkers, mostly women, are making a variety of precise trail decorated beads in many forms: Dan Adams, Michael Barley, Patricia Frantz, Kate Fowle, Kristina Logan, Michael Max, Patricia Sage, James Smircich, Cheryl Spence, Suzanne Stern, and Pati Walton (*see pages 204, 208, 209, 218*). Smircich also makes sculptural glass of

GALINA REIN Only 2.9 cm high, the intricacy and precision of Rein's work is amazing; the porcelain bead suggests a miniature marine environment.

POLYMER BEADS Made in the United States and England from 1988 to 1993, these are a minute sample of the polymer universe, 0.8 to 4.0 cm diameter. *Clockwise from nine o'clock:* Kathleen Dustin (three beads), Jamey Allen (five beads including face canes and glass simulations), Akiko Kase of London (face/chequer), Mike Kury (Kiffa), and Nan Roche (center five, including three plaques or tabular beads).

KIFFA PENDANTS *Left to right:* Kiffa made of powder glass by an unknown artist, flameworked and trailed glass by Patricia Frantz, and polymer (2.7 cm long) by Mike Kury.

abstract Venuses or goddesses. Frantz has the longest history of lampworking and consequently a strong repertoire of styles (Atkins 1992). Others like Cay Dickey, Inara Knight, Kris Peterson, Rene Roberts, and Alice Zimmerman (*see page 209*) expertly use the popular dichroic glasses. Dennis Briening's sculptural botanical beads show great promise. Helga Seimel, a German lampworker with a great deal of technical virtuosity, uses methods rarely seen in the United States (Hopper 1994; *see page 199 and chapter seven*).

While many glass beadmakers are still developing their already considerable skills, one of the most impressive is Tom Holland. Self taught and a bead collector for the last twenty-five years, he has integrated skills as a potter, blacksmith and mason into his beads. Damascene steel, faience, faience and glass, as well as lampworked, cane and ground glass beads are all within his repertoire. His replications of ancient Chinese glass and composite beads, the latter also in glass, are closest to Warring States originals (Liu 1994). Potentially a great beadmaker, Holland would make an excellent collaborator with any bead researcher interested in ancient faience and glass. An artist's technical ability to illuminate the past is one of the benefits of the current interest in glass beadmaking.

Even with the amount of support for their work, contemporary beadmakers find it difficult to make a living solely by creating and selling their beads. For example, Tom Boylan's daily production

of collectors; if we want to follow the maturing skills of today's artists, we must nurture them so that their careers can continue. And beadmakers need to improve their aesthetics and turn their work into forms which will sell in appropriate venues, like galleries. Responsible collecting of contemporary beads makes it possible to be both an artist's

TORY HUGHES Ranging from 1.0 to 7.8 cm long, these polymer beads and pendants simulate a variety of natural materials. The ornaments represent (clockwise from top left) fired clay, various turquoise beads, an incised bone pendant, coral with inset turquoise, and two precolumbian jade beads. (See Cuadra 1993b, 1994). *Courtesy of Tory Hughes.*

is three dozen beads maximum (*pers. comm.* 1990); others likely produce fewer beads. The intense concentration and neuromuscular skills required of beadmaking precludes such work on a sustained basis. Equally damaging is the lack of realization by buyers and collectors that beads made on a production basis or by Third World beadmakers, while much lower in price, differ crucially in quality.

Contemporary beadmakers deserve the support

patron and collect with a clear conscience, since no harm will afflict another's cultural heritage. American bead collectors are among the few who place as much priority on contemporary beads as ethnic or ancient ones. Foreign collectors appear to see no value in new beads, yet they too must become more aware of the destructive results of collecting any country's past material culture.

FAKES AND SIMULATIONS

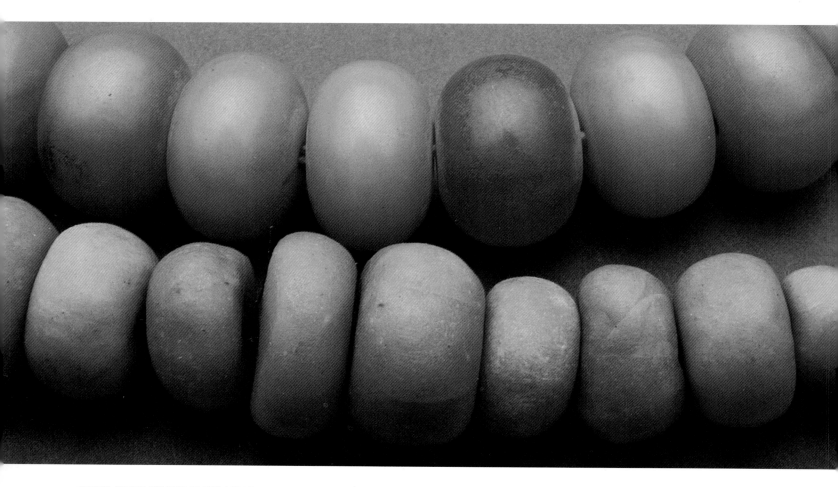

COPAL SIMULATIONS FROM AFRICA AND MOROCCO Among the most numerous copies, copal simulations from Africa are possibly made of phenolic plastic (2.4 cm diameter). The lower strand is ceramic and sold by weight in Morocco, costing about $18 to $31 per strand in the late 1980s. *Courtesy of Rita Okrent.*

CORAL AND TURQUOISE AND THEIR IMITA-
TIONS IN GLASS AND PLASTIC The coral
beads are Chinese and Middle Eastern; the
turquoise pieces are Chinese and Tibetan;
the glass and plastic copies are primarily
Indian, Chinese and Nepalese; and the
diamond-shaped glass bead (2 cm long) is
Japanese. The Czechs were prolific pro-
ducers of turquoise glass beads, spawning
the continuing controversy over what constitutes a Hubbell bead (named for the
Hubbell trading post in the United States
southwest). *Courtesy of Joyce Hundal and
Marion and Murray Winagura.*

W hile simulations and imitations are eagerly
sought by bead collectors as rare and highly
desirable items, fakes and forgeries shake the
confidence of even knowledgeable collectors. Presently
they are an area of concern because of financial loss, but
fakes and forgeries actually occur with low frequency.
Tibetan dZi beads, Phoenician mask pendants, Roman
mosaic face beads, and other ancient Middle Eastern
glass or faience beads have been subject to faking
(*see page 226*). Fantasies and marriages or conglom-
erates (von Saldern 1972) are other categories of
misrepresentations that might be more common than
fakes and forgeries. Here parts of artifacts are combined to create non-existent categories of ornaments
or to compose something which may or may not have
existed (*see page 225*). Unique beads, for which there
are no comparable examples, pose another predica-
ment—an Iranian etched carnelian bead with human
figures constituted just such a challenge, as figurative
representations on etched beads are extremely rare
and human ones are not known to exist (Davis-Kimball
and Liu 1981; *see page 101*). Misattributions, whether
intentional or accidental, are far more widespread,
although misrepresentations of all types certainly
will increase as beads become even more collectible
and expensive to purchase.

Faking of beads has received little published attention (Dale 1978, Liu 1980b, 1992, Ogden 1982). Much
of the information I referenced in 1980 still holds
true, except that glass bead industries have greatly
expanded. Fakes made in Third World countries are
cause for the greatest concern because some are meant
to copy ancient prototypes (*see page 225; chapter three*).
These industries are now producing beads with dis-
continued techniques, for example, Indian millefiori
beads with mosaic face canes, or beads made in the
same styles as European factories, exemplified by the

STONE AND SILICONE RUBBER BEADS imitating stone, ca. 2 cm wide,
from Upper Volta (now Burkina Faso). A fairly unusual material for
making copies, silicone rubber becomes sticky with age; these
beads appear in a variety of colors and shapes. The stone beads
are probably from Mali. *Courtesy of Ann Maurice.*

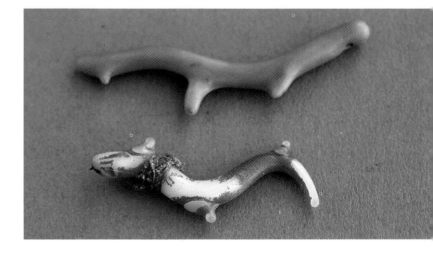

BRANCH CORAL BEAD AND PAINTED GLASS IMITATION from
Morocco (but probably not made there), reflecting the skillful
ingenuity characteristic of some copies. The lampworked glass
version is tied and not perforated, 3.6 cm length. *Courtesy of
Liza Wataghani.*

221

good quality contemporary Indian millefiori and lampwork beads. Such beads also have been misrepresented as ancient or antique (Harris 1991, van der Made 1988). Glass beads are currently lampworked in a large variety of styles, which makes it difficult to keep abreast of them and identification a challenge.

Misattributions that become embedded in literature cause the otherwise well intentioned to err. Chevrons were once thought to be ancient: one modern chevron was dated as first to third century, from Gilan province in Iran (Fukai 1977). With Fukai's article as a reference, a major British auction house gave the same attribution last year to two strands of seventeenth to nineteenth century chevrons from Egypt. Misattributions with similar beads are still extant in certain Middle Eastern and European museums (J. Picard, *pers. comm.* 1994).

Another type of misrepresentation arises from claiming incorrect origins for a bead. For example, European glass beads actually used in the American fur trade are scarce and highly valued. The same type may be more abundant elsewhere, such as Africa, so they are imported from there but attributed to the American trade. Disproving these deceptions is difficult, although glass beads do wear or abrade differently in the Americas than in Africa due to differences based on climactic conditions, clothing or lack thereof and how frequently beads are worn.

As published information increases, people have more access to accurate information, especially to good quality photographs of large numbers and varieties of beads and pendants. Knowing what an original looks like is absolutely critical to detecting an imitation, although this crucial information may be applied to increasing the forger's accuracy. In addition, as skilled beadmakers such as the Japanese (Yoshimizu 1989) replicate ancient beads, or resurrect ancient techniques for making mosaic face canes in both glass and polymer, unscrupulous people may alter them to simulate genuine antique or ancient ones. Faking has occurred frequently with contemporary beads that have been treated to simulate iridescence or corrosion from burial (*see this and opposite page*).

Since a prototype's accuracy is paramount, matching the original's material, shape, color, size, and weight

POWDER GLASS EMBEDDED IN PLASTIC RESIN These beads from Lebanon first appeared in the early 1980s. Some were artificially aged to suggest the faded and grainy look of corroded ancient glass. When exposed to a flame, they burn and fuse into glass with continued heating (Liu 1984). Center bead is 1.3 cm length. *Courtesy of Anahita Gallery and Albert Summerfield.*

ANCIENT GLASS BEAD FROM TURKEY AND GLASS FRAGMENT from a sewer, both displaying iridescence. Exposure to sewer contents is one way of inducing this phenomenon, although the iridescence is easily abraded. Most of the iridescence is in the bead's pitted portions, 1.5 cm diameter. A corroded and iridescent bead weighs less than an intact specimen of the same size. In Venice, glass beads are aged in used kitty litter.

are minimum requirements. If the original shows surface signs of burial, then the replica also needs to indicate patina, wear, iridescence, or other byproducts of decomposition, as well as use. Iridescence is one of the most desirable qualities of ancient glass, thus often imitated. Acids like hydrofluoric may be used both to corrode the glass and to give it a patina (Ogden 1982). Francis (1979c) has noted artificial weathering of beads in Turkey. A hit or miss method involves fusing powdered mica onto glass by prolonged heating in an iron box (B. Bates, *pers. comm.* 1979). Modern fuming of glass, which mimics iridescence, is accomplished by spraying an aqueous solution of stannous or ferric chloride on hot glass, devitrifying it (D. Bloch and K. Feldman, *pers. comm.* 1985).

Most simulations lack accuracy in some aspect. Some appear to have been made without benefit of an original; in others, size and color are altered, so there is no real possibility of close matches. Copying a prototype clearly entails so many variables that it is nearly impossible to do so with complete fidelity and still have an economically viable product. When attempting to duplicate indigenously made ornaments, beadmakers have difficulty reaching a substantial level of accuracy since so much variation exists, even when originals are available as models. Only a few Czech molded glass copies have attained such status (*see chapter one*), but even these have easily differentiated characteristics. When coupled with the astute observation of many native peoples, it is difficult to believe that the market is fooled by most copies. No study has attempted to survey the indigenous customers of such simulations. In most circumstances where people were deceived by imitations,

they were not familiar or lacked access to the original. In situations where copies are part of the commerce of everyday life, it is harder to conceive of deception due to a buyer's ignorance in differentiating between a genuine and a copy. (Their desire to obtain a bargain also plays a role in collectors being duped by fakes.) The acceptance of phenolic plastic as genuine amber by Africans (J. Allen, *pers. comm.* 1994) is an example of the simulation accepted as an economically accessible version of the desired original. Gradually the onus of a simulation may even be lost and the imitation becomes just another

CONTEMPORARY INDIAN GLASS BEADS The beads at the left were treated with possibly acid to simulate iridescence (2.9 cm maximum). The aged strand was listed at $800 by an antiquities dealer; the untreated strand was sold by a Senegalese runner. Other beads from Africa and the Middle East have been treated to simulate aging. *Courtesy of Paul Johnson.*

CARVED AND PLAIN COPAL IMITATIONS of thermosetting plastics, heat-treated to enhance color. This strand is one of four claimed to be carved amber from Tibet, where no such tradition exists. They were selling for more than $1,000 each in Arizona, an example of outrageous fraud that may not have tricked any collectors, ca. 3.2 cm diameter each. *Courtesy of Gabrielle Liese.*

ornament on the market and eventually takes on value, especially for bead collectors.

Detecting simulations requires knowledge of materials used for imitations and the ornaments being copied. The ability to identify material enables determination of authenticity, except perhaps for copies of antiquities. In ancient cultures, the Egyptians were adept at imitations; in the past two centuries, the most prolific simulators were from Czechoslovakia and China. Currently, most fakes and forgeries come from the Middle East, while increasing numbers of imitations derive from Southeast Asia.

Most commonly used materials for simulations, in order of increasing frequency, are shell, faience, bone, glass, and plastic, with the last two the most numerous. The combination of glass powder bound with plastic resin is now being used successfully for fakes. Yet the majority of imitations are detectable if one is familiar with glass and plastics. Many empirical tests can be applied, but rubbing or tapping a bead against one's incisors is an excellent practical method (Allen 1976b). The sensation is hard to describe, but testing beads of

known materials will easily teach one how to distinguish among glass, stone and plastic.

Using natural materials to simulate prototypes made from other natural materials is usually confined to ancient cultures and non-Western societies. When synthetics are used to copy natural materials, less working time, labor-saving or lower costs are achieved. Substances that can be molded like faience, glass and plastic are the most useful and amenable to production processes.

Examples of natural substances simulating other natural substances include shell for coral and teeth; bone for coral (often used by Chinese with dyed bone) and teeth; ivory for stone (Chinese dyed walrus tusk ivory to simulate jadeite or malachite); and stone for other stones (dyed steatite for lapis lazuli). The Chinese made many imitations in this category, often expending as much labor on the copy as on the real bead. Cammann (1950, 1962, 1979) has written extensively on this subject and a number of the materials are illustrated in Liu (1980b).

Synthetics simulating natural substances comprise the majority of imitations. The term synthetics is used here to mean that they were made by humans (not the definition used for synthetic gemstones, which are simulations with the same hardness, chemical composition, etc. as the prototype). There are many faience substitutes for stones; ceramic substitutes for faience (modern Egyptian), stone and shell; glass substitutes for stone, coral, teeth, amber or copal, hornbill, and dyed sperm whale tooth (*see page 221 and chapters one, two, three*); cement substitutes for glass (Adhyatman and Arifin 1993); silicone rubber imitations for stone (*see page 221*); and plastic for glass, coral, amber or copal (Allen 1976a, b), ivory, and stone. In capable hands, polymer makes very convincing imitations (Cuadra 1993). Current fake turquoise and coral beads in Tibet are still good enough to fool the buyer into thinking they are genuine, not plastic (possibly vinyl) and glass copies.

Synthetic substances simulating other synthetic materials include beads imitating other beads, either older versions or those popular in other markets (Francis 1979b), and copies of other copies. Chevrons made by trailing, etched patterns replicated in trailing, and glass powder applied by templates and duplicating European trail decorated wound beads by African powder glass are a few examples of common methods of simulation.

BIRD BEADS FROM INDONESIA The left specimen, an ancient glass bead with trailed bird and sunburst designs, is genuine, 1.5 cm diameter. The center is an authentic Indo-Pacific bead (as are the red glass ones alongside) with a bird design ground into it; the depression then is filled with a water-soluble material. The right specimen is a contemporary wound bead with a poor copy of the bird design in trailing. Many glass imitations are made in Java, which has an active glass bead industry. *Courtesy of Elizabeth J. Harris and Cecilia Molano.*

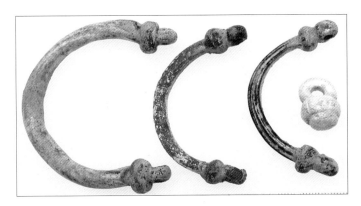

FANTASIES COMPOSED OF POSSIBLY BRACELET FRAGMENTS AND BEADS form a loop bead. These were detected when the glue (probably cyanoacrylic) failed on one end. Maximum loop size is 5.5 cm wide. The authentic bead is similar to the ends of these fakes. Similar glue was used on the other conglomerate; both have Middle Eastern origins. *Courtesy of Dr. Tobey.*

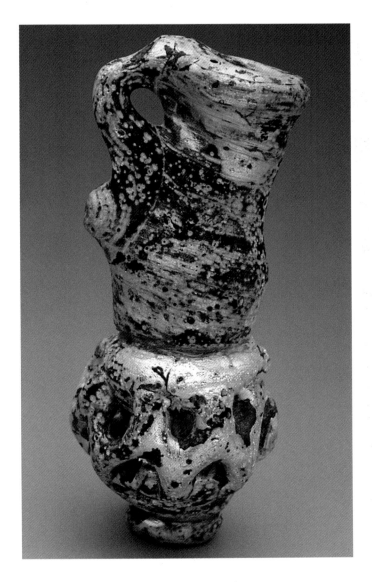

BEAUTIFULLY IRIDESCED CONGLOMERATE formed by gluing together amphora and lattice beads, detected by antiquities dealer and author Derek Content. Fakes made from ancient components are most convincing; specimen is 3.8 cm high. *Courtesy of Joel L. Malter.*

AUTHENTIC ROMAN MOSAIC FACE BEAD AND CONTEMPORARY
FACE CANE Brian Kerkvliet was the first to revive this technique in
the United States. He had been making mosaic face canes for
just two months when this photograph was taken; now they are
much more refined and complex. Face plaque is 0.8 cm high.

FAKE PHOENICIAN MASK PENDANT AND ROMAN MOSAIC FACE
BEAD from Italy and Syria. The pendant required grinding an
ancient glass bead to represent the core (dark brick red) and
then grinding or gluing components onto it, possibly with hot
glasswork. It broke during an earthquake, revealing separated
glue joins (2.7 cm diameter). As for the face bead, a face was
merely painted onto an ancient eye bead,1.35 cm diameter.
Courtesy of Cay Dickey and Rita Okrent.

CONTEMPORARY INDIAN MILLEFIORI BEADS WITH MOSAIC
FACE CANES, probably made with the hot-strip or layering
method, ca. 1.5 cm high. These beads appeared on the
market in the 1980s. *Courtesy of Elizabeth J. Harris.*

Transpositions and degradations may be mistaken
for imitations or fakes. Transpositions are duplications
in another material of the original item: the intention
is not deception but to create the desired ornament in
another medium (Zeltner 1931). Degradation applies
primarily to Egyptian amulets (Brunton 1928), whereby
degraded examples show progressively poorer form,
detail, size, glazing, and other aspects of crafting.
Examples at the lower end of the continuum resulting
from degradation become almost unrecognizable as
poor versions of the prototype (Liu 1987a; *see page 109*).

Blatant attempts to misrepresent beads as antique
or ancient are often achieved through certificates
of authenticity, used as a disarming device on the
novice or inexperienced collector. One dealer supplied a certificate for a necklace which mixed old and
new elements, costing an American couple two thousand dollars when they purchased the necklace in
Israel during 1980 (Liu 1983a). An American woman

MODERN FACE BEAD with same cane as upper left, 2.1 cm wide.
Courtesy of Brian Kerkvliet.

TABULAR BEAD WITH MOSAIC FACE Accomplished by cold-
bundling (Liu 1989b), many of these Venetian face beads from
the nineteenth and twentieth centuries may be confused with
ancient ones, 2.2 cm length. This one was secured through the
African trade. *Courtesy of Boyd W. Walker.*

recently bought a fake dZi in Venice for one thousand dollars, also accompanied by such a document. The seeding of otherwise fake beads with a few ancient ones occurs with powder glass embedded in plastic resin; one such necklace sold for four hundred dollars in Rotterdam during 1979. These resin or powder glass beads, probably from Lebanon or Syria, are among the most widespread frauds (Liu 1984b, Ogden 1982; shown in a lecture by G. Dale in 1981).

Most convincing forgeries are those reconstructed from actual ancient fragments, but they often exceed the boundary of credibility and are purely fantasies (*see page 225*). More cautious forgers succeed better, as with the ingenious faking of Indonesian bird beads (*see page 225*). Indonesian beadmakers now rank among the most prolific in copying antique and ancient beads, but most such imitations are very obvious (Adhyatman and Arifin 1993; *see chapter three*). Ban Chiang glass beads are also faked. Now there are terra cotta and porcelain fakes of ancient Chinese glass beads, made respectively in the People's Republic of China and Taiwan (D. Ross, *pers. comm.* 1994). Usually the more well known and valuable beads are faked; these include Phoenician mask pendants and Roman mosaic face beads (*see opposite page*). A Phoenician mask pendant fake, purchased in Venice, was among the most elaborate. It was built upon a modified ancient glass bead that served as the core-formed counterpart in real ones. Prior to the renaissance of mosaic face canes in the United States, crude attempts to replicate these face canes were made in Syria (Dale 1978). Beads with facial images of humans have been made by several ancient cultures (Liu 1976, 1983a), and collectors are greatly attracted to them, so undoubtedly such fakes will continue to be produced. The best protection for collectors is a thorough knowledge of the beads intended for purchase.

KIFFA BEADS IN POWDER GLASS AND POLYMER, left and right respectively. Signed on the reverse by Mike Kury, the polymer examples were created as homage to Kiffa beads, 2.4 and 2.7 cm long. *Courtesy of Elizabeth J. Harris and Mike Kury.*

COLLECTING
BEADS

Representing a category of minor artifacts studied by only a few archaeologists and anthropologists, beads have received scant attention even though they have been treasured by millions of people throughout several millennia and remain culturally significant to many societies. Today there exists worldwide interest in beads as art objects, elements of personal adornment, as a means of artistic fulfillment or livelihood, as intriguing bits of information to be deciphered, and, of course, as collectibles. To the collector, beads are an exhilarating passion—to acquire, savor and share them with others is a stimulating and satisfying experience. Still the mere mechanics of acquisition by no means defines bead collecting, it more importantly reflects one's philosophy, aesthetics, ethics, and sense of stewardship for artifacts. Moreover, dedicated collectors promote advances in information based on the social, economic, technological, religious, political, and historical data that can be gleaned from beads. This is an important and salient development, whereby essentially self taught individuals actively contribute to a field of research.

While adding to the scientific knowledge of beads, collectors also have been educating the public. Essential to this process was the development of a focal point for those frustrated by a lack of reliable and accessible information. With the publication of *The Bead Journal* in 1974 (the title was changed to *Ornament* in 1978 to reflect the inclusion of all personal adornment), a forum for the dissemination of information on beads was established.

The nearly simultaneous and independent founding in 1975 of The Bead Society in Los Angeles, California, led to the emergence of other national and international bead societies, now totaling more than forty, as well as other organizations devoted to bead research (*see appendices;* the above number does not include foreign bead collecting groups that may exist in India, Indonesia, the Philippines, Thailand, and Hong Kong, but are unconfirmed). Domestic organizations sponsor lectures, bazaars, international conventions or conferences, award funds for bead research, and publish newsletters and other material. Newsletters are among the best sources for bead information, especially that of an ephemeral nature. Among newsletters of value for research are the Bead Forum, Bead Study Trust, Bead Society for Greater Washington, The Bead Society (Los Angeles), The Beadazzled Beadstringer, and Perles Info (the newsletter of the European Bead Network).

As a founding member of The Bead Society, I am especially proud of its grant program, the first such established; since 1987, almost twenty grants have been awarded to individuals and institutions. (Some private individuals are so committed that they directly fund research.) As part of this nurturing infrastructure, private centers for bead research developed, and museums, bead societies and bead

ANCIENT, ETHNOGRAPHIC AND CONTEMPORARY BEADS from many geographic and cultural areas. Virtually all materials except those of botanical origin are present. Beads range from highly crafted ones, such as the contemporary version of an ancient Chinese eye bead by the late Kyoyu Asao, to drilled and rounded pebbles from Precolumbian Mexico. Powder glass, mandrel wound and polymer Kiffa versions are represented. The glass replica is by Patricia Frantz and the polymer one by Mike Kury.

RARE JAPANESE BEADS and Swiss calipers used in measuring beads. Marked in millimeters (dial shows tenths of a millimeter) and inches, the caliper's plastic jaws will not harm a bead. The smaller jaws are used to measure perforation diameters. Inexpensive calipers lacking the dial are also available; see page 231. Measurements should be taken in metric units, a system which prevails in the world except for the United States. *Courtesy of Ornamental Resources.*

stores offered workshops, all providing vital means of educating those interested in beads and related topics at the community level. This supportive and sharing spirit continues today, fostering a climate in which education and collecting flourishes.

Bead research generally depends upon helpful, cooperative and generous spirits: consequently there is much lending of material to others, all of which is based on respect and trust. In addition, sharing specimens among fellow researchers and collectors greatly expands one's exposure to beads and facilitates the acquisition of bead study collections. Just as books, periodicals, newsletters, as well as measuring and viewing devices are important tools in bead research, so is the study collection. This is a tradition emanating from Horace Beck and W.G.N. van der Sleen, the founders of bead research. While modern photographic reproductions have greatly improved, nothing can replace the comparison of actual specimens while trying to make critical differentiations. Since research and collecting often involves travel, many people pleasurably combine these aspects of their lives.

Beads are durable, wearable, small, easily portable, and visually and tactilely attractive. The variety is infinite and they sometimes exist in quantities sufficient for many to share, yet are rare enough to heighten the excitement of the search. Because of the large volume of many bead types, it is possible for a collector to maintain interest and still possess depth in a collection. Objects so rare that the frequency of acquisition is not forthcoming do not make good collectibles.

Bead collecting is practiced by many, but few have written about the process: collecting, display and storage have been briefly discussed (Liu 1975, 1978); Harris wrote a series of articles on this topic in The Bead Society newsletter (1980, 1981a, b, c, d, e, 1982); Francis (1994) and Terpning (1990) wrote on collecting beads; and The Beadazzled Beadstringer has a series entitled the Collector's Eye.

Although it would be interesting to learn where collectors and collections are located, such disclosures might endanger the privacy and security of those involved, except where it is already public record. Surprisingly, I have only seen or heard about some fifty noteworthy collections, undoubtedly a fraction of those extant; a number of owners have died, and some of their collections have been donated, sold or amalgamated. Others are quasi-collections, namely those belonging to dealers. The largest bead collections, in terms of numbers, probably belong to several

Middle Eastern dealers in the United States and abroad. Many dealers also collect, retaining the best for themselves, but eventually the collections are sold when substantial offers can be resisted no longer. There are exceptions, such as the Picards, whose African trade bead collection will be housed in a museum-like setting.

Private collections are concentrated on the East and West Coasts, with the predominance located in California and Washington. Possibly twenty percent are foreign collections; many more may exist, but foreign collectors are often discreet and their organizations less well established. Thus the identities of the collections are more apt to be hidden, although evidence of their existence is apparent from publications (Adhyatman and Arifin 1993, Borel 1994, Fukai 1977, Villegas 1983, Yoshimizu 1989).

Some collections attempt to encompass most areas of the bead universe: The Bead Museum is an excellent example. Even within the better collections, there are strengths and weaknesses, with ancient Egyptian beads often underrepresented. Africa, the Middle East and Asia are preferred areas for collecting, and Africa and China are most popular. Collectors who restrict themselves to specific geographic or cultural areas often specialize. The late Michael Heide

concentrated on chevron beads; another is Jamey Allen who writes on this topic and is working on a book about chevrons, so research interests often coincide with collections. The late Isabel Kelly (1992) similarly built a collection of trade beads in association with research on the anthropology and archaeology of Mexico. Elsewhere in the Americas, the strong interest in the fur trade period has encouraged many to collect beads of that era; the donation in 1988 of the large Weida collection to the Jackson Hole Museum in Wyoming is one such manifestation of this movement. Others began collecting as a result of living in foreign countries; in fact, expatriates are often avid collectors (Liu 1982). One collector living in Tunisia restricts himself to Roman mosaic face beads. Kenoyer (1993) tells of a Pakistani school teacher who has made such a good collection from a Harappan site that an archaeology student may be assigned to document and analyze the beads.

Bead collecting does not have a particularly long history in the United States; the middle 1920s marked the beginning collections for both the late Dorothy Gerrity and the remarkable Gerald B. Fenstermaker. Most current collectors only started in the late 1960s or early 1970s; thus the bulk of extant collections are

PHOTOGRAPHIC EQUIPMENT A 55 mm macro lens and SLR (single lens reflex) camera are minimum requirements for basic bead photography; additional tools include a gray card for measuring light, Mylar for reflecting light on subjects and a caliper for measuring beads. My professional equipment consists of Nikon cameras and lenses, some of them dating from thirty years ago.

some twenty to twenty-five years old, with a sizable proportion of the owners in their sixties and seventies. Naturally, some of these collections will recycle into the marketplace; a number already have been acquired by other collectors.

While there are many ways to obtain, collect, curate, and display beads, the most important link is between the bead and the data associated with it. When and where acquired, at what price, and how the bead was used cannot be deduced from studying the physical aspects and must be noted in some form, usually with a tag, along with other characteristics derived from physical examination. [Most bead collectors dislike the museum practice of inking an accession number onto the bead surface as it may obscure details or chemically interact with the composition of the bead.] One must be consistent in cataloging, rigorously and accurately recording the information that goes with each acquisition; no matter how tedious the process, the memory should not be trusted.

Obviously an important aspect of collecting beads is how to purchase or acquire them. Currently bead shops are proliferating rapidly, so finding a source is not difficult. The Bead Society of Central Ohio lists over five hundred places to buy beads; *Ornament* magazine has more than two hundred advertisers, many of whom sell beads. For the beginner, the problems lie in too much material and in deciding what to collect. It is crucial for collectors to read and learn in order to have some basis for making decisions. Many beads shown in *Collectible Beads* are still available on the market, so it too can be used as a guide.

Having the assistance of an experienced collector as a mentor is invaluable. Once a person starts buying, developing good relationships with trustworthy dealers are important, yet personal knowledge is still the best guide and defense. In addition to stores or private dealers, some collectors suggest swap meets and garage sales, although they can be sources netting little success. Trading with other collectors is not only a good way of acquiring, it is also an opportunity to learn and to form friendships.

When one becomes experienced, traders or runners and auctions are excellent sources. Auctions are one of the best venues for ancient beads, often derived from older collections with provenance provided. Many museums have sold their deaccessioned beads and ornaments in this manner. A drawback is that auction catalog subscriptions are expensive. Most major auction houses are based in New York or London, and although bids can be mailed, one must be familiar with

BEAD COLLECTION STORAGE seems to rest somewhere between the ideal and the practical. Because I frequently consult my collection, some beads are kept in compartmentalized polystyrene boxes with identifying labels. The contents can be viewed without opening the box, which is useful when searching for a particular specimen. Generally each box contains beads from only one area, here African, the ancient Middle East and Europe. From Mali, the largest bead is 10 cm long and made of gneiss.

CARDBOARD STORAGE BOXES used when there are large amounts of material from one area (Czech and some related pendants); these flat boxes store easily on shelves. Within the box, separate acquisitions are stored in their original containers, as well as polyethylene film canisters. These are excellent for both storage and mailing.

the intricacies of auctions. Sotheby's, Christie's, Spink & Son, Phillips, and Bonhams have offered beads. The best strategy is always to buy the highest quality. For those who primarily collect for research, broken or damaged specimens offer excellent heuristic value but cost little, since most collectors will not consider them.

Photography (or even a good photocopy) greatly assists the documentation process, especially when a strand will be taken apart for restringing or sorting. (If a necklace has historic or ethnographic significance, it should be kept intact.) Photographic records are extremely helpful, especially when the collection becomes extensive or if one communicates with other collectors. Without excellent photographic reproductions of beads during the last decades, we would have experienced much more difficulty in identifying and studying beads, as well as appreciating their beauty. Although scientific articles and the publications of some researchers contain detailed monochrome drawings, these do not begin to approach photographs in their usefulness.

Records can be kept on simple index cards or on a computer data base program which can be used to cross reference a bead collection with photographic slides and location of the object. Today, the price of one good bead equals the cost of a computer, so such an investment is easily justified.

Westerners have exerted little effort in displaying beads, except possibly with their being worn. Japanese collectors consider beads as miniature art and their presentation is treated accordingly; beads and other small collectibles are elegantly stored in small, plain wooden boxes, to be brought forth and appreciated. Mounting beads not only enhances them (Liu 1975, 1978), but also resolves the problem of exhibiting. By mounting individual beads on metal rods and varying the height and distance between them, beautiful groupings that require little space on a shelf can be achieved (*see page 236*). The spatial relationship between the beads emphasizes technical or cultural facets of the specimens. Harris (1981e, 1982) has discussed other methods of display, as well as storage, which are both critical to the organization and utility of a collection (*see pages 232, 233, 234*).

There is a continuum from people who acquire beads mainly for personal adornment (*see chapter seven*), to those who collect and study, to those who create them. Many become so immersed that a considerable part of their lives is dedicated to bead-related activities. There are those who have evolved from collecting to exhibiting their collection, as has Gabrielle

Liese, director of The Bead Museum in Prescott, Arizona—of course, no museum director or curator ever really loses the collecting instinct. Prior to establishing The Bead Museum, her private collection was exhibited at the Phoenix Museum of Art. Naomi Lindstrom exhibited her collection in 1993 at the San Francisco Craft & Folk Art Museum, breaking all attendance records.

In many ways, collecting beads is easier today than two decades ago since so much more information is available and a nationwide support network exists. On the negative side, prices have increased and fewer beads, especially antique specimens, are available in many areas. The looting by Third World peoples of their archaeological sites in order to supply collector marketplaces is destructive.

Yet the collector can react positively by adapting different strategies of collecting: for those who prefer mainly to wear their collections, the use of single beads as pendants (Liu 1993) or the incorporation of a few antique beads with other contemporary elements in necklaces (Liu 1979) can decrease commercial pressures. Instead of collections of multiple bead strands, one can choose to engage in specimen collecting. In this way, it is possible to increase a collection's scope, spend less, enable others to collect the same type, and facilitate curating. Noted bead researcher Elizabeth J. Harris has a specimen collection from about twenty-five countries; single beads are strung on approximately forty-five strands and have been used in numerous lectures and demonstrations. Many others engage in this practice, including myself; since age seven, June Payne has selected two of each bead she encounters for her specimen collection.

INFORMATION SOURCES Many collectors are as diligent in their search for publications as they are for beads. Sources now include a wide selection of books, journals or periodicals, monographs, reprints, and newsletters distributed by bead societies, research organizations and entrepreneurs. Shown are the first issue of *The Bead Journal* from Summer 1974, Volume 17, No. 2 of *Ornament*, the first issue of *Beads*, Volume 5 from the African trade bead series, *The History of Beads, Perle Veneziane, Paleorient*, and newsletters produced by The Bead Society of Greater Washington and Hands of the Hills. Journal articles and newsletters are most useful for current information.

ROMAN MOSAIC FACE BEADS, both spherical and tabular, purchased at auction some twenty years apart. Some have been sanded to remove corroded glass, others are in their original condition. The price differential between the first and last batch was sixfold, but nowhere near the current market price of approximately $5,000, some one hundred times greater than two decades ago. This sample provides a basis and impetus for future research on Roman mosaic face beads, which have not been studied in detail. The beads range from 1.1 to 1.4 cm diameter.

The current surge in glass and polymer bead-making provides perfect opportunities for specimen collecting. To further our understanding, researchers can collaborate with craftspeople working in various media to replicate or reconstruct many beadmaking techniques. Jamey Allen has replicated a number of ancient glass techniques in polymer clay, Peter Francis has made core-formed and wound glass beads (Liu 1985) and Cay Dickey replicated an ancient glass bead of the Americas (Harris and Liu 1979). Tait (1991) has shown modern replications of core-formed glass pendants.

The renaissance in glass beadmaking and the increasingly sophisticated aesthetics of contemporary necklaces are among the most exciting trends to watch and are being followed closely by collectors. Contemporary beads provide an area of collecting whereby one can be a patron to the artist and know that no nation's cultural heritage is affected. But intentionally or not, a collector contributes to the destruction of a country's material culture when beads are obtained through looting or other illegal means, even though many countries attach little cultural significance to such artifacts.

Because beads have been the earliest vehicles for simulations, substitutions, or copying of precious materials, the collection and study of fakes is one of the most fascinating and rewarding areas of bead collecting. Simulations are historically and geographically widespread, and the matching of copies with their prototypes is one of the best ways to learn about bead materials, methods of manufacture, and the ingenuity of merchandising through the ages (Liu 1980, 1992). With the currently high prices for many beads, especially valuable ones from antiquity, the ability to detect fakes is good economic protection.

Remember that the difference between a valuable collection and a burden to surviving heirs rests in how well the collection is catalogued and attributed. Family members are frequently left with collec-

236

tions for which there is no information, and elderly or sick collectors often despair about the fate of their treasures. Those who fail to acknowledge the strong link that runs from collecting to research and education, leading to understanding and respect for past and present cultures, will only accumulate objects that have been wrested from their original cultural or historical context. The wise collector realizes that information about a bead is as crucial as the bead itself. However important research is to collecting, it is paramount to realize that given the vastness of the field, no one authority knows everything about beads. One of the most valuable lessons that I learned from my mentor in graduate school was acknowledging that I did not know something.

So beware of bead authorities who have all the answers.

The acquisition of knowledge is integral to collecting beads, and discovering their historical and cultural backgrounds are as rewarding as obtaining them. While many have stated that certain beads perform financially much better than stocks, it must not be forgotten that whenever one collects any art form, it should be for pleasure and enlightenment, not for financial gain or speculation.

I hope that all those who love beads as I do will sustain their passion for them and be guided with a sense of responsibility and ethics. You are only the temporary steward of your collection, the beads will last many lifetimes.

VENETIAN BEADS FROM THE AFRICAN TRADE MOUNTED FOR DISPLAY Brass wires have been silver soldered onto bronze brazing rods (any stiff wire or rod can be used), so that beads of various sizes can be mounted and easily removed by lifting. I devised this mounting almost two decades ago and it remains my favorite method of exhibiting beads. The mounted beads are inserted into holes drilled into a board or shelves. Largest bead is 3.0 cm high. *Courtesy of Liza Wataghani.*

GLOSSARY

Adjagba beads See Bodom beads.

Amazonite A bluish-green feldspar, slightly changeable in luster. Favored in ancient Egypt, it remains popular in Mauritania.

Amber The popular name for fossil resins of differing geological ages and sources, but primarily from the Baltic States and dating from the Oligocene period, forty to sixty million years ago. Its proper name is succinite. Any fossil resin of sufficient beauty and hardness to make jewelry or decorative objects, amber is found in China, Myanmar (Burma), Sicily, Romania, Mexico, and the Dominican Republic. Recent or semi-fossil resins called copals are often used as substitutes where amber is not native (Africa and South America). Copal is softer, has a lower melting point and decomposes in a relatively short time; however, copal beads are rare and most examples are plastic imitations.

Amulets and Talismans Although they share attributes, these are different prophylactics or protective objects. An amulet is usually worn on the body and provides protection from evil forces. A talisman counters a specific evil, may or may not be worn and may consist of parts or objects bound or held together (as in a pouch).

Arca shell beads From either *Arca grandiosa* or *sinilis,* these beads of various sizes and shapes are made in West Africa and incorrectly called hippo's teeth, particularly the larger rectangular forms.

Baluster beads Also balustrade or vase beads, they are typically found with prayer beads and so-called Mandarin necklaces as closures or clasps.

Bauxite beads Made from an aluminum ore stained brown by iron, in the 1970s they were a staple import from West Africa. In a variety of sizes and usually cylindrical, they are also called volcanic ash.

Bida beads From Bida, Nigeria, these are the only contemporary glass beads made by the wound technique in Africa. Crude but appealing beads have been produced recently from recycled glass bottles, shaped and drilled by lapidary techniques.

Bodom beads Older powder glass beads from West Africa, usually large and most often of yellow glass on a gray to black core. Considerable controversy exists concerning how they were made, when, and whether certain examples might be European, or at least hot-worked glass. Certainly, there are European beads made to imitate them. Similar but smaller and non-cored beads are made in the area, called adjagba and Krobo beads.

Bone Hard material forming the skeleton of most vertebrate animals, primarily made of calcium phosphate. Most beadmaking bone sources are large animals such as cows, oxen, buffaloes, and camels. Bird bones are usually hollow and make obvious beads. Vertebrae and knuckles and other joints are popular as beads.

Butterfly or Double Axe beads Flat or lenticular beads from ancient times, often thicker along the perforation channel or at the aperture, sometimes extending past the body of the bead.

Cambay, India (Khambat) The longest continuing center of stone beadmaking in the world, famous for agates and other quartz minerals. Carnelian, whose color is enhanced or created by heating procedures, is the most common stone; other colors may be artificially induced, but are not dyed. Cambay carnelians are typically orange, rather than the red to brown of German agates.

Cased glass Also called overlay or layered, one color, often bold opaque and white or a pale color, is surrounded by a different color, frequently in brilliant transparent hues. The most common are cornaline d'Aleppo beads, featuring transparent red over white glasses (or more rarely opaque yellow or pink). Beads with a white core but exteriors that are not red are called white hearts.

Ceramics Generally classified as pottery, ceramics range from earthenware to fine porcelain, and derive from clay taken from the earth, purified and formed, and sometimes glazed. They are strengthened by firing in furnaces, and it is this aspect that suggests the inclusion of artificial materials such as faience and frit or kyanos. (See Faience.)

Chevron beads Venetians invented these important glass beads about five hundred years ago, and continue to make them today. The Italian name is rosetta and refers to the pattern in the cross section of the bead, resembling a flower or twelve-pointed star, derived from a molding process. Colors for the different layers tend to be blue, white and red, but many combinations have been made. The name refers to the ends of these complex canes that have been faceted or rounded by grinding, revealing the inner structure of zig-zag or chevron lines. Such beads were also manufactured in Holland in the seventeenth century by expatriate Venetian glass beadmakers and are indistinguishable from Venetian beads.

Chinese glass beads Made at various sites in China, primarily from the seventeenth century and into modern times. This designation is preferred over Peking or Canton beads.

Cinnabar Also cinnabar lacquer, an artificial material derived from the juice of trees, colored with ground mercury-rich earth to a bright vermilion. It is often mistakenly designated as carved mercury ore.

Combed glass Also called raking or dragging, combing glass, still in use, is one of the earliest decorative techniques. A trail decorated bead is altered by stroking a pointed tool across the lines to form patterns, usually zig-zags, waves, scallops, or festoons. Frequently mislabeled feathering, a technique in which up and down strokes are alternated across close parallel lines.

Composition Non-homogenous glassy materials, such as faience or frit, often of such great age and distressed condition that their exact nature is indeterminable. The term also refers to recent reconstructed materials used in jewelry, possibly from ivory, bone, or wood dust, and fairly common in Asia.

Conus shells An important mollusk species whose shells are cone-shaped, generally thin-walled with a thick apex, the latter often cut and made into a disk. Their use dates from 3,000 B.C. or earlier and is nearly universal.

Copal See Amber.

Coral An important bead material since ancient times, coral derives from marine animal skeletons related to the anemones and consists primarily of calcium carbonate (like shells). Two varieties are used in jewelry, hard stony corals and the softer horn-like corals. The former is considered precious and color ranges from white, pink, orange, red to black. Horn corals have more color variation (yellow, blue, metallic gold, etc.); the color is also enhanced by dyeing. Primary sources of precious or noble corals are the Mediterranean and South China seas; horn-like corals are primarily from the Red Sea, the Philippines and Hawaii.

Core-formed and Rod-formed Prior to glass blowing, vessels and beads were made by this process in which a metal rod is covered by a compound that forms either the desired shape of the interior of a vessel or the bead perforation. The core has not been firmly identified, but probably consisted of a friable refractory material that would not fuse with heat, and could be scraped or removed from the glass with effort. In modern bead terminology, core refers to the base of a bead, particularly when it is a different composition, structure or color from the bead's exterior. The core of ancient beads refers to the material around which the bead is formed, later removed, leaving a perforation.

Cornaline d'Aleppo See Cased glass.

Cowrie shells An important mollusk species, related to snails (gastropods), used as money and for their symbolic shape in many areas of the world, from early to contemporary times.

Crumb beads Any faience or glass bead decorated with small, colored bits of faience or glass randomly applied. The bits may be rolled in or left raised and may be sparse or dense in covering the surface and either jagged, heated to a state that rounds them off, or melts the crumbs flush with the surface.

Dogon beads Made by the Dogon of West Africa, these beads consist of igneous rocks often made into bicone shapes of great size and weight. (See Gneiss.) Also refers to other popular beads worn by the

Dogons including small annular blue glass beads from Europe and large native-made brass beads.

Djenne (d'Jenne), Mali An ancient West African site near the Niger River where numerous stone, pottery and glass beads were recovered. Often thought to be of remarkable antiquity, these artifacts probably date from Islamic times. Stone beads, primarily carnelian and white or translucent agates, were made in Cambay, India, though certain igneous rock beads were no doubt local. (See Gneiss.) Small segmented ceramic beads are probably also local in origin. Glass beads are more problematic, possibly consisting of imported Islamic and perhaps locally made or altered varieties. Later trade beads from Europe are usually incorporated into strands of such beads, ranging from sixteenth century chevron and Nueva Cádiz beads to common nineteenth century beads.

dZi beads Various agate beads avidly collected in Tibet, of unknown age and controversial manufacture; also spelled gZi and tZi. Generally brown and white or black and white, they have linear and spot patterns (eyes) and are usually long tapered bicones or plump barrels. Tibetans regard them as natural or supernatural in origin. Superior or pure beads cost up to thousands of dollars each. Though considered mystical by Tibetans and largely misunderstood by Westerners, dZi beads are related to etched agate beads of antiquity, with similar manufacture, color schemes, designs, and shapes.

Ear spools In many ancient and present day societies, earlobes are perforated and enlarged to accommodate large ornaments, often called ear spools, ear plugs or capstan beads (erh tang in Asia). In a variety of sizes, shapes and materials, they are sometimes perforated and may be worn through the hole in the earlobe or suspended with a string or wire.

End of the day beads Popular misnomer for glass beads that, by their haphazard appearance, have been assumed to have been made from glassworking leftovers. In all likelihood they were intentionally made and continue to be produced.

Etched agate or Etched carnelian Stone beads, dating from as early as 2,500 B.C., featuring linear and dot patterns painted on the surface, which when fired become permanent–the designation etched is incorrect. Decorations are mostly white, and rarely black or gray, or combinations of both. The agate material is either color-enhanced carnelian or artificially colored brown to black. Besides such beads found in India, Pakistan, Afghanistan, and Iran, there are related beads from the Himalayas (dZi beads) and from eastern India and Myanmar (pumtek beads).

Eye beads Beads of any material decorated with circular patterns resembling human or animal eyes and desirable for symbolic and superstitious functions such as averting the evil eye. The most important eye beads are made from banded minerals, primarily agates, cut to form rounded patterns and from glass simulants of these. Glass eye beads are often classified by their decorations–usually flush with the surface, raised above it or actually horned, either sparse, dense or multiple and derived from various techniques, such as stratified or mosaic. The bead's perforation is sometimes incorrectly called its eye. (See Amulet.)

Face beads Mosaic glass beads that depict human facial images in the cross sections of complicated canes. Such work began just prior to the Roman Period, and became fairly widespread. Faces range from relatively crude to complex images with details such as jewelry and clothing. A bead may be merely a slice of cane, perforated through its length, or slices may be added to glass beads, usually around the circumference in a band, with or without additional decoration. Face beads continued to be made after the Roman Period, and became even more complex in some instances, incorporating checkered mosaic components. The work vanished until modern times, when Venetians attempted to make them but with less success. Recently, face beads have been made in India (rather poorly), by Americans (with better detail) and are also made in polymer with great virtuosity. (See Plastics.)

Faience The first synthetic material and the ancestor of glass, frequently called Egyptian paste. Like glass, it is composed primarily of silica and alkali and colored by minerals such as copper (yielding bright blues). Unlike glass, it is a non-homogenous composition, less well-fused, always opaque and often with an external glaze coating, which is actual glass. The most common Egyptian faience items are tiny disks and cylinder beads of various colors, often called mummy beads from their frequent use in funerary jewelry and beadwork.

Fused-rod beads Also called Fustat beads after the place of manufacture in Egypt, these ancient mosaic glass beads are a preformed group of six to eight compound rods, placed parallel and carefully heated until they fuse. This compound pad or plaque is then rolled upon itself around a rod that forms the perforation.

Gadrooned See Melon beads.

Giryama beads Tiny brass and copper diskoidal beads made from hammered wire in Kenya. Remarkably uniform in dimension, this has inspired the incorrect name, brass hishi. Their use by Western craftspeople since the late 1970s has been rather broad and they appear in eclectic combinations, including Middle Eastern components, and are sometimes plated silver.

Glass The preeminent bead material, glass was developed as early as the second millennium B.C. and probably derived from the practice of glazing ceramics, stones and most of all faience, the ancestor of glass. It is a super-cooled liquid that is rigid at room temperature, when heated it is less viscous and can be manipulated with simple tools. Made from silica, alkali and lime, glass is colored with mineral compounds, and may be transparent, opaque and the full range between. Earliest use was for beads and to imitate rare and costly precious stones and decorative materials–a practice which continues today. Glass paste is an archaic name for products that were probably not made from such a compound, or better applied to items such as faience or kyanos. (See Faience.)

Gneiss or granite Coarse-grained igneous rocks chiefly of quartz and feldspar, usually having a speckled appearance.

Gold sandwich-glass beads See Hot-pinched beads.

Goulimine beads A popular name from the 1960s for Venetian glass millefiori beads, collected by travelers in North Africa and brought back to the United States.

Hebron Town in Israel (formerly Palestine) where crude glass beads have been made for some time. Those from the 1960s and 1970s are basic round or square cylinders and barrels, of large size and darkly transparent, but bubbly glass. Previously made Hebron eye beads may be confused with similar beads from Turkey, and Kano beads popular in Saharan and West Africa may come from Hebron.

Heirloom or heirlooming The practice of passing cultural objects like beads within the family from one generation to the next.

Hishi beads Also heishi or heeshee, this southwestern Native American name indicates shell beads made by stringing flat drilled pieces and rolling them on or between abrasive stones to form round disks of uniform diameter or graduated diameters. The name applies to beads of any material made this way, and incorrectly to any disk beads of uniform diameter. (See Giryama, Land snail shell beads.)

Hittite An ancient culture in present day Syria, dating from circa 1600 B.C. Artistic and expansionist, they were much influenced by the Babylonians and Assyrians, whom they attempted to conquer.

Hornbill ivory Not true ivory, but rather the horn-like cask of any of several large tropical birds of the hornbill family. It is a warm yellow color with an exterior coating that may be red, reddish or other colors, and has long been admired and utilized by the Chinese and other Asians for small carvings, including beads.

Hot-pinched beads Glass tube beads that have been heated and constricted to form individual beads with simple hand tools. Made since about 300 B.C. in the Near East, the most famous variety are the gold sandwich-glass beads, made in Alexandria, Egypt and elsewhere of two layers of clear glass separated by a gold foil layer and made to imitate gold. Similar beads may have silver foil, yellow pigment simulating gold, or merely a yellow glass exterior.

Hubbell beads Named for Don Lorenzo Hubbell, a trading post operator in Arizona, the story suggests these were glass beads, made in Czechoslovakia to imitate fine Persian turquoise, and sold to Native Americans as a cheap substitute for the highly valued turquoise. This may be wrong or an exaggeration. The name currently applies to any glass bead resembling turquoise or items thought to be Hubbell beads, regardless of where such were made, how old they are, or whether they belonged to Native Americans.

Idar-Oberstein Towns in a German valley, famous for lapidary manufacture and possibly dating to Roman times. There is abundant water power to run cutting and polishing wheels and drills for perforating. Formerly, there were local sources of quartz and possibly other minerals for raw materials, but these have been largely exhausted and replaced by imported material, mostly South American. Area craftspeople excel in the artificial coloration of agates and chalcedonies, and provide the bulk of the world's commercially used onyx and carnelian. The beadmakers produced a large variety of agate beads, primarily for export.

Iridescence An aspect of glass decay in which the appearance of a metallic sheen or rainbow colors forms on the surface, thought to enhance the beauty of such pieces.

Islamic Period Era of expansion and domination by the Islam religion around the Near East and Arab states, North and East Africa, India and Southeast Asia from A.D. 632 into the seventeenth century. Near Eastern glassmaking just prior to and during this time is characterized by the continuation of Roman techniques and the development of new and original practices. Until recently these beads have not been distinguished from Roman Period products and were often dated too early or characterized as Roman.

Ivory Teeth or tusks of any vertebrate animal, but specifically elephant tusks. It is desired for its beautiful grain, creamy whiteness and relative hardness, combined with ease of cutting and rarity. Besides elephants, the hippopotamus, walrus, narwhal, sperm whale, wart hog and dugong provide teeth for carving as ivory. Most animals whose teeth are used for ivory are in danger of extinction; substitutes like Tagua nuts and plastics are encouraged.

Kaolinite An artificial compound made in the Indus Valley from kaolin clay dust, and possibly talc. It is used to make extremely small extruded beads, which are then hardened by firing.

Kiffa beads Glass beads traditionally made by women in Mauritania from recycled powdered glass formed into a paste by adding saliva and heated to fusion in an open fire. The surface is decorated by a labor-intensive process whereby powdered glass paste is applied in patterns using a metal needle.

Kirdi brass beads Lost-wax cast beads of brass or bronze, of small size and shaped as spheres, barrels and bicones as well as larger bells, rings and amuletic shapes. Popular since their importation from West Africa in the 1960s.

Krobo beads See Bodom beads.

Kyanos See Ceramics, Faience and Glass.

Lacquer See Cinnabar.

Lantana Jasper, banded agate or chalcedony beads made in Ilorin, Nigeria during the nineteenth to twentieth centuries.

Lampworking Process of heating and manipulating glass with a small apparatus, like a Bunsen burner, usually fed with liquid fuel (oil, tallow or gas) and made hot enough to melt glass by forced air. The process began in ancient times, but little is known before the sixteenth century when it came into use in Venice and other European glass centers. Lampworked beads can be monochrome or polychrome.

Land snail shell beads From the *Achatina sp.* of East Africa, these are hishi beads of diskoidal shape, usually white with brown markings and sometimes large in diameter.

Lapidary manufacture Processes of cutting, grinding, carving, and polishing minerals and other materials to form shape and decoration. In beadmaking, drilling is an important associated lapidary skill.

Lapis lazuli Mainly calcite with various blue minerals and often iron pyrites, this rock is highly desirable and rare. Only three sources are exploited today–Afghanistan, Russia and Chile, and the first is the most important. It was successfully simulated by faience, kyanos and glass in ancient times–and the desire to develop suitable substitutes may have instigated these industries.

Latticino An outdated term, originally coined to describe milk-white glass, but which has come to signify glass items decorated with fine lines, regardless of color. Another term is filigree glass, or retorte (Italian for twisted).

Leech beads Ancient beads of stone, glass or amber, thought to be shaped like a leech, being fairly flat on the underside, plump in the middle and tapered on the ends.

Lenticular Shape of the cross section of many ancient stone beads and a few faience beads from the Middle East. They are flat or tabular and the cross section is tapered like a lens. A less-tapered cross section is referred to as rhomboid.

Limoges enamel An extremely fine variety of patterned enamel made in France.

Loctite A methacrylic ester structural adhesive used for glass.

Lost-wax method Technique for casting metal objects, practiced since early times. A model is made in wax, then covered by clay slip and immersed in plaster or ceramic. The encasement is heated to melt the wax out and molten metal is poured into the resulting cavity.

Malachite A bright-green ore of copper, either botryoidal (with lines and spots) or grainy. It was used in antiquity as a pigment and cosmetic and as a decorative stone for beadmaking.

Mandrel Any rod or wire, straight or tapered and of variable diameter, used as a tool in making wound glass beads. Of such materials as iron, copper or brass, it provides a handle for working glass and forms the bead's perforation. It may be coated with slip for removal of the bead; otherwise, the bead is either knocked off, or acid is used to dissolve the wire.

Marble beads Small to very large spherical glass beads, resembling conventional marbles with perforations–which they are. However, they are not drilled marbles, but hot-pinched. Probably late nineteenth and early twentieth century products from Germany.

Marriage or conglomerate See Simulant.

Marvering A molten gather of glass is rolled across a flat surface to become amalgamated and shaped. Historically made from marble, hence the word marver, it is now usually an iron slab or sheet. Beadmakers marver beads to flatten or shape them.

Matrix Rock portion in which minerals are embedded.

Meerschaum White clay-like material, called sepiolite by mineralogists, typically from Turkey, made into beads and other small items. A similar material comes from East Africa and is likewise used for beadmaking.

Melon beads Bead shape referring to longitudinal lobes resembling the form of a typical melon. Also called lotus beads, they are somewhat similar to gadrooned beads. However, the lobes of melon beads are convex in cross section, while the spaces between gadroons are concave and the gadroons are flat in cross section.

Millefiori glass A thousand flowers in Italian, it refers to most common floral design patterns. A mosaic glass, millefiori beads were made in ancient times and had numerous sections of patterned canes placed in close proximity parallel to one another, and heated to fuse together. This pad of millefiori glass was then rolled upon itself and shaped to form a bead. When Italians reinvented millefiori glass (as early as the late fifteenth century), they usually applied the cane pieces to a separate base, often the bead's core, and fused the parts together; this is one way ancient beads may be distinguished.

Mohs scale System of relative hardness used in judging the composition of minerals. Numbers range from one to ten; one is the softest, representing talc, while ten is the hardness of diamond.

Mosaic glass Named for items that are formed in at least two operations. The glassworker begins by making various components and these preformed parts are then used to compose or decorate the desired piece. There are several types of such work, but the most popular and significant group is millefiori.

Mummy beads See Faience.

Netsuke See Toggle.

Nineveh Site of the capital of the Assyrian Empire on the Tigris River, replacing earlier cities dating back to the third millennium, and existing until 612 B.C.

Nueva Cádiz beads Primarily sixteenth century trade beads of cane manufacture, with a square straight or twisted cross section, normally long, blue and of three layers–the second layer of opaque white. Recovered at European contact sites in the Philippines, North and South America and Africa, their origin is controversial.

Ojime Japanese bead in an inro ensemble (case for tobacco, medicines and more) that serves as a slide closure for the strings holding the case. Highly collectible.

Open-face mold A mold shaped on only one side so the item can be easily removed. Ancient metal, faience and glass beads and amulets were often formed in such tools.

Pancake beads Flat or tabular beads of various materials originally appearing on the backs of Mandarin necklaces, below the baluster bead, often called a cloud bead or pei yün in China. Because they were suspended by ribbons or woven tapes, pancake beads frequently have flattened perforations.

Perlen German for beads of any variety or material, though the name implies pearls from mollusks.

Phœnician head pendants or beads Made for a long period beginning around sixth century B.C., in the Mediterranean world, these large glass pendants were made by fairly simple, sometimes crude means, probably at a glass furnace. Also called mask pendants, the head is hollow, having been made on a rod or core and open at the bottom. Usually depicted is a man's face, with large round eyes, a small protruding nose (often broken away), beard, mustache and facial ornaments, possibly representing jewelry or status marks. In ornate examples, the hair and beard are articulated curls of glass, made and applied strand by strand for an evocative effect. Animals and grotesques were also made. Female or young boy images are more rare and less well made. They are clearly related to similar eye beads of the period, consisting of stratified eyes and hemispherical bumps, set in rows around the circumference.

Plastics Artificial materials or synthetic resins made since 1869, when Celluloid was patented. There are numerous types with a variety of uses, but are mainly thermoplastic, softening when heated so they can be molded, and thermosetting, which cannot be remelted once manufactured. The latter group was invented in 1908, beginning with Bakelite. By the late 1920s, cast phenolic plastics were invented which were translucent and colorful, as well as hard and durable. Bakelite was dry-molded, always of dark opaque colors and almost never used in jewelry. Cast phenolics were abundant in the costume jewelry industries of the 1930s and 1940s, and very popular for beads, brooches, pendants, buckles, and dress ornaments. Early plastics were used to imitate natural substances used as decorative materials like ivory, amber, jet, and coral. Phenolics were also used in this manner, but eventually became original and non-imitative. Their use was labor-intensive since objects were hand-formed by lapidary techniques of cutting, grinding, polishing, and drilling. Plastics have always been used to copy favored beads for foreign markets around the world; amber continues to be the most copied substance. Beginning in the middle 1980s, doughy plastics, called polyform, polymer or polymer clay, with such brand names as Fimo, Cernit and Sculpey, began to be used by craftspeople to make jewelry based on sculptural ceramic and traditional glassworking techniques.

Polychrome beads See Lampworking.

Porcelain Somewhat translucent white ceramic, made from kaolin clay and feldspar, by the Chinese as early as the seventh century. The term comes from the Italian porcellana, little pigs, and refers to the similarity to cowrie shells, called piggy shells in Italy.

Powder glass beads A class of beadmaking in which the raw material is glass ground to a fine powder, often recycled glass or glass beads. The powder may be dry-molded or wet-packed, sometimes using saliva as a binder. When molds are used they are usually fired or unfired clay. Most are from Ghana, Nigeria and Mauritania. Among the most desirable are the old Bodom and Kiffa beads. Ghana produces a great many for export, incorrectly called sand cast beads.

Quartz Mineral family from which the greatest number of stone beads have been made, from ancient to modern times. A pure form of silica, primary varieties used in beadmaking are rock crystals, agates, chalcedonies, jaspers, and opals. Among the most popular are carnelians, banded and spotted agates, amethyst, adventurine, tiger eye, and bloodstone.

Rayed beads An ancient shape for beads of faience or other materials, consisting of a central axis on which several arms extend forming rays, producing a star-shaped exterior.

Rebus Symbolic device in China and elsewhere in which a word that sounds like another is used to represent that quality or object. For example, the Chinese words for bat and happiness sound alike; therefore, a gift of a bat carving is an expression of happiness.

Register A band of pattern(s) around the girth of a bead.

Retorte See Latticino.

Rhomboid See Lenticular.

Sassanian Dynasty The Sassanids ruled the Persian Empire after the fall of the Parthians between A.D. 224 until 640, when they fell to Arab domination. They made many varieties of beads including distinctive etched carnelians.

Scorzalite A fairly rare blue mineral, strongly resembling lapis lazuli, made into beads where it is acquired in West Africa.

Segi beads Also written seghi and seggi, these are native-made glass beads, often blue in color, acquired in Nigeria. Their manufacture may represent a crude form of cane beadmaking, though without a gather being drawn into a long tube. Historically related to much older aggrey beads.

Seed corals and pearls Tiny beads that suggest the seed of a plant. Though copied in less precious materials, seed corals and pearls were used sparingly or extravagantly for beadwork constructions and embroidery trims by Asians, Indians and Europeans. Glass seed beads were made to supplement or replace their use.

Simulant An imitation or simulant looks like the prototype, but may be a different material or may be artificial rather than natural; a replica is a duplicate of an item from the same materials and techniques. Fakes and forgeries may be either of these, but made with the intention to fool a buyer. Synthetics are man-made but chemically identical copies of a material (for instance, a synthetic ruby of man-made corundum). A transposition replicates the external shape or appearance of the prototype in another material, but is not meant to fool. Since ancient times, transpositions have been very popular. A marriage or conglomerate begins with two authentic items, originally not related or connected, that are joined together into one piece. These are again made with the intention of fooling the consumer into believing the item is authentic. Not all imitations, simulants, replications, or fakes are undesirable or uncollectible. The long practice of creating such items often means they are of great antiquity and rarity. In addition, the acceptance of these objects by those who used them makes the items culturally significant. Finally, when a popular object has been made over a period of time, its form may become degraded or less well made than the initial prototype. These degraded specimens are often thought of as being fakes of the originals, and of considerably less value, when they are merely less-refined versions of the same object.

Slurry Liquid compound developed within a stone bead during the drilling of its perforation. A combination of stone dust and water, it aids the drilling as much as the bit itself. It also refers to a similar viscous liquid compound made to enhance fusing in the manufacture of faience and ceramics. Also called slip.

Talhakimt West or North African name for ornaments typically of agate, but other materials as well, probably based on the shape of a finger ring, but most often worn on the coiffure or in necklaces. They probably originated in India, but later ones are either local or imported from Europe, and may be glass or plastic.

Terra cotta A general term for earthenwares of crude clay, and colored buff, red or reddish to brown. (See Ceramics.)

Toggle Small carvings of various materials (primarily organics, minerals and glass), usually perforated for suspension with a short off-center or back hanger. Called netsuke in Japan, they serve as belt ornaments used to hang other personal items.

Trail decoration The application of a heated, viscous stream of glass onto a base to create patterns. It is distinct from mosaic glass decoration, in which preformed elements are laid down, and consists of either creating a string of near-liquid glass directly from a crucible, or by taking a preformed rod of glass and heating it to this state.

Transposition See Simulant.

—— *Composed by Jamey Allen.*

ORGANIZATIONS

BEAD SOCIETIES

ALASKA
Juneau Bead Society
c/o The Bead Gallery
201 Seward
Juneau, AK 99801

ARIZONA
Arizona Bead Society
P.O. Box 80111
Arcadia Station 072
Phoenix, AZ 85060-0111

Tucson Bead Society
P.O. Box 14271
Tucson, AZ 85732-4271

CALIFORNIA
The Bead Society
P.O. Box 241874
Los Angeles, CA 90024-9674

Bead Society of Orange County
Bowers Museum Gallery Store
2002 N. Main St.
Santa Ana, CA 92706

Bead Society of San Diego County
P.O. Box 230325
Encinitas, CA 92023-0325

Northern California Bead Society
1650 Lower Grand Ave.
Piedmont, CA 94611

COLORADO
Rocky Mountain Bead Society
2582 Arapahoe Ave.
Boulder, CO 80302

DISTRICT OF COLUMBIA
Bead Society of Greater Washington
P.O. Box 70036
Chevy Chase, MD 20813-0036

FLORIDA
Bead Society of Central Florida
121 Larkspur Dr.
Altamonte Springs, FL 32701

Bead Society of North Florida
c/o Chevron Trading Post & Bead Co.
2320 N. Monroe St.
Tallahassee, FL 32303

Florida West Coast Bead Society
6300 Flotilla Dr. #79
Holmes Beach, FL 34217

Tampa Bay Bead Society
P.O. Box 280315
Tampa, FL 33682-0315

GEORGIA
Atlanta Bead Society
c/o Gerold Baxter
1687 Monroe Dr., Apt. C-8
Atlanta, GA 30324

HAWAII
Bead Society of Hawaii—Maui
P.O. Box 12127
Lahaina, Maui, HI 96761

Bead Society of Hawaii—Oahu
2414 Kuhio St.
Honolulu, HI 96815

Oahu Bead Society
Norma Lanai
95-128 Pipapa Dr. #405
Mililani, HI 96789

IDAHO
Bead Brains Anonymous
P.O. Box 1501
Sandpoint, ID 83864

Coeur d'Alene Bead Society
P.O. Box 5301
Coeur d'Alene, ID 83814-1955

ILLINOIS
Bead Society of Greater Chicago
P.O. Box 8103
Wilmette, IL 60091

Chicago Midwest Bead Society
1020 Davis St.
Evanston, IL 60201

LOUISIANA
Baton Rouge Bead Society
c/o Jane Olson
919 Bromley Dr.
Baton Rouge, LA 70808

MARYLAND
Baltimore Bead Society
P.O. Box 311
Riderwood, MD 21139-0311

Bead Society of Greater Washington
P.O. Box 70036
Chevy Chase, MD 20813-0036

MASSACHUSETTS
Beadesigner International
P.O. Box 503
Lincoln, MA 01773

Massachusetts Bead Society
119 Burlington
Lexington, MA 02173

MICHIGAN
Great Lakes Beadworkers Guild
P.O. Box 1639
Royal Oak, MI 48068

MINNESOTA
Upper Midwest Bead Society
c/o Beautiful Beads
115 Hennepin Ave.
Minneapolis, MN 55401

MONTANA
Billings Bead Society
1727 Miles Ave.
Billings, MT 59102

Bozeman Bead Society
Old Bozeman Gifts
321 W. Main
Bozeman, MT 59715

NEW JERSEY
Bead Society of New Jersey
P.O. Box 7465
Shrewsbury, NJ 07702

NEW MEXICO
New Mexico Bead Society
P.O. Box 36824
Albuquerque, NM 87176-6824

NEW YORK
Bead Society of Greater New York
P.O. Box 427
New York, NY 10116-0427

OHIO
Bead Society of Central Ohio
249 King Ave.
Columbus, OH 43201

OREGON
Portland Bead Society
P.O. Box 10611
Portland, OR 97210

PENNSYLVANIA
Brandywine Bead Society
1116 Dorset Dr.
West Chester, PA 19382-8008

TEXAS
Austin Bead Society
P.O. Box 656
Austin, TX 78767-0656

Dallas Bead Society
10407 Shadow Bend Dr.
Dallas, TX 75230

Panhandle Bead Association
c/o Beth Barringer
P.O. Box 3747
Amarillo, TX 79116

San Antonio Bead
  and Ornament Society
P.O. Box 700611
San Antonio, TX 78231-0611

VIRGINIA
Northern Virginia Bead Society
P.O. Box 2465
Fairfax, VA 22031

Bead Society of Greater Washington
P.O. Box 70036
Chevy Chase, MD 20813-0036

WASHINGTON
Bead Group of The Palouse
c/o Aviva Suchow
321 Webb St., N.W.
Pullman, WA 99163

Northwest Bead Society
P.O. Box 15881
Seattle, WA 98115-0881

Olympic Bead Society
P.O. Box 27
Quilcene, WA 98376

Spokane-Northwest Bead Society
P.O. Box 1208
Mead, WA 99021

WISCONSIN
Madison Bead Society
819 E. Johnson St.
Madison, WI 53703

CANADA
Bead Society of Greater Vancouver
Richmond Arts Center
7700 Minoru Gate
Richmond, B.C. Canada V6B 3AO

Calgary Bead Society
#507 320 Meredith Rd., N.E.
Calgary, Alberta Canada T2E 5A6

GREAT BRITAIN
Bead Society of Great Britain
c/o Carole Morris
1 Casburn Lane
Burwell, Cambridgeshire CB5 0ED
United Kingdom

GHANA
Ghana Bead Society
P. O. Box C788
Cantonments, Accra
Ghana

HUNGARY
Hungarian Bead Society
c/o Anna Fehér
1104 Budapest, Harmat u. 65/B.3.
Hungary

BEAD INTEREST GROUPS
National Polymer Clay Guild
1350 Beverly Rd., Suite 115-345
McLean, VA 22101
(POLYinforMER Newsletter)

The Pearl Society
Eve J. Alfillé, Ltd.
623 Grove St.
Evanston, IL 60201
(Pearl Society Newsletter)

Society of Glass Beadmakers
c/o Leah Fairbanks
12 Bayo Vista Way
San Rafael, CA 94901

RESEARCH
The Bead Museum
Director: Gabrielle Liese
138-140 S. Montezuma
Prescott, AZ 86303
(Bead Museum Quarterly)

Bead Study Trust
c/o Dr. C.R. Chippindale
University Museum of Archaeology
  and Anthropology
Downing Street
Cambridge CB2 3DZ
United Kingdom
(Bead Study Trust Newsletter)

Bead Study Trust
Mrs. M.E. Hutchinson, Secretary
29 Elliscombe Rd.
Charlton London SE7 79F
United Kingdom

Center for Bead Research
Director: Peter Francis Jr.
4 Essex St.
Lake Placid, NY 12946
(Numerous bead series, monographs
  and newsletters)

Center for the Study of Beadwork
Director: Alice Scherer
P.O. Box 13719
Portland, OR 97213
(Notes from a Beadworkers Journal)

European Bead Network
c/o Natacha Wolters
Badenallee 1
D14052 Berlin (Charlottenburg)
Germany
(Perles-Info, a French & English newsletter)

Society of Bead Researchers
c/o Lester Ross
P.O. Box 7304
Eugene, OR 97401
(Bead Forum and Beads, an annual periodical)

Society of Bead Researchers
Karlis Karklins
1600 Liverpool Ct.
Ottawa, Canada K1A OH3

PUBLICATIONS
Bead & Button
P.O. Box 1020
Norwalk, CT 06856
(Bimonthly)

Lapidary Journal
60 Chestnut Ave., Suite 201
Devon, PA 19333
(Monthly)

The Bead Directory
Linda Benmour
P.O. Box 10103
Oakland, CA 94610
(Annual)

REFERENCES AND BIBLIOGRAPHY

INTRODUCTION

Beck, H.C. 1928 Classification and nomenclature of beads and pendants. *Archae-ologia* 77, 2nd Ser.: 1-76.

Byrd, J., R. Poole and L. Byrd 1992 The olde bead monger's trade bead sketchbook. Texarkana, Rebel Publishing Co., Inc.: 64 p.

Coles, J. and R. Budwig 1990 The book of beads. New York, Simon and Schuster: 125 p.

Delarozière, M.F. 1985 Mauritanian beads. *Ornament* 8(3): 24-27.

Dubin, L.S. 1987 The history of beads. From 30,000 B.C. to the present. New York, Harry N. Abrams: 364 p.

Francis Jr., P. 1993 Ghana, West Africa, where beads are loved. Center for Bead Research, Beads and People Series 2: 22 p.

Liu, R.K. 1984 African-made glass ornaments. Survey & experimental results. *Ornament* 8(2): 52-57, 23.

——1978 Beads: Ornaments from everywhere. Time-Life, The Encyclopedia of Collectibles: 6-21.

Moss, K. and A. Scherer 1992 The new beadwork. New York, Harry N. Abrams: 112 p.

Opper, M.-J. and H. Opper 1989 Kiffa beads. Mauritanian powdered glass beads. Privately published: unpaginated

Ukai, N. 1980 Kyoyu Asao, tombodama/glass bead master. *Ornament* 4(3): 13-18.

——1984 Kyoyu Asao. Glass bead master, new work. *Ornament* 7(3): 2-5.

van der Sleen, W.G.N. 1973 A handbook on beads. Liege, Librairie Halbert: 142 p.

White, R. 1993 The dawn of adornment. *Natural History* 102(5): 60-67.

CHAPTER 1

Adamson, J. 1967 The peoples of Kenya. New York, Harcourt Brace Jovanovich: 400 p.

Allen, J.D. 1976a Amber and its substitutes. Pt. II: Mineral analyses. *Bead Journal* 2(4): 11-22.

——1976b Amber and its substitutes. Pt. III: Is it real? Testing amber. *Bead Journal* 3(1): 20-31.

——1983a Chevron-star-rosetta beads: Pt. I. *Ornament* 7(1): 19-24, 40.

——1983b Chevron-star-rosetta beads: Pt. II. *Ornament* 7(2): 24-29, 40.

——1984a Chevron-star-rosetta beads: Pt. III. *Ornament* 7(3): 24-27, 41.

——1984b Chevron-star-rosetta beads: Pt. IV. *Ornament* 7(4): 24-26, 42-47.

Beck, H.C. 1928 Classification and nomenclature of beads and pendants. *Archae-ologia* 77, 2nd Ser.: 1-76.

Bedford, E. (ed.) 1993 Ezakwantu. Beadwork from the Eastern Cape. Cape Town, South African National Gallery: 112 p.

Blauer, E. 1986 Rhodia Mann. Jewelry with an African flavor. *Ornament* 10(2): 59-61.

Borel, F. 1994 The splendor of ethnic jewelry. From the Collette and Jean-Pierre Ghysels collection. New York, Harry N. Abrams, Inc.: 256 p.

Brincard, M.-T. (ed.) 1984 Beauty by design: the aesthetics of African adornment. New York, African-American Institute: 136 p.

Carey, M. 1986 Beads and beadwork of East and South Africa. Princes Risborough, Shire Ethnography: 64 p.

——1991 Beads and beadwork of West and Central Africa. Princes Risborough, Shire Ethnography: 56 p.

Casady, D. 1986 October program review. Aesthetics and value in the wearing of African beads. *Bead Society Newsletter*, Los Angeles XII(3): 10-11.

Casady, R. and D. Casady 1974 A sample book of Venetian beads from 1704. *Bead Journal* 1(1): 19-21.

Chesi, G. 1977 The last Africans. Worgl, Perlinger-Verlags: 245 p.

Codrington, K.D.B. 1932 Tibetan etched agate beads. *Man* 32(156): 128.

Cole, H.M. 1974 Artistic and communicative value of beads in Kenya and Ghana. *Bead Journal* 1(3): 29-37.

——and D.H. Ross 1977 The arts of Ghana. Los Angeles, Museum of Cultural History: 230 p.

Creyaufmüller, W. 1983 Agades cross pendants. Structural components & their modifications. Pt. I *Ornament* 7(2): 16-21, 60-6l.

——1984 Agades cross pendants. Structural components & their modifications. Pt. II *Ornament* 7(3): 37-39.

Davis, R. 1975 Correspondence: More on S. P. Quiatoni pendants. *Bead Journal* 2(2): 1-3.

Davison, C.C., R.D. Giauque and J.D. Clark 1971 Two chemical groups of dichroic glass beads from West Africa. *Man* 6(4): 645-659.

DeCorse, C.R. 1989 Beads as chronological indicators in West African archaeology.

A reexamination. *Beads* 1: 41-53.

Delarozière, M.F. 1985a Mauritanian beads. *Ornament* 8(3): 24-27.

——1985b Les perles de Mauritanie. Aix-en-Provence, Edisud: 155 p.

——1994 Perles d'Afrique. Aix-en-Provence, Edisud: 240 p.

de Negri, E. 1962 Nigerian jewellery. *Nigeria Magazine* (74): 42-54.

Diamanti, P. 1991 Trends in the bead business. *Bead Society Greater Washington Newsletter* VIII(4): 1-3.

Diamond, H.L. 1978 Correspondence: Arca ornaments. *Bead Journal* 3(3/4): 73.

Dubin, L.S. 1987 The history of beads. From 30,000 B.C. to the present. New York, Harry N. Abrams: 364 p.

Fisher, A. 1984 Africa adorned. New York, Harry N. Abrams: 304 p.

Francis Jr., P. 1982a Bead report: Pt. VII: When India was beadmaker to the world. *Ornament* 6(2): 33-34, 56-57.

——1982b Indian agate beads. Lapis Route Books, World of Beads Monograph Series 6: 52 p.

——1988 The Giacomuzzi Venetian bead sample book. *Bead Museum Quarterly* 2(3): 3-4.

——1989 Beads of the early Islamic period. *Beads* 1: 21-39.

——1990a Beadmaking in Islam. The African trade and the rise of Hebron. *Beads* 2 [1991]: 15-28.

——1990b Bead news roundup no. 11. *Bead Study Trust Newsletter* (16): 2-4.

——1990c Beads in Ghana (West Africa) Pt. 2 *Margaretologist* 3(2): 3-12.

——1990d Bead report: The greatest trade bead of all time. *Ornament* 13(3): 78-82.

——1991 Book review: Picard and Picard: Beads from the West African Trade Series, Volumes V and VI. *Beads* 3 [1992]: 89-91.

——1992a Romancing the hidden bead. *Bead Forum* (21): 12-15.

——1992b Bead report: West African perspective. Lost-wax brass casting. *Ornament* 15(4): 98-99.

——1992c Bead report: West African perspective. The early bead trade. *Ornament* 16(1): 98-101

——1992d Bead report: West African perspective. The size of the trade. *Ornament* 16(2): 98-101.

——1993a Ghana, West Africa, where beads are loved. Center for Bead Research, Beads and People Series 2: 22 p.

——1993b Bead report: Markets and the alteration of beads in West Africa. *Ornament* 16(3): 96-97, 100-101.

——1993c Bead report: West African powder glass beads. *Ornament* 16(4): 96-97, 100-101.

Frazier, S. and A. Frazier 1993 A different money market. *Lapidary Journal* 47(7): 52-56, 58, 60, 62, 64, 66.

Garrard, T.F. 1989 Gold of Africa. Jewellery and ornaments from Ghana, Côte d'Ivoire, Mali and Senegal in the collection of the Barbier-Müller Museum. Munich, Prestel Verlag: 247 p.

Geary, C.M. 1991 Old pictures, new approaches. Researching historical photo-graphs. *In*: Special issue: Historical photographs of Africa. *African Arts* XXIV (4): 36-39.

Gumpert, A. 1985 Magical Morocco. *Bead Society of Greater Washington Newsletter* 11(4): 5-6.

——1989a Howard Opper on "Collecting beads in north and west Africa." *Bead Society Greater Washington Newsletter* VI(1): 7-8.

——1989b Collectors News. *Bead Society Greater Washington Newsletter* VI(3): 8.

——1990 Program notes: March 8, 1990. Howard Opper on Kiffa beads of Mauritania. *Bead Society Greater Washington Newsletter* VII(3): 7-8.

Haigh, J. 1991 Ghana's bead-making industry flourishes. *Appropriate Technology* 18(3): 20-23.

Harris, E.J. 1982a Nueva Cádiz and associated beads. A new look. Lancaster, G.B. Fenstermaker: 15 p.

——1982b Bead detective. [Los Angeles], *Bead Society Newsletter* VII(5): 5.

——1984a Marbeled beads. [Los Angeles], *Bead Society Newsletter* IX(5): 7.

——1984b Late beads in the African trade. Lancaster, G.B. Fenstermaker: 16 p.

——1991 Made in Africa. I. Vegetable. Prescott, *Bead Museum Quarterly* 6(1): 1.

——1992a Made in Africa. II. Animal. A. Vertebrates. Prescott, *Bead Museum Quarterly* 6(2): 3.

——1992b Made in Africa. II. Animal. B. Mollusks and coral. Prescott, *Bead Museum Quarterly* 6(3): 3-4.

——1993a Made in Africa. III. Mineral C. Silver, D. Base metals. Prescott, *Bead Museum Quarterly* 7(2/3): 6-9.

——1993b Made in Africa. IV. Glass. A. Wound beads. Prescott, *Bead Museum Quarterly* 7(4): 4-6.

——1993c Made in Africa. IV. Glass. B. Powder glass. Prescott, *Bead Museum Quarterly* 8(1): 4-6.

Harter, P. 1992 The beads of Cameroon. Translated by H. Opper. *Beads* 4 [1993]: 5-20.

Insoll, T. 1994 The illicit bead trade in Gao, the Republic of Mali. *Bead Forum* (24): 6-10.

Kaplan, J. 1993 African post cards offer rich images for historians' research. *Smithsonian Institution Research Reports* (74): 1, 6.

Karklins, K. 1982a The Levin catalogue of mid-19th century beads. *In: Glass beads. History and Archaeology* 59: 5-38.

——1982b A sample book of 19th-century Venetian beads. *In: Glass beads. History and Archaeology* 59: 39-82.

——1982c Guide to the description and classification of glass beads. *In: Glass beads. History and Archaeology* 59: 83-117.

——1985 Glass beads: The Levin catalogue of mid-19th century beads; A sample book of 19th century Venetian beads; Guide to the description and classification of glass beads. Parks Canada: 123 p.

——1992 Identifying beads used in the 19th century Central East Africa trade. *Beads* 4 [1993]: 49-59.

Kaufmann, C. 1993 The bead rush. Development of the nineteenth-century bead trade from Cape Town to King William's Town. *In:* Bedford (ed.): 47-55.

Kenoyer, J.M. 1986 The Indus bead industry. Contributions to bead technology. *Ornament* 10(1): 18-23.

Laidler, P.W. 1934 Beads in Africa south of the Zambesi. *Proceedings. Rhodesia Scientific Association* 34(1): 1-27.

Lamb, A. 1972 Some observations on glass beads in Ghana, West Africa. *In:* Annales du 5e Congrès International d'Etude Historique du Verre, Prague, 6-11 juillet 1970: 247-250.

——1976 Krobo powder-glass beads. *African Arts* 9(3): 32-39.

——1978 Some 17th century glass beads from Ghana, West Africa. *Bead Journal* 2(3/4): 23-27.

Liu, R.K. 1974a Cover story. *Bead Journal* 1(1): 3-5.

——1974b Factory-made copies of native beads. *Bead Journal* 1(1): 6-18.

——1974c African mold-made glass beads. *Bead Journal* 1(2): 8-14.

——1975a Conus shell discs revisited. *Bead Journal* 2(1): 30-32.

——1975b Editorial. *Bead Journal* 2(2): 1.

——1975c Early 20th century bead catalogs. *Bead Journal* 2(2): 31-32.

——1976a Molded and interlocking glass beads. *Bead Journal* 2(3): 33-37.

——1976b Identification. Arca copies. *Bead Journal* 3(1): 39-40.

——1977 Talhakimt (talhatana), a Tuareg ornament. Its origins, derivatives, copies and distribution. *Bead Journal* 3(2): 18-22.

——1978a Identification: Nueva Cádiz. *Bead Journal* 3(3/4): 77.

——1978b Spindle whorls. Pt. I, some comments and speculations. *Bead Journal* 3(3/4): 87-103.

——1978c Identification: Arca simulations in glass. *Bead Journal* 3(3/4): 39-40.

——1978d Followup: Snake vertebrae. *Bead Journal* 3(3/4): 42.

——1980a Simulated materials in jewelry. *Ornament* 4(4): 18-26.

——1980b Followup: [Glass talhakimt]. *Ornament* 4(4): 41.

——1982a Amira Françoise. Living with beads in the Sudan. *Ornament* 5(4): 24-27.

——1982b Exhibition review. Museum für Volkerkunde. *Ornament* 6(1): 40.

——1983a Special pictorial: Bead packaging. *Ornament* 6(3): 57-58.

——1983b Dan Frost bead collection. *Ornament* 6(3): 25-29.

——1984a The bead in African assembled jewelry: its multiple manifestations. *In:* Brincard (ed.): unpaginated.

——1984b Imported Chinese jewelry. *Ornament* 7(4): 56-61, 53.

——1984c Identification: Carnelian beads and their simulations. *Ornament* 8(1): 14-17.

——1984d African-made glass ornaments. Survey & experimental results. *Ornament* 8(2): 52-57, 23.

——1984e Identification: Plain and twisted Nueva Cádiz. *Ornament* 8(2): 68, 67.

——1985a Identification: Transpositions. *Ornament* 8(4): 67.

——1985b Identification: [Smallest and largest beads]. *Ornament* 9(1): 69.

——1985c Exhibition review: Beauty by design. The aesthetics of African adornment. *Ornament* 9(2): 56.

——1987 India, Idar-Oberstein and Czechoslovakia. Imitators and competitors. *Ornament* 10(4): 56-61.

——1988a Identification: Granitic beads and their simulations. *Ornament* 11(4): 25.

——1988b Collectibles: Kenyan necklaces. *Ornament* 12(2): 74-75.

——1990a Collectibles: Picard African necklace collection. *Ornament* 13(3): 8-9.

——1990b Wholesale to the trade: Bwanacon. *Ornament* 14(1): 86-87.

——1991a Collectibles: Conus shell ornaments. *Ornament* 14(4): 16-17.

——1991b Collectibles: Powder glass beads. *Ornament* 15(1): 8-81.

——1991c Wholesale to the trade: Wind River. *Ornament* 15(1):104-105.

——1991d Wholesale to the trade: Niger Bend. *Ornament* 15(2):104-105.

——1992a Collectibles: Imitations and fakes. *Ornament* 16(1): 16-17.

——1992b Wholesale to the trade: Picard African Imports. *Ornament* 16(2): 96-97.

Mack, J. (ed.) 1988 Ethnic jewelry. New York, Harry N. Abrams: 207 p.

Nourisson, P. 1992 Beads in the lives of the peoples of southern Togo, West Africa. Translated by P. Nadon. *Beads* 4 [1993]: 29-36.

O'Hear, A. 1986 Ilorin lantana beads. *African Arts* XIX(4): 36-39, 87-88.

Opper, M.-J. 1990 Scented magic beads in Africa. Alexandria, privately published: 26 p.

——and H. Opper 1989a Kiffa beads. Mauritanian powdered glass beads. Privately published: unpaginated.

——1989b A custom among the Laobe women of Senegal. *Bead Society Greater Washington Newsletter* VI(2): 5-6.

——1989c Diakhite. A study of the beads from an 18th-19th century burial site in Senegal, West Africa. *Beads* 1: 5-20.

——1989d Rare Mauritanian Kiffa beads. *Ornament* 12(3): 32-35.

——1989e Followup: Granitic beads and their simulations. *Ornament* 13(1): 74.

——1990a Ancient amazonite and scorzalite beads. *Ornament* 13(3): 34-37, 6, 13, 15.

——1990b Beads from the Faleme River Valley. An archaeological and ethnographic report of a research mission to eastern Senegal. Privately published: 65 p.

——1992 An update on Kiffa beads. *Bead Society Greater Washington Newsletter* IV(1): 4-5.

——1993 Powdered-glass beads and bead trade in Mauritania. *Beads* 5 [1995]: 37-44.

Osburn, A. 1992 A testament to life. Dan Telleen. *Ornament* 15(4): 66-69.

Picard, J. and R. Picard 1986a Chevron beads from the West African trade. Picard African Imports I: 16 p.

——1986b Tabular beads from the West African trade. Picard African Imports II: 6 p.

——1987 Fancy beads from the West African trade. Picard African Imports III: 16 p.

——1988 White hearts, feather and eye beads from the West African trade. Picard African Imports IV: 36 p.

——1989 Russian blues, faceted and fancy beads from the West African trade. Picard African Imports V: 44 p.

——1991 Millefiori beads from the West African trade. Picard African Imports VI: 88 p.

——1993 Chevron and Nueva Cádiz beads. Picard African Imports VII: 128 p.

Ross, A.L. 1991 Wholesale to the trade: Liza Wataghani. *Ornament* 14(3): 86-87.

Saitowitz, S. 1993 Towards a history of glass beads. *In:* Bedford (ed.): 35-45.

Schienerl, P.W. 1979 The amuletic significance of swords and daggers in Islamic jewelry. *Ornament* 4(2): 30-33.

Smith, W.H. 1979 Viewpoint: Kirdi brass jewelry. *Ornament* 4(1): 42-44.

Steiner, C. 1990 West African trade beads. Symbols of tradition. *Ornament* 14(1): 58-61.

Trebbin, C. 1985 Achate, geschliffen in Idar-Oberstein-Amulette, Schmuck und Zahlungsmittel in Afrika. Museum Idar-Oberstein 6: 39 p.

van der Sleen, W.G.N. 1973 A handbook on beads. Liege, Librairie Halbert: 142 p.

van der Zwan, N. 1985 Oog voor kralen. Berg en Dal, Afrika Museum: 44 p.

Wente-Lukas, R. 1977 Die materielle kultur der nicht-islamischen Ethnien von Nord-kamerun und Nordostnigeria. Studien zur Kulturkunde, Wiesbaden 43: 1-305.

CHAPTER 2

Abellera, B.C. 1981 The heirloom beads of Lubo, Kalinga-Apayao. M.A., Asian Center, University of the Philippines: 180 p.

An, J. 1991 The early glass of China. *In:* Brill and Martin (eds.): 5-19.

Banes, H. 1988-89 Chinese beads, their symbols and materials. *Bead Society Greater Washington Newsletter* V(5): 1-3.

Bartholomew, T.T. 1985 The hundred flowers. Botanical motifs in Chinese art. Asian Art Museum of San Francisco: 15 p.

——1988a Myths and rebuses in Chinese art. Asian Art Museum of San Francisco: 21 p.

——1988b Pious hopes carved on Chinese beads. A discussion of rebuses and legends in Chinese art. *Orientations* 19(8): 23-30.

Beck, H.C. 1928 Classification and nomenclature of beads and pendants. *Archaeologia* 77, 2nd Ser.: 1-76.

Blair, D. 1951 East Asiatic glass. Part I: China. *Glass Industry* 32(7): 347-369.

Brill, R.H and J.H. Martin (eds.) 1991 Scientific research in early Chinese glass. Proceedings of the Archeometry of Glass sessions of the 1984 International Symposium on Glass, Beijing, September 7, 1984 with supplementary papers. Corning Museum of Glass: 212 p.

——I.L. Barnes and E.C. Joel 1991 Lead isotope studies of early Chinese glasses. *In:* Brill and Martin (eds.): 65-83.

——S.S.C. Tong and D. Dohrenwend 1991 Chemical analyses of some early Chinese glass. *In:* Brill and Martin (eds.): 31-58.

Brown, C. and D. Rabiner 1987 The Robert H. Clague Collection. Chinese glass of the Qing Dynasty 1644-1911. Phoenix Art Museum: 96 p.

——1990 Clear as crystal, red as flame. Later Chinese glass. China Institute in America: 103 p.

Cammann, S.V.R. 1962 Substance and symbol in Chinese toggles. Chinese belt toggles from the C.F. Bieber collection. Philadelphia, University of Pennsylvania Press: 256 p.

——1979 Ch'ing Dynasty "mandarin chains" *Ornament* 4(1): 25-29.

Chen, C.H. 1978 Formosan primitive art. Vol. 1. Taipei, Museum of Formosan Primitive Art: 86 p.

Chen, C.L. 1968 Material culture of the Formosan aborigines. Taiwan Museum: 422 p.

Cheng, T.K. 1963 Archaeology in China. Volume three: Chou China. Cambridge, University of Toronto Press: 183-199.

Ch'in, H.Y. 1986 Catalogue of the exhibition of Ch'ing Dynasty costume accessories. Taiwan, National Palace Museum: 352 p.

Chu, A. and G. Chu 1973 Oriental antiques and collectibles, a guide. New York, Crown Publishers Inc.: 248 p.

Curtis, E.B. 1991 Glass for K'ang Hsi's court. *Arts of Asia* 21(5): 130-136.

Dale, G. 1981 London letter: Bead shopping in the Far East. *Ornament* 5(2): 59.

Darmody, L. 1987 Beads in Sarawak. *Ornament* 11(2): 28-29, 70-71.

Dohrenwend, D. 1980-81 Glass in China. *Oriental Art, NS* 26(4): 426-446.

Dubin, L.S. 1987 The history of beads. From 30,000 B.C. to the present. New York, Harry N. Abrams: 364 p.

Engle, A. 1976 Readings in glass history 6-7. Jerusalem, Phoenix Publications: 142 p.

Eyster, F.L. 1988 Bead buying in Hong Kong, Manila and Honolulu. *Bead Society Greater Washington Newsletter* V(3): 3-4.

Fan, S. and B. Zhou 1991 Some glass in the Museum of Chinese History. *In:* Brill and Martin (eds.): 193-200.

Fenstermaker, G.B. and A.T. Williams 1979 The Chinese bead. Lancaster, G.B. Fenstermaker: 51 p.

Fitzhugh, W.W. and A. Crowell 1988 Crossroads of continents. Cultures of Siberia and Alaska. Washington, Smithsonian Institution Press: 360 p.

Francis Jr., P. 1986 Chinese glass beads. A review of the evidence. Center for Bead Research Occasional Papers (2): 47 p.

——1988 Beads and bead trade in the North Pacific region. Appendix I. *In:* Fitzhugh and Crowell: 341.

——1990a Glass beads of China. *Arts of Asia* 20(5): 118-127.

——1990b Bead report: Chinese coil beads. *Ornament* 14(1): 66-67, 69-70.

——1990c Bead report: Peking glass beads. *Ornament* 14(2): 66-67, 69.

——1991a Bead report: The plumbum clue. *Ornament* 14(3): 62-63.

——1991b Bead report: Two distinctive Chinese glass beads. *Ornament* 14(4): 82-83.

——1992 Heirlooms of the hills: Southeast Asia. Center for Bead Research, Beads and People Series 1: 22 p.

Frankel, E.J. and J. Frankel 1993 Cinnabar. For lacquer of a better name. Exhibition brochure, E. and J. Frankel: 4 p.

Fukai, S. 1977 Persian glass. Weatherhill/Tankosha: 66 p., 89 plates.

Hansen, H.H. 1993 Mongol costumes. London, Thames and Hudson: 283 p.

Hardie, P. 1983 The origins of Chinese carved overlay glass. *Journal of Glass Studies* 25: 231-237.

Harris, E.J. 1983 Chinese pressed glass beads? [Los Angeles], *Bead Society Newsletter* IX(2): 6-7.

——1984a Fancy Chinese beads. [Los Angeles], *Bead Society Newsletter* IX(6): 8-9.

——1984b More Chinese beads. [Los Angeles], *Bead Society Newsletter* X(2): 10.

Jenkins, M.R. 1975 Letters: Comments on early Chinese glass beads. *Bead Journal* 1(3): 6.

Kan, P. and R.K. Liu 1984 Chinese glass beadmaking. *Ornament* 8(2): 38-40, 67.

Kano, T. and K. Segawa 1956 An illustrated ethnography of Formosan aborigines. Vol. 1, The Yami (rev. ed.). Tokyo, Maruzen Co.: 456 p.

Liu, M.C. 1979 Culture and the art of the Formosan aboriginal. Taipei, Lion Art Book Co.: 200 p.

Liu, R.K. 1974 Chinese cloisonne and enameled beads. *Bead Journal* 1(1): 27-30.

——1975a Cover story. *Bead Journal* 1(3): 10-12.

——1975b Chinese glass beads and ornaments. *Bead Journal* 1(3): 13-28.

——1975c Ancient Chinese glass beads. *Bead Journal* 2(2): 9-19.

——1980 Simulated materials in jewelry. *Ornament* 4(4): 18-26.

——1982a Exhibition review: The Manchu dragon. Costumes of China, the Ch'ing Dynasty. *Ornament* 5(4): 46.

——1982b Glass ojime. *Ornament* 6(2): 24-28.

——1982c Iranian faience. Beads/pendants of late periods. *Ornament* 6(2): 6-7, 42-43, 54.

——1982d Juxtaposition: Chinese kingfisher feather ornaments. *Ornament* 6(2): 35.

——1983 Formosan ornaments and clothing. *Ornament* 6(4): 21-27.

——1984 Imported Chinese jewelry. *Ornament* 7(4): 56-61, 53.

——1985a Asian glass ornaments: Pt. I. *Ornament* 8(4): 28-31, 25, 15.

——1985b Asian glass ornaments: Pt. II. *Ornament* 9(1): 34-36, 47.

——1985c Exhibition review: Dragons in the New World. Native Americans and the China Trade. *Ornament* 9(1): 55.

——1993 Wholesale to the trade: Abeada. *Ornament* 16(3): 104-105.

——and D.K. Liu 1982 Ch'ing Dynasty jewelry from Museum of Treasures. *Ornament* 5(3): 58-59.

Miyamoto, N. 1957 Glass beads of the Formosan aborigines. *Minzoku-Gaku Kenkyu* (Japanese Journal of Ethnography) 21(4): 89-93.

Pilditch, J.S. 1992 The glass beads of Ban Bon Noen, central Thailand. *Asian Perspectives* 31(2): 171-181.

Seligman, C.G. and H.C. Beck 1938 Far Eastern glass: some Western origins. Museum Far Eastern Antiquities, Stockholm. *Bulletin* (10): 1-64.

Sprague, R. and J. An 1990 Observations and problems in researching the contemporary glass-bead industry of northern China. *Beads* 2 [1991]: 5-13.

Taylor, Z. 1974 Ancient Chinese glass. *Arts of Asia* 4(6): 27-31.

Ukai, N. 1984 Kyoyu Asao. Glass bead master, new work. *Ornament* 7(3): 2-5.

van der Sleen, W.G.N. 1973 A handbook on beads. Liege, Librairie Halbart: 142 p.

Wang, S. 1991 Some glasses from Zhou dynasty tombs in Fufeng County and Baoji, Shaanxi. *In:* Brill and Martin (eds.): 151-156.

Woodward, A. 1967 Indian trade goods. Portland, Oregon Archaeological Society: 38 p.

Yang, B. 1987 A brief account of Qing dynasty glass. *In:* Brown and Rabiner (eds.): 71-86.

——1991 An account of Qing dynasty glassmaking. *In:* Brill and Martin (eds.): 131-150.

Yi, J. and S. Tu 1991 Chinese glass technology in Boshan around the 14th century. *In:* Brill and Martin (eds.): 99-101.

Yoshimizu, T. 1989 Eye of the dragonfly (Tombodama). Tokyo, Heibonsha: 163 p.

Zhang, F. 1991 Scientific studies of early glasses excavated in China. *In:* Brill and Martin (eds.): 157-166.

CHAPTER 3

Abellera, B.C. 1981 The heirloom beads of Lubo, Kalinga-Apayao. M.A., Asian Center, University of the Philippines: 180 p.

Adhyatman, S. and R. Arifin 1993 Manik-manik di Indonesia. Beads in Indonesia. Jakarta, Penerbit Djambatan: 164 p.

Allen, J.D. 1986 Pumtek: an introductory report upon an unusual class of decorated stone beads. *Bead Forum* (9): 6-13.

——1990 Ancient beads from Burma—notes from Jamey Allen. *Bead Museum Quarterly* 4(2): 3.

Barbier, J.P. 1984 Art of Nagaland. Geneva, Musee Barbier-Müller: 87 p.

Beck, H.C. 1976 The magical properties of beads. *Bead Journal* 2(4): 32-39.

Borel, F. 1994 The splendor of ethnic jewelry. From the Collette and Jean-Pierre Ghysels collection. New York, Harry N. Abrams: 256 p.

Brown, R.M. 1983 Thailand. A birthplace of civilization? *Sawaasdee* 12(1): 20-26.

Chang, H.S. 1993 The bewitching bijou of Tibet. A(n) illustrative study of dZi bead. Taipeh, Shu Hsin: 158 p.

Chin, L. 1984 Beads. Sarawak Museum Occasional Paper (2): 21 p.

Darmody, L. 1987 Beads in Sarawak. *Ornament* 1(2): 28-29, 70-71.

Dubin, L.S. 1987 The history of beads. From 30,000 B.C. to the present. New York, Harry N. Abrams: 364 p.

Dunning, D. and S. Dunning 1993 Indonesian beads. Borneo and the new glass-making industry. *Hands of the Hills Newsletter*: 1-2.

Ebbinghouse, D and M. Winsten 1982a Tibetan dZi beads. Pt. I *Ornament* 5(3): 19-25.

——1982b Tibetan dZi beads. Pt. II *Ornament* 5(4): 36-39.

Ellis, G. R. 1981 Arts and peoples of the northern Philippines. *In:* Casal *et. al.*, 1981 The people and art of the Philippines. University of California, Los Angeles, Museum of Cultural History: 182-263.

Engle, A. 1990 The ubiquitous trade bead. Readings in glass history 22. Jerusalem, Phoenix Publications: 99 p.

Francis Jr., P. 1979 Third world beadmakers. Lapis Route Books, World of Beads Monograph Series 3: 17 p.

——1982a Indian agate beads. Lapis Route Books, World of Beads Monograph Series 6: 52 p.

____1982b The glass beads of India. Lapis Route Books, World of Beads Monograph Series 7: 26 p.

____1983 Bead report, Part VIII: Minor Indian beadmakers. *Ornament* 6(3): 18-21.

____1985a Bead report XV: The Asian bead study tour. Part I: Beads as survivors in Korea. *Ornament* 9(1): 42-46.

____1985b Bead report XVI: The Asian bead study tour II. Thailand: Revolution and ruin, tradition and change. *Ornament* 9(2): 42-48.

____1986 Bead report XVIII: The Asian bead study tour IV. A little tube of glass. *Ornament* 10(1): 54-57.

____1987a Bead report XX: Another bead potpourri. *Ornament* 10(3): 62-63, 75-79.

____1987b Bead report: The endangered bead. *Ornament* 11(1): 64-73.

____1988 The beads of India. *Arts of Asia* 18(2): 102-110.

____1989 Bead report: Mantai, bead crossroads of the medieval world. *Ornament* 12(3): 82-85, 87-91.

____1990a Beads in the Philippines. *Arts of Asia* 20(6): 97-107.

____1990b Glass beads in Asia. Part I, Introduction. *Asian Perspectives* 28(1): 1-21.

____1990c Glass beads in Asia. Part II, Indo-Pacific beads. *Asian Perspectives* 29(1): 1-23.

____1990d Bead altering in southeast Asia. *Margaretologist* 5(2): 11.

____1990e Bead report: The greatest trade bead of all time. *Ornament* 13(3): 78-81.

____1991a Beads in Indonesia. A review of the evidence. *Asian Perspectives* 30(2): 217-241.

____1991b Bead report: Philippine National Museum. *Ornament* 15(2): 98-99.

____1991c Bead report: The glories of Kedah. *Ornament* 15(1): 98-100.

____1991d Beadmaking at Arikamedu and beyond. *World Archaeology* 23(1): 28-43.

____1992a Bead news roundup no. 13: Beads in Indonesia. *Bead Study Trust Newsletter* (19): 2-3.

____1992b Heirlooms of the hills. Southeast Asia. Center for Bead Research, Beads and People Series 1: 22 p.

____1992c Bead report: Heirloom beads in the Philippines and Borneo. *Ornament* 15(3): 98-99.

____1993a Sumatra's lost kingdom. *Lapidary Journal* 47(7): 108-112, 114, 116, 118.

____1993b Bead report: Ifugao heirloom beads. *Ornament* 17(1): 112-113.

____1994 Beads of the world. A collector's guide with price reference. Atglen, Schiffer Publishing Ltd.: 142 p.

Fukai, S. 1977 Persian glass. Weatherhill/Tankosha: 66 p., 89 plates.

Gabriel, H. 1985 Shell jewelry of the Nagas. *Ornament* 9(1): 37-41.

____1994 In search of the shadow soul. *Lapidary Journal* 48(7): 18-24.

Glover, I.C., P. Charoenwongsa, B. Alvey and N. Kamnounket 1984 The cemetery of Ban Don Ta Phet, Thailand: results of the 1980-1 excavation season. *In:* South Asian Archaeology 1981, B. Allchin (ed.). Cambridge University Press: 319-330.

Harris, E.J. 1981 Caveat emptor. [Los Angeles], *Bead Society Newsletter* VII(3): 5.

____1985 More Chinese beads. [Los Angeles], *Bead Society Newsletter* X(5): 7.

____1991 New face beads from India. [Los Angeles], *Bead Society Newsletter* (18): 13.

Herle, A. 1988 Naga body decorations. Continuity and change. *Ornament* 12(1): 28-33, 81.

Jacobs, J., A. Macfarlane, S. Harrison, and A. Herle 1990 The Nagas. Hill peoples of northeast India: Society, culture and the Colonial encounter. London, Thames and Hudson: 359 p.

Karklins, K. 1987 Some comments on mulberry and twisted square beads. *Bead Forum* (11): 12-14.

Kenoyer, J.M. 1986 The Indus bead industry. Contributions to bead technology. *Ornament* 10(1): 18-23.

____1991 Ornament styles of the Indus Valley tradition. Evidence from recent excavations at Harappa, Pakistan. *Paléorient* 17(2): 79-98.

____1993 Bead news. *Madison Bead Society Newsletter* 2(4): 4-5.

Kessler, E. 1992 New territories. *Bead Society Greater Washington Newsletter* IX(3): 1-2.

Kinsey, R.O. 1991 Ojime. Magical jewels of Japan. New York, Harry N. Abrams: 64 p.

Lewis, P. and E. Lewis 1984 Peoples of the golden triangle. Six tribes in Thailand. London, Thames and Hudson: 225 p.

Liu, R.K. 1976 Followup. *Bead Journal* 3(1): 42.

____1980a Identification: Tzi beads. *Ornament* 4(4): 56-59.

____1980b Simulated materials in jewelry. *Ornament* 4(4): 18-26.

____1982a Followup: Tibetan dZi beads. *Ornament* 6(2): 55.

____1982b Glass ojime. *Ornament* 6(2): 24-28.

____1983 Special pictorial: Ojime. *Ornament* 7(1): 25-26.

____1984 Identification: Carnelian beads and their simulations. *Ornament* 8(1): 14-17.

____1985a Asian glass ornaments: Part I *Ornament* 8(4): 28-31, 25, 15.

____1985b Identification: [Smallest and largest beads.] *Ornament* 9(1): 69.

____1986a Followup: Asao bead components. *Ornament* 9(3): 48-49.

____1986b Followup: Indonesian glass beads. *Ornament* 9(4): 64-65.

____1986c Identification: Tibetan eye beads. *Ornament* 9(4): 9.

____1987 India, Idar-Oberstein and Czechoslovakia: Imitators and competitors. *Ornament* 10(4): 56-61.

____1988 Collectibles: Philippine shell ornaments. *Ornament* 12(1): 46-47.

____1989 Collectibles: Mosaic face beads. *Ornament* 12(3): 22-23.

____1990a Wholesale to the trade: Jackie Little.*Ornament* 13(3): 74-75.

____1990b Wholesale to the trade: Art Expo. *Ornament* 13(4): 16-17.

____1991 Exhibition review: Beads, beadwork and adornment of Indonesia, the Philippines and island Southeast Asia. *Ornament* 14(4): 67.

____1992a Wholesale to the trade: Hands of the Hills. *Ornament* 15(4): 96-97.

____1992b Collectibles: Imitations and fakes. *Ornament* 16(1): 16-17.

____1993a Wholesale to the trade: Ornamental Resources. *Ornament* 16(4): 104-105.

____1993b Collectibles: Himalayan ornaments. *Ornament* 17(1): 24-25.

Munan, H. 1985 Common Borneo beads. *Sandfly* 1(3): 13-15.

____1991 Land Dayak beads. *Bead Forum* (19): 3-11.

____1993 Lun Bawang beads. *Beads* 5 [1995]: 45-60.

Munan-Oettli, H. 1983 Bead cap 64/88 in the Sarawak Museum collection. *Sarawak Museum Journal* XXXII (53): 89-96, plate

Picard, J. and R. Picard 1993 Chevron and Nueva Cádiz beads. Volume VII-Beads from the West African trade. Picard African Imports: 128 p.

Pilditch, J. 1992 The glass beads of Ban Bon Noen, central Thailand. *Asian Perspectives* 31(2): 171-181.

Ritzenthaler, R.E. 1954 Native money of Palau. Milwaukee Public Museum, Publications in Anthropology (1): 1-46.

Shaw, J. 1985 Tak hilltop burial sites. *Arts of Asia* 15(4): 95-102.

Stark, P. 1992 Gold & silver auction. Part I, Ancient to tribal [Burma (Myanmar), Khmer-Cambodia, Thailand, Classical Java, Indonesia, Philippines, India, China, Tribal]. Singapore, Taisei Gallery: 356 p.

Ukai, N. 1980 Kyoyu Asao, tombodama/glass bead master. *Ornament* 4(3): 13-18.

____1984 Kyoyu Asao. Glass bead master, new work. *Ornament* 7(3): 2-5.

Untracht, O. 1988 Chapter 3 Asia. India. *In:* Ethnic jewelry. J. Mack (ed.), New York, Harry N. Abrams: 64-93.

van der Made, H. 1988 Report on some face-beads. *Bead Forum* (13): 4-5.

van der Sleen, W.G. N. 1973 A handbook on beads. Liege, Librairie Halbart: 142 p.

Villegas, R. N. 1983 Kayamanan. The Philippine jewelry tradition. Manila, Central Bank of the Philippines: 210 p.

Weihreter, H. 1988 Schmück aus dem Himalaja. Graz, Akademische Druck u. Verlagsanstalt: 303 p.

Yoshimizu, T. 1989 Eye of the dragonfly (Tombodama). Tokyo, Heibonsha: 163 p.

zu Windisch-Graetz, S. and G. zu Windisch-Graetz 1981 Juwelen des Himalaja. Götter, Völker und Kleinodien. Luzern, Reich Verlag: 192 p.

CHAPTER 4

Aldred, C. 1971 Jewels of the pharaohs. Egyptian jewelry of the Dynastic Period. New York, Praeger Publishers: 256 p.

Alekseeva, E.M. 1971 Miniature mosaic in glass ornaments, first century B.C. second century A.D. [in Russian] Moskow, *Sovetskaia Arkheologiia* 4: 178-185.

Andrews, C. 1990 Ancient Egyptian jewelry. New York, Harry N. Abrams: 208 p.

____1994 Amulets of ancient Egypt. Austin, University of Texas Press: 112 p.

Anonymous 1972 Antiquities and Oriental art. The Thomas Barlow Walker collection. New York, Sotheby Parke Bernet Inc.: unpaginated.

____1974 Jewelry from Persia. The collection of Patti Birch. Pforzheim, Schmuckmuseum: unpaginated.

____1985 Antiquities and Islamic works of art. New York, Sotheby's: unpaginated.

____1986 Antiquities and Islamic works of art. New York, Sotheby's: unpaginated.

____1994 Fine antiquities. London, Bonhams: 105 p.

Beck, H.C. 1928 Classification and nomenclature of beads and pendants. *Archaeologia* 77, 2nd Ser.: 1-76.

____1931a Beads from Nineveh. *Antiquity* 5: 427-437.

____1931b Notes on glazed stones. Part I-Glazed steatite. *Ancient Egypt and the East*, December: 1-15.

____1935 Notes on glazed stones. Part II-Glazed quartz. *Ancient Egypt and the East*, June: 1-19.

____1941 The beads from Taxila. Delhi, *Memoirs of the Archaeological Survey of India* (65): 66 p., plates X-XII.

Brosh, N. 1987 Islamic jewelry. Jerusalem, Israel Museum: 71 p.

Brovarski, E., *et. al.* 1982 Egypt's golden age. The art of living in the New Kingdom 1558-1085 B.C. Boston, Museum of Fine Arts: 336 p.

____Callmer, J. 1977 Trade beads and bead trade in Scandinavia ca. 800-1000 A.D. *Acta Archaeologica Lundensia* 4(11): 229 p., map, plates, color plates.

Camps-Faber, H. 1990 Bijoux Berberes d'Algérie. Grande Kabylie-Aures. La Calade, Edisud: 145 p.

Content, D.J. 1992 Gold & silver auction. Part II. Ancient to Renaissance. Singapore, Taisei Gallery: 267 p.

Dale, G. 1978 Fake Roman glass. *Antique Collector* 1: 80-82.

— 1981 Ancient beads upgraded. *Antique Collector* 3: 72-75.

— 1982 Third millennium beads from Euphrates region. *Ornament* 5(3): 30-32.

Davis-Kimball, J. and R.K. Liu 1981 Identification: An etched carnelian bead with human images. *Ornament* 5(1): 34-35.

Dayton, J.E. 1993 The discovery of glass. Experiments in the smelting of rich, dry silver ores, and the reproduction of Bronze Age-type cobalt blue glass as a slag. American School of Prehistoric Research, *Bulletin* 41: 72 p.

Dayton, J. and A. Dayton 1978 Minerals, metals, glazing and man. London, Harrap: 496 p.

Dubin, L.S. 1987 The history of beads. From 30,000 B.C. to the present. New York, Harry N. Abrams: 364 p.

During Caspers, E.C.L. 1971 Etched carnelian beads. London, Institute of Archaeology *Bulletin* 10: 83-98.

Eisen, G. 1916 The characteristics of eye beads from the earliest times to the present. *American Journal of Archaeology*, 2nd Ser. 20: 1-27, plate.

— 1930 Lotus and melon beads. *American Journal of Archaeology*, 2nd Ser. 34(1): 20-43.

Engle, A. 1990 The ubiquitous trade bead. Readings in glass history 22. Jerusalem, Phoenix Publications: 99 p.

Fisher, A. 1984 Africa adorned. New York, Harry N. Abrams Inc.: 304 p.

Foster, K. P. 1979 Aegean faience of the Bronze Age. New Haven, Yale University Press: 205 p.

Francis Jr., P. 1979a Bead report I: Iran, Part 1A. *Ornament* 4(1): 44-46.

— 1979b Bead report I: Iran, Part 1B. *Ornament* 4(2): 34-35.

— 1979c Third world beadmakers. Lapis Route Books, World of Beads Monograph Series 3: 17 p., color plates.

— 1980a Bead report II: Etched beads in Iran. *Ornament* 4(3): 24-28.

— 1980b Bead report III: Beads in Egypt. *Ornament* 4(4): 15-17, 49-50.

— 1981a Bead report IV: Beads in Afghanistan. *Ornament* 5(1): 24-25, 54-56.

— 1981b Bead report V: Pt. I Beads in Turkey. *Ornament* 5(2): 38-39, 58.

— 1982 Bead report VI: Pt. II Beads in Turkey. *Ornament* 5(3): 25-27.

— 1988 Nishapur. An early Islamic city of Iran. *Ornament* 12(2): 78-80, 82, 84-85, 87, 88-93.

— 1989 Beads of the early Islamic period. *Beads* 1: 21-39.

— 1990 Beadmaking in Islam. The African trade and the rise of Hebron. *Beads* 2 [1991]: 1-28.

— 1994 Beads of the world. A collector's guide with price reference. Atglen, Schiffer Publishing Ltd.: 142 p.

Fukai, S. 1977 Persian glass. Weatherhill/Tankosha: 66 p., 89 plates.

Gitin, S. 1992 Last days of the Philistines. *Archaeology* 45(3): 26-31.

Glover, I. 1994 Bead notes from southeast Asia. *Bead Study Trust Newsletter* 23/24: 7-11.

Goldstein, S.M. 1979 Pre-Roman and early Roman glass in the Corning Museum of Glass. Corning Museum of Glass: 312 p.

Green, C.I. 1993 Ancient Egyptian glass and faience from the 'Per-neb' collection, Part III. London, Christie's: 85 p.

Gwinnett, A.J. and L. Gorelick 1991 Bead manufacture at Hajar ar-Rayhani, Yemen. *Biblical Archaeologist* December: 186-196.

Haevernick, T.E. 1968 Doppelköpfchen. *Wissenschaftliche Zeitschrift der Universität Rostock* 17: 647-653.

— 1972 Perlen mit zusammengesetzten Augen (compound eyebeads). *Prähistorische Zeitschrift* 47: 78-93.

— 1977 Gesichtsperlen. *Madrider Mitteilungen* 18: 152-231.

Hansmann, L. and L. Kriss-Rettenbeck 1977 Amulett und talisman. Erscheinungsform und Geschichte. München, Verlag Georg D. W. Callwey: 444 p.

Harden, D.B. 1981 Catalogue of Greek and Roman glass in the British Museum. Vol. I, Core- and rod-formed vessels and pendants and Mycenaean cast objects. British Museum Publications Ltd.: 187 p., 29 plates, 19 figures.

Harris, E.J. 1993 An end and new beginning. *Bead Museum Quarterly* 7(4): 4.

Hasson, R. 1987 Later Islamic jewellery. Jerusalem, L.A. Mayer Memorial Institute for Islamic Art: 160 p.

Insoll, T. 1994 The illicit bead trade in Gao, the Republic of Mali. *Bead Forum* (24): 6-10.

Jenkins, M. and M. Keene 1982 Islamic jewelry in the Metropolitan Museum of Art. New York, Metropolitan Museum of Art: 160 p.

Jereb, J. 1989 The magical potency of Berber jewelry. *Ornament* 13(2): 4-43, 69, 73.

Jick, M. 1990 Bead-net dress from Giza tomb G7740Z. Old Kingdom, Dynasty IV, Reign of Khufu. *Ornament* 14(1): 50-53.

Kaczmarczyk, A. and R.E.M. Hedges 1983 Ancient Egyptian faience. An analytic survey of Egyptian faience from Predynastic to Roman times. Aris & Phillips Ltd.: 587 p.

Kelly, I. 1977 Some sixteenth-century jet imports to the New World. *Bead Journal* 3(2): 24-28.

Kennedy, S. 1979 Aqd Mirjan. A ceremonial necklace from Yemen. *Ornament* 4(1): 2-3.

Kenoyer, J.M. 1986 The Indus bead industry. Contributions to bead technology. *Ornament* 10(1): 18-23.

— 1991 Ornament styles of the Indus valley tradition. Evidence from recent excavations at Harappa, Pakistan. *Paléorient* 17(2): 79-98.

— 1992 Lapis lazuli. Beadmaking in Afghanistan and Pakistan. *Ornament* 15(3): 70-73, 86-87.

— 1993 Bead news. *Madison Bead Society Newsletter* 2(4): 4-5.

— 1994 Faience from the Indus valley civilization. *Ornament* 17(3): 36-39, 95.

Kolbas, J.G. 1983 A color chronology of Islamic glass. *Journal of Glass Studies* 25: 95-100.

Küçükerman, O. 1988 Glass beads. Anatolian glass bead making. The final traces of three millennia of glass making in the Mediterranean region. Turkish Touring and Automobile Association: 102 p.

Kurinsky, S. 1991 The glassmakers. An odyssey of the Jews. The first three thousand years. New York, Hippocrene Books: 434 p.

Liu, R.K. 1974a Glass mosaic or millefiore beads. *Bead Journal* 1(1): 22-26.

— 1974b Cover story. *Bead Journal* 1(2): 5-7.

— 1975a Chinese glass beads and ornaments. *Bead Journal* 1(3): 13-28.

— 1975b Faience. Technical aspects and beads of simple form. *Bead Journal* 1(4): 24-41.

— 1976 Ancient glass ornaments with human facial images. *Bead Journal* 2(3): 27-32.

— 1977 Exhibitions and shows: Phase I of the reinstallation of the Egyptian collection, Metropolitan Museum of Art. *Bead Journal* 3(2): 4-5.

— 1979 Review of exhibitions: New Mesopotamian Hall, the Oriental Institute. *Ornament* 4(2): 37-40.

— 1980 Simulated materials in jewelry. *Ornament* 4(4): 18-26.

— 1981 Carol Strick. Artist in faience. *Ornament* 5(2): 34-37.

— 1982a Exhibition review: Phase II of the reinstallation of the Egyptian collection, Metropolitan Museum of Art. *Ornament* 5(3): 46-47.

— 1982b Iranian faience. Beads/pendants of the late period. *Ornament* 6(2): 6-7, 42-43, 54.

— 1983a Followup: Iranian faience and glass amulets. *Ornament* 6(4): 45.

— 1983b Identification: Phoenician mask pendants. *Ornament* 7(1): 58.

— 1983c Juxtaposition: Iranian amulets. *Ornament* 7(1): 59.

— 1983d Identification: Afghani stone beads. *Ornament* 7(2): 34-35.

— 1983e Followup: Miniature talhakimt. *Ornament* 7(2): 45.

— 1984a Exhibition review: Islamic jewelry in The Metropolitan Museum of Art. *Ornament* 7(3): 18-19.

— 1984b Exhibition review: Ancient Mesopotamia. The royal tombs of Ur, University Museum. *Ornament* 7(4): 40-41.

— 1984c Special pictorial: Saudi Arabian jewelry components. *Ornament* 7(4): 10-11.

— 1984d Identification: Rock crystal ornaments. *Ornament* 7(4): 54.

— 1984e Exhibition review: Third phase of the reinstallation of the Egyptian collection, Metropolitan Museum of Art. *Ornament* 8(2): 15-17.

— 1985a Identification: Transpositions. *Ornament* 8(4): 67.

— 1985b Identification: [Smallest and largest beads.] *Ornament* 9(1): 69.

— 1986 Iridescence and related phenomena. *Ornament* 9(3): 31-36.

— 1987a Identification: Degradation. *Ornament* 10(4): 37.

— 1987b Exhibition review: Elba to Damascus: Art and archaeology of ancient Syria, Natural History Museum of Los Angeles County. *Ornament* 11(1): 23.

— 1989a Collectibles: Mosaic face beads. *Ornament* 12(3): 22-23.

— 1989b Collectibles: Faience ornaments. *Ornament* 13(2): 16-17.

— 1990 Identification: Ancient Egyptian glass. *Ornament* 13(4): 66-67.

— 1992a Collectibles: Questions about amulets. *Ornament* 15(3): 16-17.

— 1992b Collectibles: Ancient European glass beads. *Ornament* 15(4): 16-17.

— 1992c Museum news: Prähistorische Staatssammlung. *Ornament* 16(1): 28-29.

— 1992d Wholesale to the trade: Lost Cities. *Ornament* 16(1): 96-97.

— 1993a Museum news: Royal Ontario Museum. *Ornament* 16(4): 76-77.

— 1993b Museum news: British Museum. *Ornament* 17(1): 92-93.

— 1994 Conference: Bead Expo '94. *Ornament* 17(4): 120-121.

— and D.J. Content 1979 Ancient jewelry molds. *Ornament* 4(1): 30-39.

— and L. Wataghani 1975 Moroccan folk jewelry. *African Arts* VIII(2): 28-35, 80.

Maxwell-Hyslop, K.R. 1971 Western Asiatic jewellery. c. 3000-612 B.C. London, Methuen and Co. Ltd: 286 p., illus.

McGovern, P.E. 1990 The ultimate attire. Jewelry from a Canaanite temple at Beth Shan. *Expedition* 32(1): 16-23.

— S.J. Fleming and C.P. Swann 1991 The beads from tomb B10a B27 at Dinkha Tepe and the beginnings of glassmaking in the ancient Near East. *American Journal of Archaeology* 95: 395-402.

Moscati, S. 1988 The Phoenicians. New York, Abbeville Press: 768 p.

Muzzy, S. 1993 Glass beadmaking. The ring of fire. *Ornament* 16(4): 56-59.

Negahban, E.O. 1964 Preliminary report on Marlik excavation, Gohar Rud Expedition, Rudbar 1961-1962. Special Publication, Ministry of Education Iran: 9-47, figure 63.

Newton, R.G. and C. Renfrew 1970 British faience beads reconsidered. *Antiquity* 175: 199-206.

Nicholson, P. T. 1993 Egyptian faience and glass. Princes Risborough, Shire Egyptology Series (19): 80 p.

Ogden, J. 1982 Jewellery of the ancient world. New York, Rizzoli: 185 p.

Opper, M.-J. and H. Opper 1990 Ancient amazonite and scorzalite beads. *Ornament* 13(3): 34-37, 6, 13, 15.

Petrie, Sir W. M. Flinders 1972 Amulets. J. L. Malter & Co., Aris & Phillips Ltd.: 58 p., plates.

Pilditch, J. S. 1992 The glass beads of Ban Bon Noen, central Thailand. *Asian Perspectives* 31(2): 171-181.

Quillard, B. 1979 Bijoux Carthaginois. I, Les Colliers. Louvain-la-Neuve, Institut Supérieur d'Archéologie et d'Histoire de l'Art: 133 p., plates.

Raschka, M. 1994 Salvaging a scarred land. *Archaeology* 17(1): 64-67.

Riefstahl, E. 1968 Ancient Egyptian glass and glazes in the Brooklyn Museum. Brooklyn Museum: 118 p.

Ross, A.L. 1991 Wholesale to the trade: Liza Wataghani. *Ornament* 14(3): 86-87.

Schienerl, P.W. 1982 Crescent to cross. Roman and Byzantine glass pendants from Egypt. *Ornament* 6(2): 8-9, 54.

—— 1985 Major trends in the historical development of amulets. *Ornament* 9(2):19-25.

Schmidt, E.F. 1933 Tepe Hissar excavations 1931. *Museum Journal* XXIII(4): 323-487.

Scott, N.E. and R.K. Liu 1979 Notes on construction of Egyptian broadcollars. *Ornament* 4(2): 11-14.

Seefried, M. 1982 Les pendentifs en verre sur noyau des pays de la Méditerranée. Collection de l'Ecole Française de Rome 57: 186 p.

Sono, T. and S. Fukai 1968 Dailaman III. Excavations at Hassani Mahale and Ghalekuti 1964. *Tokyo University Iraq-Iran Archaeological Expedition Report* 8: 1-73, tables, plates I-LXXXVII.

Spaer, M. 1993 Gold-glass beads. A review of the evidence. *Beads* 5 [1995]: 9-25.

Stawiarska, T. 1985 Glass beads of northern Poland in the period of Roman influence [in Polish]. *Biblioteka Archeologiczna* 28: 158 p., charts, maps.

Stout, A.M. 1986 The archaeological context of late Roman Period mosaic glass face beads. *Ornament* 9(4): 58-61, 76-77.

Tait, H. 1976 Jewellery through 7000 years. British Museum Publications: 276 p.

—— 1991 Glass 5,000 years. New York, Harry N. Abrams: 256 p.

Tatton-Brown, V. 1981 Rod-formed glass pendants and beads of the 1st millennium B.C. *In*: D. B. Harden, Catalogue of Greek and Roman glass in the British Museum: 143-155, plates XXIII-XXIX, figures 11-19.

Templeman-Maczy'nska, M. 1985 Die Perlen der römischen Kaiserzeit und der frühen Phase der Völkerwanderungzeit in mitteleuropäischen Barbicum. Verlag Philipp von Zabern, *Römisch-Germanische Forschungen* 43: 399 p., Tafeln 1-80, Beilagen 1-3.

Tite, M.S., I.C. Freestone and M. Bimson 1983 Egyptian faience. An investigation of the methods of production. *Archaeometry* 25(1): 17-27.

Tosi, M. 1974 The problem of turquoise in protohistoric trade on the Iranian plateau. *Memorie dell'Instituto Italiano di Paleontologia Umana* II: 147-162.

van der Sleen, W. G. N. 1973 A handbook on beads. Liege, Librairie Halbart: 142 p.

Vandiver, P. 1982 Technological change in Egyptian faience. *In*: Archaeological Ceramics. J.S. Olin and A.D. Franklin (eds.) Smithsonian Institution Press: 167-179.

—— 1983a Appendix A: The manufacture of faience. *In*: Kaczmarczyk and Hedges: A-1-A-144, figures 23-46.

—— 1983b Glass technology at the mid-second millennium B.C. Hurrian site of Nuzi. *Journal of Glass Studies* 25: 239-247.

Venclova, N. 1983 Prehistoric eye beads in central Europe. *Journal of Glass Studies* 25: 11-17

Weinberg, G.D. 1971 Glass manufacture in Hellenestic Rhodes. *Deltion* 24: 143-151, plates 75-88.

Westlake, F. 1976 Horace C. Beck, "The Bead Man", 1873-1941. *Bead Journal* 2(4): 30-31.

—— 1993 Effects of Gulf War. *Bead Study Trust Newsletter* (22): 1-2, 5.

Wilkinson, A. 1971 Ancient Egyptian jewellery. London, Methuen & Co. Ltd.: 266 p., plates.

Yoshimizu, T. 1989 Eye of the dragonfly (Tombodama). Tokyo, Heibonsha: 163 p.

CHAPTER 5

Anonymous 1981 The Bogousslavsky collection of pre-columbian art. New York, Sotheby's: unpaginated.

Armstrong, W.P. 1993 Neotropical amber. *Ornament* 17(1): 58-61, 108.

Balser, C. 1980 Jade precolombino de Costa Rica. San José, Instituto Nacional de Seguros: 128 p.

Benson, E.P. (ed.) 1979 Pre-columbian metallurgy of South America. A conference at Dumbarton Oaks. October 18th and 19th, 1975. Washington, D.C., Dumbarton Oaks Research Library and Collections: 207 p.

Bray, W. 1978 The gold of El Dorado. Times Newspapers Ltd.: 240 p.

Digby, A. 1964 Maya jades. British Museum Publications: 32 p., 16 plates.

Donnan, C.B. 1993 Royal tombs of Sipán. Moche ornaments of Peru. *Ornament* 17(1): 44-49.

—— and C.J. Mackey 1978 Ancient burial patterns of the Moche Valley, Peru. Austin, University of Texas Press: 412 p.

Dubin, L.S. 1987 The history of beads. From 30,000 to the present. New York, Harry N. Abrams: 364 p.

Easby, E.K. 1968 Pre-Columbian jade from Costa Rica. Andre Emmerich: 103 p.

Fogelman, G.L. 1991 Glass trade beads of the Northeast. And including aboriginal bead industries: stone-bone-shell-catlinite-cannel coal-teeth. Fogelman Publishing Co., Pennsylvania Artifact Series Booklet (70): 44 p., 1 color chart.

Foshag, W.F. 1957 Minerological studies on Guatemalan jade. *Smithsonian Miscellaneous Collections* 135(5): 60 p., plates.

Francis Jr., P. 1984 Bead report XI: Beads and the discovery of America, Part I. Beads of the Native Americans. *Ornament* 7(4): 16-19, 48-49.

—— 1994 Beads of the world. A collector's guide with price preference. Atglen, Schiffer Publishing Ltd.: 142 p.

Gessler, T. 1988 Precolumbian jewelry from Peru. *Ornament* 11(3): 50-55.

Haviser, J. B. 1990 Perforated prehistoric ornaments of Curaçao and Bonaire, Netherlands Antilles. *Beads* 2 [1991]: 85-92.

Jernigan, E.W. 1978 Jewelry of the prehistoric Southwest. Santa Fe, School of American Research and Albuquerque, University of New Mexico Press: 260 p.

Jones, J. 1988 The Americas: Precolumbian America. *In*: Ethnic jewelry. J. Mack (ed.) New York, Harry N. Abrams: 134-147.

Kelly, I. 1992 Trade beads and the conquest of Mexico. Windsor, Rolston-Bain: 291 p.

Kessler, E. and S. Kessler 1978 Beads of the Tairona. *Bead Journal* 3(3/4): 2-5.

—— 1986 Ecuadorian beads, ancient to modern. *Ornament* 10(2): 48-52.

—— 1988 Beads of ancient Panama. *Ornament* 11(4): 20-24.

Keverne, R. (ed.) 1991 Jade. New York, Van Nostrand Reinhold: 376 p.

King, C.D. 1981 Prehistoric and early historic California beads. *Ornament* 5(1): 11-17.

—— 1990 Evolution of Chumash society. A comparative study of artifacts used for social system maintenance in the Santa Barbara Channel region before A.D. 1804. New York and London, Garland Publishing, Inc.: 296 p.

Labbé, A.J. 1986 Colombia before Columbus. The people, culture, and ceramic art of prehispanic Colombia. New York, Rizzoli: 207 p.

Lange, F. W. (ed.) 1993 Precolumbian jade. New geological and cultural interpretations. Salt Lake City, University of Utah Press: 378 p.

Liu, R.K. 1978 Spindle whorls: Pt. I Some comments and speculations. *Bead Journal* 3(3/4): 87-103.

—— 1983 Pre-columbian necklaces, then and now. *Ornament* 7(1): 2-5, 14-15, 44-45.

—— 1984 Followup: Ecuadorian spindle whorls. *Ornament* 7(3): 28.

—— 1985a Special pictorial: Chumash Indian ornaments. *Ornament* 8(3): 44-45.

—— 1985b Identification: Transpositions. *Ornament* 8(4): 67.

—— 1985c Identification: [Smallest and largest beads.] *Ornament* 9(1): 69.

—— 1985d Identification: Broadwing pendants. *Ornament* 9(2): 26-27.

—— 1987 Exhibition review: Maya. Treasures of an ancient civilization, Los Angeles County Museum of Natural History. *Ornament* 10(3): 21.

—— 1989 Identification: Precolumbian jewelry materials. *Ornament* 12(4): 38-39.

—— 1991 Exhibition review: Hall of South American peoples, American Museum of Natural History. *Ornament* 15(2): 29.

—— 1992a Collectibles: Questions about amulets. *Ornament* 15(3): 16-17.

—— 1992b Exhibition review: Mesoamerican Gallery, the University Museum. *Ornament* 15(3): 29.

—— 1992c Precolumbian personal adornment. *Ornament* 16(1): 50-55.

—— 1993 Exhibition review: Museo Arqueológico de la Costa Grande. *Ornament* 16(4): 29.

Lothrop, S.K. 1937 Coclé, an archaeological study of central Panama. Part I. Historical background, excavations at the Sitio conte, artifacts and ornaments. *Memoirs Peabody Museum of Archaeology and Ethnology,* Harvard University VII: 327 p.

—— 1950 Archaeology of southern Veraguas, Panama. *Memoirs Peabody Museum of Archaeology and Ethnology,* Harvard University IX(3): 116 p.

—— 1955 Jade and string sawing in northeastern Costa Rica. *American Antiquity* 21: 43-51.

Mason, J. A. 1936 Archaeology of Santa Marta, Colombia. The Tairona culture. Part II, Section l. Objects of stone, shell, bone and metal. Field Museum of Natural History, Anthropological Series XX(2): 418 p., plates.

McEwan, C. and M. van de Guchte 1992 Ancestral time and sacred space in Inca state ritual. *In*: The ancient Americas. Art from sacred landscapes. Townsend, R. F. (ed.) Art Institute of Chicago: 358-371.

McGuire, J.D. 1896 A study of primitive methods of drilling. *Annual report, 1894* Smithsonian Institute: 625-756.

Mirambell, L.E. 1968 Técnicas lapidarias prehispánicas. XIV Instituto Nacional de Antropología e Historia México: 115 p.

Mujica Gallo, M. 1959 The gold of Peru. Recklinghausen, A. Bongers: 285 p.

Orchard, W.C. 1975 Beads and beadwork of the American Indians. *Contributions from the Museum of the American Indian XI:* 168 p.

Plazas, C. (ed.) 1986 Metalurgía de América precolombina. Precolumbian American Metallurgy. 45th International Congress of Americanists, Universidad de los Andes, Bogotá, Colombia, 1985. Bogotá, Banco de la República: 435 p.

Rowe, A.P. 1984 Costumes and featherwork of the Lords of Chimor. Washington, D.C., The Textile Museum: 190 p.

Tanner, C.L. 1976 Prehistoric Southwestern craft arts. Tucson, University of Arizona Press: 226 p.

Treviño de Sáenz, H. 1947 Perú. Joyas, telas, cerámica. México, D.F., Xavier Gomez: 235 p.

Tushingham, A.D., K.C. Day and L. Rosshandler 1976 Gold for the gods. Toronto, Royal Ontario Museum: 146 p.

——U.M. Franklin and C. Toogood 1979 Studies in ancient Peruvian metalworking. Monograph 3, History, technology and art. Royal Ontario Museum: 103 p.

Wassén, H. 1934 The frog motif among South American Indians. *Anthropos* 29:319-370.

Yoshimizu, T. 1989 Eye of the dragonfly (Tombodama). Tokyo, Heibonsha: 163 p.

CHAPTER 6

Allen, J.D. 1982a Cane manufacture for mosaic beads: Part I. *Ornament* 5(4): 6-11.

——1982b Cane manufacture for mosaic glass beads: Part II. *Ornament* 6(1): 13, 43, 17.

——1993 Publication review: James Byrd, Roger Poole and Linda Byrd 1992 The olde bead monger's trade bead sketchbook. Texarkana, Rebel Publishing Co., Inc.: 64 p. *Ornament* 17(1): 100.

Armstrong, W.P. 1991 Beautiful botanicals. Seeds for jewelry. *Ornament* 15(1): 66-69.

Benesh, M. 1994 Museum news: State Historical and Art Museum. *Ornament* 18(1): 68-69.

Brain, J.P., T.M. Hamilton, I.W. Brown, V.P. Steponaitis, M. Gerin-Lajoie 1979 Tunica treasure. *Papers Peabody Museum Archaeology and Ethnology,* Harvard University 71: 329 p.

Callmer, J. 1977 Trade beads and bead trade in Scandinavia ca. 800-1000 A.D. *Acta Archaeologica Lundensia* 4(11): 229 p., map, plates, color plates.

Casady, R. and D. Casady 1974 A sample book of Venetian beads from 1704. *Bead Journal* 1(1): 19-21.

Converse, R. N. 1976 Beads. *Ohio Archaeologist* 26(1): 6.

Cordry, D. 1975 Pendant glass beads from San Pedro Quiatoni, Oaxaca, Mexico. *Bead Journal* 1(4): 10-12.

Cuadra, C. 1993 Wholesale to the trade: Folk Art International. *Ornament* 17(1): 120-121.

Davis, R. 1975 Correspondence: More on S. P. Quiatoni pendants. *Bead Journal* 2(2): 1-3.

DeCarlo, G. 1987 Jacopo Franchini: Miniature portraits in glass. *Ornament* 10(4): 46-47.

de Williams, A. A. 1975 Sea shell usage in Baja California. *Pacific Coast Archaeological Society Quarterly* 11(1): 1-22.

Déchelette, J. 1927 Les verroleries, Perles et bracelets. *Manuel d' Archaeologie Prehistorique Celtique et Gallo-Romaine.* Paris, Editions Auguste Picard 4: 820-838.

Dubin, L. S. 1987 The history of beads. From 30,000 B.C. to the present. New York, Harry N. Abrams: 364 p.

Fenstermaker, G.B. 1974a Susquehanna, Iroquois colored trade bead chart 1575-1763. Lancaster, G. B. Fenstermaker I: 8 p.

——1974b Early Susquehanna Iroquois colored trade bead chart 1550. Lancaster, G. B. Fenstermaker III: 4 p., 1 tipped in color illus.

——1976a First Northwest coast colored trade bead chart. Lancaster, G. B. Fenstermaker VI: 4 p., color plate.

——1976b South American colored trade bead chart 1850-1870. Lancaster, G. B. Fenstermaker VII: 3 p., color plate.

——1976c Mississippi colored trade bead chart. Lancaster, G. B. Fenstermaker VIII: 4 p., color plate.

——1976d Northwest colored trade bead chart. Lancaster, G. B. Fenstermaker IX(2): 4 p., color plate.

——1977a Mardi Gras colored bead chart. Lancaster, G. B. Fenstermaker X: 6 p., color plate.

——1977b Pennsylvania Conoy colored trade bead chart. Lancaster, G. B. Fenstermaker XI: 4 p., color plate.

——1978 Tennessee colored bead charts. Lancaster, G. B. Fenstermaker XIII: 12 p., color plates.

Fogelman, G.L. 1991 Glass trade beads of the Northeast. And including aboriginal bead industries: stone-bone-shell-catlinite-cannel coal-teeth. Fogelman Publishing Co., Pennsylvania Artifact Series Booklet (70): 44 p., color chart.

Francis Jr., P. 1984a Bead report XI: Beads and the discovery of America, I. Beads of the Native Americans. *Ornament* 7(4): 16-19, 48-49.

——1984b Bead report XII: Beads and the discovery of America, II. Beads brought to America. *Ornament* 8(2): 24-27.

——1985 Bead report XIII: Beads and the discovery of America, III. The later bead trade. *Ornament* 8(3): 47-51, 53.

——1986 Bead report XIX: Beads and the discovery of America, IV. Did beads buy Manhattan Island? *Ornament* 10(2): 55-58, 73-76.

——1988 The glass trade beads of Europe. Their manufacture, their history, and their identification. Lake Placid, World of Beads Monograph Series 8: 69 p.

——1994 Beads of the world. A collector's guide with price reference. Atglen, Schiffer Publishing Ltd.: 142 p.

Glumac, P.D. 1985 Earliest known copper ornaments from prehistoric Europe. *Ornament* 8(3): 1-17.

Good, M.E. 1972 Guebert site: an 18th century historic Kaskaskia Indian Village. *Central States Archaeological Societies, Inc. Memoir II:* 194 p.

Green, C.I. 1993 Ancient Egyptian glass and faience from the 'Per-neb' collection, Part III. London, Christie's: 83 p.

Guido, M. 1978 The glass beads of the prehistoric and Roman Periods in Britain and Ireland. Society of Antiquaries of London: 249 p.

Gumpert, A. 1989 A breathtaking bonanza of African beads. *Bead Society Greater Washington Newsletter* VI(1): 1-3.

Haevernick, T.E. 1981 Beiträge zur Glasforschung. Die wichtigsten Aufsätze von 1938 bis 1981. Verlag Philipp von Zabern: 440 p.

Handler, J.S., F.W. Lange and C.E. Orser 1979 Carnelian beads in necklaces from a slave cemetery in Barbados, West Indies. *Ornament* 4(2): 15-18.

Harris, E.J. 1979 American Indian glass beads. [Los Angeles], *Bead Society Newsletter* IV(6): 8.

——1982 Nueva Cádiz and associated beads. A new look. Lancaster, G.B. Fenstermaker: 15 p.

——1985 The Russian bead. Northwest colored bead chart. Lancaster, G. B. Fenstermaker XXI(3): 14 p.

——1993 An end and new beginning. *Bead Museum Quarterly* 7(4): 4.

——and R.K. Liu 1979 Identification: Mold-made (?) glass beads from Ecuador/Peru. *Ornament* 4(2): 60.

Hayes, C.F. (ed.) 1983 Proceedings of the 1982 glass trade bead conference. Rochester Museum and Science Center, Research Records (16): 284 p.

Henderson, J. 1988 Glass production and Bronze Age Europe. *Antiquity* 62: 435-451.

Jargstorf, S. 1991 Glass in jewelry. Hidden artistry in glass. West Chester, Schiffer Publishing Ltd.: 175 p.

——1993 Baubles, buttons and beads. The heritage of Bohemia. Atglen, Schiffer Publishing Ltd.: 176 p.

Jenkins, M. 1975 Glass trade beads in Alaska. *Bead Journal* 2(1): 23-26.

Johnson, E. 1975 Notes from a bead buying trip to Europe. *Bead Journal* 2(2): 30.

Johnson, S.C. 1975a The intriguing mystery of the Quiatoni beads. *Bead Journal* 1(4): 13-16.

——1975b Living beads in Guatemala. *Bead Journal* 2(1): 18-22.

——1976 An "undescribed" bead from Central America. *Bead Journal* 3(1): 37-39.

Karklins, K.1974 Seventeenth century Dutch beads. *Historical Archaeology* 8: 64-82.

——1985a Early Amsterdam trade beads. *Ornament* 9(2): 36-41.

——1985b Glass beads: The Levin catalogue of mid-19th century beads; A sample book of 19th century Venetian beads; Guide to the description and classification of glass beads. Parks Canada: 123 p.

——1993 The *a speo* method of heat rounding drawn glass beads and its archaeological manifestations. *Beads* 5 [1995]: 27-36.

——and C.F. Adams 1990 Dominique Bussolin on the glass-bead industry of Murano and Venice (1847). *Beads* 2 [1991]: 69-84.

——and N.F. Barka 1989 The beads of St. Eustatius, Netherlands Antilles. *Beads* 1: 55-80.

Kelly, I. 1992 Trade beads and the conquest of Mexico. Windsor, Rolston-Bain: 291 p.

——and I.W. Johnson 1979 The squiggle. An 'undescribed' bead from Central America. *Ornament* 4(1): 4-8.

Kessler, E. and S. Kessler 1986 Ecuadorian beads. Ancient to modern. *Ornament* 10(2): 48-52.

Kidd, K.E. 1979 Glass bead-making from the Middle Ages to the early 19th century. Parks Canada, History and Archaeology 30: 104 p.

King, C.D. 1981 Prehistoric and early historic California beads. *Ornament* 5(1): 11-17.

Liu, R.K. 1974 Glass trade beads from an early eastern North American site. *Bead Journal* 1(2): 23-26.

——1975 Early 20th century bead catalogs. *Bead Journal* 2(2): 31.

——1978 Identification: Nueva Cádiz, *Bead Journal* 3(3/4): 77.

____1983 Dan Frost bead collection. *Ornament* 6(3): 25-29, 44-45.

____1985a Special pictorial: Chumash Indian ornaments. *Ornament* 8(3): 44-45.

____1985b Exhibition review: Dragons in the New World: Native Americans and the China Trade. *Ornament* 9(1): 55.

____1986a Special pictorial: Venetian bead factory. *Ornament* 9(3): 50-52.

____1986b Exhibition review: Jivaro, expressions of cultural survival. *Ornament* 9(4): 66.

____1987 Exhibition review: California State Indian Museum. *Ornament* 10(3): 20.

____1992a Collectibles: Ancient European glass beads. *Ornament* 15(4): 16-17, 95.

____1992b Museum news: Prähistorische Staatssammlung. *Ornament* 16(1): 28-29.

____1993 Wholesale to the trade: Ornamental Resources. *Ornament* 16(4): 104-105.

Lundström, A. 1976 Bead making in Scandinavia in the early Middle Ages. Stockholm, *Early Medieval Studies* 9: 3-19.

Marascutto, P.R. and M. Stainer 1991 Perle Veneziane. Nuove Edizioni Dolomiti S. r. l.: 183 p.

Mille, P. 1975 An historical explanation of Alaskan trade beads. *Bead Journal* 2(2): 20-24.

Miller, P.G. 1994 Glass trade beads in Alaska. Bead Society of Central Florida, Research Monograph: 44 p.

Moltz, L. and P.D. Schulz 1980 European "trade" beads from old Sacramento. *California Archaeological Reports* (19): 49-68.

Morlot, A. 1992 On the date of the copper age in the United States. *Beads* 4 [1993]: 39-48.

Moscati, S. (coor.) 1991 The Celts. Milano, Bompiani: 799 p.

Murdoch, T. (comp.) 1991 Treasures & trinkets. Jewellery in London from pre-Roman times to the 1930s. Museum of London: 208 p.

Neuwirth, W. 1994 Perlen aus Gablonz, Beads from Gablonz. Vienna, Druckhaus Grasl. 560 p.

Ninni, I. and L. Segatti 1991 L'impiraressa: The Venetian bead stringer. *Beads* 3 [1992]: 73-82.

Opper, M.-J. and H. Opper 1991 French beadmaking. An historical perspective emphasizing the 19th and 20th centuries. *Beads* 3 [1992]: 47-59.

____1993 Gougad-Pateraenneu. Old Talisman necklaces from Brittany, France. Bead Society Greater Washington Monograph Series (1): 18 p.

____1994 Exotic Czech beads from the 1920s. Alexandria, Moon Dust Publications: 4 p.

Orchard, W.C. 1975 Beads and beadwork of the American Indians. *Contributions from the Museum of the American Indian XI*: 168 p.

Picard, J. and R. Picard 1989 Russian blues, faceted and fancy beads from the West African trade. Picard African Imports V: 43 p.

____1991 Millefiori beads from the West African trade. Picard African Imports VI: 87 p.

____1993 Chevron and Nueva Cádiz beads. Picard African Imports VII: 128 p.

Ross, L.A. 1974 Hudson's Bay Company glass trade beads: manufacturing types imported to Fort Vancouver (1829-1860). *Bead Journal* 1(2): 15-22.

____1990 Trade beads from Hudson's Bay Company Fort Vancouver (1829-1860), Vancouver, Washington. *Beads* 2 [1991]: 29-67.

____and B. Planz 1989 Bohemian glass beadmaking. Translation and discussion of a 1913 German technical article. *Beads* 1: 81-95.

Rumrill, D.A. 1991 The Mohawk glass trade bead chronology. *Beads* 3 [1992]: 5-45.

Seaman, N.G. 1946 Indian relics of the Pacific Northwest. Portland, Binfords & Mort: 157 p.

Sharlach, L. 1992 Beads from West African markets. *Bead Society of Greater Washington Newsletter* IX(4): 5-6.

Slemmons, R. 1987 The Frank Fiske collection. Portraits of Native Americans. *Ornament* 10(3): 51-53.

Smith, M.T. 1976 Additional notes on Alta Verapaz eye beads. *Bead Journal* 2(3): 37-38.

____1977 The chevron trade bead in North America. *Bead Journal* 3(2): 15-17.

____1981 European and aboriginal glass pendants in North America. *Ornament* 5(2): 21-23.

____and M.E. Good 1982 Early sixteenth century glass beads in the Spanish Colonial trade. Greenwood, Cottonlandia Museum Publications: 64 p.

Sorenson Jr., C. 1971 The enduring intrigue of the glass trade bead. *Arizona Highways* XLVII (7): 10-37.

____and C.R. Le Roy 1968 Trade beads. The powerful companion of the explorer. San Diego, Brand Book Number One, San Diego Corral of the Westerners: 35-48.

Sprague, R. 1985 Glass trade beads. A progress report. *Historical Archaeology* 19: 87-105.

Springett, C. and D. Springett 1987 Spangles & superstitions. C. and D. Springett: 38 p.

Stawiarska, T. 1985 Glass beads of northern Poland in the period of Roman influence [in Polish]. *Biblioteka Archeologiczna* 28: 158 p., charts, maps.

Strong, E. 1960 Stone age on the Columbia River. Portland, Binfords & Mort: 254 p.

Strong, M.B. 1983 Glass trade beads in North America, Part I. *American Rendezvous Magazine* 2(2): 29-35.

Taylor, M.E. and R.A. Robinson 1979 Trilobites in Utah folklore. *Ornament* 4(1): 40-41.

Tempelmann-Maczyn'ska, M. 1985 Die Perlen der römischen Kaiserzeit und der frühen Phase der Völkerwanderungszeit im mitteleuropäischen Barbicum. Verlag Philipp von Zabern, *Römisch-Germanische Forschungen* 43: 339 p., Tafeln 1-80, Beilagen 1-3.

Todd, J. M.(ed.) 1985 Special issue: Studies in Baltic amber. *Journal of Baltic Studies* XVI (3): 183-320.

Tomalin, S. 1988 Beads! Make your own unique jewellery. David & Charles Craft Book: 128 p.

Trebbin, C. 1985 Achate, geschliffen in Idar-Oberstein-Amulette, Schmuck und Zahlungsmittel in Afrika. Museum Idar-Oberstein 6: 39 p.

van der Made, H. 1978 Seventeenth century beads from Holland. Lancaster, G.B. Fenstermaker XIV: 10 p., color plates.

van der Sleen, W.G.N. 1973 A handbook on beads. Liege, Librairie Halbart: 142 p.

Venclova, N. 1972 Celtic glass in Czechoslovakia. Annales du 5e Congrès de l'Association Internationale pour l'Histoire du Verre. Prague 6-11 Juillet 1970: 41-46.

____1983 Prehistoric eye beads in central Europe. *Journal of Glass Studies* 25: 11-17.

White, R. 1993a The dawn of adornment. *Natural History* 102(5): 60-67.

____1993b Technological and social dimensions of "Aurignacian-Age" body ornaments across Europe. *In*: Before Lascaux: The complex record of the early Upper Paleolithic. Boca Raton, CRC Press: 277-299.

Wilcox, U.V. 1976 The manufacture and use of wampum in the Northeast. *Bead Journal* 3(1): 10-19.

Yoshimizu, T. 1989 Eye of the dragonfly (Tombodama). Tokyo, Heibonsha: 163 p.

CHAPTER 7

Allen, J.D. 1989 Millefiori polyform techniques. *Ornament* 12(4): 46-49.

Anonymous 1975 How to string beads and make jewelry professionally. New York, Sheru Bead: 16 p.

Applegate, J. 1989 Rita Okrent. Majestic artifacts for the body. *Ornament* 13(2): 50-53, 23.

Barnard, S. 1987 Jewelry showcase: The Flying Shuttle. *Ornament* 11(2): 56-57.

Benesh, C.L.E. 1979 The ceramic jewelry of Parrot Pearls. *Ornament* 4(2): 2-10.

____1981 Angela Cummings, a designer for Tiffany. *Ornament* 5(1): 28-33, 56.

____1983 Collaboration. Lucia Antonelli, Martin Kilmer, Laura Popenoe. *Ornament* 7(2): 2-5, 42-43.

____1985 News: Barbara Natoli Witt. *Ornament* 9(2): 50.

____1986 Newcomb Company. Fine porcelain jewelry. *Ornament* 10(4): 26-31.

____1989 Ramona Solberg's jewelry. "I'm sort of the Henry Ford of jewelry." *Ornament* 13(1): 58-63.

____1990 Extracting the infinite. Jeff Wise. *Ornament* 14(1): 54-57.

____1994 The creative spirit. Flora Book. *Ornament* 17(3): 46-51.

Blauer, E. 1986 Rhodia Mann. Jewelry with an African flavor. *Ornament* 10(2): 59-61.

____1987 A basic palette. The fine jewelry of Jan Yager. *Ornament* 10(4): 48-55, 68.

____1990 Robert Ebendorf. A vision freely shared. *Ornament* 12(4): 32-37, 88, 90.

Booth, J. 1975 Glass and silver. *Bead Journal* 2(1): 9-17.

Brownrigg, L.L. 1985 Exhibition review: Oxford Gallery. *Ornament* 9(1): 57-58.

Bullis, D. 1992a A generous spirit. Sandra Sakata. *Ornament* 15(4): 60-65, 79, 83.

____1992b Making a difference. Tabra Tunoa. *Ornament* 16(2): 36-39.

____1993 Auspicious emblems. Pat Au-Young Tseng. *Ornament* 16(3): 34-39.

Butts, G. 1971 Restringing beads and pearls. Los Angeles, Products & Systems: 36 p.

Casady, D. 1994 February program review: Designing jewelry with contemporary art glass beads. [Los Angeles], *Bead Society Newsletter* XIX(4): 4.

Champion, D. 1985 The basics of bead stringing. Santa Monica, Borjay: 47 p.

Clark, G. 1986 Symbols of excellence. Precious materials as expressions of status. Cambridge, Cambridge University Press: 126 p.

Coles, J. and R. Budwig 1990 The book of beads. New York, Simon and Schuster: 125 p.

Cuadra, C. 1991 Discovery: Tom André. *Ornament* 15(2): 88-89, 101.

____1993a Master class on knotting. Judith Ubick. *Ornament* 16(4): 60- 65, 83, 90.

____1993b Master class on fancy knotting. Judith Ubick. *Ornament* 17(1): 84-89.

____1993c Master class with Tory Hughes: Polymer clay simulations, [Coral and jade]. *Ornament* 17(2): 84-91.

____1994 Master class with Tory Hughes. Polymer clay simulations, Ivory and turquoise. *Ornament* 17(3): 84-89.

Dale, G. 1983 London letter. *Ornament* 6(3): 60-61, 51.

____1984 Wendy Ramshaw and David Watkins. *Ornament* 8(2): 28-33.

Diamanti, J.S. 1991 Keepsakes: Agnes Stewart. *Ornament* 14(3): 16-17.

Dierks, L. 1994 Creative clay jewelry. Asheville, Lark Books: 144 p.

DiNoto, A. 1985 Surface and edge. Designs in laminate. *Ornament* 8(4): 32-37, 46-47.

Donnan, C.B. 1993 Royal tombs of Sipán. Moche ornaments of Peru. *Ornament* 17(1): 44-49, 115.

Drew-Wilkinson, K. and C. Haynes 1993 Complete guide to wire work for bead jewelry. Ashland, Nomad Press: 90 p.

Dubin, L.S. 1987 The history of beads. From 30,000 B.C. to the present. New York, Harry N. Abrams: 364 p.

Dustin, K. 1988 The use of polyform in bead-making. *Ornament* 11(3): 16-19.

Ebbinghouse, D. 1989 Michael Winsten. Being inspired by the muse. *Ornament* 13(2): 36-39.

Fitzgerald, D. 1991 Rich tapestries. The jewelry of Helen Banes. *Ornament* 14(4): 52-55.

—— and H. Banes 1993 Beads and threads, a new technique for fiber jewelry. Rockville, Flower Valley Press: 144 p.

Goebel, E. 1987 Portable treasures. The jewelry of Judith Ubick. *Ornament* 10(4): 32-36.

Goldberg, J. 1987 Exhibition review: Breon O'Casey. *Ornament* 10(3): 22-23.

Gosselink, M.B. 1990 Elizabeth Ward's step by step guide to professional bead stringing. Washington, D.C., Elizabeth Ward & Co.: 21 p.

Greenbaum, T. 1992 Luminous plastic jewelry. Cara Croninger. *Ornament* 15(4): 56-59, 18.

Hamaker, B. 1989 Tory Hughes jewelry. "Art is a conversation, not a conversation piece" *Ornament* 13(2): 60-63, 6.

—— 1990 Evoking gentle beauty. Fumiko Ukai. *Ornament* 13(4): 32-35.

—— 1991 Voices from antiquity. Natalia Josca. *Ornament* 14(3): 50-53.

Hancock, D. and M. Hancock 1991 Artist's statement: Doug and Mary Hancock. *Ornament* 15(1): 88-89.

Jackson, G. 1989 Exhibition review: Three bead designers. *Ornament* 13(2): 28.

Kangas, M. 1995 The age of Solberg. *Metalsmith* 15(1): 24-29.

Kennedy, S.S.J. 1983a News: Kai Yin Lo at Neiman Marcus. *Ornament* 6(3): 57.

—— 1983b Marketplace: Kathlean Gahagan. *Ornament* 7(2): 38-39.

—— 1985a Kiff Slemmons. A study in continuity and change. *Ornament* 9(1): 16-20.

—— 1985b Nyhus design glasswear. *Ornament* 9(2): 12-17.

Kestler, C.S. 1977 Viewpoint: Cultural by-products in jewelry. *Ornament* 3(2): 22-23.

LeGardeur, L. 1994 The business decision. Sometimes, your first idea is the best. *Crafts Report*, January: 9.

Liese, G. 1993 The work of contemporary glass beadmakers. July 9th to August 28, 1993. Prescott, The Bead Museum: 16 p.

Liu, R.K. 1974 Materials and techniques for stringing necklaces. *Bead Journal* 1(2): 27-32.

—— 1976a The Kulicke-Stark Academy of Jewelry Art. *Bead Journal* 2(3): 21-26.

—— 1976b Exhibitions and shows: California Design 76. *Bead Journal* 2(4): 5-6.

—— 1977 Marketplace. *Bead Journal* 3(2): 52.

—— 1979 Mounting small artifacts in contemporary jewelry. Oriental material. *Ornament* 4(2): 54-59.

—— 1980a Marketplace: Art Necko. *Ornament* 4(3): 56-58.

—— 1980b Review of exhibitions: Joyce Whitaker and Sauny Dils, Mini-show. Museum Shop of the Craft and Folk Art Museum, June, 1978. *Ornament* 4(4): 27.

—— 1981a Marketplace: Phyllis Woods. *Ornament* 5(1): 36-37.

—— 1981b News: Wendy Ramshaw/David Watkins slide lecture at California State University, Los Angeles, CA, Oct. 15, 1980. *Ornament* 5(1): 27.

—— 1981c Review of exhibitions: Collaborations: Robin Casady, Sue Kingsley, Judith Ubick. Precious Objects Gallery, Los Gatos, California; September 5-30, 1980. *Ornament* 5(1): 48-49.

—— 1981d Carol Strick. Artist in faience. *Ornament* 5(2): 34-37.

—— 1981e Marketplace: Debbie Hetrick shell jewelry. *Ornament* 5(2): 54-55.

—— 1982 Marketplace: Alternate Marketing-Gift shows/Home shows. *Ornament* 5(4): 40-43.

—— 1983a Special pictorial: Clasps. *Ornament* 6(3): 38-40.

—— 1983b News: Fashion Accessories Expo West '82. *Ornament* 6(3): 37.

—— 1983c News: Rose Garfunkel of Santa Monica, died July 1983. *Ornament* 7(1): 36.

—— 1983d Pre-Columbian necklaces, then and now. *Ornament* 7(1): 2-5, 14-15, 44-45.

—— 1983e Department store promotions. *Ornament* 7(2): 37.

—— 1984a News: Les Halles. *Ornament* 7(4): 15.

—— 1984b Competition analysis. *Ornament* 8(1): 62-63.

—— 1984c Special pictorial: Clasps. *Ornament* 8(2): 46-47.

—— 1985a Design exercise. Use of metal tubing in necklaces/findings. *Ornament* 8(3): 28-30.

—— 1985b Identification: Transpositions. *Ornament* 8(4): 67.

—— 1985c Special pictorial: International Bead Conference 1985. *Ornament* 9(2): 10.

—— 1986a Identification: Celtform jewelry. *Ornament* 10(1): 64-65.

—— 1986b Recent work: Martin and Lucia. *Ornament* 10(2): 64-65.

—— 1987a Exhibition review: Art to wear. *Ornament* 11(1): 22.

—— 1987b New work: Elisabeth Cary. *Ornament* 11(1): 38-39.

—— 1987c Recent work: Heyoehkah Merrifield. *Ornament* 11(1): 18-19.

—— 1987d New work: Dorothy Feibleman. *Ornament* 11(2): 54-55.

—— 1989a Recent work: Nancy Aillery. *Ornament* 12(3): 50-51.

—— 1989b Keepsakes: Laura K. Popenoe. *Ornament* 12(4): 56-57.

—— 1990 Findings: Tina Johnson Depuy. *Ornament* 13(3): 70-71.

—— 1991 Conference: Second International Bead Conference. *Ornament* 14(3): 13.

—— 1992 Collectibles: American ceramic beadmakers. *Ornament* 16(2): 16-17.

—— 1993 Experiment: Bead pendant design. *Ornament* 17(1): 104-105.

—— 1994a Beads from Africa. *Ornament* 17(3): 52-57.

—— 1994b From the heart. Valerie and Benny Aldrich. *Ornament* 18(2): 46-49.

—— and S.S.J. Kennedy 1986 A 10th anniversary celebration: Neckpieces. A selection from past issues. *Ornament* 10(1): 36-41.

Moss, K. and A. Scherer 1992 The new beadwork. New York, Harry N. Abrams: 112 p.

Mujica Gallo, M. 1959 The gold of Peru. Recklinghausen, A. Bongers: 285 p.

Myhre, S. 1987 Bone carving. A skillbase of techniques and concepts. Reed Methuen: 116 p.

Osburn, A. 1992a Treasure necklaces. Nance Lopez. *Ornament* 15(3): 66-69, 100-101.

—— 1992b Trusting the eye. Barbara Zusman. *Ornament* 16(2): 62-65.

Poris, R. 1984 Step-by-step bead stringing. A complete illustrated professional approach. Farmington Hills, Golden Hands Press: 45 p.

—— 1989 Advanced beadwork. Tampa, Golden Hands Press: 148 p.

Prichett, J. 1990 Ancient echoes. The jewelry of Annette Bird. *Ornament* 14(1): 32-36.

Roche, N. 1991 The new clay. Techniques and approaches to jewelry making. Rockville, Flower Valley Press: 144 p.

Ross, A.L. 1991 Exhibition review: Jacqueline Lillie. *Ornament* 14(3): 35.

Scott, N.E. and R.K. Liu 1981 Notes on construction of Egyptian broadcollars. *Ornament* 5(2): 11-14.

Slemmons, K. 1978 Viewpoint: Combining beads and metal in contemporary jewelry. *Bead Journal* 3(3/4): 78-81.

Solberg, R. 1972 Inventive jewelry-making. Van Nostrand Reinhold Co.: 128 p.

—— 1988 Museum news: Bellevue Art Museum. Ubiquitous bead. *Ornament* 11(3): 48-49.

Tomalin, S. 1988 Beads! Make your own unique jewellery. David & Charles Craft Book: 128 p.

Virchick, H. 1989 Pearl and beadstringing with Henrietta. Linecraft, Inc.: 89 p.

Waltz, C.L. 1994 Making odd ends meet. Cap your necklaces with cones. *Bead & Button* (3): 5-6.

Weiner, M. 1992 Serendipitous discoveries. Klaus Dietz, Gabrielle Späth. *Ornament* 16(2): 58-61.

Wilson, M. 1985 Create your own fashion jewelry. Mele Ana, Inc.: 64 p.

CHAPTER 8

Adhyatman, S. and R. Arifin 1993 Manik-manik di Indonesia. Beads in Indonesia. Jakarta, Penerbit Djambatan: 164 p.

Allen, J.D. 1989 Millefiori polyform techniques. *Ornament* 12(4): 46-49.

Atkins, R. 1992 Patricia Frantz. *Ornament* 15(3): 80-81, 95.

Benesh, C.L.E. 1986 Newcomb Company. Fine porcelain jewelry. *Ornament* 10(2): 26-31.

—— 1992 Gallery showcase: HumanArts. *Ornament* 16(2): 8-9.

—— 1994 Exhibition review: Contemporary glass beadmakers. *Ornament* 17(2): 31.

Booth, J. 1975 Glass and silver. *Bead Journal* 2(1): 9-17.

Cuadra, C. 1993a Master class on fancy knotting. Judith Ubick. *Ornament* 17(1): 84-89.

—— 1993b Master class with Tory Hughes. Polymer clay simulations, [Coral and jade]. *Ornament* 17(2): 84-91.

—— 1994 Master class with Tory Hughes: Polymer clay simulations, Ivory and turquoise. *Ornament* 17(3): 84-89.

Dubin, L.S. 1987 The history of beads. From 30,000 B.C. to the present. New York, Harry N. Abrams: 364 p.

Dunham, B.S. 1993 Contemporary lampworking. A practical guide to shaping glass in the flame. Pre-publication edition. Prescott: unpaginated.

Dustin, K. 1989 The use of polyform in bead-making. *Ornament* 11(3): 16-19.

Foreman, R. 1978 Disc beads. Production by primitive techniques. *Bead Journal* 3(3/4): 17-22.

Hopper, S.M. 1994 Bead arts: Helga Seimel. *Ornament* 17(4): 60-61.

Kan, P. and R.K. Liu 1984 Chinese glass beadmaking. *Ornament* 8(2): 38-40, 67.

Kennedy, S.S.J. and R.K. Liu 1983 Jean Stark. Neoclassical jeweler. *Ornament* 6(4): 2-5, 40-41.

—— 1985 Contemporary cane beadmaking. *Ornament* 8(3): 18-23.

Kenoyer, J.M. 1992 Lapis lazuli. Beadmaking in Afghanistan and Pakistan. *Ornament* 15(3): 70-73, 86-87.

Kinsey, R.O. 1987 The lacquered ojime of Tomizo Saratani. *Ornament* 10(3): 56-60.

—— 1991 Ojime. Magical jewels of Japan. New York, Harry N. Abrams: 64 p.

Liese, G. 1993 The work of contemporary glass beadmakers. Prescott, Bead Museum: 16 p.

Liu, R.K. 1981 Carol Strick. Artist in faience. *Ornament* 5(2): 34-37.

—— 1983 Special pictorial: Ojime. *Ornament* 7(1): 25-26.

—— 1986 Followup: Asao bead components. *Ornament* 9(3): 48-49.

—— 1987 New work: Elisabeth Cary. *Ornament* 11(1): 38-39.

—— 1989 Collectibles: Mosaic face beads. *Ornament* 12(3): 22-23.

____1990 Collectibles: American glass beadmakers. *Ornament* 14(1): 16-17.

____1991 Conference: Second International Bead Conference. *Ornament* 14(3): 13.

____1992 Collectibles: American ceramic beadmakers. *Ornament* 16(2): 16-17.

____1993a Experiment: Bead pendant design. *Ornament* 17(1): 104-105.

____1993b Collecting beads. *Ornament* 17(2): 38-43.

____1994 Conference: Bead Expo '94. *Ornament* 17(4): 120-121.

McCarthy, C. 1994 Puttin' on the glitz. *Lapidary Journal* 48(7): 34-38.

Muzzy, S. 1993 Glass beadmaking. The ring of fire. *Ornament* 16(4): 56-59.

Picard, J. and R. Picard 1993 Chevron and Nueva Cádiz beads. Vol. VII-Beads from the West African trade. Picard African Imports: 128 p.

Reynolds, G. 1990 The fused glass handbook. (rev. ed.) Scottsdale, Hidden Valley Books: 80 p.

____1992 What's hot?—glass beads. *Glass Art* 8(1): 14-16.

Roche, N. 1991 The new clay. Techniques and approaches to jewelry making. Rockville, Flower Valley Press: 144 p.

Ross, A.L. 1991 Innovation: City Zen Cane. *Ornament* 15(2): 70-71, 87.

____1994 Master Class with Molly Vaughan Haskins. Kiln-formed glass beadmaking. *Ornament* 18(1): 90-95.

Searle, K. 1992 Glass lampworking workshop. *Ornament* 15(4): 104-105.

Tomalin, S. 1988 Beads! Make your own unique jewellery. David & Charles Craft Book: 128 p.

Ukai, N. 1980 Kyoyu Asao, tombodama/glass bead master. *Ornament* 4(3): 13-18.

____1984 Kyoyu Asao. Glass bead master, new work. *Ornament* 7(3): 2-5.

Waggoner, S. 1993 Lewis C. Wilson. From lampworking to beadmaking. *Glass Art* 8(6): 4-7.

Weiner, M. 1992 Serendipitous discoveries. Klaus Dietz, Gabriele Späth. *Ornament* 16(2): 58-61.

Yoshimizu, T. 1989 Eye of the dragonfly (Tombodama). Tokyo, Heibonsha: 163 p.

Zimmerman, A.F. 1993 Lampwork beads. The book. KBA: unpaginated.

CHAPTER 9

Adhyatman, S. and R. Arifin 1993 Manik-manik di Indonesia. Beads in Indonesia. Jakarta, Penerbit Djambatan: 164 p.

Allen, J.D. 1976a Amber and its substitutes. Pt. II: Mineral analyses. *Bead Journal* 2(4): 11-22.

____1976 Amber and its substitutes. Pt. III: Is it real? Testing amber. *Bead Journal* 3(1): 20-31.

____1982 Correspondence: Tibetan dZi beads. *Ornament* 6(2): 57, 60.

Brunton, Sir G. 1928 Qua + Badari, Vol. II. London, British School of Archaeology in Egypt: 7-25, plates.

Cammann, S.V.R. 1950 The story of hornbill ivory. *University Museum Bulletin* 15(4): 19-47.

____1962 Substance and symbol in Chinese toggles. Philadelphia, University Pennsylvania Press: 256 p.

____1979 Ch'ing dynasty "Mandarin chains" *Ornament* 4(1): 25-29.

Cuadra, C. 1993 Master class with Tory Hughes. Polymer clay simulations, [Coral and jade]. *Ornament* 17(2): 84-91.

Dale, G. 1978 Fake roman glass. *Antique Collector* (1): 80-82.

Davis-Kimball, J. and R.K. Liu 1981 Identification: An etched carnelian bead with human images. *Ornament* 5(1): 34-35.

DeCarlo, G. 1987 Jacopo Franchini. Miniature portraits in glass. *Ornament* 10(4): 46-47.

Ebbinghouse, D. 1982 Correspondence: Dzi beads. Rebuttal. *Ornament* 6(2): 60-61.

Francis Jr., P. 1979a The story of Venetian beads. World of Beads Monograph Series 1: 19 p.

____1979b Czech bead story. World of Beads Monograph Series 2: 19 p.

____1979c Third world beadmakers. World of Beads Monograph Series 3: 19 p.

____1980 Bead Report III: Beads in Egypt. *Ornament* 4(4): 15-17, 49-50.

____1982 Followup: Dzi beads. *Ornament* 6(2): 55-56.

____1992a Heirlooms of the hills. Southeast Asia. Center for Bead Research, Beads and People Series 1: 22 p.

____1992b Letters from the readers: imitation beads. *Ornament* 16(2): 4-5.

Fukai, S. 1977 Persian glass. New York, Weatherhill/Tankosha: 66 p., 89 plates.

Harris, E.J. 1991 New face beads from India. *Bead Forum* (18): 13.

Liu, R.K. 1974a Factory-made copies of native beads. *Bead Journal* 1(1): 6-18.

____1974b Glass mosaic or millefiore face beads. *Bead Journal* 1(1): 22-26.

____1975 Conus shell discs revisited. *Bead Journal* 2(1): 30-32.

____1976 Ancient glass ornaments with human facial images. *Bead Journal* 2(4): 27-42.

____1977 T'alhakimt(Talhatana), a Tuareg ornament. Its origins, derivatives, copies and distribution. *Bead Journal* 3(2): 18-22.

____1980a Identification: Tzi beads. *Ornament* 4(4): 56-59, 36.

____1980b Simulated materials in jewelry. *Ornament* 4(4): 18-26.

____1982a Followup: Tibetan dZi beads. *Ornament* 6(2): 55.

____1982b Glass ojime. *Ornament* 6(2): 24-28.

____1983a Identification. *Ornament* 6(3): 53.

____1983b Identification: Phoenician mask pendants. *Ornament* 7(1): 58-43.

____1984a Identification: Carnelian beads and their simulations. *Ornament* 8(1): 14-17.

____1984b African-made glass ornaments. Survey & experimental results. *Ornament* 8(2): 52-57, 23.

____1985a Asian glass ornaments: Part I. *Ornament* 8(4): 28-31, 25, 15.

____1985b Identification: Transpositions. *Ornament* 8(4): 67.

____1985c Asian glass ornaments: Part II China. *Ornament* 9(1): 34-36, 47.

____1986a Iridescence and related phenomena. *Ornament* 9(3): 31-36.

____1986b Followup: Indonesian glass beads. *Ornament* 9(4): 64-65.

____1987a Identification: Degradation. *Ornament* 10(4): 37.

____1987b India, Idar-Oberstein and Czechoslovakia. Imitators and competitors. *Ornament* 10(4): 56-61.

____1988 Granitic beads and their simulations. *Ornament* 11(4): 25, 8.

____1989a Collectibles: Faience ornaments. *Ornament* 13(2): 16-17.

____1989b Collectibles: Mosaic face beads. *Ornament* 12(3): 22-23.

____1992 Collectibles: Imitations and fakes. *Ornament* 16(1): 16-17.

Ogden, J. 1982 Jewellery of the ancient world. New York, Rizzoli: 185 p.

____1993 Fool's gold. *Gem and Jewellery News* 1: 8-9.

Stout, A. M. 1986 The archaeological context of late Roman period mosaic glass face beads. *Ornament* 9(4): 58-61, 76-77.

van der Made, H. 1988 Report on some face-beads. *Bead Forum* (13): 4-5.

von Saldern, Axel 1972 Originals-Reproductions-Fakes. *In:* Annales du 5e Congrès International d'Etude Historique du Verre, Prague, 6-11 juillet 1970: 299-318.

Yoshimizu, T. 1989 Eye of the dragonfly (Tombodama). Tokyo, Heibonsha: 163 p.

Zeltner, F.D. 1931 La bijouterie indigene en Afrique occidentale. *Journal Société des Africanistes* 1(1): 4-48, 4 plates.

CHAPTER 10

Adhyatman, S. and R. Arifin 1993 Manik-manik di Indonesia. Beads in Indonesia. Jakarta, Penerbit Djambatan: 164 p.

Borel, F. 1994 The splendor of ethnic jewelry. From the Collette and Jean-Pierre Ghysels collection. New York, Harry N. Abrams, Inc.: 256 p.

Casady, D. (ed.) 1985 Bead news selected from ten years of the Bead Society Newsletter, 1975-1985. Los Angeles, Bead Society: 101 p.

Diamanti, J. (ed.) 1993 The Beadazzled Beadstringer. News and views, tips and tales for bead fanciers and fanatics. Falls Church: 20 p.

Francis Jr., P. 1994 Beads of the world. A collector's guide with price reference. Atglen, Schiffer Publishing Ltd.: 142 p.

Fukai, S. 1977 Persian glass. New York, Weatherhill/Tankosha: 66 p., 89 plates.

Harris, E.J. 1980 Bead collecting. [Los Angeles], *Bead Society Newsletter* VI (3): 9.

____1981a Starting a specimen bead collection. [Los Angeles], *Bead Society Newsletter* VI(4): 9.

____1981b Bead collecting. A specialized specimen collection. [Los Angeles], *Bead Society Newsletter* VI (5): 3.

____1981c Documenting your bead collection. I. Numbering. [Los Angeles], *Bead Society Newsletter* VI (7): 7-8.

____1981d Documenting your bead collection. II. Historical and descriptive record.[Los Angeles], *Bead Society Newsletter* VII(2): 9.

____1981e Storing and displaying, Part I. Specimen bead collecting. [Los Angeles], *Bead Society Newsletter* VII (3): 5-6.

____1982 Specimen bead collecting. Storing and displaying, Part II. [Los Angeles], *Bead Society Newsletter* VII (7): 8-9.

____and R.K. Liu 1979 Identification: Mold-made (?) glass beads from Ecuador/Peru. *Ornament* 4(2): 60.

Kelly, I. 1992 Trade beads and the Conquest of Mexico. Windsor, Rolston-Bain: 290 p.

Kenoyer, J.M. 1993 Bead news. *Madison Bead Society Newsletter* 2(4): 4-5.

Liu, R.K. 1975 General considerations on the storage and display of beads, with a method for the display of single beads. *Bead Journal* 1(4): 17-23.

____1978 Beads: Ornaments from everywhere. Time-Life, The Encyclopedia of Collectibles. 6-21.

____1979 Mounting artifacts in contemporary jewelry: Oriental material. *Ornament* 4(2): 54-59.

____1980 Simulated materials in jewelry. *Ornament* 4(4): 18-26.

____1982 Amira Françoise. Living with beads in the Sudan. *Ornament* 5(4): 24-27.

____1985 Special pictorial: International Bead Conference 1985. *Ornament* 9(2): 10.

____1992 Collectibles: Imitations and fakes. *Ornament* 16(1): 16-17.

____1993 Experiment: Bead pendant design. *Ornament* 17(1): 104-105.

____1994 Master class: Photographing beads. *Ornament* 17(4): 90-95.

Tait, H. (ed.) 1991 Glass 5,000 years. New York, Harry N. Abrams: 256 p.

Terpning, S. 1990 Guidelines for starting your own bead collection. Tucson: 43 p.

Villegas, R.N. 1983 Kayamanan. The Philippine jewelry tradition. Manila, Central Bank of the Philippines: 210 p.

Yoshimizu, T. 1989 Eye of the dragonfly (Tombodama). Tokyo, Heibonsha: 163 p.

INDEX